$65,-
48
15
G

JOŽE PLEČNIK

'For in truth, art invents nothing – everything it deals with is in fact already there, it only has to re-evaluate it!', Semper, *Der Stil*, II, 91.

1. Wall fountain in Prague Castle, 1923/4

Damjan Prelovšek

JOŽE PLEČNIK

1872–1957

Architectura Perennis

Translated from the German by
Patricia Crampton and Eileen Martin

Yale University Press
New Haven & London
1997

For Professor France Stele

Set in Ehrhardt by Best-set Typesetter Ltd., Hong Kong and
printed through World Print Ltd., Hong Kong

Library of Congress Cataloging-in-Publication Data

Prelovšek, Damjan.
    [Josef Plečnik, 1872–1957.   English]
    Jože Plečnik, 1872–1957: architectura perennis / Damjan Prelovšek:
    translated from the German by Patricia Crampton and Eileen Martin.
        p.   cm. – (Architectura perennis)
    Includes bibliographical references and index.
    ISBN 0–300–06953–7 (cl.)
    1. Plečnik, Jože, 1872–1957 – Criticism and interpretation.
    2. Architecture, Modern – 20th century.   I. Title.   II. Series.
NA1455.S563P643613   1997
720′.92 – dc21   96-48899
                                                                                          CIP

For the Yale University Press edition the book has been revised and
altered in several parts. The chapter on Plečnik's activity at Prague Castle has
been practically written anew, based on thorough archival studies during the
course of preparatory works for the 1996 Plečnik Exhibition in Prague. The
footnotes include the latest bibliography, and some illustrations have been
exchanged for the ones that exhibit the present state of monuments.

CONTENTS

1 YOUTH AND EDUCATION

Jože Plečnik came from the same generation as Josef Hoffmann and Adolf Loos. He was born on 23 January 1872 in the former Austro-Hungarian provincial capital of Ljubljana, the third child of Andrej and Helena Plečnik (fig. 2). From early childhood he was expected to inherit his father's modest cabinet-maker's workshop, and to earn his living by repairing and making furniture. His temperament was inherited from both parents: his father was a gentle, melancholy man, with an artist's understanding; his mother was more decisive and ambitious. As a result the young Plečnik would fluctuate between dreams and reality. Both his elder brother Andrej and the younger one, Janez, finished their college education but he gave up in despair in the very first class of secondary school, preferring to return to his father's workshop. In natural sciences and in mathematics his marks were too poor for his mother to be able to boast of three academic sons. During lessons he preferred to observe the teachers' manner and clothing rather than follow the lesson.[1] The young Plečnik loved drawing, but often had to conceal his passion from his father, who, with his bourgeois outlook, feared his good reputation would be threatened: the family did not want a bohemian for a son. Jože enthusiastically collected illustrations from the various journals published at the time in Slovenia, though the selection available was limited. Reproductions of the works of Slav, and above all Czech artists predominated, for their plates, once used, were bought by editors abroad in order both to reduce printing costs and to awaken an enthusiasm for pan-Slavism among their readers.

During Plečnik's early years the social climate of Ljubljana then the capital of the province of Carniola, which had belonged to the Hapsburg crown ever since the thirteenth century (and now the capital of the republic of Slovenia), was determined by the quantitatively smaller, but economically and culturally stronger German-oriented population. The Slovenes, regarded as a people without a history, tried to extricate themselves from their subordinate situation by means of a fictional and romantic glorification of their own past, or by cultural attachment to other, larger Slavic countries. With some 30,000 inhabitants, its characteristic low-rise building style and poorly developed industry, Ljubljana really looked more like an extended village than a town.

Political conflicts with the Germans led to Slovenian expectations that Ljubljana would gradually develop into the centre of the entire Slovenian territories, which, except for Carniola, had been divided ever since the Middle Ages between the provinces of Carinthia, Styria, Gorizia and

2. Family photo of 1889: Plečnik's mother Helena and his father Andrej with their children, Jože, Andrej, Janez and Marija

Istria. However, it would be a long time before Plečnik's vision of a modern capital, which he saw crowned by a monumental parliament building, could be realized. Only a few of the town's inhabitants could boast non-peasant origins going back more than two generations.

Plečnik grew up in this small-town climate, which was influenced on the one hand by the dominance of the Catholic church and on the other by a moderate liberalism, without any major social upheavals. His father came from the village of Hotedršica, south-west of Ljubljana, in the Karst region where the continental architecture begins to make way for Mediterranean stone buildings. He did not move to Ljubljana until the mid-1860s, after spending some time fighting in North Italy; his mother, on the other hand, was a native. At first his parents' origins were of no great importance to Plečnik. However, as he came to maturity as an artist he became more aware of them and tried to use them to escape the influence of the Germanic north which had for centuries decided the fate of his homeland. In 1888 he attended the School of Crafts in Graz with a state bursary, and received an excellent training as a cabinet-maker and in some related crafts (figs 3–4). The boys were taught daily from 7 am to 7 pm, with theoretical disciplines supplemented by time in the workshops. He had a fruitful association with the school's building department pupils, learning so much that Professor Leopold Theyer took him into his atelier as a draughtsman, where Plečnik worked after school hours and on Sundays. The completion of the southern railway connecting Vienna with Trieste had resulted in a real renaissance for the Styrian capital. Theyer employed Plečnik mainly in work on the redesign of the former Joanneum Park, where a ring road was built for Graz on the Viennese pattern.

Theyer was one of those talented graduates of the Viennese Technical University (Technische Hochschule) and the Academy of Fine Arts (Akademie der Bildenden Künste) whose career had taken them through various provincial capitals of the Austro-Hungarian monarchy. Plečnik remembered Theyer with gratitude, aware that without a knowledge of such disciplined architectural drawing he would never have crossed the frontier of craft pure and simple. 'Theyer was of course a Renaissance man – but a little smithy dust from Schmidt[2] still clung to him – and it was that that made Theyer so dear to me',[3] Plečnik wrote years later in his brief autobiography, high-lighting the fine tradition of the Viennese School of Architecture. Technical training was at an enviably high level in Austria at that time. After the World Exhibition of 1873 and the stock exchange crash of the same year, people in Vienna were once again aware of the need to link art, craft and industry together, a

2

problem already recognized and debated after the London World Exhibitions of 1851 and 1862. Education was reorganized on Western European patterns; English models of education and training were adopted. All of this was to leave lasting traces on Plečnik's views.

Plečnik would probably not have found a particularly successful career as an independent cabinet-maker in Ljubljana – he lacked the business sense for that – but in any case the unexpected death of his father gave his life a different direction. His mother and elder brother agreed that Jože was still too young to take over his father's workshop. So in 1892, instead of returning home, he moved on without really wanting to, to Vienna, taken there by Theyer's pupil Leopold Müller, owner of the respected. Imperial and Royal J.W. Müller Court Carpentry business. Two years of factory work were a good, but harsh discipline for Plečnik. It is difficult to reconstruct this period, because Plečnik did not enjoy looking back on it. Later he told his first biographer, Kosta Strajnić, that in Graz he had learned to draw, build models, carve and engrave, as well as being instructed in practical matters, such as the maintenance of a gas engine.[4] The experience he had gained through working with other teachers in Graz was extremely useful to him in Vienna, since besides his work as a draughtsman he was also expected to supervise the output in the workshops. Müller often used leading architects, since his clients included the imperial court as well as the rich Viennese and Hungarian aristocracy. The fact that many of the drawings were by Plečnik himself is shown by the manufacturer Zacherl's family chronicle, where the architect's first visit is recorded. Plečnik recognized the rustic-style furnishings as having been designed by himself.[5]

It will never be possible to reconstruct everything that passed through his hands in the two years he spent working with Müller. Much of the historical furniture of the new wing of the Hofburg, in the Burgtheater and other imperial buildings, might have been made by the young Plečnik. The fundamental knowledge of historical styles he acquired in Graz and in this work in Vienna was just as important to his future development as his interest in the practical and technically perfect English interior, which in Austria was valued as an ideal model for cabinet-makers.

The move to metropolitan Vienna represented a decisive turning-point in Plečnik's life. The city was changing almost before his eyes into the monumental capital of the Danube monarchy. Plečnik was one of the countless workers and craftsmen whose handiwork contributed to this vast wealth, and he saw more than its dazzling glamour. He found the material poverty of his fellowmen hard to bear, and the dirt and stench of the suburbs distressed him. 'I

could write Dante's Journey through Hell,'[6] he complained later. Nevertheless, the lively political climate of the time, with the first public workers' rallies, held little attraction for him.

Philosophically Plečnik was closer to Christian Socialist ideals than to the anti-clericalism of the Social Democrats. He was an enthusiastic supporter of the Vienna mayor Karl Lueger, the leader of the Austrian Christian-Socialist movement, but he never joined his party, although for a time he collaborated in the Leo Society which through its scientific and educational activities, popularized the ideas of Christian Socialism. Political writings did not interest Plečnik; his philosophy was determined more by the workers' physical environment. Exposed to the harsh struggle for survival, and by no means settled ideologically or spiritually, he took refuge in his leisure time in the First District of Vienna where he enjoyed the metropolitan buzz of the central Ringstrasse, which mirrored for him another, apparently more beautiful and well-ordered world. At that time he was still an extremely undecided youth, lacking in self-awareness and confidence, and not really knowing how to shape his life, despite the paternal care bestowed on him by his elder brother. He even dreamed briefly of a literary career. But he found consolation in art and conscientiously looked at what the capital could offer him in this respect. On his visits to the city's exhibitions he felt that his work in the factory would soon destroy him. Deciding that his future lay exclusively in applied art, in 1893 he applied to the School of Arts and Crafts of the Austrian Art and Industry Museum (Museum für Kunst und Industrie), but was turned down by the director of the architectural department, Hermann Herdtle.

Later Plečnik enthusiastically described his visit to the third International Art Exhibition in Vienna's main exhibition place, the Künstlerhaus, in the spring of 1894, which encouraged him to study architecture:

And then, one fine Sunday afternoon, I came to the Künstlerhaus – and as God wills – I saw exhibits of sketches by Otto Wagner – I think the collection was shown on his appointment as Professor – I don't know how and what – any more than I know where I took courage and ideas from – other than God any my stupidity I had no one in the whole of great Vienna. Rudolf Berndt (sic). I knew by sight from the atelier – I went up to him and asked him for a recommendation. Yes – he said – I will recommend you, but not to Wagner – to Luntz. In God's name – so I went to Luntz and there met – as I later realized, his son. He let me go – and I went back to the assembly hall from there with my roll of

3 and 4. Plečnik when a pupil at Graz School of Crafts and as furniture draughtsman in Vienna

drawings – applying without a recommendation – to Wagner . . .[7]

In fact his brothers Andrej and Janez had advised him to follow an academic career. After the death of his father, the elder, Andrej, looked after his mother and supported the education of his two brothers from his modest income as a priest. Andrej's naturally unstable character led him to a Jansenist approach to life. He spent the majority of his days, bitter and introverted, in self-imposed isolation. He had few friends and even among his ecclesiastical superiors he found no understanding, with the result that he gave up his ambition to become a canon. Jože always admired his brother and confided everything to him, seeing him as a decent and good-natured man with an unusual gift of observation. His brother had a profound knowledge of theology, and was a reliable support to him later on, in his efforts to revive church art. It was also Andrej, however, who, after the death of their father, extinguished the last breath of moderate liberalism in the family, which their father had represented, replacing it with his strict Catholicism. The younger Janez was the first to withdraw from the authority of his elder brother. He was of a much more genial temperament and did not choose to take all the sufferings of the world on his shoulders, although he too believed that one must serve the people by working hard.

A year later in 1894 Janez followed his brother Jože to Vienna as a medical student. He had to put up with Jože's indecisiveness for much of the time, and try to help him resolve his existential problems. Janez had an extremely fiery temperament and he did this with only moderate patience. When the brothers argued in Vienna chairs were said to fly out of the window. Plečnik later told his pupils, 'As a child I could get so angry with my brother Janez that I would run after him with a knife. Thank God I never caught him, because I do not know what would have happened',[8] in order to show them that passion had pulsed through his veins too in early years.

Only after lengthy persuasion by the family did Plečnik decide to leave Müller and try his luck again at college, although he had left higher education so ingloriously years before. When he returned to Vienna after the holidays in October 1894 he had forgotten almost all this good advice and was ready to flee to Prague, where he hoped success would come more easily among his Slavic brothers than he could expect in the apparently hostile atmosphere of the multi-national capital. Janez had to exercise some skill in persuading his brother to call on Wagner's colleague Rudolf Bernt at the Academy of Fine Arts, with three drawings and a recommendation from Müller. 'You will be notified,' Wagner is said to have remarked as he looked at the drawings.[9]

Later, Plečnik said that it was only Wagner's 1891 designs for the new Berlin cathedral, which he had seen in the Künstlerhaus, that had moved him to take this step. He had not liked them, but he had sensed the mind of a great artist. Although Plečnik had an excellent command of the heterogeneous vocabulary of decorative late historicism at that time, he had no firm artistic philosophy of his own. The few sheets of drawings preserved show him as a conscientious draughtsman of details and plant studies. He oscillated between self-doubt and exaggerated self-esteem, and did not pay much attention to the progressive tendencies of contemporary Viennese cultural life.

OTTO WAGNER'S PUPIL

In 1894 Plečnik came to Otto Wagner at the Academy of Fine Arts without the relevant education in architecture and the humanities. Almost all of Wagner's pupils came from distinguished bourgeois families. In the very first lesson he heard Wagner's well-known inaugural lecture. Like all newcomers, he was overwhelmed by the manner in which the professor expounded his architectural credo. It was also the first time he had heard the Semper quotation adopted by Wagner: 'Artis sola domina necessitas', which he himself converted nearly thirty years later into 'Nécessité est la mère de l'industrie'.[10] By this Wagner meant that true art is greatly superior to pure functionalism. However, Plečnik's enthusiasm faded when Wagner began to hand out work to the various student years, since he did not feel capable of designing a block of flats. So he buried his hopes of making an impression in front of his colleagues through his skill as a draughtsman, but remained at the Academy despite Wagner's advice 'not to push his way into such things' and to acquire some preliminary knowledge in an atelier.[11] During the academic year of 1894/95 Plečnik worked in Wagner's private atelier and soon acquired some of the basic technical mathematical formulae. Later he said that Wagner had recommended an excellent teacher of applied geometry: 'It is impossible to describe how this man was able to explain everything to me and represent everything pictorially. I can claim that free drawing had never caused me any problems before, but later technical drawing no longer did, either.'[12]

Freed from the oppressive, endless weekly repetition of drawings of Greek, Roman, Gothic and Renaissance decoration with Müller, Plečnik was at last able to breathe in his new milieu. He told Strajnić later that Müller and Wagner were completely different personalities.[13] Wagner was a *grand seigneur* in the best sense of the words and maintained discipline at work through his own example. Since he began work on the projects punctually, he was able to finish them at the agreed time. In addition he was never bad tempered with his fellow-workers. In the course of time he became a father figure to Plečnik. Although Wagner accepted commissions for blocks of flats, Plečnik sensed that his teacher adhered fundamentally to the ideals of art. He particularly liked to recall how lovingly Wagner created little sketches, needed by his fellow-workers in order to work out his plans. Work in his atelier made good progress, because all the workers there were paid by the hour and the conditions were clearly set out. Wagner arrived every morning at 8.0 am from his villa in Hütteldorf and corrected the plans in the atelier until midday. At 1.30 pm he returned from lunch in his town residence and went on working until 5.0 pm. He had eighteen workers, to whom Plečnik was the youngest addition. Plečnik enjoyed many interesting and happy hours in this environment. Strajnić recorded the anecdote of the Monarch Franz Josef's visit to the atelier. Wagner proudly presented his fellow-workers to the monarch as 'hungry royal tigers', to which the Monarch apparently replied: 'But, Herr Oberbaurat, these are royal rabbits, not royal tigers'.[14]

The year with Wagner came to an end and Plečnik was once again at a loss. Only when Wagner let him know that he would be glad to have him as a pupil did he pluck up his courage and register at the Academy again.

There is no doubt that Plečnik's vehement efforts to compensate for the painful failure of his first attempt to enter the Academy made a decisive contribution to this unexpected development. The following comment by Josef Hoffmann is

5. Study trip to Munich, summer 1897: Wagner's students at St Peter's cemetery in Salzburg

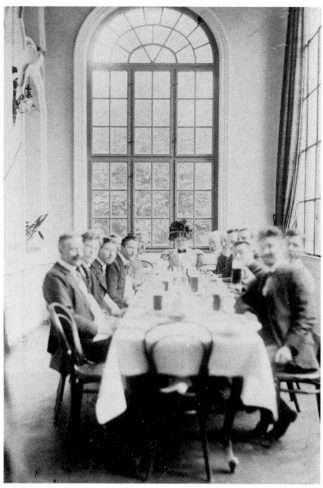

6. Study trip to Munich, summer 1897: Plečnik (third from the left), between F. Matouschek and A. Ludwig; in the background Fr. von Thiersch, Frau Wagner, A. Streit and Otto Wagner

evidence of his persistence: 'He was completely absorbed in his work and his plans, and thought of nothing else. Thanks to this intense concentration he was very withdrawn and completely dedicated to his task.'[15]

Plečnik completed his studies within the prescribed three years. Though he greatly appreciated student life, he nevertheless remained closely linked with the atelier, because the Academy left him sufficient time for himself. His colleagues also earned their money in various ateliers or by drawing at home. At the end of the study year the students showed Wagner what they had done and, according to Plečnik, they made considerable use of him.[16] 'You did not know him well', Plečnik wrote in 1929 to his earlier fellow-student Alfred Castelliz. 'Most people in the atelier had no notion of him at all – but perhaps I saw into him more deeply because I was from a more southern spot, grew up under the walls of Emona (the Roman forerunner to Ljubljana, author's comment) and he was such a father to me!'[17] A somewhat unusual comment which it is impossible to understand without knowledge of his later reflections.

Wagner's first years at the Academy were crucial to the development of modern architecture in Austria. Everything Plečnik heard initially at the Academy was based on Wagner's recognition that his architecture must follow the revolutions taking place in Europe. Work on predominantly utilitarian tasks, such as the building of the Viennese municipal railway, which began in 1894, or the regulation of the Danube canal, hastened the process of maturity. Since the commissions for the Ringstrasse, and hence all the prestigious building commissions, had already been handed out, Wagner had to fall back on the area of technology. His maxim that the artist had to take over the reins from the engineers was thus the result of a painful personal experience. Wagner involuntarily confirmed Semper's prediction that increasingly the architect would be obliged to take on utilitarian tasks, leading to the birth of a new style.[18]

Wagner provided Plečnik with a fundamental grammar which at that time seemed to be the only way to achieve the morphological and syntactical continuance of Classical Antiquity. Plečnik achieved real mastery in the renewal of the traditional language of form and was thus able to avoid short-lived fashions. Even if later on he often doubted his own abilities, he was always convinced of the rightness of his aesthetic judgment, and he remained true to himself even when the emergence of Functionalism cast some doubt on his universalist views, accepting his place on the margin of current trends.

To Plečnik, the part of Wagner's architectural theory drawn from the German architect and theorist Gottfried Semper was of particular significance. Only by considering

Semper's theories can we follow the thread of Plečnik's beliefs, which, proceeding from Schinkel's engagement with Antiquity, led via Vienna to Prague and Ljubljana. Before this, it is worth remembering his origins as a poorly trained cabinet-maker, one who after one year's preparation and three years' study in Wagner's special class at the Vienna Academy, developed into a famous artist, praised even by the critical Adolf Loos.

SEMPER'S PRINCIPLE OF CLADDING

In his mature years Plečnik scarcely ever mentioned Gottfried Semper, whom he wrongly regarded, probably throughout his life, as Swiss;[19] nevertheless he owed the greater part of his morphological knowledge to him. His striving for absolute art – Stele speaks of the 'architecture perennis' – corresponds to Semper's understanding of style. Semper thought, to put it simply, not of a specific historical style, but of a method of processing building material according to function, that is, the rules of the process of creation should be a synopsis of historical development. Hence they can continue to apply in all times and everywhere. However, Semper saw function considerably more comprehensively than Wagner's positivistically oriented generation, who were concerned only with its rational material dimension. This concept of style represented for both Semper and Plečnik the standard for distinguishing between utilitarian buildings and true architecture.

Semper's influence on Viennese art theory was fundamental. Arts and crafts – or industrial art (Kunstindustrie) as Semper called it – were also taken by the co-founder of the Viennese School of Art History, Franz Wickhoff, whose teacher had been Semper's pupil Alexander Conze, as the point of departure for his theories.[20] Following Wickhoff and his younger colleague Alois Riegl, art historians turned away from the exclusive consideration of the great classical themes and devoted themselves to previously undervalued epochs and peripheral areas of art history as well, which was also a result of the multitude of artistic monuments of only provincial quality that were spread throughout the Austro-Hungarian empire. This disconcerted the young Plečnik and shook his faith in the inviolability of fixed values; it brought the art of his Slovenian homeland closer to him.

In Vienna at the turn of the century, Semper's theories, based on German idealistic philosophy, increasingly lost their original significance and became synonymous with a materialistic view of art. Riegl, who introduced the concept of artistic intention (Kunstwollen) into the history of art,

was basically settling accounts with the then customary view of Semper's theories rather than with Semper himself. Riegl's views were also followed by Max Dvořák. He was, among other things, the teacher of Plečnik's biographer and apologist France Stele, who attached very little importance to Semper's influence on Plečnik. Plečnik himself could not completely bypass Riegl's theories, of which more later.

Although Wagner accused Semper of inconsistency with regard to the interpretation of functionality in architecture,[21] he nevertheless quoted him frequently. Semper's theoretical maxims bear witness to an extraordinary knowledge of archaeology and the history of art, but seen as a whole they were not revolutionary enough to be taken over without amendment as the basis of a manifesto of modern architecture. This is clearly apparent in the matter of iron construction work. Whereas Wagner was an enthusiast for iron, Semper warned against its excessive use for monumental building projects.[22] For him iron was a universal building material which one could pour, hammer, roll, press, in short, submit to all the methods of technical processing. He therefore did not award iron the rank of a primary building material, although he included it in all four classes of the technical arts: textiles, ceramics, tectonics (carpentry) and stereotomy (stone construction). In his fundamental work *Der Stil* (*Style*) he allots no more space to iron than to rubber. Semper continued to regard stone as the most important building material, valuing iron more for its decorative possibilities. It worried him that the minimal use of material in iron constructions, as for instance the extremely slim but still classically designed columns of modern buildings, did not appear to have the same stability and solidity that the traditionally trained eye saw in the Greek temple.

An understanding for the meaningful relationship of function, building material and construction was passed on to Wagner by his two teachers, van der Nüll and Sicardsburg. When he accepted the chair at the Academy in 1894 he needed an appropriate theoretical superstructure for his practical work. This he took over almost word for word from Semper's *Stil*. However, he latched onto the more radical theories in Semper's early papers, which contain the first seeds of theories later worked out in more detail, but never fully concluded. The motto referred to, 'Art knows only one master: necessity', appears in the paper written in 1834 on the polychromy of antique architectural sculpture.[23] With this the young Semper was declaring war on eclecticism, and he came into conflict with two authorities of his time: with Durand's schematized historical typology and with Winckelmann's idea of the 'white' art of Antiquity.[24]

However, Wagner did not share Semper's opinion with

regard to construction. In contrast to Semper, he believed that construction was the original cell of architecture and the seed of the new modern forms.[25] In daily practice, he continued to make use of the wealth of symbolism offered him by Semper's principle of cladding (Bekleidungsprinzip), paying more attention to traditional ornament than to modern construction, in which, according to him, the ornament should originate. Thus, modern architecture in Austria proceeded not from radical changes but from the adaptation of traditional ornament to modern needs; so the ornament became the symbol of the new aesthetics. One need only think of the florid literary style of his study for the new building the Imperial and Royal Academy of Fine Arts in Vienna in 1898, on which Plečnik also worked.

Wagner's book *Moderne Architektur* (*Modern Architecture*), apart from its importance in the context of the development of European architectural theory, is a compendium of his own experience, of faith in the future and of Semper's views, but it is not a complete system of architectural philosophy.[26] Semper did not complete *Der Stil*; the third and last part – the comparative doctrine of style in which he intended to apply his knowledge to the practice of architecture in order to indicate guidelines for contemporary architecture – is missing. So Wagner had plenty of scope in his book. Plečnik's generation, which in one way or another was involved in the debate on architectural theory between the end of 1894 and the publication of the book in the summer of 1896, was already able to distinguish the foundations of Semper's grammar of form from the declared ideals of the new architecture. Wagner employed cultivated, imaginative and skilled draughtsmen,[27] who were capable of adapting Semper's language of form to contemporary taste. It was a question of the process of renewal, or, according to Semper, of invention,[28] the magical word of the nineteenth century, which Plečnik also used later in his School in Ljubljana.

The fact that Wagner did not distance himself greatly from Semper on many points is evident from his broad interpretation of the concept of style, or perhaps even more from the marginal comment on the traditional study trips to Italy, in which he says that young architects are not yet sufficiently mature to be capable of reconstructing the genesis of forms and their justification.[29] Here he was referring to Semper's theory of metabolism, which states that specific original forms of one material are converted into another. Wagner modernized the classical language of architecture by stressing surfaces and geometrizing ornament to suit contemporary design and the new technology.

By working daily on their concrete tasks, Wagner's students were diverted from theoretical writings. Plečnik was no exception in this. In the spring of 1903 he wrote to his brother Andrej: 'It is easy to talk – but to do – this is what I would like to tell everyone: work and leave the writing alone. A critic should be nothing but a chronicler. Philosophers and other scholars can be leaders – encouraging the artist – the man of finance who can see a little deeper – the conductor . . .'[30] For the rest of his life Plečnik remained true to the pragmatic style of Wagner's atelier.

Impelled by his own particular social, cultural and national origins, Plečnik selected from Semper's writing the points which were significant for his needs. The symbolism of ornamentation and the question of professional ethos meant more to him than the problems of the big city or modern technology. In this way he remained in many respects more strongly linked than Wagner with Semper's basic thinking. Whereas, for instance, Wagner allotted no more than a marginal position to the arts and crafts, for Plečnik they always remained the seed of all monumental art. Later Plečnik opposed Wagner's demand for the 'flat handling of the surface'[31] and set against it his expressly Mediterranean feeling for plasticity.

The intensity with which Plečnik adhered to Semper's theories changed over the years, without in any way affecting his agreement with the content. This was apparent in his period as professor at the Prague College of Arts and Crafts and at the time of the more intense concern with arts and crafts caused by the shortage of major commissions after the Second World War. Whenever Plečnik talked about the existence of two original styles – the Antique and the Gothic – the role of architecture, the demand for monumentality or the like, we can always hear the echo of the more or less covert philosophy of Semper's *Stil*. Also the denial of the Baroque, which he came to understand better only through contact with his native monuments, is not the fruit of his own, but of Semper's historical experience in the mid-nineteenth century.

Let us try to define that part of Semper's theory which directly affected Plečnik. Impressed by the exact sciences, during his journeys through southern Italy and Greece the German architect was working to achieve a normative system of architecture.[32] On the question of the polychromy of antique architecture he referred back to the findings of his contemporaries Jakob Ignaz Hittorf and Henri Labroust, whereas it was the Englishman, Thomas Hope, who gave him an understanding of the material-specific and climatic conditions.[33] Before Semper, Carl Bötticher had reached similar conclusions by separating core form and art form.[34] In order to underpin the phenomenon of the organic growth of classical architecture the archaeologically experienced Semper turned from Greek Antiquity to the Assyrian and

Babylonian area. Semper's somewhat exotic theory, as Wagner called it, contains *a priori* reasoning as well as surprising, if logical reversals. For instance, he contradicts the view that art developed from simplicity to richness and from there to excessively cluttered forms;[35] such a view was later officially introduced into the history of art by Heinrich Wölfflin.

The focal point of his theory is the primacy of what he called industrial art, from which, according to him, architecture could take 'ready-made' decorations. This is supposed to pass on to monumental architecture the language of forms already developed. According to Semper, this can also be understood in reverse: whenever art loses its true direction, it has to refer back to the arts and crafts, in order to reestablish a harmony between construction and decoration.[36] This also became Plečnik's maxim for life. He impressed on his pupils: 'If you devote yourselves to arts and crafts you will become alive and only this will make you into proper architects.'[37] Semper touched on classical German idealistic philosophy with his explanation of the relative autonomy of architectural symbols. In *Der Stil* he wrote: 'The tectonic structure achieves monumentality only by emancipation from structural and material realism, by the symbolic spiritualization of the expression of its purpose.'[38] He developed his theory of cladding, an area in which textile art assumes a central role. Textile art and ceramics, according to Semper, produce the initial symbols which are subsequently converted by architecture. They are either borrowed from nature or they are the traditional forms of different social eras and their industrial art. Thus for Semper the symbolic forms refer to the function of the individual parts of the building, the whole, the purpose, etc.[39]

Semper assumes that the products which serve the basic needs of humanity have not changed as much as their material and technology.[40] Since the properties of the material affect the method of processing, there are metamorphoses during the development period between the original material and the final stage – Semper sums this up under the concept of metabolism – although the memory of the original form is preserved. In accordance with the principle of cladding, architecture should thus be a kind of palimpsest on which varied ornaments of past times, conditioned by current technologies should be loaded over the centuries. With reference to classical Greek architecture Semper contradicted Vitruvius's theory, according to which wood construction passed straight into stone construction. Semper held the theory that there was an interim phase, of which metal cladding of all kinds had been characteristic, which enriched Greek temple building with dynamism.[41]

He called this the 'tubular principle' or 'tubular style', which for him meant a hollow 'body', consisting only of 'cladding'.

Those chapters of Semper's *Stil* in which he deals with the classification of different races in terms of the step they have reached on his speculative ladder of development are also crucial to an understanding of Plečnik. The ideal synthesis of structural and symbolic form, bestows eternal validity on the Greek temples. This unusual thought already contains all the elements of Plečnik's later idea of the 'architectura perennis'. Semper writes:

> When we go through the history of architecture and compare the different types of style, we are struck by the fact that almost all of them are based on very sound principles of statics and construction; however, only one nation has succeeded in breathing organic life into its architectural creations and its industrial products. Greek temples and monuments were not built, they grew, they are not, like those of the Egyptians, simply externally adorned by the addition of vegetable embellishment; their forms are in themselves such as organic life produces in its struggle against gravity and substance. In no other way can we explain the incomparable charm of a Greek column.[42]

It was in this sense that Plečnik also saw architecture as an organism. He used it, not knowing that it was a characteristic concept of the mid-nineteenth century,[43] which Semper had defined precisely for the first time.

The point of departure for Plečnik's emphasis on the moral element in architecture must be sought in Semper's treatise 'Die vier Elemente der Baukunst' ('The Four Elements of Architecture'). These are the hearth, the roof, the enclosing wall and earthwork, corresponding to the four basic materials and techniques.[44] The hearth plays a central ethical role, since it is simultaneously the symbol of settlement, of civilization and humanity, or, the centre of society, the family, the place where the first social orders and religion are founded. Wagner contradicted this theory, while Plečnik, with his more traditional outlook, saw nothing wrong with it. Indeed he later bestowed on his pupils the symbolic title of 'Hearth of Academic Architects'.

At first sight it looks as if sheathing and concealing the building structure contradicts precisely the definition of the relationship between building material and construction determined as far as back the eighteenth century by Lodoli and Laugier. Viollet-le-Duc actualized this definition in the nineteenth century and it was transferred directly from him to the twentieth-century aesthetics of Functionalism. If one takes Semper's individual ideas out of their overall context they may sound very misleading, as for instance when he speaks of colour as the most perfect means of dispelling reality.[45] That the protagonists of Viennese architecture nevertheless well understood the German theorist is evident from Loos's article 'Das Prinzip der Bekleidung' (The Principle of Cladding), in which he sheds light on the question of morality in art with the help of Semper's maxim and states that no material allows interference with its own particular range of forms. 'Anyone who nevertheless risks such an invasion will be branded by the world as a forger. But art has nothing to do with forgery. Its ways are full of thorns, but pure'.[46] Loos was echoing the ideas of Semper and Wagner.

Plečnik adopted Semper's doctrine without hesitation, convinced of its high moral value. His understanding of polychromy as the introduction of pigment into the very material instead of as an addition on the surface also comes from Semper. Semper claimed that textile dyeing had a more ancient origin than painting.[47]

However, the concepts of colouring, cladding, masking and decorating did not make Plečnik turn away from the technologically correct treatment of material. If Wagner reduced Semper's complex theory to the direct causal relationship between construction and form, or between function and form,[48] the more poetic Plečnik adhered to its idealism as well. Their differing views may also have resulted from the generation gap, as the younger Plečnik was more strongly influenced by the fin-de-siècle climate than his teacher. However, this did not prevent the uncompromising Loos from continuing to value Plečnik as an artist who was on the right path.

In the 1834 text referred to above, Semper also speaks fleetingly of faith. These statements could not, of course, greatly impress Wagner, but they had more effect on Plečnik, ending as they did with an appeal against the tendency to art for art's sake. 'Religion has at all times been the nursemaid of the arts,' wrote Semper, and continued:

> They aged with her. To this extent their stages of life can be defined by the age of religious concepts and forms. The history of art passed through mysticism, symbolism and allegory. In its last period of degeneration it loses all meaning and lays itself open to general reproach for sophisticated stimulation of the senses. The representation of the beautiful should never be the purpose of a work of art. Beauty is a necessary property of the work of art, like the extension of the bodies. It has never occurred to anyone to represent the mere concept of size by erecting a colossus.[49]

To overcome the 'styleless' present, Semper proposed two principles in which Plečnik also believed: convention and taste.[50]

Despite lack of scientific proof, Semper's cladding principle, which discusses the textile origins of the walls and coverings of the earliest constructed human dwellings, was of great practical significance in Vienna. The Secessionists enthusiastically delved into arts and crafts and looked for inspiration in the ornaments of the colourful Persian carpets and other oriental textiles. Wagner was not opposed to such trends in the development of Viennese art, and he himself encouraged his students to take creatively from the treasures of traditional ornaments.[51] Semper's theory enabled Wagner to observe and analyse historical forms in themselves, with the eyes of the practical creative artist. This approach was detached from the scientific archaeological and art-historical viewpoint, which it actually contradicted in some points. Such findings out of the genesis of individual forms, based entirely on artistic intuition, was very suitable for Plečnik in view of the gaps in his education, especially as in this respect he had something of a lead over his colleagues thanks to his experience of the arts and crafts. He even believed himself to be closer to the true spirit of antiquity than any scholar. Looking at forms he already knew through Semper's eyes brought him closer to the justification of every individual form and confirmed his belief in the possibility of their use in a new syntactic order.

Visits to museums, the study of ethnological collections and his interest in illustrated art books played an essential part in Plečnik's academic studies. The parallels between art and music to which Semper refers[52] opened up to him the world of cadences and other rules of composition which could be applicable to fine art. We can see that Wagner too attached importance to his pupils' musical gifts from the fact that when he was trying to obtain a professorship for Olbrich at the School of Arts and Crafts of the Austrian Museum, he made much of his musical interpretive abilities.[53] In contrast to his younger brother, Plečnik was no instrumentalist, but he was very musical and liked to whistle arias from operas as he worked. When Wagner saw the dedication with which Plečnik tackled the problems of the fine arts, he referred to him one day as Pygmalion.

Wagner enabled Plečnik to develop his talent freely while at the same time imbuing him with the conviction that architecture was the most important social task. Semper had already made the same claim.[54] However, he had not linked this with the idea that only spiritual suffering leads to human greatness. Plečnik's teacher, on the other hand, whose views of modern architecture met with great opposition, warned his pupils of a thorny future;[55] because only a few of the elect understand the language of architecture, the architect is not bound to respect public opinion. Plečnik, the believer, interpreted the professor's warning principally in the sense of strict Christian morality: repentance, enlightenment and sacrifice. Few students were later prepared to follow him in the asceticism which already bordered on a monastic way of life. It is striking that in his early period the young Le Corbusier was concerned with similar issues.[56] Wagner, on the other hand, aligned himself with Michelangelo and his superhuman struggle with art and God.

The situation altered fundamentally with the emergence of Functionalism. While the generation of Giedion and Pevsner attributed the development of modern architecture to technology, under Semper's influence Plečnik adhered to the evolution of traditional form. Semper explained the difference between Functionalism and monumentality with the example of the Caribbean hut, which displays all the four architectonic elements, yet lacks the cohesive force of creativity to elevate it from pure technique to the level of art.[57] With the notion 'to elevate', which Plečnik liked to use as a description of intervention in existing architecture, he also remained true to Semper's phraseology.

Wagner was among the most constant spokesmen for this chapter of Semper's doctrine. In 1893 he was already stressing in the explanatory report on the Master plan for the regulation of Vienna that it is for the artist to take charge of town planning. He repeated this idea in his inaugural speech, already referred to, as well as soon afterwards in his book *Moderne Architektur*. Such an idea fell on fruitful ground with Plečnik. As Wagner put it: 'Since the engineer is seldom born an artist, while the architect can generally be made into an engineer, it may safely be assumed that in time art, or the architect, must succeed in expanding his influence to the area now occupied by the engineer, so that here too the legitimate aesthetic demands are satisfied.'[58] A basic dilemma of the second half of the nineteenth century is being addressed here, and Wagner offered Plečnik eloquent argument in support of the theory that someone trained only in technology would be incapable of creating full-scale architecture. Nevertheless, this was still the period of the elegant metal constructions of the church designed for Osijek, the antique-type pylons of the Vienna municipal railway and similar technologically influenced building works by Otto Wagner. When, under the influence of the new trends in architecture, Wagner greatly simplified his formal vocabulary, Plečnik was disappointed: 'In any case,' he wrote, 'the man would perhaps later have preferred to become an engineer – earlier – before that discovery, he was an architect.'[59] As the steel and concrete spread, Plečnik must have felt that a part of architecture was being withdrawn from him; nonetheless he clung to his belief that the most important part of architecture was a monumental building.

Plečnik's studies under Wagner were helped by various favourable factors without which he might at best have become a fashionable arranger of Viennese interiors. Wagner equipped him to carry out every kind of architectural commission. Plečnik's theoretical knowledge alone would not have been enough seriously to contradict any of the chapters from Semper's *Der Stil*. Of course, as a sensitive artist he could always be influenced by his surroundings but remain true to himself on fundamental issues. As he strongly sensed, especially after the First World War, Semper's fate became his own. In the 1930s a point was reached where even his immediate pupils were no longer able to understand his method of composition. Plečnik became a unique phenomenon on the European architectural scene, and he could work only under the quite specific conditions of a provincial milieu on the margin of current trends. All the same, unless he wished to be untrue to almost all his youthful ideals concerning the ethics of architecture, he had to keep to this path.

While he attended the Viennese Academy he showed no particular sympathy for other architectural theories. A good example of this is Semper's contemporary, Viollet-le-Duc. While Wagner followed Viollet-le-Duc's statements on the functional, national and social elements in architecture with interest – themes which should actually have been close to Plečnik's thinking – he attached more value to the practical application of Viollet-le-Duc's texts. For Plečnik Viollet-le-Duc's huge lexicon of French medieval architecture[60] represented a welcome supplement to Semper's *Stil*. It made him aware of the purely technical aspects of classical architecture as well as the typology of liturgical art, and awakened his interest in everyday history. He actually copied a few of the illustrations. For instance, in the chapter entitled 'Tombeau' he was interested only in the baldachin over a tomb, not in the tombstone itself, which had nothing in common with Semper's cladding principle. In the chapter entitled 'Maison' his attention was caught by a stone house near Avallon, whose three long walls are pierced by the facade and project above its surface; he sketched this too. He adopted these ideas in the late 1920s when building the mountain church on the Krvavec. Similarly, in his mature years Plečnik used Auguste Choisy's *Histoire de l'Architecture* (Paris 1899) as a manual on building techniques in Antiquity. This work offered him a lot of creative ideas on the explanation of the genesis of individual architectural elements. So, in many ways, the manual served him as an indispensable source for metamorphosing forms of Antiquity.

11

Some of the English theorists would surely have been closer to Plečnik, since they espoused similar aims.[61] The equation of the Gothic with Christianity by Pugin, and its association with morality and democracy, Ruskin's moral doctrine, William Morris's veneration for arts and crafts, his utopian Socialism and the revival of the Guild system, or Ebenezer Howard's idea of the garden city could have had a greater influence on him than was actually the case. These authors were available to Plečnik only in translation, although it must be said that even before Hermann Muthesius the German-speaking area was familiar with trends in England. Besides the French journals *L'Art et Décoration* and *L'Art Décoratif*, Wagner's students were interested in the British journal *The Studio*. Nevertheless these theories reached Plečnik relatively late. Some of Morris's ideas, however, were close to his own. In Prague, and later on in Ljubljana, he tried to raise the level of the native arts and crafts by producing objects d'art with his students, but the revival of medieval crafts and their techniques was not his ideal. That would have been in contradiction to Semper's ideas in *Stil*, which was intended as a manual for the renewal of an industrial art based on machine work.

Plečnik's assertion to his brother that he did not know Ruskin well enough was true up to a point. He felt drawn to some of Ruskin's ideas. He particularly liked to quote the statement that good art was always the result of a morally sound society, but since both the good and the bad could be inherited, we should not be indifferent to how we shape our life and what we bequeath to future generations.[62]

There are considerably fewer theoretical agreements between Howard's garden city and Plečnik's idea for the planning of the northern part of Ljubljana in 1929 although at first sight they seem very similar. Their starting points were in fact quite different, but more of this later.

Like Plečnik, the Dutch architect Hendrik Petrus Berlage also based his work on Semper's theory, although he was influenced by Viollet-le-Duc and Camillo Sitte as well.[63] Plečnik actually described one of Berlage's texts, presumably because of the social aspects which Berlage was trying to associate with aesthetic criteria, as 'the most interesting work by an architect that I have ever read'.[64] With regard to Berlage's modular experiments he said:

I have always followed such studies with great interest, since I myself am not versed in such canons. Who indeed should be versed in them? The purpose of the canon is merely to awaken people's interest, after which anyone can assimilate it and interpret it independently. I, being more idle, use the square, of course – pure theory does not help here either, it is merely a check '*for discipline*'. No law is of use here. It is a completely individual matter. We must not become slaves to such a canon, nevertheless it undoubtedly gives us a scaffolding. The fact is that I, when I examine a ground plan in accordance with these principles, create great order and a clear rhythm . . .[65]

Of the Viennese theorists Alois Riegl, who 'dethroned' Semper's theories in art history, seems to have exerted the greatest influence on the young Plečnik. Plečnik was not much concerned with Riegl's two major works, *Stilfragen* (*Questions of Style*) and *Die Spätrömische Kunstindustrie* (*Late Roman Industrial Art*), but some of their theories must have been known to him, since they were so topical at the time. Riegl had nothing essentially new to say to him, nor could he shake his faith in Semper. Nevertheless, Plečnik's description of the 'inner nerve of art'[66] is close to Riegl's concept of the 'will to art'. In this way Plečnik more or less intuitively realized that the art of individual geographic areas developed according to its own immanent logic; this idea was later formulted by F. Stele as the 'geographic constants of art history'. Plečnik's conviction that the simple forms of early Christian architecture were not the result of a 'barbarization' of Antiquity but were based primarily on a deliberate will[67] can certainly be attributed to Riegl. The same is true of his concern, when he was already a college professor, with a common national will in architecture and art.[68]

Indirectly one can find one idea of Riegl's in Plečnik's correspondence, but, in contrast to the work of the Viennese art historian, it is of an emphatically Christian nature. It is a bizarre flash of ideas on the fringe of mysticism, which Riegl discussed in his work on the Dutch portrait. According to Riegl, the artistic genius is none other than the unconscious, though at the same time perfect, executor of the artistic will of a particular nation.[69] For Plečnik's client Johann E. Zacherl and probably also in the architect's interpretation, the will of God replaced the artistic will. In this case it was possible that this idea was a latent romantic thought which was introduced as early as the second half of the eighteenth century into German art philosophy by J. G. Hamann, who interpreted the gift of a genius as a reflection of the original image of all creation; so it was a case of imitating God himself.

Plečnik also acquired something from Max Fabiani, his professional colleague and a native from the Slovenian Karst region in Wagner's atelier. Fabiani had been interested for some time in the question of race or the national element in architecture,[70] in the sense of Semper's comparative doctrine of style, which interpreted, for instance, the difference between the two basic vessel shapes of Antiquity, the Egyp-

12

tian *situla* and the Greek *hydra*, as the expression of opposite poles of civilization.[71] In his classification of art according to material, technical, climatic, religious, political, national and personal factors, Semper left the door open to various theories, as for instance Hippolyte Taine's theory of the importance of the environment. For Wagner, material and technology were in the foreground, and the geographical, national and cultural history factors adduced by Semper were of only marginal interest to him.[72] Plečnik, as a member of a small and constantly threatened nation, had sufficient grounds to pay attention, like Semper, to Fabiani's reflections mentioned above on the differences in the character of national expression in architecture.

Wagner was convinced that Plečnik lacked a general humanistic education, for which he was trying to compensate by reading, rather than a knowledge of aesthetic theories. In his letters to his brother Andrej, Plečnik mentions here and there the author and title of a work he had read, though these were primarily works of religious literature. In the first decade of the twentieth century Plečnik was intensely preoccupied with modern Christian thought. However, he also enjoyed reading the Classics: Plato, Dante, Pascal, and above all the Russian writers. His favourites were Dostoevsky's *Brothers Karamazov*, Cervantes' *Don Quixote* and the novels of Dickens.[73] Plečnik was relatively unversed in modern Viennese literature. His rather conservative outlook can to some extent be seen as a rejection of the worldly Wagner. Nevertheless, Plečnik did not go as far as Tolstoy, for instance, and reject all contemporary art. In 1898 he recommended Tolstoy's book *Against Modern Art* to his brother for its Christian views, although he himself did not share all the maxims it contained.[74] However, he vehemently rejected Nietzsche, whose works – in his opinion – expressed an arrogance which he found barbaric.[75]

It is scarcely possible that Otto Weininger's book of 1903 *Geschlecht und Charakter* (*Sex and Character*), which was very popular in its day, ever came into Plečnik's hands. The anxieties of society at the turn of the century which it describes and which led Weininger to aggressive anti-feminism,[76] were in any case in general circulation in Vienna. People spoke of the feminization of art. The ascetic way of life was seen as an alternative, a means of preserving its ethical and cultural virility. Under the spiritual guidance of his morally strict brother Andrej, Plečnik was predestined for this. He had already begun to lead an almost monastic life, without pondering much over the real reasons for his decision.

Life in the capital did not loosen Plečnik's close ties with his home; on the contrary, for fear of losing himself in Vienna,

he clung all the more firmly to his homeland. He told his brother: 'The capital promotes talent – but it destroys every man's soul.'[77] His constant reappraisal of anything new and strange with the help of Christian ethics indicates the dominant influence of his brother and of the traditional milieu from which he came. His loyalty to his small country weighed on him, since all his life he felt obliged to make good some of the shortcomings in its culture. 'It seems that I live in poor company,' he complained to his brother Andrej:

> This is a German Vienna – and I want nothing more than to be increasingly a Carniolan – a Slovene – in the same way as my parents on the one hand – and on the other hand – not to distance myself, in progressing or rather developing, from what is native to me. It is in fact all waste land – we have nothing – and yet in this period I have observed our character – and I was taken by it.[78]

What is surprising about the above quotation is that Plečnik stresses character and not national artistic peculiarities. Only in this way, however, could he avoid including ethnography in art, which to his compatriots in the Viennese Association for Fine Arts, *Vesna* (*Spring*)[79], was the mainspring of their aims.

The mechanical transposition of Semper's methods to popular art was a trap in which the friend of Plečnik's youth, the technically trained architect Ivan Jager, was caught, seeking original artistic forms in decorations on Easter eggs, fur garments and peasant barn buildings. Plečnik never fell victim to the vulgarization of Semper's doctrines, nor was he particularly well versed in Slovenian fine art.

Against the glorification of Germanhood which became more and more manifest before the approaching world war he set the whole cultural tradition of the Slavs. The Czechs played a particularly élite role in his ideas. It is no accident that he soon formed a friendship with the Czech Jan Kotěra, a year older than himself, who also gathered other Wagner pupils about him. For Plečnik, Kotěra personified the best tradition of the people he so greatly admired. On the other hand, Kotěra believed in Plečnik's great gifts and missed no opportunity to recommend him to his fellow countrymen. When in 1900 Kotěra joined the publishers of the journal *Volné směry* (*Ways of Freedom*), the Czechs were able consistently to follow Plečnik's rise. The latter's preoccupation with the fame of Czech history awakened feelings of inferiority in Plečnik which he tried to counter by seeking a specific form of expression for Slavic fine art, hoping in this way to reap success with the Czechs as well. He was particularly attracted by the needlework in the ethnographic museum in Prague and while looking at it was guided only by his artistic taste. He discovered the very things he himself was striving for, those simple, clear classical forms, expressed with a certain austerity. According to Kotěra, Plečnik regarded astringency and lyricism as specifically Slavic character traits.[80] In order to withdraw from Wagner's influence, Plečnik began to stress more emphatically the emotional element of art. According to his fellow pupil Hans Kestranek, this would lead him back to his 'true and best virtues'.[81] In Vienna Plečnik was pleased by every success attained by Kotěra and the Czechs.

Plečnik regarded Slavic art as a kind of sleeping beauty, which would awake in the twentieth century. 'There is a suffering, silent energy within us,'[82] he wrote after the successful exhibition by the Polish association 'Sztuka' in the Viennese Secession in 1902. He frequently reminded his Czech friend not to be unfaithful to Slavic austerity. A momentary euphoria actually moved him to the following statememt:

> Perhaps I err in my simplicity – we artists – Kotěra can be assured we are artists – are God's elect – the blessing of nations – but we must know – that we are not artists in order to make works of art – but that in pain and suffering we bring ourselves in the search for the beautiful and good – possibly close to God – to the understanding of justice, and make good people – good righteous men as perfect as possible! Everything else is added to us.[83]

At that time Plečnik was already convinced that he had found the specific expression of Slavic art, including his particular homeland. He declared his work to be national art valid for the whole Slavic world, and Kotěra and Fabiani acknowledged this.[84] However, it is important to remember that Plečnik did not thereby move away from the classical repertory of forms.

THE LANGUAGE OF FORMS MATURES

Plečnik's period at the Academy occurred as the Austrian variant of Art Nouveau was developing. Wagner followed the Western decorative fashion with reservation, restricting vegetable ornamentation to limited geometrical surfaces in order not to smother the building structure. Plečnik's approach was different. For him Secessionist art represented a state of mind, which he linked with concepts such as lightness, tenderness, poetry, spring budding and the like. This, as we have seen, also corresponded to his ideas of a national art. At last he was able to give free rein to his lyrical nature, suppressed until then by the strict framework of late historicism. This was something like a psychoanalytical attempt at liberation, connected with the memory of home, childhood, and after his return from his study tour in Italy and France (1898–9), his mother. He did not need a new language of form in order to do justice to modern architecture, being able to adapt the traditional forms to the desired expression. Wagner also valued this ability in Plečnik.

His first drawings to be published in the journal *Der Architekt* (*The Architect*) are a conglomerate of Mediterranean elements, and we can easily see what inspired him. As we know he showed a great interest in Ancient Greece and Egypt. 'I knew him to the bottom of his soul. His love of Greek art – unless it happened to be ceramics – is insignificant.'[85] Fabiani was to write after Plečnik's death, with the intention of shielding him from the then current accusation of eclecticism. Without Semper, Plečnik would not have discovered the painted Greek vases of which traces can be found in some of his early drawings, like the 1896 competition design for the poster for an English printer.[86] He was later to produce variations of the shapes of the ceramic vessels in metal, wood, stone and artificial stone. Apparently not even Fabiani was aware how much freedom Plečnik was able to create for himself within the fixed typology of arts and crafts. Another aspect of this is his admiration of Classical Greek architecture, which up to 1927 he knew only from museum fragments and literature.

None of the Eastern or antique models, however, made as much impression on him as Ancient Egyptian art, to which Semper had in fact not attached great value, although he often referred to it when defining the various concepts. On Sundays Plečnik spent hours admiring the rich collection of coffins and sculpture in the Viennese Kunsthistorisches Museum. He would imagine the distant, alien age in which, with such huge effort, the temples and pyramids had grown up out of the desert sand, their timeless monumentality drawing him with almost magical power. He adopted a number of Ancient Egyptian themes into his architectonic vocabulary, like the winged sun and stylized birds' wings. Other Secessionist motifs, the fan-shaped leaves and fluttering veils of the dancers, which became his favourite motifs for a time, filled the pages of the journal *Ver sacrum* around the year 1900.

In Wagner's studio Plečnik was presented with three projects for rented premises which were particularly significant for Viennese modern architecture. The Neumann department store in Kärntner Strasse was already being built when the professor handed over the detailed planning for the entrance and the glazed floors with a metal grille and a glass roof over the courtyard (fig. 7).[87] Had Plečnik not later recorded his share in a photograph, we would be unable to distinguish it from Wagner's own work. Although the building appears to derive its style from the rented blocks of the late 1860s, its facade contains some remarkable innovations, which we will find again in late works by Wagner. The facade is enclosed in a large rectangle, delimited above by a roof cornice and framed on each side by a pilaster crowned by a figure. His composition scheme follows Semper's explanation of eurhythmics as closed symmetry,[88] and in Secessionist Vienna the frame became the most important manifestation of this. With its concentric hierarchy, it brings order into the whole composition. Semper's next guiding principle led to a revolution in facades: 'The panel and the frame are permissible only in panelling, which may also of course be carried out in stone, in which case, however, the joint must not stand out as such.'[89]

In contrast to former practice, the facade of the Neumann department store, although carried out in plaster and ceramic from the Zsolnay factory in Hungary, was considerably flatter in design, almost like a canvas stretched on a frame. The upper part also functioned as the background for large advertising posters, while the two uniformly glazed lower floors served as displays. Wagner responded to Semper's demand that a building should be structured with logical tectonics, by placing the two-storey show-windows, as a secondary facade 'skin', before the pillars which carried the upper floors. Thus he avoided the illogical impression of the building floating over a transparent base.

The Neumann building was not yet finished when Wagner designed the row of housing blocks on the Wienzeile avenue. This was a new street along the river Wien which was to link the town centre with the Palace of Schönbrunn, a Viennese version of Berlin's magnificent boulevard Unter den Linden.[90] Wagner wanted to give the houses along the Wienzeile an expressedly modern appearance. Owing to the complicated ground plan situation, it was also necessary to solve the basic question of the harmony of the two different facades, one of which had a noticeably projecting corner. In accordance with his working methods, at the end of 1895 and the beginning of the next year he collected a great number of feasible ideas from his students. Plečnik was probably also highly praised for the design of the facade composition for the left-hand house, later named the 'Majolica House'. His drawing shows some console cornices decorated with lion heads. For the upper floors he planned to use stucco from the formal vocabulary of Wagner's municipal railway project. Wagner later used a similar motif of lion heads to terminate the upper part of this facade which indicates that Plečnik's school drawings were not without influence on the final solution.[91]

7. Otto Wagner: The Neumann department store, frame by Plečnik, 1896

During the planning phase fundamental innovations were introduced for the two buildings on the Wienzeile. With their freer interpretation of Semper's *Stil*, Wagner's younger collaborators and pupils[92] created a greater wealth of Secessionist ornament and used unconventional building material. They replaced the Renaissance, Baroque and Rococo forms with a more neutral plant ornamentation which merged into the plaster, ceramic and iron. The originally monochrome exterior turned into a colourful, smooth surface, with painted or applied decoration. In the houses on the Wienzeile the Viennese Secession attained its classical dimension between structure and symbolism. Plečnik's share in this is not inconsiderable, since Wagner had left the planning of the main entrance of the corner house to him.[93] Plečnik discreetly applied laurel leaves, in Ancient Greece the symbol of the god Apollo, to the iron entrance gate. Wagner used them to typify the imperial metropolis. In comparison with his colleagues, Plečnik was content with a small selection of forms, though he used them with all the more elegance. As they were partly changed in the course of their execution, they appear less logically composed than in the sketch preserved from 1897.

The extent to which Plečnik was then bound to the architecture of his teacher is demonstrated by a drawing of the facade of a monumental public building, dated 1 June 1898 (see fig. 20).[94] The dome and the two narrow side projections imitate Wagner's project, produced at the same time, of the new Academy of Fine Arts in Vienna, on which, besides Olbrich, Plečnik and his colleagues Hubert Gessner, Marcel Kammerer and Alois Ludwig also worked. Despite the rich figurative ornament, it is not possible to see what purpose the building was meant to serve. Without written explanation, however, the same might be said of Wagner's Academy project, the central part of which positively overflows with a wealth of varied symbolism.

In the 1930s Plečnik returned to the idea of the dome above a central space, a theme that interested him throughout his working life. Even on his deathbed he was thinking about a monumental circular church building before the entrance to the cemetery in Ljubljana; it was intended to realize the project for the Academy of Fine Arts which he had once pursued with the youthful enthusiasm typical of his generation.

RECOGNITION – THE GUTENBERG MONUMENT

Some of Plečnik's Viennese works were particularly close to his heart because they reminded him of his youthful ideals. When, after the Second World War, his field of activity gradually narrowed, he often sought stimulus in his early drawings, and these include the competition design for the Gutenberg monument in Vienna,[95] through which he first found public recognition (figs 9–10). Like Wagner – we can see this from the example of the project from the Academy of Fine Arts – Plečnik was also inevitably influenced by Olbrich's dome on the exhibition pavilion of the Secession Association. All three buildings have a common point of departure. This is the choragic Lysicrates memorial in Athens, which according to the attempted reconstruction passed on by Semper, had once been crowned with a metal tripod.[96] Plečnik translated this motif into three dimensions. With reference to the relationship between the leafy sphere on the Secession building and Plečnik's globe, overgrown with plants, on the memorial (both 1897), it is not absolutely clear whether the architects might have arrived simultaneously at similar solutions. Plečnik's memorial plinth with the five border stones bears witness to a meticulous study of Greek column profiles. Plečnik unified the forms in a masterly way, breathing into them, in the words of Kotěra, the pure spirit of Antiquity.[97]

The figurative ornamentation on the Gutenberg monument was modelled in outline by Wagner's colleague Othmar Schimkowitz. It was strewn with literary references:

Gutenberg sits, gives birth to an idea – supports himself on his left arm – under which is the parchment or paper, as the case may be – behind him grows a tree, thrusting upwards until it reaches the terrestrial globe on which he supports himself – on the globe – in which the boughs branch out – there is a frieze representing humanity – the power of humanity is braced against the sphere – a male figure – richly muscled – gives it a new direction. On the third side sits scholarship, a grave female figure, one hand stretching out into the distance – with the other she supports herself on a tawny owl – a tender youth listens to her raptly. The entire monument is round and is framed by five border stones with small spheres – 5 continents.[98]

Mention must also be made of the colour. A reddish marble from Untersberg was to provide the plinth, with snow-white Carrara marble for the figure of the printer, and for everything else, lead: a polychromy similar to the one used later in Max Klinger's Beethoven memorial.

Besides Wagner's city railway station, Plečnik's Gutenberg memorial was in fact the first herald of the Viennese modern school, since all the other buildings now regarded as milestones of Austrian architecture at the turn of the century were either not yet under construction at the beginning of 1898, or were still in the planning stage.

8. Otto Wagner with his staff around 1898: Olbrich is first from the left, Plečnik, second from the right, and behind him is Hoffmann

Among forty-three different proposals, Plečnik's design aroused great interest and split the jury into two camps. He did in fact win the highest distinction, but had to share it with the far more conventional design of Max Fabiani and the sculptor Hans Bitterlich, who were then also entrusted with the execution of the memorial. Plečnik's prediction that 'there would be something of a stir',[99] was thus realized. To the Secessionists, on the other hand, the outcome of the competition was a welcome opportunity to criticize Viennese conservatism.[100]

Plečnik did not have to wait long for further recognition. The Arts and Crafts Association of Lower Austria wanted to display its members' creations at the Jubilee Exhibition in the Prater in 1898.[101] A well-known government architect, whose name Plečnik withheld from his biographer Strajnić, had been entrusted with setting up the exhibition in the north-western section of the former rotunda built for the World Exhibition of 1873 in Vienna, but proved not to be up to the task, upon which the directors of the association

turned to Wagner. Commenting that he would have the area designed by the next day according to his best endeavours, Wagner passed the job on to Plečnik (fig. 11). Convinced that this was a whim of his teacher's, Plečnik drew a sketch which Wagner sent to the Arts and Crafts Association. At the same time Wagner passed on both the fee and the supervision of the design's execution to his pupil.

Plečnik transformed the makeshift arrangement of the irregular space between the central part of the rotunda and the lateral wing into a large oval with the help of draped white material. He had the floors covered with red carpeting, set a statue of the Emperor in the centre of the space and placed chandeliers on the two supporting pillars which stood more or less at the focal points of the ellipse. The arrangement of the exhibits in groups also represented an innovation with regard to previous exhibition practice. He draped the pedestals in light green silk with silver embellishments. In one of the booths he placed Wagner's famous bathroom with the glass bathtub. The only decisive inter-

17

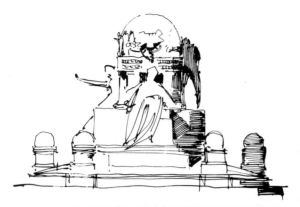

9–10. Competition for the Gutenberg memorial in Vienna, 1897: sketch and model

vention was five arches which opened the side wing and linked the hall with the other exhibition areas.

Plečnik's design was far more than an instant sensation. Wagner apparently said: 'Even a classical artist could have done no better in his day.'[102] Ludwig Hevesi, Richard Muther and Adolf Loos were equally enthusiastic. Loos wrote: 'One has only to look at the public, the rapt attention with which they walk through these rooms. Even the shoe-scraper is zealously used.'[103]

In the four months following the competition for the Gutenberg memorial, the situation of the Viennese Moderns altered considerably. Visitors to the Jubilee Exhibition were confronted with Secessionist forms at every turn. However, Loos conceded that Plečnik had found the first satisfactory solution to the stretched and draped textiles (*velum*) in Vienna.[104] Plečnik adopted the idea of the oval from the classical solutions in urban architecture, such as St Peter's Square in Rome or the Place de la Concorde in Paris, particularly beloved of Wagner. He found all the rest of his inspiration in Semper. He implemented the basic grammar of the German architect's textile art, which had its beginnings in the seam, the mesh and the plait and its continuation in various textiles and their patterns. The obviously Wagneresque pillars (with O. Schimkowitz's sculptures) in front of the hall constitute a vivid example of Semper's explanation of the ancient art of upholstery.[105] Plečnik attached ribbons, carpets and two tablets with inscriptions to the two pillars. He did not solve the question of lighting with conventional lustres, but following the example of many older interiors by his teacher, used luminous spheres which hung on wires like bunches of grapes from the ceiling. In turn, the luxuriousness of Plečnik's lamps inspired Wagner when he was furnishing the church Am Steinhof. Plečnik actually transformed the basic decoration of ribbons and knots into two-dimensional appliqué work, or copied them in stucco. Between the arches he used the contours of the antique altar which he adopted from Semper's chapter on stone constructions;[106] Wagner too, used these forms frequently in his metropolitan railway stations.

THE DIPLOMA AND THE PRIX DE ROME

Plečnik completed his studies at the Academy in the summer term of 1897/98 with a utopian commission characteristic of the Wagner School, the urban plan for the Scheveningen seaside resort at the Hague.[107] Plečnik's first attempt at urban design was not entirely successful. The solution is reminiscent of Wagner's idealistic plan for the

'Artibus' museum district of 1880, and it was symmetrically monumental rather than practical. Some of the recent experience gained from building the city railway – like the traffic junction without crossroads – did not meet the functional requirements of a bathing resort sufficiently to convince Loos when he visited the exhibition by Wagner's students at the end of July 1898.[108] For the central spa building Plečnik intended to use stone, concrete, iron and glass. He tried to make the building look as technical as possible, like a station hall, or the 'Galerie des Machines' by Dutert, Contamin & Pierron at the Paris World Exhibition of 1889, but he was unable to conceal the fact that Wagner's plans for the Academy of Fine Arts and the architecture of the two municipal railway pavilions on Karlsplatz were closer to his heart.

A characteristic feature of the design is the four observation towers[109] beside the spa building (see fig. 21), which the architect had adopted from Wagner's Academy project. The latter was a more conventional design, and its towers were intended to represent 4,000 years of art history. Plečnik was pulled between technical bravura, with which he hoped to win his teacher's approval, and his love of historical anthropomorphic sculpture. We can see a similar solution the year before this in Plečnik's competition design for the new Vienna gas lighting.[110] The design of the observation towers was also influenced to some extent by the unexecuted model of the clock candelabra in front of the entrance to the railway stations on Karlsplatz. Plečnik's architectural sculpture no longer represents figures of victory with raised wreaths, which had adorned Wagner's Academy project; it is concerned with an apotheosis of the power that creates world order, and it is pure fin-de-siècle. (The theme of the mast, held up by three suspension cables, was repeated by Plečnik some thirty years later in the war memorial at Lány in Czechoslovakia.) In the detail referred to in Plečnik's diploma work there is a spatial concept which was later aptly described by Le Corbusier with reference to a similar example as the 'promenade architecturale'. Like the relief lines on the pillars in front of St Charles Borromeo's church in Vienna, the visitor's path travels spirally upwards on the outside or within the spindle-shaped observation towers. Almost forty years later we find this theme again in the bell tower of St Michael's Church in Barje, on Ljubljana Moor.

With his diploma work Plečnik won a travel bursary, the Prix de Rome, which had been awarded in the previous year by the Board of the Academy's professors to his friend Jan Kotěra for a similarly utopian design for the entrance gates to a channel tunnel between France and England. 'And yet justice was done,' wrote Loos: 'The prize was not awarded to the square metre of drawing paper, but to Pletschnik. And

11. The Lower Austrian Arts and Crafts Association section at the Jubilee exhibition in Vienna, 1898

this is an extremely rare human being, a man who needs the air of Italy as much as a slice of bread. For Pletschnik is the hungriest of our young architects. He must therefore be fed. Of one thing we are certain: whatever he takes he will repay us a thousandfold in strength.'[111]

Plečnik, who till then had travelled no further than Graz and Vienna, was now able to fulfil his great desire to visit some European countries. First among them was France, where, in Paris, the preparations for the new World Exhibition in 1900 were in progress. French was also the only foreign language that he knew, at least partially, since in 1897 he had already seriously considered the possibility of seeing contemporary Parisian architecture,[112] of which he had heard a great deal in Wagner's atelier. Here, suddenly, was the opportunity to visit England too, with its architecture inspired by comfort and livability, as well as Belgium and Germany.

In accordance with the rules of the prize every recipient was obliged to undertake a freely selected artistic task on his journey. Plečnik chose modern church building as his theme, since this had preoccupied him most during his period as Wagner's pupil, although he had had no opportunity to become more intensively involved with it. On 2 October 1898 he received his passport for Italy, Spain, Portugal, France, Belgium and Germany,[113] but did not begin his journey at once; instead he spent almost a month and a half at home. The unexpected successes of his last student year had to some extent bolstered his self-confidence. He planned to begin his journey by visiting those places in Northern Italy which were considered essential for the study of the history of art and repertory obligatory for Austrian architectural scholarship holders.

12. A page from Plečnik's Rome sketchbook: the garden wall of the Palazzo Zuccari, 1899

So, on a cold November night, after an uncomfortable trip by gondola, he landed on the Piazzetta in the middle of Venice, and as he looked around he was unable to believe his eyes. He told Strajnić later that the Venetians must definitely be of Slavic origin,[114] although at the time such thoughts did not occur to him. For the first time in his life Plečnik was really free. The architecture of the Rennaissance and the Baroque overwhelmed him. Beadeker in hand, he walked the streets, whenever possible, buying Alinari's photographs of the artistic monuments rather than making sketches, which he did only occasionally. The influence of Semper and Wagner paled beside the multiplicity of new impressions. 'My God, what barren straw we have been threshing in Vienna, but we had to thresh it, otherwise we would be quite unable to understand these things,'[115] he wrote later in Rome.

From the fragments preserved of his diary and his correspondence it is not always possible to work out his precise itinerary. For his family he liked recording his encounters with historical places or Christian monuments, for which he often adapted his route. In Venice the felt drawn above all by the buildings of Palladio, which he followed as far as Vicenza, but we do not know how intensively he studied these works. His drawing of Giorgio Massari's Pietà Church on the Riva degli Schiavoni[116] gives us no more information on Plečnik's stay in Venice.

Only when he reached Padua did he slowly begin to turn his attention to his task, and leaving Vicenza and Verona for Milan, he began to study the problem of the dome by examining the early works of Bramante: 'After the impact of these great ones I am likely to make their mistakes,' he wrote to his mother from Turin. 'I have spent some days thinking about domes; it seems to me that not only is this problem still unsolved, it is insoluble as long as the transition into the square is forced; it is also unaesthetic to divide the transepts, the intersections are not beautiful, all in all, the enforced effort is detectable, whereas the Romans in the Pantheon quite soberly and logically placed the round cap on the round cylinder. I hope that I shall compete what I spoke of in Rome.'[117] The modern architecture of Milan and Turin did not interest Plečnik. He remained reserved even in the face of Guarini's chapel of Santa Sindone, which seemed to him more original than beautiful. However, in the high dome of the Superga Basilica by Turin he did recognize that Wagner could no longer be his sole exemplar in sacred architecture.

Filled with doubt, in the middle of December he reached Florence by way of Genoa, Pisa and Livorno. He became increasingly aware that the great masters had also been outstanding technicians: 'What a different man I might have become, I admit, had I paid more attention to the human body and had the opportunity to be an engineer – that is a mathematician – and if I had mastered more or less all the philosophical areas; but I am only a desperately poor man, and I come closer to fiasco day by day.'[118]

Plečnik regained his self-confidence after his encounter with Brunelleschi and Michelangelo, since in their divine genius he could also perceive human fallibility. Michelangelo in particular made a great impression on him. Away now from Wagner, Michelangelo became his model, because in Plečnik's eyes he was the one Renaissance architect who had been able to shape the building of Antiquity into a new architecture. In the Biblioteca Laurenziana he admired Michelangelo's boldness in dealing with the traditional rules of style. More than two decades later he made use of a similar procedure. While he also swore by Michelangelo in sculpture, in painting Fra Angelico was his model. This discrepancy is not only characteristic of Plečnik, it also contributes to an understanding of his belief in the then popular painters from the Benedictine monastery of Beuron, who wanted to see sacred art purified of sensuality.

Whatever Plečnik saw, the conclusions he drew were always transferred to his homeland. Before the Santo Spirito Church in Florence he found a model for the design of the square before the cathedral in Ljubljana, Pisa seemed to him to be the ideal town, and in Rome he realized that even a capital city can retain something of a rural character. In Bologna he expressed his dilemma: 'I come with the tradition of my homeland; its tradition and its needs are rooted in me; and now I doubt whether I am seeking the right thing, in which points I ought to part from them, etc. Apart from this, the memories and knowledge of Graz and Vienna are in me.'[119] In the church of San Miniato al Monte in Florence he actually contradicted Semper with regard to the ceiling that the latter had so greatly admired: '. . . very interesting, but not for us (open roof-truss).'[120] It was not until he was in Pistoia that he declared that he could envisage a church with a polychrome, properly lit flat ceiling and slender pillars which did not spoil the effect of space. Later he tried to realize these ideas in his church in Vienna. His tastes were becoming increasingly simple and he delighted in early Christian monuments at the end of his stay in Florence.

The visit to Bologna moved him to reflections with regard to plaster; however, this can be seen more as the expression of his momentary disinclination for modern architecture and it had no far-reaching consequences on his work. The further he was from Vienna, the more alien Secessionist art seemed to him. He even put it to Wagner that he was wrong and should work out new forms with regard to plaster. 'If you are in fact a verist, which I think is right, let it be completely. Stone, tile, or if you like, in my view, a mixture; they should always be compact masses, no fiddling about, and it's good. I am honestly glad to have reached this conclusion; I believe that much can be solved, if only one uses good terracotta for it and exploits the possibilities of polychromy,'[121] he said of his visit to the late Gothic church of San Petronió. The facade of the library in Ljubljana is clear proof that Plečnik always remembered this journey, which he never repeated.

The basilicas in Ravenna fulfilled his expectations. Overwhelmed by them, he fell victim to self-pity, convinced that he was one of the few Slovenes who had experienced a revelation at the source of true art but continued to be

13. A page from the Rome sketchbook: a monument to Victor Emmanuel, 1899

unrecognized and ignored by their homeland. He also visited the tomb of Theodoric, which was the best-known archetype of tomb architecture at the turn of the century;[122] he particulary admired its mighty monolithic dome of Istrian limestone.

Plečnik spent four months in Rome. The feverish search for his own identity was finished, soothed by the realization that his forefathers had learned much from the Italians. Thinking of the Slavs, he said: 'We have our own original force, but we too will have to go to Rome a few more times for this.'[123] However, another reason kept Plečnik in the Eternal City. In contrast to Olbrich and Josef Hoffmann, who were in sympathy with the anonymous architecture of the southern Mediterranean countries because they found nothing of relevance for the modern age in the capital, Plečnik was convinced that he had come upon the true roots

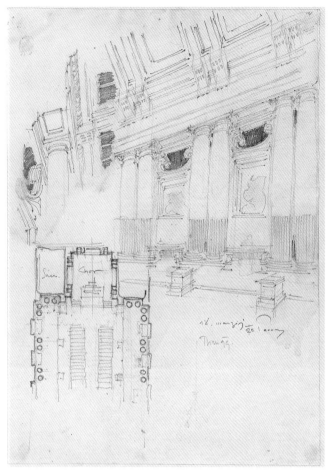

14. A page from the Rome sketchbook: study for a modern church, 1899

consider why 'the ancients built thus and not otherwise,' in an attempt to persuade him to travel on as soon as possible to the Riviera and then to Paris and London.[125] But Plečnik had no wish to leave Rome: 'If I could get work for a while, I would like to stay here for a long, long time. That Paris could give me as much as Rome I do not believe.'[126] The models he had already found were joined in Rome by Bernini, Borromini and Peruzzi. From a sketch of the entrance gate to the garden of the painter Frederico Zuccari's house (fig. 12),[127] which displays a florid hypertrophy, typical of some of Plečnik's drawings from the period around 1897, we can detect that Mannerism also appealed to him. What might have been expected was a similarly intensive study of Antiquity, but with the exception of those buildings which time had transformed into Christian holy places, Plečnik saw few of the ancient Roman monuments. He devoted more attention to the tombs along the ancient Via Appia, which corresponded to his idea of the architectural prototypes. Similarly, for instance, the lively cubic masses of the village houses in Capri were Josef Hoffmann's models for a long time. The difference lay simply in the fact that Plečnik was envisaging ideal commissions: chapels, monuments, mausoleums and the like.

Particularly instructive in this regard is his imaginative drawing of a rocky Italian landscape (fig. 13). There is an equestrian statue positioned in front of a precipitous wall composed of blind arches;[128] it is not difficult to recognize the architecture of the Roman aqueducts. The drawing was made in Rome and is dated 1899. According to Strajnić it was to be a memorial to Victor Emmanuel. This could be right, since Plečnik was undoubtedly inspired to handle this theme from the memorial of the same name by Giuseppe Sacconi, erected at that time right in front of his Roman lodgings. But this is also a favourite theme of the Wagner School, and other competitions held around the turn of the century, like the one for a Battle of the Nations memorial at Leipzig, may have aroused the imagination of the young artists. The drawing of the Victor Emmanuel memorial later particularly influenced Plečnik's younger, very sensitive fellow-pupil Mario Sandonà,[129] who was one of his great admirers.

In Rome Plečnik resumed contact with Vienna and his homeland. He received letters from Wagner and son, Kotěra and some fellow-pupils, who supplied him with news and suggestions. He turned his attention enthusiastically to the theme of the modern church and asked his brother Andrej to send him a town plan of Ljubljana so that he could put in place what he had seen and experienced. He was particularly surprised to realize how perfectly the monumental buildings of the Eternal City are adapted to human dimensions. Con-

of Wagner's art. After his return to Vienna he wrote to his brother:

> This is interesting – they obliged me – to write a Text on the Rome tour for the Wagner Volume – I wrote – I said, among other things: on surveying O.W's ground plans a thinker said: as often as I see this – I remember Letarou(i)illy (illustrations of classical works of the Renaissance by Letar(ouilly)). That is his backbone – and look, these lines were not crossed out in O.W's censorship – is that not delightful – I am happy to have been enabled to see this backbone in Italy – happy – in the Christian sense to have found his stone-bone as the foundation from which he grows.[124]

While all Plečnik's fellow pupils and colleagues were looking for ways into the future, he turned to Wagner's historical work. The postcards he sent to the atelier prompted Wagner's fatherly advice that he should above all

22

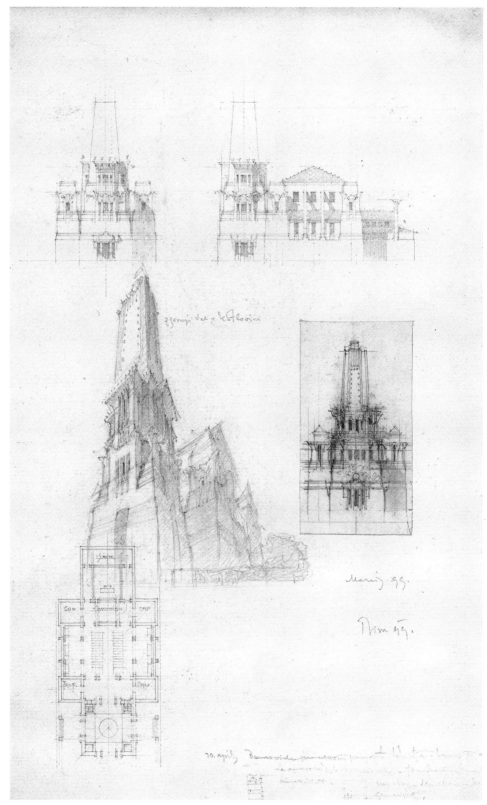

15. A page from the Rome sketchbook: study for a modern church, 1899

vinced that he had found the source of pure, clear art, he wrote to his brother: 'I tell you, in Rome you will find everything modern heated up again at least once. The wretched English, that's what they hang about here for, and the Germans, too, but we are at home and buy their rubbish.'[130]

In Rome Plečnik's solitude also came to an end. He became friendly with Alfred Castelliz, a colleague and compatriot from Celje two years older than himself, and the Hungarian painter Oszkár Mendlik, who had taken over the tower of the former Little Palazzo Venezia,[131] in which the Austrian scholars were housed before his arrival. Mendlik introduced him to the attractive Polish painter Irma Dutczýnska, a pupil of his later friend Ferdinand Andri. However, as we learn from Castelliz's diary notes, the painter's mother soon put an end to any hopes cherished by the young architect with regard to her daughter.

From Rome, Plečnik was able to go on excursions, like the one to Naples and Pompeii at the end of Arpil 1899, when he went on by steamer to Palermo and Monreale. The fact that he had expected something from the ruined city under Vesuvius is demonstrated by his early sketches which often depict Pompeiian motifs. He went to Monreale principally on the advice of Kotěra, but was a little disappointed by what he found there. He also visited Taormina, Agrigento and Segesta, which had always been a favourite goal of study tours, and where Semper had also spent some time. After his return from Naples he wrote home: 'I have already seen something that I shall never forget, all the same I shall stick to Rome. It is simply among the best that Lower Italy has to offer.'[132]

From Italy he travelled to Spain. It was not the modern Barcelona, but the medieval cathedrals and distant Batalha in Portugal that led him to visit the Iberian peninsular. However, he reconsidered the idea soon after crossing the frontier, after seeing some children in one town tormenting cats and he went to Lourdes, probably travelling directly to Paris from there. The news of his mother's death, which reached him shortly after his arrival in Paris, presumably contributed to his aversion to the French and modern French art. The 'restrained elegance' that he ascribed to French Gothic, and the city that stood for national greatness, nevertheless remained in his memory for ever.

WORK IN WAGNER'S ATELIER

Plečnik returned to Ljubljana from Paris, and did not then immediately travel back to Vienna. After the severe earthquake in 1895 his home town was being rebuilt, but nobody remembered the young architect. After designing a modest private nursery garden in July 1899 almost free of charge,[133] nothing pointed to any further commissions, so he returned to Wagner in the autumn of 1899. As he explained later, it was a difficult step to take, because he had 'seen too much beauty in Rome and Florence'[134] and was no longer interested in Secessionist architecture. His erstwhile teacher received him with open arms. Olbrich had since made himself independent and he was in need of a capable colleague for the creation of the Vienna city railway. Plečnik was thus one of the few to see this project through from start to finish.

He had begun as a technical draughtsman in Wagner's atelier in 1894, and now, at the end, he was designing city railway stations independently. Unfortunately only a few drawings which reliably bear his characteristic drawing style have been preserved, some of them only in reproduction, such as the signed perspective of the railway gallery by the Danube Canal (1895), published in Wagner's publication *Einige Skizzen, Projekte und ausgeführte Bauwerke*. It seems that he worked first of all on the design of the viaduct in Währing. The sketches by Wagner, preserved in Ljubljana, of the Burggasse railway station with the chapel of St John in Währing which was also a part of the Vienna railway project,[135] indicate that Plečnik was involved in the planning of both buildings. Still more revealing is the detail of the banisters at the Michelbeuren stop, from 1897,[136] which is identical to the decorative frame in the photograph of Wagner's Neumann store, which Plečnik had drawn a few months earlier (fig. 7).

The project for the Viennese city railway, took on an increasingly coherent form. In the design, the treatment of the aesthetic potential of iron in accordance with Semper's four basic techniques for the processing of material was important. From a comment on a photograph and from a letter to Kotěra we know that after his return Plečnik designed the metropolitan stations of Schottenring (fig. 16) and Roßauerlände.[137] This is also confirmed by analysis of the form. In both cases we have a so-called normal type – a smaller station raised over the tracks – over an underground stop. Up to 1897 Wagner had given these a standard form in the Wientallinie section: a cube with a tent roof, surrounded by four pylons and lean-to roofs on the lower side sections. Plečnik altered this type considerably. He placed the roof ridge in the right-angle to the direction of the rails. Over this he led a saddle back roof made as if it were a metal canopy. He decreased the slope of the lean-to roofs so that the central part of the roof would be brought into better prominence. Instead of the pylons he unified the building with two higher walls, whose termination in profile represents the motif of an Antique altar. The textile inter-

24

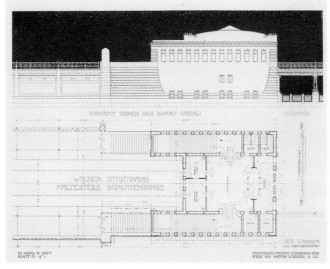

16. Plečnik's drawing of the Vienna city railway Schottenring station, 1900

17. Plečnik in Otto Wagner's atelier, February 1900

18. Plečnik's drawing of Otto Wagner's Modern Gallery, 1900

pretation of the architecture is further emphasized by the unified facade, rhythmically linked by narrow windows, and inside by the gentle transition from wall to ceiling.

The Roßauerlände station was built a few months after the Schottenring stop, which no longer exists. Influenced by the then almost completed building for the firm of Portois & Fix by Max Fabiani, Plečnik was able to bring out the transition between wall and roof even more subtly. In the plaster he actually succeeded in creating a fictional contrast between the 'textile' sheathing and the profiled 'stone' cornice.

Plečnik's contribution to the Vienna city railway ended with this station. The next station, Brigittabrücke, now Friedensbrücke, is similar to the other stations in appearance, but lacks Plečnik's consistency is terms of the textile interpretation of architecture.

Two uncompleted perspective drawings and a ground plan drawing[138] also indicate Plečnik's collaboration in Wagner's project for a Gallery of Modern Art on the eastern end of the Ring. The drawings of the facade give a little more information on the secondary ornamentation (fig. 18), which we also find in the railway stations; otherwise they still follow Wagner's architectural direction.

In time Plečnik began to tire of his work with Wagner. As we have seen, he had returned from Rome with new views which he was forced to deny in Vienna. In the summer of 1900 he first visited Kotěra in Prague. Kotěra introduced him to the central group of the Czech Moderns, concentrated round the journal *Volné směry* (*Ways of Freedom*) they were the painter Jan Preisler, the sculptor Stanislav Sucharda, František Xaver Svoboda, a man of letters, and the publisher Jan Štenc. These contacts strengthened Plečnik in his pan-Slavism. Previously the idea of going into partnership with Wagner's son Otto, also an architect, had seemed desireable. However, on their very first commission, the interior decoration of the new luxury Hotel Bristol in Warsaw, the two had come into conflict. When Plečnik realized that the young Wagner was proposing to charge too much he withdrew at once and would have nothing more to do with the matter.[139]

On leaving the Wagner atelier he became a freelance artist, and, as one of the great hopes of the Viennese Moderns, enough doors seemed to be opening for him. All the same, Andrej knew his brother better and advised him to seek a safer source of income. 'How long does it take to finish eight high school classes – even this thought is a torment,'

Plečnik objected, knowing that without the relevant certificates he was barred from serving the state:

'How, Andrej, can you recommend Mrs. von Hohenwart to me? Andrej – I have quarrelled with the Kofrat – and also with the rest of the mighty – Andrej, I can't do it – why seek my ruin – I fight off any post in the public service – you urge me – perhaps I am doing the wrong thing – but I know about my short life – that's why I love freedom all the more – I love it – hungry or full – God must look after me, not the damned – I name them – authorities – and not all power is from above – and if it were – we do not orawl before it.'[140]

Between the lines we can read that he himself did not attach any very great value to the only post he might have obtained, at the School of Arts and Crafts of the Austrian Museum. However, he was very pleased by Kotěra's invitation to join the College of Arts and Crafts in Prague, which he received in the summer of 1901, and would have been prepared to leave Vienna immediately. Nevertheless this intention was not realized until ten years later, when Prague was to offer him escape from the problems of his life. Before this, Plečnik hoped for some material advantage from his formal allegiance to the Secession in Vienna.

VIELES UND GROSSES IST IN ÖSTERREICH, IST IN WIEN UNTER DER GLORREICHEN REGIERUNG EUERER MAJESTÄT ENTSTANDEN. AUCH DER KÜNSTLER IST EIN SOHN SEINER ZEIT UND FÜHLT DAS WEHEN DES GEISTES AUCH AUSSERHALB DES EIGENSTEN GEBIETES RINGS UM IHN HER.

DIE STADT IN IHREM GEWALTIGEN WACHSTHUM WIRD AUCH AUF DIE GESTALTUNG DER KUNST IHREN EINFLUSS ÜBEN. WOHIN DER BLICK FÄLLT, STELLEN SICH WERKE VON GIGANTISCHER GRÖSSE DEM AUGE DAR — WIENS WASSERLEITUNG, DIE REGULIERUNG DES DONAUSTROMES, DER AUSBAU DES BAHNNETZES, DESSEN VOLLENDUNG IM HERZEN DER STADT SICH EBEN VOLLZIEHT, DIE VÖLLIGE UMGESTALTUNG GANZER STADTTHEILE ERFÜLLEN DEN BETRACHTER MIT BEWUNDERUNG UND EHRFÜRCHTIGEM DANK GEGEN DEN FÜRSTEN, UNTER DESSEN MÄCHTIGER ÄGIDE DIESE WERKE DES FRIEDENS ENTSTEHEN KONNTEN. SCHON SIND DIE ÄUSSERSTEN WÄLLE DER ALTEN STADT GEFALLEN, UND BIS AN DIE HÄNGE DES GEBIRGES, BIS AN DIE UFER DES STROMES DEHNT SICH IHR RIESENLEIB. SOWEIT ABER DIESE STADT SICH BREITET, SCHWELLT EIN INBRÜNSTIGER WUNSCH ALLE HERZEN, RINGT SICH EIN HEISSES GEBET VON ALLEN LIPPEN:

GOTT ERHALTE, GOTT BESCHÜTZE, GOTT SEGNE

EUERE MAJESTÄT

UND DAS ALLERHÖCHSTE KAISERHAUS!

19. The last page of the codex dedicated to the Emperor by the Vienna Academy of Fine Arts, 1898

20. Study for a public building, 1898

28

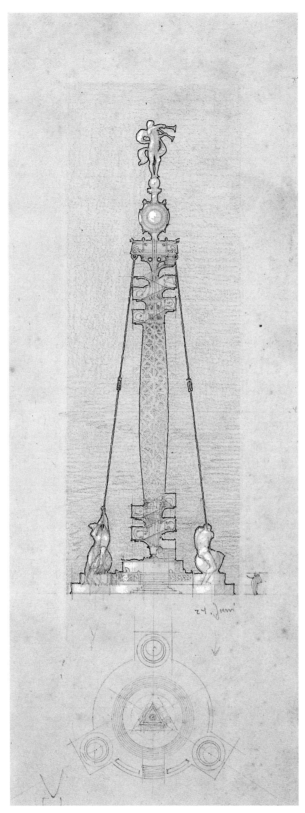

21. Plečnik's diploma work of 1898: an observation tower for the seaside resort of Scheveningen

22. The Zacherl House in Vienna: study for the facade, 1904

30

23. The Zacherl House in Vienna, 1903–5, contemporary photograph

24. The Zacherl House in Vienna, 1903–5: top storey, telamons by Franz Metzner

25. The Zacherl House in Vienna, roof and top storey

26. The Zacherl House in Vienna, vestibule

27. The Zacherl House in Vienna, stairway

28–30. The St Charles Borromeo
Fountain in Vienna, 1906–9

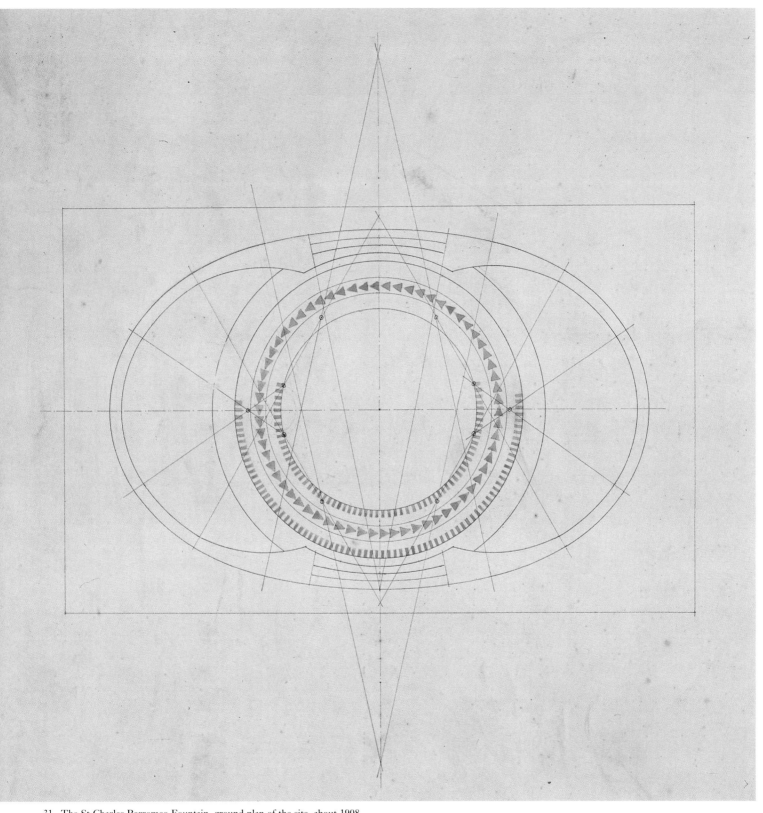

31. The St Charles Borromeo Fountain, ground plan of the site, about 1908

32. A memorial stone for a grave, 1901

38

33. The church of the Holy Spirit, Vienna, 1910–13

34. The church of the Holy Spirit, Vienna, crypt, 1910 (fitments 1911/12)

35. The church of the Holy Spirit, Vienna, crypt, 1910

36. Design for the competition for a monument to Jan Žižka in Prague, 1913

37. Study for a church, around 1913

2 A FREELANCE
ARCHITECT IN VIENNA

Plečnik's work of 1900 coincided stylistically with his brief but expressive Secessionist phase. Characteristic of this were the elegant pylons, with their round tapering tops and organic, vegetable forms. He enjoyed sketching various brick arches recalling his impressions of Italian Antiquity, creating lively colour contrasts by adding stone and other materials. He revived these ideas in his late years. Increasingly his imagination moved away from Wagner's vocabulary of forms and caused him to stylize other plant species instead of laurel. The Villa Langer[141] in the Viennese suburb of Hietzing is a good example of Plečnik's concern for stylistic independence (fig. 38). French and Belgian models guided him as he moved away from Viennese influences. Of course, his adherence to Semper's cladding principle meant he did not escape Wagner's influence entirely.

Master builder Karl Langer had already begun the foundations of his villa when in August 1900 he involved Plečnik in the planning. Unfortunately we know no more than this of their two-year collaboration. Probably thanks to the opportunities which seemed to be opening up for him everywhere at that time, Plečnik did not want to attach himself permanently to Langer, whom he had met when working together on the Neumann department store.

According to the original design the villa was planned very conventionally. Plečnik created something which at first sight seems impossible. He retained Langer's ground plan and modernized the entire facade as well as the staircase. Instead of the planned wooden oriels he created a convex wall at the front of the salons. This wall was to be interrupted on both upper floors by two big windows. He repeated the motif of the rounded segment in the smaller bedroom windows, thus achieving the impression of a lively band of glass stretching across the facade, ending with the studio windows. In order to re-emphasize this movement he repeated it on the roof in the form of arches. He neutralized the extreme right axis of the kitchen windows by setting back the body of the building, following Wagner's example. As he could not take the salon oriel down to the ground floor because the foundations were already built, he supported it with an organically shaped pillar. He repeated the street facade on the garden side, replacing the luxuriant ornamentation by a simpler one.

The central composition theme lay in the textile interpretation of the facade cladding. While Wagner had considered the direction and density of ornament for the Majolica House, Plečnik chose the vertical wavy line which remains neutral both upwards and downwards. Regardless of the window openings, he covered the entire facade with a

38. The Langer House in Vienna, 1900/1, contemporary photograph

44

regular pattern. Under the eaves he set a narrow ceramic band or took the smooth plaster back slightly, thus strengthening the impression of wall hangings or tapestry. Following the example of the Portois & Fix building by Fabiani, he designed a rounded transition from the decorated facade to the kitchen windows, which simultaneously limits the facade decoration. Compared with Wagner, Plečnik's choice of material is a compromise. The decoration on the street facade is not worked in stucco but consists of applied ceramic. For this reason the surface of the facade is not homogeneous either.

His intense concern with the question of plaster or stucco, which had caused him doubts even during his Italian journey, led him occasionally to reject this material although it was later to play a role once again. In August 1901 he wrote to Kotěra:

> Of course it's all lies and nonsense – What is plastered can't be good. It can be stupid – it can be showy – it can be sentimental – so full of 'silent poetry' – but endowed with masculine – and youthful – soundness it is not. Even the staircase should not be done in plaster – only the rooms – all that I want made in plaster is the three-dimensional forms – which are bricked-up – covered over with it – and soon reach the state that makes them enjoyable. [142]

Nevertheless, it was precisely the coarse white plaster juxtaposed with the bright green tiles and red bricks which helped the architect to produce the desired poetic expression on the facade. Here, it must be stressed, Plečnik made a strict distinction between sentiment and sentimentality, regarding the latter as one of the greatest dangers of modern times. The Villa Langer represents an important victory for the character and symbolism of a building – which for Wagner constituted the moral guidelines of his compositions.[143]

Plečnik tried to attain perfection through self-discipline. He wrote to Kotěra: 'I know myself – I have a peculiar (unlucky) nature – capable of attracting extremely – but unfortunately no less capable of taking the slightest unpleasantness seriously – so seriously that it is a misery. What have I not done – to root out this devilishly womanish trait – and still do.'[144] In dialogue with Wagner he had reached a dilemma that characterizes the range of his later search: 'Otto Wagner meddled and suppressed what had gone before. Architecture of usefulness, of life there – architecture of the imagination elsewhere; as in the music of Richard Wagner versus Mozart, Beethoven, Bach, etc. Where is the boundary, what is relative, what absolute, more valuable.'[145]

39. The Villa Loos in Melk, 1901, contemporary photograph

In the Villa Langer Plečnik believed he had created something novel, indeed something positively pure and fresh. The realization that the architectural vocabulary of forms could be treated freely, and thus endow building with an expression appropriate to one's convictions, is also important for an understanding of the Zacherl House built a few years later.

Where did Plečnik's ideas for his first architectural work come from? Even if inwardly he remained true to the restrained austerity of Wagner's city railway stations, with the stylized rose ornamentation of the facade of the Langer Villa he was approaching the manner of the circle of illustrators of the journal *Ver Sacrum*, especially Olbrich, from whose Stöhr House in St Pölten he had adopted some motifs. Fabiani's Artaria building was the source of the convex windows which he later repeated in the Zacherl House. One element imported to Vienna, employed particularly in Wagner's city railway stations, is the metal border which copies the crossbeam above the windows on the first floor. Here we can detect the influence of Belgian Art Nouveau and above all of the architect Victor Horta, as we can in the pylons of the garden fence, although these seem to be derived more from some buildings by Paul Hankar. Plečnik's pleasure in organic ornament and figured work can also be seen in the metal girders of the guttering and the goosehead on the second floor. This is reminiscent of the sea horse on Hector Guimard's Castel Béranger in Paris, which Plečnik either visited during his study tour or knew from the Guimard monograph in Wagner's library. Last but not least, there is the terrazzo pattern of the entrance area, with which Plečnik immortalized the moss that as a child he had gathered for the Christmas crib. Such memories of his birthplace were always a component of his Viennese architecture, but they were always kept so personal that they can scarcely be deciphered.

THE VILLA LOOS IN MELK

The villa for Hans Loos, the notary, of Loosimfeld[146] is an important example of Plečnik's early rejection of the forms of the Secession. From a letter to Kotěra we learn that he was offered the commission by master builder F. Czastka,[147] and succeeded in winning complete artistic freedom for himself.

The earlier planning of the 'House on the Lake'[148] for the Viennese dentist and town councillor Carl Schuh, had taught Plečnik, so he said, to understand the concept of the villa. This commission had been primarily inspired by Hoffmann's artists' colony on the Hohe Warte in Vienna. Plečnik had given the exterior of this building a purely Mediterranean air. This is expressed not only in his favourite polygonal oriels, but above all in the disposition of the areas round the hall which rose to the height of two storeys, the staircase and the gallery. The client then changed the plans and had a small Renaissance castle built instead of a modern villa, and Plečnik embarked on the design of the Villa Loos in Melk on the Danube in the spring of 1901 (fig. 39) with all the more energy and determination to remain serious and level-headed.[149]

The ground plan is almost square and is symmetrically organized. The composition is based on the theme of frame and content. In contrast to Wagner, Plečnik did not involve the facade as a whole, but divided the surface into rectangles of different sizes which neutralize the tectonic forces. Although he had begun to move away from Wagner, he was still fully aware of the 'incompleteness' or – as he himself would certainly have put it – the non-organic solution of the facade for the Villa Loos. On the principal facade he varied the oriel window motif of the Villa Langer, combining it

40. The Langer apartment block, 1901/2, contemporary photograph

with semi-circular windows adopted from Belgian Art Nouveau. Nevertheless, he could not succeed in uniting it organically into the whole, which is not in itself particularly homogeneous. Instead of imitating textile models, he drew in this case more on Semper's chapter on carpentry.[150] He also ascribed great significance to colour. He remained undecided as to the contrast between the white and blue ceramics and the tactile contrast between smooth and rough plaster surfaces. Unlike his teacher, he drew the frame elements out over the corners of the building, anticipating his later solution of a continuous outer surface to the building, running across all parts of the facade, which he then realized in the Zacherl House.

In many respects, Plečnik was looking for solutions similar to Josef Hoffmann's. He is also linked with the latter by the process he used in the dining-room on the wooden ceiling demanded by the client. Later Plečnik returned to classical joinery, giving up the 'two-dimensional' excision of

46

forms from boards which had been characteristic of the liveliest Secessionist phase of Hoffmann and Olbrich.

LANGER'S APARTMENT HOUSE

The archetypal apartment block in Vienna allowed for no innovation in the division of space. The proximity of the Wagner houses on the Wienzeile obliged Plečnik to take a very fundamental approach to the design of the facade of the Langer apartment house, built there between 1901 and 1902. His aim was to achieve the maximum clarity and delicacy.[151] The problem lay in combining three different heights of building. His design was influenced by Wagner's 1888 building in Universitätsstrasse, which has a characteristic vertical arrangement. Although, as we have seen, he had objections to plaster, he used it on the house on the Wienzeile. In relation to the competition for the Zacherl House, he actually said: 'This noble old technique which I was trying to revive this time – demands intensive study . . .'[152]

Langer's apartment house on the Wienzeile[153] followed the villa in Melk chronologically. After several attempts, Plečnik found the final solution in the summer of 1901, when instead of the smooth surface of the Wagner building, enriched with Secessionist ornamentation, on the opposite side of the Wienzeile, he chose an elegant, many-layered facade for his building. The transformation of the lisenes between the windows of the upper floors of this house on Universitätsstrasse into pilasters almost invisibly tapering downwards, was perhaps inherited from ancient Egyptian architecture. (At the end of the 1920s the architect designed the facade of the offices of the Vzajemna insurance company in Ljubljana in similar form, but executed it with greater plasticity.) On the Langer House, however, he interpreted the classical Rustic style with horizontal incisions in the more solid parts of the plaster. Since these incisions no longer had any tectonic function and can be regarded simply as ornamentation, he introduced a wavy line as an optical pendant, using it to surround the entire top floor of the building in the manner of the Rustic style. This is an ornament adopted from the Villa Langer in Hietzing, but simplified. The square frames between the storeys form a neutral accompaniment to the calm contrapposto of the facade. The lowest front of the house on Hamburger Strasse displays an egg and dart moulding. The facade is given additional rhythm by the coils inspired by metal processing, which are repeated on the roof cornice. Whereas we know a good deal about the provenance of the decoration of the Villa Langer in Hietzing, that of the Langer House on the Wienzeile has

41. The Langer apartment block, stairwell, 1901/2

already become so abstract that one can only guess at the models, although the cartouches between the windows of the upper part of the building are more traditional.

Emphasized corner columns would have destroyed the homogeneity of the facade and Plečnik therefore modified their vertically divisive effect with balconies which he allowed to run round the relevant corners; in this he may have been inspired by Schinkel (the pavilion in the Schlosspark at Charlottenburg). However, in order not to allow this to overshadow the rest of the ornamentation, he used filigree grilles and glass floors. Individualizing parts of buildings which looked onto different streets, a characteristic of Wagner's architecture, was, as Plečnik showed, not the only way of interpreting Semper's principle of the textile-covered frame, which played a crucial role in the composition of facades in Vienna around 1900. Plečnik made important innovations, though he did not see them as such, or in terms of a personal manifesto.

Delicate forms also characterize the entrance area and the staircase. The wave-like forms of the stucco running along the staircase deserve particular attention. Although the idea did not originate with Plečnik – the railway entrances on Karlsplatz were once similarly decorated – it nevertheless shows that in Vienna ornamentation was a functional component of architecture. Plečnik provided the stair transitions with narrow ribs underneath, which give his last Secessionist building additional lightness.

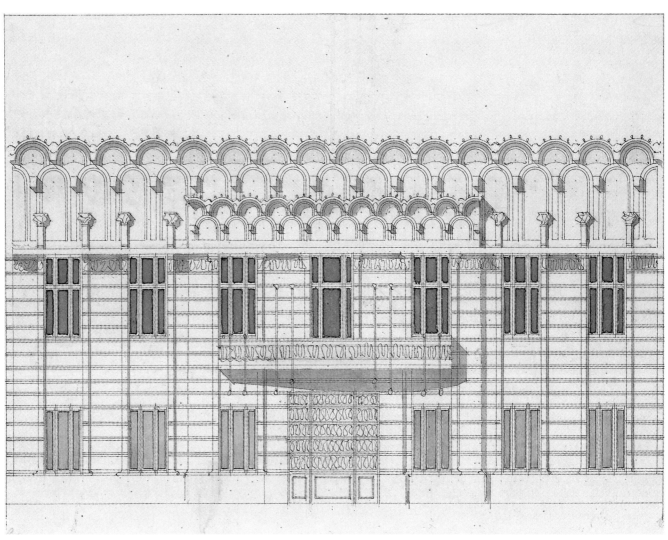

42. Plečnik's first design for the facade of the Weidmann House in Vienna, 1902

The Langer apartment house on the Wienzeile had more or less exhausted the possibilities of plaster, so this theme could be regarded as concluded for some time. Plečnik's temporary return to historicist architecture did not, of course, fill his teacher with enthusiasm, although they continued to keep in touch. Wagner wrote to him with regard to the adaptation of the facade of the Weidmann House[154] in the spring of 1902: 'I am not in agreement with everything and it seems to me that in Hietzing the Weidmann has *too many* puttis, fewer would have been better.' But he gave fatherly comfort to the young architect: 'Times are bad now, I hope they will get better.'[155]

Like Langer, Plečnik also knew the fashion accessories manufacturer Weidmann from Wagner's atelier. In 1898, in Wagner's School, he had decorated some pages of a codex dedicated to the Emperor (see fig. 19),[156] with a binding made by Weidmann according to Wagner's instructions. His new client was artistically more knowledgeable than Loos the lawyer. The soundness and care taken in the manufacture of his products were famous beyond the frontiers of Austro-Hungary. He was a passionate collector of Italian antiquities and as enthusiastic a character as Plečnik, and he enjoyed being involved in the architect's work. This time Plečnik was collaborating with his colleague Josef Czastka, a year older than he was, probably the son of the master builder with whom he had worked on the planning of the villa in Melk. However, Czastka, also a pupil of Wagner, only played a subordinate role.

First Plečnik attended to the courtyard, in which he placed a garage with a Mediterranean pergola on it. As the house looked on to the street opposite Schönbrunn castle, the owner wanted to give it the appearance of a small palace. Plečnik first proposed a facade arranged along horizontal lines and a windowless parapet to conceal the unprepossessing roof (fig. 42). This composition relied on the contrast between the organization of the lower part and the superstructure. The two parts would have been linked by rod-like pilaster strips. These were intended to interrupt the strict caesura above the windows on the first floor and to end in front of the arches of the parapet in the form of a flower-like decoration. The existing, but scarcely visible jutting projection was to be crowned with smaller blind arcades. It is difficult to say what prompted Plečnik to this solution, in which elements of the Zacherl House were already visible. The semi-circular arches of the parapet are certainly of Venetian origin, though the direct model was probably

43. The Weidmann House in Vienna, 1902, contemporary photograph

the so-called Teyn School on Old Town Square in Prague.

The decision to use the roof space as well made Plečnik alter the plans for the facade fundamentally. Instead of the windowless parapet he now planned above the mansard windows a narrow roof supported by double columns beginning at the height of the window crosses. Setting back the upper part of the building made the facade more dynamic. Plečnik was aware that the unproportioned columns were the weakest element in the facade. In the final correction he tried to clear this up, which led to a more conventional arrangement. Was he motivated here by the closeness of Schönbrunn, or the client's wishes? At all events it is certain that Plečnik was undergoing a personal crisis at that time:

Nothing – I stand here with empty hands – and am sorry for myself and the others. Alone – alone – among millions of people – perhaps a crowd of acquaintances. That is why I like to go into the city, seeking out old places – the

49

old palace of the Liechtensteins – of the Kinskys – and enjoy the life of the long-dead – what power – what plasticity, how luxuriant it all is – full – and so proportioned – for this reason I avoid the ruinous Moderns – I have howled – now I no longer howl.[157]

Plečnik discovered that vital force which the Secession had by now lost for him in the high Baroque. For this reason he contrasted the clearly organized lower part of the building against the almost Baroque-inspired upper half, which he decorated with playful realistic putti that show some likeness to Donatello's choirstalls in the cathedral museum in Florence. The same dynamic is demonstrated by the cornice of the roof-bearing columns. This is no longer designed on the lines of the antique altar – a motif characteristic of Plečnik's early work – it has a Baroque liveliness. Originally there was to be a similar motif on the fencing of the front garden. An exception to this liveliness is seen in the balcony, with its standard industrial profiles and glass floor which conveys something of Plečnik's lingering Secessionism (fig. 43).

Plečnik greatly regretted that he was unable to think through the external facade down to the last detail because the client drove him on mercilessly. 'My house in Hietzing is a miscarriage. Everyone says excellent but something – the donkeys do not know that I was not my own master – I cannot stand another master besides myself. It's a question of money here – *pay Crovat*',[158] he complained to his brother. He was satisfied only with the furnishing of the dining-room, which will be discussed elsewhere (see figs 60–1).

A MEMBER OF THE SECESSION

From the start in Wagner's atelier Plečnik was familiar with the ideas and work of the members of the Viennese Secession. In the spring of 1901, hoping to improve his opportunities for employment and to bridge the financially not very promising start of the year, he formally became a member of the Secession.[159] This link with modern Austrian and European art brought him a very important source of information. Despite his critical distance from everything new, he admired, often unconsciously, those artists in particular who had already greatly valued Wagner. Ultimately it was the Secession that kept him from moving to Prague.

Around the turn of the century, arranging exhibitions represented a considerable part of an architect's work. The relatively high expenditure invested in this by the Secessionists raised the general level and in part actually dictated

44. The wall fountain in the XVth exhibition of the Vienna Secession, 1902

the fashion of Viennese domestic culture. Moreover, the exhibitions offered artists a good opportunity to establish themselves quickly, although they also demanded a constant flow of new ideas and a sense for improvization, for which a feeling for space and good taste were crucial. Colours, curtains, canopies, veiling, screens, carpets, panelling plinths, showcases, lighting fixtures and plants had forced some of the previously binding rules of architectural design into the shade. Now art, which in architecture as traditionally practised was subject to the delay between idea and realization, could be presented to the public with great topicality. Conversely, architects succeeded in transforming the stimuli resulting from exhibition practice into something lasting and absolute.

Plečnik was positively predestined to such work. If we compare how Olbrich and Hoffmann organized the first Secession show in the horticultural halls immediately before the opening of the Jubilee Exhibition of 1898,[160] we realize that Plečnik employed almost exactly the same tricks as they did. However, with the organization of the exhibition for the Arts and Crafts Association of Lower Austria (see fig. 11) he far transcended the still rather traditional colour and clutter of the Secession Exhibition in the Horticultural Society building. Plečnik had already worked elegantly and grandly on the symbols of the new age. The Secession welcomed him with open arms. In the spring of 1901 we find him among the organizers of the extremely popular tenth exhibition of the Secession,[161] devoted to Austrian art, where the central work was Gustav Klimt's *Medicine*.

Towards the end of the following year Plečnik was appointed to the working committee of the fifteenth Secession exhibition[162] and he arranged one of the halls with paintings by Wilhelm Leibl, who died in 1900. The organizational level of the previous, fourteenth, exhibition had been very high, thanks to the participation of Josef Hoffmann. It had ended in the summer, recording the second largest number of visitors up to that time. The centrepiece was Max Klinger's figure of Beethoven.

In preparing the fifteenth exhibition Plečnik concentrated on the interior and was annoyed that in the end he had to do without the planned parquet flooring,[163] so that a continual transition from the wooden floor into the low panelling could not be realized. Nevertheless – and more or less involuntarily – Plečnik found that what was left of his idea (the panelling) was the cheapest and most lasting wall covering. He later used it in the most varied contexts, beginning with the staircase of the Zacherl House; another case was the bottom parts of the two bridges between the galleries in the big reading room at the Ljubljana library. In the window area he covered the ceiling and wall of his Secessionist inte-

45. The salon at the World Exhibition in St Louis, 1904

rior with plaster of Paris ribbing, which gave the impression of geometrically decorated carpets. On a narrow strip under the wall showcase of miniatures by a Scottish painter he executed a negative impression of the same pattern, subtly converting it into wood. He repeated the same motif on a smaller scale under the glass structure of the writing-desk (see fig. 59), thus including it stylistically in the area design.

In the opposite corner of the hall he placed a wall fountain with a dog leaning over the basin (fig. 44). The sketch shows a human figure, instead of a dog, against a varied background of stone and tiles, although for this he later had to be content with stucco. The richly contoured background of the fountain can be compared with Josef Hoffmann's abstract sopraporta from the previous Secession exhibition, which can also be traced in the cornice of the Zacherl House. There can scarcely be a better illustration of the distinct development of the two architects, whose work for a time was stylistically very closely related: Hoffmann was objective, simple and attracted by geometrical forms; Plečnik was full of imagination and poetry and was also a master of melody and composition. One inconspicuous and inventive detail will serve as an example: a column-shaped sculpture plinth made only of material stretched over a stand. This solution is proof of the ease with which Plečnik moved between Semper's metaphors and a textile metamorphoses of antique building elements.

In the first eight years of its existence the Secession was very cosmopolitan, and it is interesting to observe the impression that some of its artists made on Plečnik. In the first exhibition he was very attracted by Pierre-Cécil Puvis de Chavannes, while he could not muster any enthusiasm for the work of contemporary German painters. Later still, he admired some of the second-rate fellow-travellers of

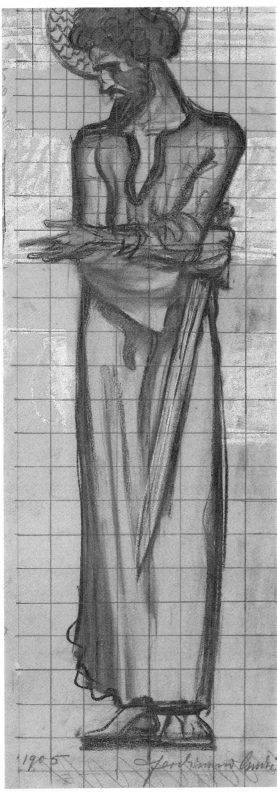

46. Ferdinand Andri: Plečnik as the Apostle Paul, sketch for the 'altar wall' at the XXIVth exhibition of the Vienna Secession, 1905

Modernism more than its protagonists. Early in 1900 he expressed praise for Japanese art,[164] although, to judge by the number of visitors, it did not convince the Viennese public. One of the undoubted high points was the eighth Secession exhibition, devoted to arts and crafts, in the autumn of 1900. Although we do not know of any comments on this by Plečnik, it can be assumed that he had closely examined the furniture of Henry van de Velde, C.R. Ashbee and the Glasgow School. This exhibition was probably his first proper encounter with contemporary English arts and crafts. In the work of Charles Rennie Mackintosh and his wife Margaret MacDonald he must have found a kindred poetic feeling, though it was too redolent of a northern gracefulness for him. Closer to his inclination, however, was the harmony, influenced by the Alpine landscape, of Giovanni Segantini, whose works he learned to appreciate at the next, ninth Secession exhibition. He described him as 'the purest soul that had ever appeared before his eyes'.[165] Segantini's general popularity among Slovenian artists at that time makes it probable that Plečnik too, despite his declared commitment to Mediterranean art, never fully discarded the Alpine side of his character. At the same exhibition he praised the French artists again; however, he had little enthusiasm for Max Klinger, the favourite of the Viennese public. The plaster model by Auguste Rodin of the Burghers of Calais seemed to him to be 'indescribably' beautiful; he called the French the 'substratum' of painting; with regard to the Spaniard Zuloaga he said in connection with Ruskin's views on inheritance that 'he illustrated in a healthy way many of the weaknesses of his people'.[166] Though Plečnik found it difficult to tolerate the German ambience on which he was in many ways dependent, he felt all the more attracted by Scandinavian art,[167] from which in his opinion a veiled, mystical poetry emanated.

His relations with Gustav Klimt are a another matter and he never expressed a definite opinion about him. It appears, however, that he was prepared to ignore the sensuality in his works. He was less tolerant of Egon Schiele, Oskar Kokoschka and other young Austrian artists.[168] He followed the work of Koloman Moser and Josef Hoffmann with mixed feelings; in the latter he took particular exception to the 'neo-pagan' display of Klinger's statue of Beethoven.[169] Early in 1904, at the nineteenth Secession exhibition, he met Ferdinand Hodler, whom he placed on an equal footing with his two favourites, Puvis de Chavannes and Segantini: 'Of course I know little of this world – but this greatness and simplicity – for me evangelical clarity – is something splendid.'[170]

The severe shortcoming of the Secession exhibitions of fine arts, which was not put right until the beginning of 1903 with a big international exhibition, was the lack of Impressionists, or, rather, of the French avant-garde of the end of the nineteenth and beginning of the twentieth century. In moving words Plečnik described to his brother what the President of the Secession, Wilhelm Bernatzik, who had just returned from Paris, said about the painter Van Gogh, of whom Plečnik had known nothing until then.[171] As yet neither he nor the Viennese 'Stylists' were able to appreciate true Impressionism.

Plečnik worked in the Secession from the spring of 1904 until the building of the Zacherl House two years later, without becoming involved in the fateful quarrels of its members. At the beginning of 1904 he helped the respected Viennese cabinet-maker Sándor Járay with the design of an interior for the World Exhibition in St Louis in the USA (fig. 45).[172] Plečnik practically created the design in a day, so it is understandable that in many respects it is not of the same quality as the interior in the fifteenth Secession exhibition. Some of the solutions, like the built-in show windows or pictures set between the rectangular frames of the wall covering, were part of his constant repertoire at that time. Surprising for Vienna in those days was his choice of the unusually dark colours which he had come to enjoy in Czech folk embroidery. In complete contrast was Hoffman's bright and thoroughly modern interior of the School of Arts and Crafts of the Austrian Museum, also shown in St Louis. In comparison with his professional colleague Hoffmann, Plečnik created a modern design with straight lines, smooth surfaces and an elegant contrast between the black polished wall panelling – the latter appropriate to the dedication of the room to the late Empress – and the yellow silk damask wallpaper. For the first time he gave up the fashionable Secessionist fabrics in favour of a classical material. The large mirror above the sofa used in his American interior was almost certainly inspired by the exhibition room of the telegraph office 'Die Zeit' set up by Wagner. Similarly, his massive furniture was an answer to Wagner's bentwood armchair in the ground-floor rooms of this office. Where Wagner had provided the arms of the chair with aluminium fittings, in order to endow the furniture with a contemporary yet lasting character, Plečnik gave priority to user comfort with the upholstery. The interior for the World Exhibition brought a definite caesura in Plečnik's expression. The granite table top designed for this interior contributed to the darkish impression of the furnishing; thus it coincides with the facade of the Zacherl House.

At the end of January 1905 Plečnik, was obliged to replace Leopold Bauer on the committee of the Secession.[173] Relations between the members of the association were by then already very strained. On the occasion of the twenty-third exhibition of the Secession[174] Plečnik once again declared his great respect for his teacher. He decided that the model of the church Am Steinhof was to be the central exhibit, and designed a real, small-scale avenue leading up to it.[175] He opened up the view on to the green with a large window, thus suggesting the position planned for the church. This arrangement was one of the first realizations of a theme loved by Plečnik, namely the way out of semi-darkness into light, which he had adopted from ancient Egyptian religious architecture.

A few weeks before the fateful general meeting of the Secession, at which the Klimt group only narrowly missed winning the vote, Plečnik represented the Secession in the design of the Austrian section at the ninth International Art Exhibition in Munich in 1905.[176]

Towards the end of the same year Plečnik fulfilled within the context of the Secession a wish he had cherished for years, with the twenty-fourth exhibition devoted entirely to religious art. The fact that this unusual idea could be realized can no doubt be attributed to the chairman of the association, his like-minded friend Ferdinand Andri; he had already supported Plečnik in the spring of 1905, when the Secession outwardly at least still appeared to be unified.[177]

Plečnik wanted his exhibition to counter the low level of the two previous, similar exhibitions by the newly-founded art section of the Austrian Leo Society, which he had had to organize, to some extent against his will.[178] He worked with the Munich Association for Christian Art and the artist monks of Beuron. Plečnik won the cooperation of the Beuron monks with the help of Zacherl, who put him in touch with the conservative Catholic publicist Richard von Kralik. Surviving sources do not reveal whether the exhibition was intended to counter-attack the more liberal-spirited artist group round Klimt. After the Klimt group left the Secession this kind of intention was attributed to it willy-nilly.

During the preparatory period of the exhibition Plečnik often travelled to Germany and he also went to the Abbey of Monte Cassino, where the Beuron monks were painting at that time. Iconographically he placed the sacrament of baptism at the centre of the exhibition and erected a painted apse with a font at the end of the room (fig. 46). Despite the participation of numerous native and foreign members of the association, the exhibition did not have the expected financial success. The absence of Klimt and the 'Stylists', initially a relief to many people, had weakened the Secession irreparably.

It is not easy to explain what moved Plečnik, despite the

47. The XXXIVth exhibition of the Vienna Secession in 1909, devoted to J. Engelhart

apparent poverty of the majority of the Beuron works, to look with such confidence to the future of the artist monks and to believe in their redemptive mission. What also seems unusual is the partially positive verdict with which Viennese art critics reacted to this, virtually the first joint appearance of the Beuron monks to take place in Vienna. Even the well-known Viennese art critic, Hevesi, actually described them as the forerunners of the Secessionists.[179] The rejection of classical perspective and illusion as well as the transition to linear superficiality and immateriality evinced by a Peter Lenz were ideas that at that time were already forty years old, but apparently to Secessionist Vienna they were up to date again from a pure aesthetic viewpoint. For Plečnik Beuron art meant cleansing contemporary art of sensuality and sentimentality. He was convinced that only art created behind monastic walls could express the highest moral values, and he was not disturbed by the fact that the founder of the School, Peter Lenz, reinforced the demand for hieratically authoritarian religious forms with the dogmatic emphasis of the papal ultramontanism of his age.[180] The move towards elementary simplicity coincided with Plečnik's idealistic concept of original Christianity. Admiration of Egypt as the cradle of human civilization led Lenz to speculate that ancient Egyptian art contained the rules of divine creation, to which contemporary creativity should also be subject.[181] In this respect as well, Lenz found fruitful ground in Plečnik. Plečnik admired the same works as he did and, inspired by Semper, was intensely preoccupied with the art of the ancient cultures, whose originality and unadulterated quality he tried to penetrate.

To Plečnik the monk's search for the ancient canon of beauty seemed less attractive, if not quite pointless. Of the Beuron works, he attributed lasting validity to only two, by Lenz: the Egyptian figure of Mary and the Maurus chapel at Beuron, which he commended to his brother as a model when the latter was considering the building of a votive chapel in Idrija. He was also inspired by this in the workshop building of the Žale cemetery in Ljubljana, which exhibits almost the same supporting columns. During the preparations for the Viennese exhibition Plečnik met Jan Verkade, a former member of the Nabis Group. His hieratically decorative interpretation always served Plečnik as the ideal of sacred painting. Nevertheless, he had to admit that Father Willibrord, as he called himself after becoming a Catholic, was rather alone with his talent in the ranks of the monks.

Before Plečnik withdrew from the Secession in 1906 for a few years, he worked with his fellow-pupil Leopold Bauer on the twenty-seventh Secession Exhibition,[182] which was largely dedicated to the French painter Eugène Carrière, a member who had died that year. He used red material with a pattern by Koloman Moser, inlays and for the first time white Doric pillars, over which he stretched a dark canopy to tone down the bright lighting of the pictures. 'I am a son of darkness,'[183] he wrote jocularly in a letter to Kotěra.

Plečnik's enjoyment of his work for the Secession, which did not have much more to show for itself, and began increasingly and provocatively to turn to Germany, petered out. For his friend, the sculptor and painter Josef Engelhart, he organized one more big one-man exhibition in the autumn of 1909 (fig. 47),[184] but without allowing his name to appear, and then left the association together with Andri, Hanak and Lederer. To Plečnik's dismay Engelhart had contributed, but, leaving Plečnik to battle with all the unpleasantnesses in the preparatory period, he had not allowed his holiday on the Attersee to suffer.

THE ZACHERL HOUSE

The four-year planning of the Zacherl House[185] (see figs 22–7) coincided with an intensive search for new possibilities of application of Semper's principle of cladding. With his rationalist outlook, Wagner had abandoned all Semper's symbolism, and justified the cladding of facades with shorter building times and lower costs, the final result would be the same as in the Classical style of building with stone blocks. Although expert literature has only emphasized so far the avant-garde aspect of Wagner's fastening facade stone slabs with metal knobs which give the impression of a new 'technical' ornamentation of the twentieth century,[186] the impetus for such a solution had rather come from tradition. Wagner might have followed Semper's speculation that the mail heads or rosettes belonged to textile elements.[187] However, in a very concrete way he could apply Choisy's explanation of fastening decorative slabs below the corona of a Greek temple. On page 288 of his book *Histoire de l'architecture* it is shown very illustratively that the guttae were derived from wooden bungs.

In 1898 Wagner, working with Olbrich, had completed the two city railway pavilions on Karlsplatz, where there are no traces of 'nails' to be found. The thin sheets of homogeneous Carrara marble were set in metal frames like window panes. Even the ornamentation still had nothing in common with the technoid aesthetics of Wagner's later work. There is little fundamental difference between the ornaments of Plečnik's interior from the Jubilee Exhibition in the Prater in 1898, cut out of cardboard and covered with material, and the gilded flowers engraved in the pavilion facades. Fabiani went a step further in fastening the marble slabs of the 'Artaria House' with bronze anchors,[188] but he did not lay claim to a new type of decoration.

For some time after the publication of his book, Wagner adhered in part to the massive building method with stone ashlar blocks in the study for the new building of the Imperial and Royal Academy of Fine Arts. The Viennese modern architectural scene had initially inclined towards plaster and ceramic, which led primarily to the realization of Semper's cladding theory. Wagner's 'Majolica House' and its perfected variant, Fabiani's 'Portois-&-Fix' building, which was clad with pyrogranite from Zsolnay, illustrate just before the turn of the century the entire span of facade design. In the 'Majolica House' the arrangement follows the example described by Semper of the glazed ceramics of the old Assyrians.[189] Wagner hung the cladding like a great tapestry on the lion-heads adopted from the Greek sima under the cornice with the decoration of the classical Greek geison. In contrast, when composing the mosaic-style tiles on the pattern of Venetian architecture,[190] Fabiani did not consider Semper's recommendation to arrange the ornamentation more densely above, thus enabling it to spread freely. He 'stretched' the cladding across an imaginary blind frame, which he expressed by avoiding sharp facade edges. By doing without the protective cornice Fabiani was also trying to give proof of the durability of the ceramic cladding, thus taking a further step towards the aesthetics of the curtain wall.

In some respects it was Josef Hoffmann who came closest to the later 'white functionalism'. On the facade of the Stoclet Palace in Brussels he renounced the visibility of the tectonics altogether. The building no longer hints at the

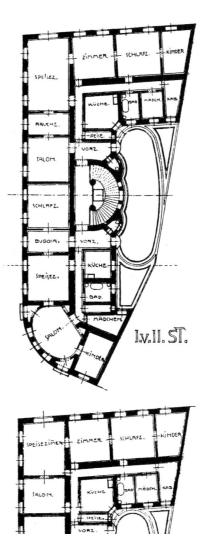

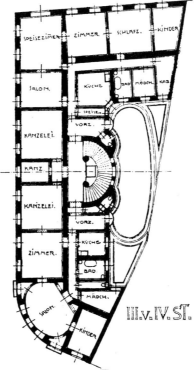

48. Competition design for the Zacherl House, 1900

49. Competition design for the Zacherl House, 1900

massive stone construction method.[191] Each of the facade surfaces is edged with a kind of gilded band, or enclosed in a frame, and along its edge touches only the adjacent band. Despite the emphatically 'atectonic' architecture the palace gives the impression of a free composition of different sized cubes; however, these are still subject to the traditional alignment and symmetry.

When the manufacturer Johann Evangelist Zacherl turned to Wagner for his building project in autumn 1900 on the advice of Josef Maria Auchentaller, a family friend and member of the Secession, almost all these possibilities of facade designs were still open. Among his colleagues and pupils Wagner selected Max Fabiani, Otto Schönthal, Carl Fischl and Plečnik for the internal competition for the residential and business premises.[192] Zacherl also proposed his former architects Franz Krauss and Josef Tölk. Plečnik won the competition and with it the prize of 250 gulden.

At the turn of the century, some streets in the centre of Vienna were radically widened (as they were in Prague and some other European cities). Zacherl's business premises on the Bauernmarkt in central Vienna, renovated barely a year and a half before, fell victim to this rebuilding. An irregular site became available. The planned building bordered on

three narrow alleys. Two of these met at an extremely obtuse angle and called for a rounded corner facade. The ground plan itself was not a problem, since it was possible to plan for the larger rooms on the sides facing the street, while all the other rooms, including the kitchen, bathrooms, minor rooms and servants' quarters, were accommodated on the courtyard side. The competitors were free to plan for two or three flats on each floor. A third flat would of course have had economic advantages but would have inevitably meant narrowing the staircase and the light-well, which would have made conditions worse for the service personnel. Plečnik proposed a smaller number of more spacious flats, with a central staircase and a correspondingly large and bright courtyard (fig. 48).

The facade studies were decisive for the outcome of the competition. As the excellent position in the centre of town called for a prestigious exterior, the question for Plečnik was how to achieve a more decorative appearance for the upper part of the building with marble cladding. The only model at that time was Fabiani's 'Artaria House' but the different storeys are treated uniformly there. To avoid this problem, Plečnik compromised: he proposed cladding the building with stone up to the second floor and rendering and decorat-

56

ing the remaining storeys in the manner of the Langer House in Hietzing (figs 38 and 49).[193]

In deciding on stone he was also following Fabiani's example. He wanted to apply a row of polished marble slabs with visible 'metal nails' to the columns of the ground floor and mezzanine; a second row was to be hung on the next two floors, although the sketch does not give a clear idea of how this was to be done.[194] He envisaged the building to be roughly the same colour as Fabiani's 'Artaria'.

In Plečnik's proposal the most important innovation is the unification of the facade sections. Where Wagner would have introduced a strict vertical caesura, Plečnik altered the rhythm. Because the Zacherl House stands in the near vicinity of Vienna Cathedral, Plečnik paid particular attention to its view from this direction. The reduced window intervals would have given the impression of a continuous outer wall. The two planned vertical rows of balconies were later abandoned as the residue of Wagner's composition scheme, and so were the figures of the Four Seasons with which Plečnik planned to emphasize the entrance and the rounded corner of the building. However, nothing came of all this, because he was prevented from any further work by disagreements with the client's contractors, Krauss and Tölk.

In the autumn or winter of 1902 Plečnik became more closely connected with Zacherl through his work in the Leo Society. When in his youth, he had taken over his father's prosperous insecticide business, Zacherl had not been interested in religion. Later on he underwent a fundamental conversion and devoted himself primarily to social work with young people. His society included amongst its menbers the most important representatives of the Austrian Christian Socialists. He was also personally acquainted with the Mayor of Vienna, Karl Lueger. One result of his position was that he was able to steer Plečnik on to the path of a reformer of sacred art. Plečnik's astonishment and fascination with Zacherl was principally over the completely worldly, and to him at that time unimaginable, nature of the battle with the Social Democrats for power over the Viennese working class. If we also mention the anti-Semitism of these social circles in this connection, which Plečnik himself partially supported, we should remember that this was manifested at various significant levels. Up to the end of the first decade of the twentieth century Zacherl was intensely preoccupied with the romantic glorification of Richard Wagner as an ideal Catholic musician, at the expense of the Jews, although he was not among the militant protagonists of anti-Semitism. His work in the Party's youth organization brought him closer to the controversial fanatical supporter of Austrian Christian Socialism, Anton Orel.[195]

The book Das Weltantlitz (The Face of the World) written by Zacherl and Orel under the joint pseudonym Johannes Aquilla[196] was published in 1919 with the church's imprimatur. At the same time Zacherl also published his work Die Glaubensfrage (The Question of Faith),[197] in which he similarly attempted to prove the historical guilt of the once chosen and later rejected people. But the books remained insignificant and had little impact on an Austria described by Karl Kraus, an ironic critic of Austrian narrow-mindedness and intolerance, as 'an experimental station for the end of the world', and found scarcely any seriously interested readers. Plečnik's anti-Semitism was of a completely verbal nature and restricted to generalized prejudices, incited by the spiritual father of Austrian Christian Socialism, Karl von Vogelsang, against the alleged damaging power of Jewish capital.[198] At the same time Plečnik honestly admired the genius of this persecuted people.

In Zacherl Plečnik had found a patron who was always prepared to support him with advice and money. For this reason too, the architect stayed on in Vienna longer than he had perhaps planned. He frequently visited the manufacturer's family and found a friend in Maria Peham, Zacherl's somewhat older sister-in-law, who was able to lend a motherly ear to his sensitive artistic soul. However, he continued to refuse the idea of marriage, for fear of concessions to family life which might have jeopardized his ideals. As he was a believer in a national elite to which his education and work made him feel he belonged, it seemed to him that he had no time for marriage. On a later occasion he stated: 'I too could have married, and when I was in Vienna I did consider it. Yes, I could have married more easily than anyone, but I did not do it. I told myself: It is written: a man cannot serve two masters and architecture remained my beloved.'[199]

It should be mentioned in passing that as an amateur botanist Zacherl also awakened in Plečnik an interest in the symbiosis between plants and architecture which far transcended his initial love of plant decoration which the organization of exhibitions had fostered in him.

'I torment myself as much as I can – to satisfy him with my work (he has an extremely refined sensitivity) but it goes very slowly. Of course there are some things I did well – in which he gained great confidence in me –'[200] he wrote to his brother Andrej when he resumed work on the Zacherl House in the spring of 1903. In the next planning phase he had to reconsider the use of the rooms economically. The first major redesign, in which he fell in with the demands of his client and his technical colleagues Krauss and Tölk, concerned the use of reinforced concrete.[201] This was intended to lower costs and give greater mobility to the business areas.

50. Johann Evangelist Zacherl and his wife, 1904

Reinforced concrete – in the Zacherl House it was used for the supporting columns of the two lower floors and ceilings – was not then a traditional building material. Since its qualities were not fully understood and tested, several building firms offered different schemes, but all more or less based on the traditional ideas of bearing and loading structural elements. The most progressive, with his system of monolithic joining of all construction elements – which found its expression in less use of concrete and iron, and consequently in much lower prices – was the French engineer François Hennebique, a licence from whom had been procured by the master builder Eduard Ast in Vienna in 1899. As Zacherl had approached him even before 1907 as Hennebique's most important patents were running out, he was acquiring the appropriate renown for his building in Viennese architectural history in technical respects as well.[202]

The conversion of the ground plan made it necessary to redesign the staircase. The shape of the neighbouring house enabled Plečnik to take the staircase out of the mass of the building and place it independently on the court-side building line (fig. 52). Instead of a semi-circle, he gave it the shape of a flattened oval. At the same time he moved the entrance to the shorter facade side on Wildpretmarkt (see fig. 23). This change also owed something to the idea of preserving the memory of one of the most beautiful late Baroque oval stairways in the Gruber Palace in Ljubljana, which was then threatened with demolition. The fact that this and similar ideas often influenced Plečnik's decisions is borne out by the following extract from a letter to his brother Andrej:

> When my house is finished you absolutely must come and look. I will stand there more or less without competition – whether good or not good. I want to make sure that you take it in and confirm it – so that all my passion and my struggle and everything – for my homeland is not lost for ever. My parents are contained in it – and if anyone wanted to dispute it – then my homeland must learn – that I have thought it through from bottom to top – and in a time of suffering – in which artists are not generally used to work –.[203]

In the arrangement of the facade Plečnik adhered to some ideas from the competition design, others he altered fundamentally. In planning to use ceramic cladding (fig. 51) he wanted to avoid the combination of marble and plaster of which he was still unsure. He wished to enliven the upper part of the building, like the facade of the Wiedmann House, with putti. Here he was following Semper's pronouncement, according to which the people of Antiquity made use of anthropomorphic building sculpture more in a decorative than in a structural sense.[204]

Plečnik wanted to cover the whole residential part of the building evenly with a pattern of rectangular frames. He also changed the proportions of the windows, making them almost square. A further important area in which Plečnik was distancing himself from Wagner's practice was in the treatment of the mezzanine, which was to be divided from the ground floor by an emphatic cornice, whereby the composition would have been symmetrically balanced vertically as well. Semper compares facade cladding with a large stretched carpet, and speaks of an upper and lower edge, though he actually advises against lateral edges unless they are structurally necessary.[205] At the same time he points out that the horizontal edges – in concrete terms the fourth floor and the mezzanine – must be treated differently. Plečnik achieved this by differing the proportions, changing rhythms and redirecting the decoration; for instance, the down-turned lamps in the mezzanine.

Plečnik would probably not have changed his plans any more had not Zacherl drawn his attention to the facade of an old grey house in the neighbourhood which he particularly liked. Plečnik explained to him that a similar effect could be achieved with granite cladding, to which Zacherl is said to have replied: 'Cost what it may, it is all feasible.'[206] In Wagner's atelier the idea of a granite facade had been very topical and we also come across it in the unrealized project of

58

the Academy of Fine Arts. Once again Semper is in the background. Although the latter looked upon Egyptian architecture as an example of an inferior developmental stage if compared to Greek Antiquity, he nevertheless spoke enthusiastically about the monumentality of old-Egyptian temples:

> The granite and porphyry monuments of Egypt exert an unbelievable power over every mind. In what does this magic consist? No doubt partly in the facet that they are the neutral ground where the hard resistant material and the soft hand of man with his simple tools (hammer and chisel) meet and conclude a pact. 'Thus far and no further, thus and not otherwise.' That has been their silent language for millennia.[207]

Later on we read that some of the properties of granite, such as the 'splendid calm, massiveness, the somewhat angular and flat refinement of its lineaments, temperance in the treatment of the difficult material, of which it makes one aware, its entire habit' increasingly lose their significance with the new technical possibilities of working it. On this point Loos also agrees with Semper.[208] Nevertheless, we can regard his explanation of the competition design for the *Chicago Tribune* building in 1923 primarily as a great concession to Plečnik's Zacherl House for Loos intended to design the exterior of his building in the same way: 'My teaching that the ornaments of the ancients should be replaced by us with noble material is intended to be expressed here in gigantic form: only one material should be used, *black, polished granite*.'[209] Despite the lively debate about granite, before Plečnik no one in Vienna had dared to clad an entire building with it. Up to then granite had been used almost exclusively for monuments and funeral architecture.

Plečnik's creative process begins at the point at which Semper concludes the explanation on the decoration of ancient Egyptian smooth granite pylons with rod-like profiles. This procedure appealed to him all the more because Semper derived this motif from carpentry.[210] The difference lay simply in the fact that Semper speaks of a surround for the corners, while Plečnik separates the individual slabs with extremely narrow granite lisenes. The strips are similar in cross-section to the letter T and thus not only conceal the points of intersection of the individual slabs, but also serve to fasten them. By comparison with Wagner's 'nails', Plečnik's solution was closer to Semper's idea of organic architecture, although it lays no claim to modernity. Fundamentally this principle of fixing has the advantage that the cladding is not tightly stretched, so that the risk of damage caused by extending is avoided. Of course the most important point was the anchoring of the heavy granite slabs. In

51. Variant of the Zacherl House design, 1903

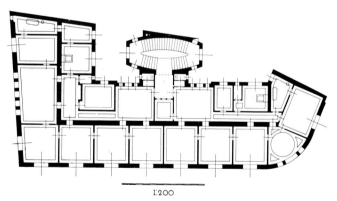

1:200

52. The Zacherl House, ground plan of the upper floors, 1903/4

59

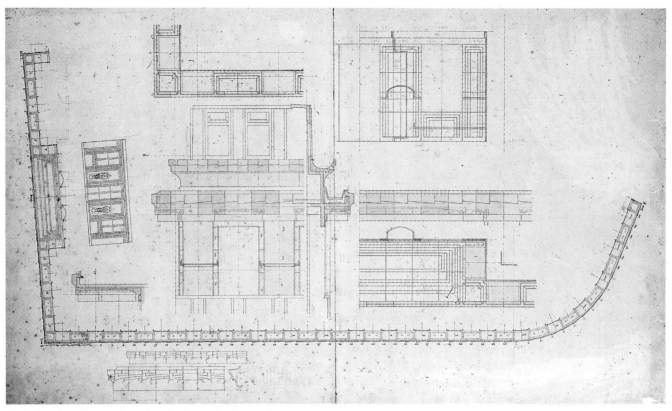

53–5. Drawing of the cornice and studies for the facade of the Zacherl House, 1904

54

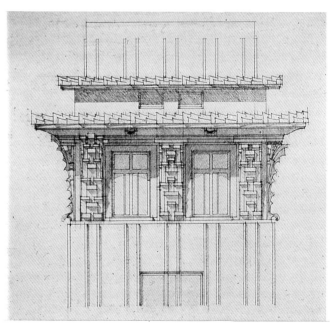

55

60

contrast to Wagner, who solved this problem with the help of mortar and the additional 'nails', Plečnik did without mortar and fixed the slabs with profiles and additional iron anchors.

Plečnik omitted any decoration of the stone, he neither bevelled the right-angles, a motif – very popular at the time – which had found its way into architecture from carpentry, and which he intended to imitate in his ceramic façade variant, nor indicated the centre of the slab, a characteristic that Hoffmann had adopted from Antiquity. By the rhythmic alternation of wider and narrower vertical granite strips, he accepted Semper's principle of alternating eurhythmia, which derives from decorative mouldings as well as the interchanging of triglyphs and metopes on the entablature of Doric temples.[211] For the sake of the unified surface of the building Plečnik waived a vertical strengthening strip on the facade corner. The entrance facade differs from the others only in the altered rhythm of windows and the inserted balcony which marks the centre (see fig. 23). The windows are set flat in the facade and follow the basic compositional scheme; the window crosses determine the size of the granite slabs.

One last major intervention in the design before the plan was presented was the regrouping of the attic windows above the cornice. When the plans were submitted in the spring of 1904 there were unexpected difficulties. The municipal council of Vienna demanded a change in the pitch of the roof. This meant that Plečnik felt obliged to find a different top for the building. This unappealing decision forced him to rethink the basic question of the building material, which Semper regarded 'not merely as a passive mass, but as a means, as a cooperative element in the stimulus to invention'.[212]

Because of the expressed verticalism of the narrow lisenes, the cladding no longer formed a neutral transition between the upper and lower cornices, but became a surface on which the solution for the facade tectonics had to be found. A solution was offered in the telamons of the Czech-German sculptor Franz Metzner,[213] exhibited at this time in the Secession; they arrived as a positive blessing to Plečnik because they radiated the spirit of that new mythical solemnity which corresponded to the architect's ideas of the character of the building. In order to create an anology with ancient Egyptian architecture, Plečnik proposed earthenware.[214] The numerous sketches (figs 22, 54, 55) prove that the ultimate solution was not so easy to find, and in this Semper's opinion of the higher intellectual level of stylized plant ornamentation as opposed to the realistic telamons certainly played a role.[215]

Metzner's sculptures gave stronger emphasis to the cor-

56. The Zacherl House, 1903–5

nice. Plečnik preserved the memory of the original decorative function of the cornices with a band of leaves. He filled the space between the heads of the rather too low telamons and the height of the cornice with an abacus on each (see fig. 24). The fundamental problem of composition, however, lay in the intertwining of the vertical and horizontal tectonic forces, which might have been affected by the emphasized, decorated cornice. After lengthy experiment Plečnik succeeded in restoring the balance by continuing the pilaster strip to the attic floor, over the cornice, and by doubling the crown cornice (fig. 56). The telamons thereby carried enough weight optically, and the conflict between the forces behind their backs was relaxed in the transition from granite to copper cladding. The very plastic frieze, which is underlined still further by the semi-circular domed projecting windows between the telamons, was given its compositional pendant in the stricter convex windows on the first floor. In many respects Fabiani's architecture was responsible for this and other details which were tested by Plečnik in new compositional connections.

The architect was also given some headaches by the rounded corner of the building which, because of the exposed position, he did not want to leave unemphasized. Driven practically to despair, the problem finally virtually solved itself: during a conversation he unintentionally overturned a box of tooth powder and placed it negligently on the model of the house. Like the decision not to have projecting shop windows he created a complete novelty. The corner of the Zacherl House was topped with a high drum-

57. The insect powder shop on the ground floor of the Zacherl House, contemporary photograph

by small light bulbs in concealed positions (see fig. 26). Owing to the irregularity of the site the axis does not run parallel to the main facade. Optically, however, this shift is concealed by the slightly turned elliptical stairway. It is not lit from the side, but the big windows are distributed at the end of each flight of stairs, so that a visitor is repeatedly led from darkness to light (fig. 27). The unusual organically-shaped candelabra placed on the longitudinal axis create a contrast to the all-embracing strictness of form and hinted symbolically at the insects on whose destruction Zacherl had founded his fortunes. The lamps are like soap bubbles which might fall at any moment from the candelabra. But where the architect makes them hang from the roof one has the impression that they are being released from their bonds and floating slowly to the floor like flares. For the manufacturer's office to the left of the main entrance he used broad fluorescent tubes made of opalescent glass instead of the flares (fig. 57).

The entrance area of the Zacherl House represents the clearest and most deliberate expression of space on the pattern of ancient Egyptian temple architecture.[217] In this respect too, Plečnik distanced himself from Wagner's ideal of a harmonically perfected but static central space. From the Zacherl House it is apparent that Plečnik shared Semper's conviction that art must always be didactic. Architect and client decorated the entire stairwell, like an exhibition, with reproductions of Old Masters.

When in November 1905 the scaffolding was removed, the building was revealed in all its strangeness. Zacherl's opponents immediately spread the rumour that the granite cladding caused damp in the rooms. Peter Altenberg, a friend of Loos, composed one of the classic hymns of praise to modern architecture, saying among other things:

Your building seems to have grown of itself from the earth of a great city! I never dream. But it is the house of my dreams. It is the fulfilment of my architectural dreams! In this house there must be living on the various floors: Beethoven, R. Wagner, Schubert, Ibsen, Maeterlinck, Hamsun, Strindberg, Jonas Lie, Grieg, Tchaikovsky, Maxim Gorky, and an attic for myself![218]

Aware of the amount of youthful courage contained within the granite walls of the Zacherl House, in later years Plečnik placed under the cornice of his residence in Ljubljana a reduced relief of the Metzner telamons. For him the Zacherl House remained a treasury of creative themes until his death. It aroused unconventional ideas in him which kept pace with those of his contemporaries and often actually overtook them.

like roof, which gives an impression of a cylinder inserted in the facade coating. This impression is further strengthened by a changed rhythm of windows on this part of the house. Plečnik was of course aware that he had not adhered to the normal practice of a solid lower section of the building, and had the roller-blinds of the display windows pulled down for photographing.

The Zacherl House transcended Wagner's relatively simple facade scheme by combining different, parallel compositional themes. Plečnik described the building as 'an organism that grew out of function and material'.[216] As a final element in 1909 he added Ferdinand Andri's statue of the archangel Michael to celebrate the birth of Zacherl's son Michael. Plečnik had the statue, which the sculptor had made according to Antique methods from copper sheet, placed at the most visible point of the facade.

The long, narrow landing to the staircase is clad to the ceiling with black marble. Before the stairway it widens into a small peristyle with natural top lighting, replaced at night

58. Study for a facade, 1914

With regard to the interior, Plečnik had an advantage over his colleagues, who proceeded from modern forms but were not well-versed in the production of furniture or the properties of wood. In the area of classical carpentry even Semper could not tell him anything really new, although the particular stress laid on the possibility of translation from one material to another allowed him to expand his technical ability to the point of virtuosity.

The tradition of Biedermeier and the English cabinetmaker's culture propagated in particular by Arthur von Scala, Director of the Austrian Museum of Art and Industry, created a situation particular to the Viennese arts and crafts sector: the Art Nouveau flourishing in Roman lands was unable to gain a foothold in a climate determined by a healthy balance between structural design and form. The 'two-dimensional' interior with dynamic outlines, and the flat decor, the so-called 'Brettl style', typical of the early work of Hoffmann, Moser and Olbrich, was the modest answer to Art Nouveau. The imagination of the Viennese furniture designers was also kept in check by the late Biedermeier bentwood furniture, which offered only limited ornamental possibilities in contrast to carved wood.

The Secession enriched this tradition with a few classical chair designs. A further characteristic worth mentioning was the practice in the Wiener Werkstätte – founded on the model of the English Guild of Handicraft – around 1905 of decoratively rubbing white colour into the wood pores, to emphasize the grain. If we add a few technical improvements, such as the processing of the wooden seats and backs by hydraulic presses, we have mentioned the most important creative innovations of the Viennese architects before World War I.

Admiration for British furniture design culminated in Vienna at the end of 1900 with the eighth exhibition of the Secession, which was dominated by the Glasgow School. That period saw the establishment in Vienna of the frames and screens made up of narrow borders, the slender, columnar struts with flat capitals, the characteristic door and cupboard closures and the high, slatted seat-backs.

Plečnik preferred to follow tradition and relied on the expert fitting of the wooden parts, strengthening them by applying veneers. In his furniture designs, in contrast to architecture, he felt less strongly bound to his teacher. His desire to carry on the tradition of the paternal workshop went hand in hand with his search for a national identity and a reinforcement of his own self-awareness. Thus for in-

63

stance in the autumn of 1902 he wrote very enthusiastically about his share in the fifteenth Secessionist exhibition:

> Today I saw the writing desk (fig. 59) that I made for the Secessionist exhibition. I believe this is my best piece of craftwork so far. I am very happy about it – and hope – God willing, for a spectacular effect. You really wouldn't dream – what ideas one can get in such fun and games. And everything with such clarity and fluidity – that my heart laughed aloud – Vederemo. My greatest pleasure, however, is that in the writing desk and armchair I am honouring a technique that Father used to use.[219]

If we leave aside the fact that Plečnik, describing his writing desk, used the words 'honouring a technique', thus even adopting Semper's ways of expression, we can recognize the young architect's very heterogeneous wealth of imagination for furniture design. The table was made up of a polygonal lower part, which looked to Van de Velde's dynamic, and a light showcase top with rounded glass panes. Although this writing desk is sublimated to the last degree, it is still a classic product of classical joinery, because it was designed and executed in wood.

However, we can only speak of the use of Semper's theory of metamorphosis in the designs of the same date for a desk set of turned wood,[220] which has its origins in Greek and Egyptian arts and crafts. Despite the parallel with the copies of Egyptian chairs by Loos, this was an episode without direct consequences. Plečnik continued to work in the tradition of the Viennese Biedermeier which he tried to enrich with constructive peculiarities of English furniture, thus trying to approach the fashionable forms of the Secession.

As a trained cabinet-maker, he frequently returned to historical styles, in contrast to his colleagues from the Secession who readily followed the new fashions. In his interiors, like Loos, he preferred to put in period furniture. But the two architects differed in that Loos was an enthusiast for Anglo-Saxon culture as a whole, while Plečnik was interested only in British technological solutions. For this reason, he never used the inglenook seats so popular at the turn of the century, but preferred ceramic and iron stoves which gave him a feeling of homely familiarity.

To free himself from historical influences, in about 1900 he turned his attention to the rejuvenating dynamic forms and polygonal volumes inspired by English bay windows. The furnishing of the drawing-room in the Weidmann House in Hietzing, also belongs to this phase (figs 60–1).[221] This consoled Plečnik a little for the architecture of the house which was not entirely successful. Despite his inter-

ests, which inclined towards the historical, he did follow the fashion trends of his time with great sensitivity. For instance, he enriched Wagner's chair from his own appartment in Köstlergasse, Vienna, with spiral profiles, diagonally linked and organically strengthened, which we also find in Van de Velde and his German colleagues Richard Riemerschmied, Bernhard Pankok and Bruno Paul. In the elegantly shaped legs and armrests of the Weidmann chairs Plečnik did, however, come face to face with the conflict between organically evolved and rational structural design. For this reason, and also because of the high costs of carving, he soon stopped experimenting in this area.

The chairs of simple design inspired by English Arts and Crafts were of special importance to the further development of Plečnik's furniture designs. Thus for instance in the fifteenth Secession exhibition already referred to, besides the writing desk set, he also exhibited an armchair with a slatted back and cushion hung on it. Later in 1903 mature variants of this model of chair were made for Dr Jernej Demšar from Ljubljana[222] and for the consulting room of Emil Knauer, the gynaecologist (a son-in-law of Zacherl) in Graz (fig. 62).[223] Stylistically the two types of chair are very similar to the anteroom furnishings for Dr Hans Salzer and the office for Dr Hugo Henneberg by Josef Hoffmann. However, differences are visible in the design. Whereas Hoffmann tightly linked together the bars, of equal thickness, and with a square cross-section, in the form of a rectangular frame, Plečnik stressed the elasticity of the slats by arranging them in a fan shape, to give an optical impression of comfortable seating. An important factor is the upholstery hung on or attached to the chair. Here Plečnik was literally following Semper's observation that the upholstery must first simply lie on the furniture.[224] Plečnik's chair for the Graz consulting room is a work of classical joinery, composed of a supporting glued frame and thinner slats stretched within it like strings. The inspiration not only comes from the English interior but partly also the antique tripod. Plečnik's imagination was always set alight by the most varied associations, but owing to his aim to combine everything in one organic whole the individual elements cannot always be recognized. We can make the same claim for the chairs from Zacherl's business premises (see fig. 57), made in 1905,[225] since these display both modern English and ancient Greek influences.

With the furnishing of Dr Heinrich Peham's waiting-room,[226] (he was another of Zacherl's sons-in-law), in 1905 Plečnik paraphrased the beloved Secessionist bentwood chair with the low semi-circular back (fig. 63). Hoffmann gave this chair its classical form one or two years later, when

59. The writing desk at the XVth exhibition of the Vienna Secession, 1902

60–1. Interiors of the Weidmann House in Vienna, 1902

he did the designs for the cabaret *Fledermaus*. Plečnik's chair has three legs, which for reasons of stability are held underneath by a horseshoe-shaped support. The tapering elements, resembling Minoan columns, are repeated in other parts of the fittings and give a hint of archaism. The essential innovation lies in the Biedermeier combination of the lighter softwood and harder dark wood. The contrast is not simply one of design but also one of content. The darkly polished parts raise the fittings above the level of mass production, among which Hoffmann's furniture referred to earlier can be included. Plečnik's interpretation of historical models is extremely complex. As regards composition, Plečnik often used compasses to define proportions. In the fittings for Dr Peham's appartment there is a striking emphasis on the numbers three and four, particularly in the unusual division of a reproduction of Leonardo's *Last Supper*, used as a wall decoration.

When wood with a colourless varnish or painted in lively colours came into fashion, scarcely any of the Secessionist artists continued to use veneer. If one of them did resort to this technique he generally tried to enliven it with inlays. Plečnik too adopted the practice of decorating his furniture with rectangular frames in veneer, but in his arts and crafts work, in contrast to his architecture, he used this to indicate the centre of an area. His preference was for gilded square inlays (fig. 64), with which he divided a larger area into several smaller ones, the middle of which he decorated with delicate geometrical intarsia. Veneers can be applied in various ways. By applying smaller and smaller pieces one on top of the other he achieved a relief enhancement of the 'negative' frame. On the other hand, by a special combination of veneer grains, he could produce the illusion of various interlocked rectangles. Another type of decoration that he used in Knauer's interior in Graz was an arrangement of the wood's age rings round the centre; in this way he obtained a pattern resembling the Greek meander. He neutralized the movement with an apparent turn in one direction or the other. According to Semper, one of the fundamental wisdoms of Antiquity was balancing the direction of the ornament.

Besides the chairs, sideboards were among the most important furniture of Plečnik's Viennese period. From the polygonal sideboard in the Weidmann House (fig. 60) he soon went over to cubic volumes, which he combined with the peculiarities of English furniture; one beautiful example of this is the sideboard in Dr Knauer's flat in Graz with small stylized metal columns supporting the top board extending over the lateral sides of the sideboard's middle part. However, Plečnik also produced variations on a more conventional type of a sideboard by his Secession colleague

62. Chairs for Dr Knauer's waiting room in Graz, 1903

63. Dr Peham's waiting room in Vienna, 1905

64. Interior at the winter exhibition of the Austrian Museum of Art and Industry, 1903

Koloman Moser, which is known as 'The miraculous draught of fishes'.[227] Plečnik was attracted above all by the dynamic contrast between the convex lower and the concave upper part. In 1903 in the winter exhibition of the Austrian Museum of Art and Industry, he exhibited an interior,[228] far more elegant than Moser's arrangement (fig. 64). Between the straight side panels of the cupboard he captured an animated play of lines, eradicating anything which might have hinted at the massiveness of Moser's furniture.

Just as it should not be overlooked that in his dialogue with the Secession Plečnik incorporated Baroque and Biedermeier models, so too is it obvious that the black polished furniture surface can be regarded as one of his most aesthetic experiments on the route to the granite facade of the Zacherl House. However, until his arrival in Prague in 1911, Plečnik concerned himself less and less with furniture design. With the interior for the winter exhibition of 1903 the period of his classical cabinet-making ended. Circumstances changed after the First World War, and growing importance was attached to symbolism, which Plečnik realized with the help of Semper's principle of cladding.

In furnishing residences Plečnik converted the idea that textiles were the primary skin of architecture into reality with floor-length curtains. In many cases he also covered the walls with the same material. In Weidmann's town residence[229] he used heavy brocade, thus allowing the ambience of his client's period-furniture to dominate but this step should not be regarded as a return to the heavy historicist textiles, typical of Makart's epoque in Vienna. A few months later, in the autumn of 1905, Plečnik designed the domestic furnishings mentioned earlier for Zacherl's son-in-law Dr Heinrich Peham; these are stylistically quite different, with no traces of historicism or Secessionist ornamentation (fig. 63). He reported on this furnishing to his brother:

> The gynaecologist's residence – which was finished about a month ago – is praised and esteemed – this seems to me to be one of my most mature works. The entire residence is painted in white – from this alone you can see my complete radicalism – or it would be more correct to say democratism – and nevertheless although it is serious and severe – they say the women are quite crazy, and are complaining of their own residences . . .[230]

By dropping the Secessionist ideal of the total work of art, Plečnik, like Loos, subsequently appeared simply as a sensitive arranger of period furniture.

Even while the Zacherl House was being built, Plečnik began work on the redesign of Zacherl's one-storey house in Döbling,[231] opposite his factory. Some initial operations went on up to the beginning of the First World War. With the completion of this extra building, which because of economic changes turned out to be more modest than originally planned, Plečnik's contact with Johann Evangelist Zacherl was finally at an end.

The house, which is no longer standing, was not one of Plečnik's greatest achievements, but during the long years of planning it did lead to certain ideas which were echoed in almost all his later work. The commission strengthened his Catholic ideal of the preservation of traditional family integrity. At the same time he tried to restrain his client's desire for a homely idyll by means of whitewashed walls, large glass areas and a practical English interior.

The problem of the stains caused by moisture which kept on appearing on the upper part of the facade was resolved in 1910 by a natural wood cladding which he arranged ornamentally with slender turned columns. This was apparently a metamorphosis of Giulio Romano's mannerist architecture of the Cortile della Cavallerizza in the Ducal Palace in Mantua. The solution aroused great admiration and earned Plečnik the nickname of 'the Baroquist gone mad'.[232] The remaining sketches show that he proceeded from classical monumental architecture, which he then moved closer to popular art in the final version. Particularly in his later work, Plečnik loved to convert stone Renaissance shapes into wood (as in the 'Križanke' convent in Ljubljana, and a church in Stranje near Kamnik).

Plečnik had already faced the problem of the profane use of classical forms in 1907 when building a boarding school in Währing.[233] The work came to him through Zacherl, who was a member of the committee of the Catholic charity Kinderschutzstationen (Child Protection Society). As the building was to take in young people without money Plečnik attached particular value to a friendly atmosphere, to be conveyed by lively decoration. He framed the facade with two Secessionist type pylons, and brought them into line with the rules of Ionic column order by means of architrave, cyma and the pilasters which in the planning phase still display classical capitals. Only the space between the windows on the first floor was filled with fashionable rectangular frames. The ornamental strips worked in the plaster or in the sgraffito technique represent a loose paraphrase of the Ionic sima and thus take from the building the severity characteristic of the Zacherl House. Even Plečnik could not avoid the Neo-Classical

spirit that prevailed in Vienna from the middle of the first decade of the twentieth century after the exhaustion of all the Secessionist forms. Since he was always interested in Antiquity, he was able to adorn the change of style with a number of decorative neologisms. A letter he wrote to Kotěra in the autumn of 1902 is evidence of the early reorientation of his ideas. 'In Vienna there are said to be 800 buildings today – but it's all the Tower of Babel. That is more than sad. Of course everything is modern. I assure you that I have long wished – somebody would start to build again in the "Classical style". That will be our one salvation.'[234]

The Ionic pilasters which he attached to the facade of the villa built in 1908 and 1909 for the Viennese Professor of Hygiene, Dr Roland Graßberger,[235] are the clearest signs of the new Classicism. The architecture of the first half of the twentieth century was certainly fond of manifest rhetoric, but it gained its concrete form primarily through one-family houses. Plečnik was deeply involved with the problems of this building challenge – he told Strajnić that the reason for this was in the first place the marketing of the Viennese flat houses, which he disliked because it was profit-oriented[236] – but since the building of the Villa Loos in Melk he had had no other realistic opportunities.

A fundamental revolution in the traditional space hierarchy in the Graßberger project did not bring the desired success. The client's wife blamed him for the undersized squaring, which he then enlarged by broadening the ground plan with a wide staircase, symmetrically repeating beside it the original extent of the building (fig. 68). The central axis of communication thus occupied almost one third of the entire usable area. Plečnik's 'promenade architecturale' acquired a stone washbasin on every floor, which, like the lights in the Zacherl House, symbolically indicated the client's profession.

Largely as a consequence of his intense concern with sacred art, Plečnik gradually revised his views on architecture. His awareness of the social mission of his chosen profession became stronger, and he liked to stress the educational components, which are relatively alien to our age. The central, communicating part of the Villa Graßberger, which he connected with individual living cells, corresponded to these ideas: he attributed to it a bonding role, promoting family life, and assumed that the inhabitants of this monastic way of life would come together, which of course did not happen, as each one took refuge in his own room, so that the community rooms were largely unused. Still under the influence of this bitter experience, he wrote to Zacherl in 1913: 'I am still not quite clear as to the extent to which separate living is useful to a human being's education, but it is quite

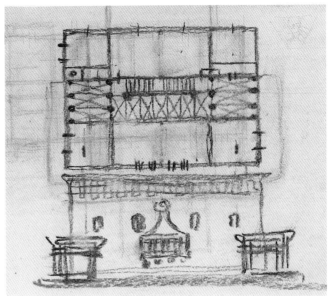

65–8. Facade studies for the Graßberger Villa in Vienna, 1908

certain that without it, at least at times, the human being would be forced to despair.'[237]

The villa's staircase also reflects contemporary efforts to bring the beginnings of a space plan into the architecture of the residences. Plečnik knew in what direction modern architecture was tending, but he was not prepared to follow it unconditionally. He remained true to Schinkel in the strictly organized symmetrical composition of cubes, although with this he was involuntarily already moving towards the radicalism of the twenties.

Plečnik never completely lost his link with modern architecture. The large glass areas and the typographical aesthetics of the firms' names in the design for the reinforced concrete facade of the warehouse and offices of the Viennese branch of the Stollwerk chocolate factory[238] in 1910, are somewhat bewildering compared with the exterior of the contemporary Zacherl Villa and its turned pillars (fig. 69). The discrepancy can be explained only by Semper's differentiation between functional and monumental architecture. The experience of new materials gathered by Plečnik since the planning of the church of the Holy Spirit in Vienna (1910–13) is also reflected in the sketches for the Stollwerk factory facade. The use of wooden boarding called for an extreme simplification of the ornamental vocabulary, and simultaneously gave him the idea that he could achieve better lighting for the rooms by means of slanted window openings. The visible reinforced concrete skeleton, which was already an accepted idea in France, for instance in the architecture of Auguste Perret, was partly influenced also by his Zacherl

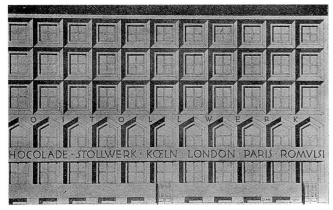

69. Facade study for the Stollwerk factory in Vienna, 1910

House. Whereas the uniform, glittering granite surface is characteristic of the latter, for the Stollwerk facade it was the glass surfaces with frames used in Vienna at the turn of the century which represented his point of departure for a carefully proportioned rhythm. The windows, seemed to stretch up from the two lower floors and end at the top in triangles. They are accompanied by a band of lettering stretching across the entire width of the facade. Within this system the hierarchy of the window axes is completely removed. All this contributed to the Viennese city council's rejection of Plečnik's design 'on aesthetic grounds'.[239]

THE ST CHARLES BORROMEO FOUNTAIN

After completion of the Zacherl House in 1905, Plečnik received no major commissions for a long time and was more or less dependent on the occasional work offered him by his friend Zacherl. In fact his intensive concern with liturgical art and his move towards ecclesiastical clients greatly narrowed the circle of his potential clients in view of the extremely conservative taste of the Austrian clergy. Plečnik himself, however, was convinced that since the building of the Zacherl House he was being blacklisted by the heir to the throne, Francis Ferdinand,[240] who owned the quarry in Moravia from which the granite slabs for the Zacherl House had come. Even though the contract had been signed, the director there had departed on honeymoon during the work, which had caused the whole process to come to a stop for some time. On his return he was called to account by Zacherl, and the heir to the throne lost out on other commissions because work was being done exclusively for Zacherl.[241] All this, of course, does not justify Plečnik's over-sensitivity. For instance, at the last moment he broke off the construction of the boarding school in Währing mentioned above,

after which the building had to be completed in accordance with his plans by the architects Krauss and Tölk.

The elegant 'Viennese Apollo', as friends of the Secessionist artist Josef Engelhart called him, was in many respects the opposite of the anti-social Plečnik. Engelhart had married one of the Mautner-Markhof sisters, who belonged to the rich family of the Viennese food-industrialists. He travelled the world and acquired a large studio for himself. His invitation to Plečnik to collaborate on the St Charles Borromeo fountain (figs 28–31)[242] came at an opportune time, as the sculptural work in the studio brought him out of his melancholy (fig. 70). A whole year of planning already lay behind the story of the fountain. The local councils of Vienna's third district wanted to erect the fountain in honour of Mayor Karl Lueger's 60th birthday. Lueger's political career had begun in this district. Engelhart designed four realistic groups intended to represent scenes from the life of St Charles Borromeo, the politician's name saint. The water was intended to pour into four bowls over the groups standing on a rectangular stone block.

Plečnik followed his friend's work with interest and in the autumn of 1906 proposed a circular fountain with the figure of a boy, since he believed that this would be more appropriate to the unfavourable site of the square, which was squeezed between four narrow streets. Finally Engelhart left the decision in Plečnik's hands. By which time Plečnik was no longer able to make anything of Engelhart's Secessionist, narrative work, and he attempted to unite the heterogeneous ornamentation more firmly and steady the rhythm. Plečnik replaced the square ground plan with a triangular one and placed the bronze bowls above the putti, with the intention of stressing the tectonic as against the literary aspect. The introduction of a different scale for the figures corresponded to the different levels of the places where viewers would stand, which he created by the oval depression round the fountain. This was how he resolved the problem of the site, unattractive in itself, and protected the visitors from traffic. A small park with a low surround was created, with seats, lawns and poplars, from the centre of which the richly structured fountain rose from a circular basin. He finished off the whole ensemble with a neutral obelisk. It is not difficult to find a parallel to the Baroque fountain of the three Carniolan rivers erected in the middle of the eighteenth century by the Venetian sculptor Francesco Robba in front of the town hall in Ljubljana. As we have already seen in the example of the Zacherl House, it was not by chance that Plečnik transferred the memory of some of the most important monuments of his home town to Vienna. When, after numerous complications with the committee members, work on the fountain was coming to an end in 1908, the anniversary celebrations

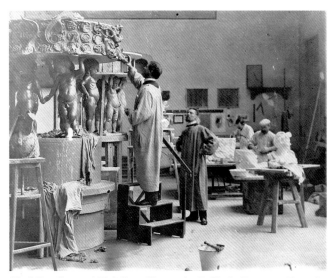

70. J. Engelhart and Plečnik working on the St Charles Borromeo Fountain, 1908

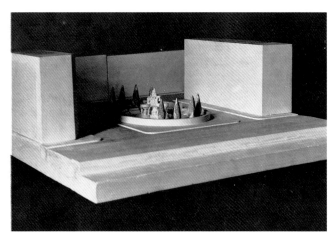

71. The model of the St Charles Borromeo Fountain, 1908

were long over. A few months before the dedication of the fountain he wrote home despairingly:

When will the water flow – I don't know – perhaps on 3 April. I quake at that day and the one after. It will be a misery – I keep on telling Engelhart: both of us will have to emigrate – but the man does not quite understand me. The thing is wild – without harmony – without will – altogether, I don't know what it is, waltz, polka or mazurka – perhaps a czardas – all things must be made with 'reverence' – anything not so made has no value.[243]

Plečnik's participation as a sculptor was not insignificant in this case. He modelled the granite plinth of the obelisk, covered with acanthus and two pairs of matching bronze vases on the park wall (figs 29–30). The stylized eagles and mountain goats reveal an understanding of the monumentality of sculptural expression which is congenial with Antiquity.

REFORMER OF RELIGIOUS ART

Plečnik's faith fostered an idealized association with his home. He told Strajnić of his mother's fervent belief: she had attended morning Mass daily, often taking him with her. The church interior, the figures, the paintings and the light took her out of the monotony of everyday life.[244] Her death in 1899 had affected Plečnik greatly. He turned all the more to his elder brother, the priest, who with Jansenist sternness maintained the moral values of the lost family home. The roots from which Plečnik's religious art grew are best seen from an excerpt in which the generally taciturn architect describes a religious ceremony in Ljubljana in 1905:

As always I greatly admired the wonderful interior proportions of St James's. It was Sunday and High Mass . . . throughout the Mass I stood below the choir admiring what was offered to me there. In front of the altar, whose height was in sound taste – comparable to few Austrian ones in height – so that the priest could be seen at eye level, the priests read the Mass in golden vestments. Through the windows, which are very successfully placed on either side of the forward area, the sunlight fell on the shimmering vestments and the colourfully clad children before the altar . . . From the choir came singing such as one cannot hear elsewhere in Ljubljana. And I tell you: this powerful, healthy brightness in these noble spatial proportions and before the altar that spirited priest, reading the Mass with such ardour, as if he were saying: Children, quickly, freshly, skilfully and then with healthy human intelligence and cheerful thoughts, to work! I tell you, to see that and to take courage for our work and for our people is one and the same.[245]

On the basis of this paragraph it is not difficult to see that Plečnik and Wagner had different views in some areas. For Plečnik the church was a place of profound, intimate experience of the Eucharist, a holy space which should not be heated and, as the popular Catholic author, Alban Stolz, demanded, should not really be provided with seats either, since the question arises as to 'how valuable a prayer made sitting can possibly be'.[246] His teacher, on the other hand, had nothing but functional issues in mind in his religious commissions. Wagner's indifference to religion irritated Plečnik especially during the period when the church Am Steinhof was being built, since his own efforts in respect of similar commissions were unsuccessful.[247]

Plečnik's faith was not simply provincial and conservative; it also had social aspects. He believed that the return to faith could prevent social revolution; this belief of his was similar to Le Corbusier's, who thought that the same result could be achieved by providing clean and healthy human dwellings. For instance, Plečnik had designed the church of the Holy Spirit in Vienna from the very beginning as both a religious and a social institution for the Ottakring working class district. He took Semper's search for originality to heart to such an extent that he tried, with the help of art, to create the conditions for a renaissance of the original 'unspoilt' society, which was supposed to have prevailed in the church in the first centuries of its existence.

His first attempts at religious architecture took place in 1897, in the School competition for the Füger medal. Together with his Czech colleague, Gustav Rossmann, and still obviously influenced by fear of the empty space, he proposed, entirely in the spirit of his teacher, an oval chapel for the site beside the city railway in Währing.[248] A year later he sketched a church facade,[249] which with its basilica-like design and bell tower on the long side, indicates his emancipation from Wagner's influence. Religious theme's however, were treated quite marginally by the school throughout the period of Plečnik's studies. Yet, this changed fundamentally in 1898, with the announcement of a competition for the Jubilee church in Vienna and the death of the Austrian Empress inspired Wagner to take an interest in religious architecture. The unfortunate events surrounding the competition, in which the jury excluded the designs by Olbrich, Hoffmann and Bauer in the first round,[250] convinced Wagner

that he must become more fully committed in this area.

Wagner's designed the church in the Währing cemetery in the summer of 1898. At this time Plečnik was still spending some time on his diploma work, but although he was not involved in the planning of the church he followed the project with great interest. The same applies to the Capuchin church project in Vienna, of which he preserved an early sketch by Wagner,[251] which his teacher must have given him immediately before he left for Rome.

In the explanatory text for the study of the church in Währing Wagner clearly defined the points of departure for the church building, in which economic considerations were of primary importance. He proposed the shape of a gasometer, which not only seemed to him to be the cheapest variant in relation to the usable space, but also corresponded optically, acoustically and hygienically to his ideas, since a space without intermediate supports opens up the view of the altar and provides good sound diffusion.[252]

From a religious standpoint Plečnik preferred a longitudinal nave with the traditional hierarchical organization of space, but he was not unimpressed by Wagner's wellfounded and logical arguments. In his Viennese period he countered Wagner's 'non-denominational style' with the image of the basilica, though later he himself returned frequently to the round space, which Wagner derived from the antique Pantheon.

The hope of finding answers to the questions that concerned him through contact with ancient art accompanied him to Italy in 1898. When, early in 1899, he applied to the Rector's office of the school for payment of the second instalment of his grant, he was still not quite clear how to combine Wagner's maxims with his own new discoveries. Working in Rome on the task set by the school, he completely avoided the problem of the dome, which had concerned him throughout his journey through northern Italy. However, he was permanently interested in the question of central versus longitudinal construction. His interest in the question of centrally planned space reflects his desire to please his teacher, whereas longitudinal construction reflected his personal interest, although he knew that he would find no sympathy for this in Vienna.

He concentrated on the problem of the entrance area, that is, the route of the procession to the high altar,[253] a subject which was quite alien to Wagner. The longitudinal church was naturally more suited to the solution of this problem. In a sketch which certainly belongs to the project he finally completed in Rome, Plečnik proposed a kind of ambulatory with altars, which were to alternate rhythmically with double pillars in a variant of the longitudinal church (see fig.

72. Sheet of sketches showing studies for a church and a house, 1899

74

14).[254] A centrally planned church recorded in a sketch from Rome also presented him with major difficulties (see fig. 15).[255] He composed the ground plan in squares of different sizes, but indicated a longitudinal axis with the bell tower and presbytery. While the west tower was in the Alpine or Slovenian tradition, in the pylons, the lean-to roofs, basilica windows and vegetable ornamentation he was guided by Secessionist examples. However, he took no pleasure in the design, especially as he was also extremely dissatisfied with the arrangement of the facade.

After his return to Ljubljana in the summer of 1899 he once again turned to his Roman study of a modern church and tried to combine the two types (fig. 72).[256] He resorted once more to the dome and other traditional structural elements. The exterior of the building lost part of its dramatic monumentality and its organization came closer to Wagner's project for Währing. We do not know whether Plečnik retained this solution, or whether he developed the idea further, since the report of the school exhibition, where he exhibited his drawings after returning from his travels, mentions no variants of a modern church.[257]

Some drawings of church facades from 1901 have been preserved. They open to their surroundings in various ways and invite visitors to enter through monumental entrances. The tall Venetian campanile became an essential component of Plečnik's religious work at this time. The fantastic sketch of the 'Crown of the City',[258] a monumental temple on a hill, approached by a winding road, passing by Stations of the Cross or statues of famous men, deserves special attention (fig. 73). Regardless of his tendency in those days towards Egyptian and Mesopotamian architecture, this sketch plays quite a significant role in Plečnik's art later on. For want of an actual commission for a church building, he designed chapels and wayside shrines for places in his homeland, trying to match modern forms to the sentiments of the population.

His first real encounter with modern architecture took place on the occasion of the competition for the newly-founded art section of the Austrian Leo Society in October 1901.[259] Plečnik participated in three of the prescribed themes, an ideal study for a parish church, an altar and a Holy Sepulchre. For the church he chose the longitudinal shape (fig. 74), and divided it according to functional criteria, in contrast to his Roman studies, where the arrangement of space had resulted primarily from the symmetry of the ground plan. He placed the tower, the chapel and the sacristy in a row along the long side, thus resolving the strict symmetry of his previous solutions. On the other hand, in placing the choir gallery above the entrance he adhered to

73. 'The Crown of the City', 1901

tradition. The altar area bears witness to a committed approach to the role of worship in the modern church service. In memory of his mother, who had been a fervent worshipper of the Sacred Heart of Jesus – a devotion very popular among Catholics at that time – he sketched a large chapel to the left of the presbytery. Its uniqueness lies in the diaphanous division of a slim line of pillars. It is possible that Palladio's division of the church of San Giorgio Maggiore between the monastic choir and the presbytery served as a model.

In the first place the pillars in the presbytery aroused objections from the jury, but its more conservative members were also upset by the flat roof. The carefully designed lighting of the nave and altar area, on the other hand, went completely unnoticed.[260] We know from the description above of the Mass in St James's in Ljubljana that Plečnik felt particularly attracted by the theme at that time. He was also influenced by this church in determining the fundamental relationship between the length and breadth of the area in question.

As he was unsuccessful with the first competition theme, he involved himself all the more intensively with the Holy Sepulchre. This section of the competition was repeated three times and at the beginning of 1903 the first prize was awarded to Plečnik. The jury justified its hesitation by the liturgical inadequacy of the proposals; in fact most of the jurors would have preferred a kind of stage set, with an artificial rock relief. Supported by his brother, Plečnik kept to the altar form, justifying it on the basis of historical development. He designed four variants with geometrical patterns, plant decoration and wooden designs draped in

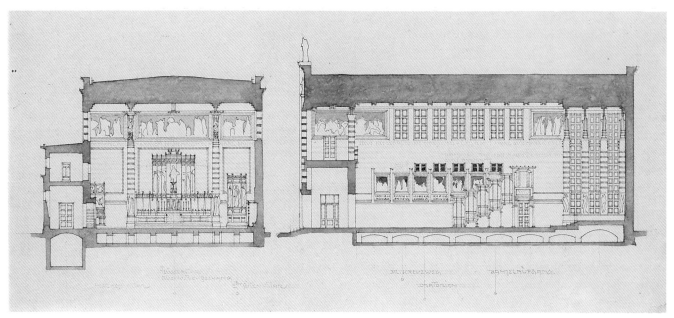

74. Competition design for a modern church, 1902

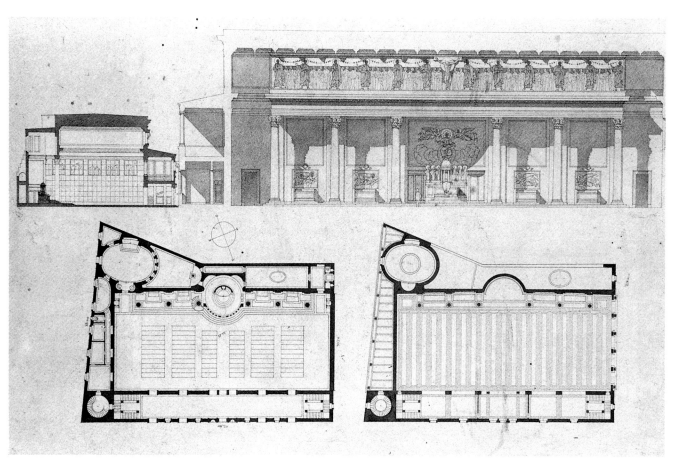

75. Project for a church in Vienna, 1906

76

material. Only the cheapest variant was approved by the jury.

In the course of the competition Plečnik met the founder of the art section, the court chaplain Heinrich Swoboda, who was regarded as the supreme authority in sacred art. In 1906 he commissioned from Plečnik a church in a Viennese suburb (fig. 75).[261] The site was enclosed between two narrow streets, opening to the park on one side. It seems that at first the shape of the plot was not completely clear to Plečnik, because he wanted to go back to his solution for the competition design of the Leo Society. In accordance with the guidelines imposed by a parish centre, he placed the sacristy, the library and the meeting-room along the narrow, winding building line, which bordered on the neighbouring apartment block. On the model of the Xaverius Chapel of St James's in Ljubljana he filled the dead east corner with an adjacent rotunda.

Plečnik neutralized the irregularity of the plot on the ground floor by means of side rooms, while on the upper floor he clearly indicated the difference between the core of the building and its outer skin. Only the side of the building facing the park was appropriate for the entrance area. Several doors were planned for this area. Since the church was shorter than the site, Plečnik filled the remaining corner area with a bell tower which allowed him to retain the symmetry of the main façade.

His work in the Leo Society encouraged Plečnik's intention of reforming religious art. This is also revealed in the following letter:

> I have changed greatly in my longings and my inner self. I have so little love of riches in the church – I want to see form there only insofar as it is intended to be the most necessary vessel of thought and purpose. This does not mean that I am thinking of an empty Protestant church – no I want – I in fact think of everything as inexhaustibly rich – in experience – in though – but not in riches. I hate that.[262]

In another place Plečnik says: 'St Peter's – the colonnades – the Renaissance is aristocratic – tyranny – absolutely involuntary subjection – organization. The early Christian churches: democracy – voluntary joyful subordination – organization – that is my formula – which has quite a lot to it.'[263]

Thus the draft study for the church in the Viennese suburb (which was later built according to other plans) in many respects confirmed Plečnik's views and distanced him still further from his teacher. Nevertheless something of Wagner is still detectable in the study. Wagner's principle of the unimpeded visibility of the main altar led Plečnik to replace the longitudinal axis by a transverse axis. He told his pupils in Ljubljana that it was a church in Prague with a decorated long side which inspired him to take this step.[264] However that may be, the solution resulted from the given situation and from the conviction that the entrance and the presbytery must lie on one axis. A novelty was the physical closeness of the faithful to the priest, which was completely in line with Plečnik's understanding of the old Christian fraternal divine service. Despite the attempted return to hieratic beginnings, which the ecclesiastical power in Ljubljana was not always prepared to tolerate, Plečnik did not go as far as the more practically inclined aesthete Wagner, who was of the opinion that the priest should face the people.[265]

Immediately before the building of the church of the Holy Spirit, in Vienna in 1909, Plečnik was busy with the expansion of the Franciscan monastery in Trsat near Rijeka,[266] where he applied the idea of modern church building by historical means again. At the same time he raised the question of the collaboration of old and new which was to play a significant role in his later works. Since the origin of the church in Trsat is linked with a saintly legend which in former centuries had already prevented any sizeable encroachments on the existing building, Plečnik also advised the Franciscan monks not to destroy it. Originally the monks had wanted a new Neo-Gothic building, but after protests and interventions by the monument preservation office in 1908, they entrusted the Benedictine priest and architect Anselm Werner with the task. Persuaded by the Viennese master builder Benno Brausewetter, Plečnik went to Rijeka in 1908, but had to admit that he had come too late. From personal interest he committed himself deeply to this difficult task. In May of the following year, Crown Prince Francis Ferdinand, as the highest authority in the Austrian imperial and royal *Zentralkommission* for the preservation of monuments, approved Plečnik's plans which gave him false hopes. At the end of 1909 Plečnik returned to Rijeka with the reworked sketches. It turned out that the months of work had been in vain. Who was most responsible for his disappointment will probably never be quite clear. The monks trusted their own architect; in the Croatian capital, in turn, other interests prevailed, and ultimately the Crown Prince himself bore no small share of the responsibility.

In his designs for Trsat Plečnik solved the question of the procession round the main altar with a new circular church linked with the old presbytery. In this way he was trying to ensure that the course of the divine service would be undisturbed. He adopted the basic idea for this central new building from his 1906 project for the suburban church mentioned above.

The fundamental compositional problem related to the interaction of the different structural bodies. The extension was to carry a dome, twenty metres in diameter and easily visible from the sea. As a counterweight to this Plečnik planned a new bell-tower beside the old one, in the Venetian style. The central church, open to the cloister, would in many respects recall early Christian architecture. With the dome, the portal, influenced by Michelangelo, and the colonnades, on the other hand, he was returning to Renaissance models, because in his opinion they best corresponded to the elevated situation of the monastery above the bay of Rijeka. Plečnik was highly delighted with the plans for the building of the dome; he frequently recalled it later on, although he was never able to realize it in such mighty dimensions. Of course, Wagner was no longer able to applaud this obvious tendency towards ancient architecture. When the project was published he is supposed to have said: 'I do not understand why Plečnik has let himself go so far astray.'[267]

THE CHURCH OF THE HOLY SPIRIT

On Swoboda's recommendation, at the beginning of 1908 the Ottakring priest, Franz Unterhofer, made contact with Plečnik and asked him to build a church[268] in one of the most neglected Viennese working-class districts. Plečnik willingly agreed to the building of this kind of missionary centre for Christian Socialist projects, although after his unfortunate experiences with the ecclesiastical authorities he scarcely dared to believe in its realization. Moreover, another architect was already working on the project. From a later letter by Plečnik we can conclude that in this building he also wanted to find an answer to the problem of a 'community hall with speaker's platform' for the workers, which was particularly topical at the time when he was studying.[269] Convinced that the world must return to Christianity, which, in his view, the foundation of technical colleges had helped to weaken, he did not see the future in Social Democracy, nor did he look for it in socially committed art, but in creative work capable of uplifting both heart and spirit. Later on, he commented on Kollwitz, the highly important German representative of socially inspired art: 'Käthe Kollwitz is not a saviour.'[270]

The honesty and cosmopolitanism of Unterhofer impressed him so much that, following his advice, he turned his attention to some modern Anglo-American church buildings,[271] which corresponded more closely to his aims than the historical models. Nevertheless, where usefulness had to prevail over monumentality, Plečnik put his trust in Otto Wagner's engineering solutions. His teacher had in fact

designed different variants of a so-called interim church between 1906 and 1907. In these drafts he was experimenting with wood and metal constructions such as were used in the construction of temporary exhibition pavilions or halls. With his expressivity he succeeded in giving these buildings a religious character. Plečnik followed Wagner's experiments with great interest, but he called his church Am Steinhof a failure in both functional and liturgical respects.

With similar dedication to Wagner's with regard to the technical issues, Plečnik was seeking clear formal expressions. In 1907, looking for an architectural language which would correspond to the technology of the cheaper reinforced concrete mode of construction with the help of wooden pannelling, he allied himself with Cubism, thus finding a connection with the experiments of the Wagner School in which Karl Maria Kerndle in particular had attacked the question of the geometrical reduction of form a few years earlier,[272] although with a different feeling for plasticity. In contrast to his colleagues, Plečnik saw the problem of formal language with the eyes of the ancient master builders. In the archaic Mediterranean pseudo-vaults built from heavy stone blocks he found a simplicity and usefulness for the new reinforced concrete technique, similar to those which the polygonal proto-Doric Egyptian columns with simple capitals. When monumentalizing Wagner's technical ideas Plečnik was not content only to change the material, he had to rework it fundamentally along Semper's lines.

The planning of the church turned into a real tale of woe, as the members of the building committee changed their demands frequently in the expectation of new sponsors. Ultimately, they were forced to realize that the money was not enough for even the cheapest variants. On their very first meeting Unterhofer showed Plečnik an empty plot in the sixteenth district of Vienna, between Herbststrasse and Koppstrasse, which the members also wanted to use for residential building in order to finance the building of the church. For this reason initially a less well-situated area in the middle of the building plot had been set aside for the church. However, Plečnik's proposal for a church standing at right-angles to the streets proves that the decision had not yet been made as to the final site.[273] As that part of the plot slopes, he tried to arrange the interior on two levels. The altar was to stand at the beginning of the higher part, under which he planned a crypt. However, his solution for the altar to be in the middle of the church was apparently too unusual even for him, because it no longer appears in further plans.

After Plečnik submitted the first drawings to the building committee there was a delay. The clients had come to realize

76. The church of the Holy Spirit, variant, 1910

that they would have to sacrifice the plot along the higher main road for the church. Consequently, in the spring of 1910 there was a new project for a disproportionately long, narrow 'hall' church. The two drawings dated in early April, with several rows of expressive dormer windows, influenced by the second variant of Wagner's interim church, also fall into this planning phase (fig. 76).[274]

But the difficulties were by no means at an end. The change of site again raised the question of the parish house, for which those responsible had planned to use the site on Koppstrasse. Plečnik had to revise the finished plans and arrange for additional rooms to be fitted in beside the church. His proposal that until the church was finished

Mass should be read in the crypt, which would later be converted into a hall, gave the clients a vision of a pastoral, cultural and political centre for the Ottakring Catholics. As the clients were expecting massive financial help from the Jesuits (who, however, made only a small contribution in 1912) they commissioned another new project, with a large parish hall under the church.

The planning then moved into a new phase, in which liturgical issues predominated (fig. 77). 'Unterhofer mentioned something – and I made a mountain out of a molehill',[275] we read in a letter from the architect. He was particularly attracted by the idea hinted at in the early drafts of using the crypt, visibly linked with the church above it,

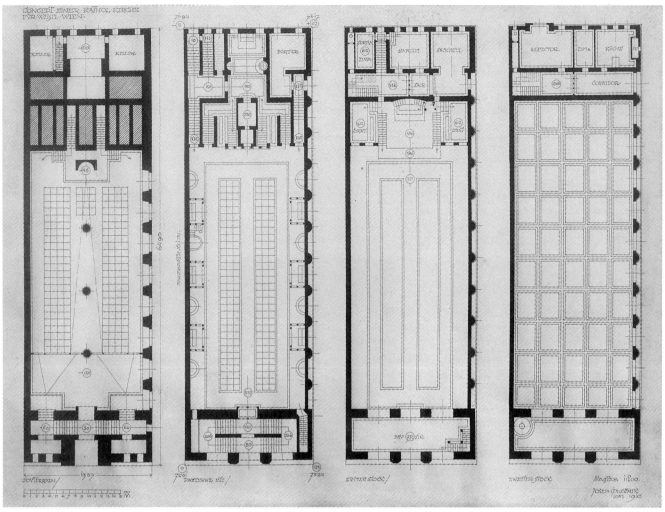

77. The church of the Holy Spirit, variant, 1910

for the sacraments of baptism and marriage. For the church he now chose the shape of an unarticulated hall, lit on the model of a basilica. The presbytery would have to be raised because of the extraordinary length of the space. Along the two long sides he arranged, as in his Roman studies, alternate altars and confessionals. The single, rather striking, architectural ornament would have been a richly decorated wooden ceiling, but he later had to abandon this owing to the fire regulations. The combination of the parish hall on the lower floor, the church, the lower crypt partly underneath the presbytery, and the four floors of the parish house called for an extremely complicated spatial plan, of which Loos himself could have been proud. Plečnik ended the building with an integrated, almost flat saddleback roof. Because the costs were rising too fast he abandoned for the time being the Venetian campanile planned in front of

the entrance and contented himself with an open belfry.

With this, Plečnik's job was provisionally over. He wrote to his brother Andrej that in some respects this was his most mature work: 'The whole has no decor other than the purest of architectonic organization – and this is always utility. Only at the front does everything develop into an arc de triomphe . . .'[276] The same applies to the facade of his later Franciscan church in Šiška, which appeared so poverty-stricken to his pupils by comparison with the interior that they tried to call his attention to it.[277] The extent to which Andrej identified with his brother's work is revealed by his impulsive reaction to Stele's positive criticism of Wagner's church Am Steinhof, which appeared in the Slovenian press in 1911.[278] He adopted his brother's argument that the social problems of the city could be overcome only with the help of cheap and functional churches.

The Ottakring building committee succeeded in gaining the Crown Prince's wife, the Duchess of Hohenberg, as its patroness in the summer of 1910. At her wish the church was dedicated to the Holy Spirit. The clients' optimism now knew no bounds. The building site was widened by nearly 16 metres, while the rest of the block was sold. As the size of the plot was sufficient for a block of flats, Plečnik included this in his plan as a pendant to the parish house. Thanks to the increase in the size of the plot, he was no longer bound by the unusually narrow building space and could give the church a more spacious form. He decided on an almost square area, acessible from the main street (fig. 78), which in pastoral respects offered the best possible link between the congregation and the altar. To achieve better acoustics and a better overall view, he abandoned the traditional segmentation of the space by pillars or columns. On the side walls he planned two concrete choir lofts with a span of 20.7 metres. This was the first time he had introduced a completely secular, industrial element of bridge building into religious architecture. Understandably, it earned him vehement protests from the Crown Prince. From the original longitudinal church variant he adopted the elevated presbytery, which allowed for visual communication between the nave and the crypt.

The sketch of the church with the planned decoration testifies that Plečnik had in mind a proto-Christian basilica, here built of conrete and adapted to Wagner's principle of religious architecture. The fact that Plečnik had envisaged this type of ecclesiastical area is further demonstrated by the many symbols used, as for instance the lustre with the dolphins in the crypt, the ornamentation on the metal doors of the communion rail, etc.

Independently of the Ottakring project he was looking for new solutions within the basilica type of church. On 31 October 1910 he designed two variants of an interior with brick arches (fig. 79),[279] which replace the straight concrete choir lofts and link the entrance with the altar. Between these the narrow, high 'central nave' has been inserted, which meant that he had abandoned ceilings in favour of an open roof truss. He adopted these ideas again later for the church in Bogojina. A further extreme is represented by a small sketch made in Prague, which shows a church expanded at the height of the galleries (see fig. 37).[280] This bold constructional idea is practically extracted from the lit part of the church of the Holy Spirit in Vienna. In this and similar studies Plečnik worked with more expressive forms, as he knew very well that the church building,

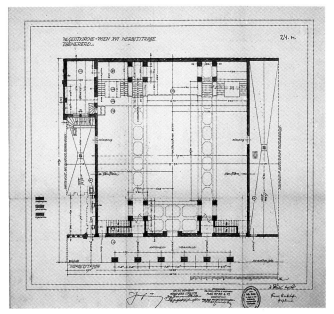

78. The church of the Holy Spirit, ground plan of the ground floor, 1910

however well chosen the proportions, must be more than a functional hall.

The altered site in Ottakring enabled the architect to deal more freely with the arrangement of the building masses. He moved the church a few metres back from the street making the narthex, while he wanted to arrange the parish house with the parish hall on the ground floor as well as the block of flats symmetrically on both sides (figs 82–3). The fundamental motif of the composition lies in the wall between the two buildings flanking the church, before which he planned to place the extended line of columns of the church facade. The theme of transparency, or the double 'facade skin' was frequently adopted by Plečnik when he was monumentalizing existing buildings. Of the early attempts, the design for the reconstruction of a chemist's shop in Vöcklabruck in 1905 is certainly one of the most interesting proposals.[281] Although the theme points to Semper, Plečnik might also have adopted it from Palladio's basilica in Vicenza.

Plečnik now returned to the tower, which was functionally linked with the parish house, and brought dynamism to the symmetrical organization. As in the project for the Franciscan monastery in Trsat, Plečnik was intensely concerned with the balance of the building masses, trying to heighten the block of flats, place the tower above the church entrance, and so on.

The motif of the stylized papyrus in the narthex and on the tower (fig. 83) in the version selected for construction confirms Strajnić's assumption that Plečnik greatly admired

79. A study for a church, 1910

with the words 'Andreas famulus Christi'. The emphasis is on the Eucharist with the altar in the form of a table which is raised simply for better visibility. The choir lofts give the impression of a longitudinal space directed towards the altar. The apparent purpose of the pillars, which naturally also have a load-bearing function, lies in the rhythmical subdivision of the space.

Plečnik also changed the lighting of the church area. This meant that the presbytery had no light source of its own, because he wished to leave the altar wall with its painted frescoes in semi-darkness, in order to increase the mystical effect of the Eucharist. He wanted his friend Jan Verkade to represent 'The seven gifts of the Holy Spirit' in the form of a tapestry stretched across the wall. To judge by the drawing that has been preserved,[285] this was intended to recall the tradition of the Lenten veils. His departure for Prague prevented the fulfilment of this wish and the subsequent construction of the altar wall which took place without Plečnik's knowledge actually contradicted his original ideas to a great extent.

Industrial aesthetics are visible in the galleries and still more strongly in the metal windows of the crypt and the extremely secular appearance of the wired glass in the entrance hall. What we have here is a concept of art extraordinarily influenced by social concern. If in Wagner's church Am Steinhof we speak of technoid ornamentation raised to a new aesthetic level, in Plečnik we find ourselves confronted with an 'unembellished' quotation from the everyday life of working people.

The lower church is more conservative in conception and reflects Plečnik's ideal of an early Christian sanctuary divided up by pillars, with which he had already been concerned during his Italian journey (figs 34–5 and 80). Only with the help of reinforced concrete could he realize the slender pillars which maintain the idea of the basilica without concealing the view of the altar. Plečnik approached the issue of the new material from the point of view of the aesthetics of texture. The design of the crypt partially follows Wagner's solution for the hall under the famous main hall of the Vienna Post Office Savings Bank. In more complicated technical commissions Plečnik continued to feel strongly committed to his teacher, though he tried to perfect the latter's solutions in formal terms. Plečnik gave the trapezoid capitals inherited from Wagner an octagonal section and by bevelling the corners, a sensual transition from vertical to horizontal (figs 34–5). Although the capitals can be seen as part of the traditional construction system, nevertheless they also point to the possibility of transition to the mushroom ceiling. Plečnik himself did not of course consider this tendency and adhered to the expressive slanting

the rigour and calm of ancient Egyptian temple architecture.[282] Similarly Plečnik was concerned for a time with the palm capitals in the interior of the church. This syncretism can also be explained in Semper's words: 'What is the western basilica whose last expression is fixed in the Gothic dome, but an Egyptian priest's temple? The Ecclesia has devoured the temple, the church has become master to the god; not even the tall Egyptian pylons are missing here.'[283] The facade of the church of the Holy Spirit was intended by Plečnik to be enlivened with different materials. From the combination of the dark red brick, plaster and granite pillars he was looking to achieve the lively appearance of eastern Christian church buildings.[284] All this was to be completed by rich sculpture, for which, however, the money could not be obtained.

The interior of the church bears witness to Plečnik's and Unterhofer's reforming ambitions. These even apply to the role of the priest, who was not simply to read the Mass and bestow God's blessing but to function as the link person between God and the community of the faithful. Plečnik formulated this idea on the first two chalices for his brother surfaces, which soon afterwards became a favourite motif of Czech Cubist architecture. In addition he had some hopes of the overall decorative impression produced by the Beuron versions of early Christian ornamentation (fig. 80).[286] The prevalent Pompeiian red was meant to interrupt the monotonous grey of the concrete. The introduction of red powder from crushed bricks into the concrete mass of the walls has its origins in Semper's polychromy. The contrast between smooth surfaces and surfaces roughened with a granulating hammer is consistently carried out, despite the lack of painting, according to the principle of the tectonic delimitation between load-bearing and resting-weight parts. The exposed concrete of the main facade is also one of the experiments with different textures (see fig. 33).

Even before the building of the church of the Holy Spirit it had become customary to replace the stone building methods used in vaults, domes and other technically complicated constructions with reinforced concrete. By about 1910 the method of building with reinforced concrete had already gained so much ground that there were no longer any fundamental objections as regards safety. Nevertheless, there was still resistance to the use of exposed concrete in monumental architecture. This applied above all to religious architecture, which adhered most tenaciously to the historical models. Plečnik was certainly performing pioneer work in this respect.

The first exposed concrete church in Europe was built by Anatole de Baudot as early as 1904. Plečnik may have seen it in a half-finished state on his visit to Paris on the way from the church of the Sacré Coeur in Montmartre. However, it left no visible traces on his work. Baudot's church of St Jean-de-Montmartre is the concrete version of the French Neo-Gothic cast-iron structures of the 1860s. However it is influenced too much by the technical language of cast iron for Plečnik to have seen it as the beginning of a monumental form of expression of the new material.

Much more advanced is the reinforced concrete church by István Benkó Medgyaszay, Plečnik's younger colleague from the Wagner School. It was built in the outlying village of Mul'a in an area settled by a mixture of Hungarians and Slovaks in 1909/10. Medgyaszay had spent some time before that in François Hennebique's atelier, where he was able to learn the technical possibilities of the new building material. This was how he was able to realize Wagner's ideal of a centrally planned building with an extraordinarily thin shell – only a few centimetres thick at the apex of the dome.[287] Despite the technical bravura the church in Mul'a remains in formal respects committed to the romanticism of

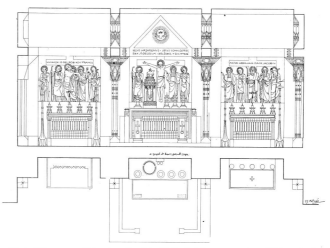

80–1. The crypt of the church of the Holy Spirit, perspective, 1910, and plan of the altar wall, 1911

the Hungarian national style, without offering any new ideas worth mentioning in liturgical terms.

At least ten years later Auguste Perret's famous church of Notre-Dame was built in Raincy near Paris. In the first place it represents an apotheosis of reinforced concrete building, but if we set aside Plečnik's ascetic version of modern Christianity, it still lacks that contemporary mysticism which Le Corbusier breathed into his church in Ronchamp. Perret filled the interior with the vivid light of French Gothic. As regards design it was really a successor to the great medieval cathedrals, but formally its religious area differed from his industrial buildings only in its colourful windows. When Plečnik saw a picture of Perret's church he could not deny its specific qualities and 'esprit', but remarked with reference to his own Viennese Experiences:

I do not know where it stands – but it must be in proletarian surroundings . . . I believe that this and similar

CONCEPT·DER·FACADEN·IN·DER·HERBSTRASSE /VNTEN·KLAVSGASSE/

DOMINE·NON·SVM·DIGNVS·VT·INTRES·SVB·TECTVM·MEVM·SED·R·

NACHBARGEBÄVDE.

DOMINE·EXAVDI·NOS·MISERERE·NOBIS·DOMINE

1910

82–3. Variants of the facade for the church of the Holy Spirit, with the priest's house and the apartment building, 1910

84

over-transparent designs cannot satisfy. Nowhere does a human being have more desire for a feeling of extraordinary security than in church. We are living in a new – completely new time – and yet sadly no one has yet discovered the church of our time.[288]

Plečnik had no objection to reinforced concrete when economic considerations obliged him to use it. Semper's theories and his practical work with Wagner helped him to find his way into the aesthetic and technological peculiarities of the new material; on the other hand, the issues of construction interested him less. He controlled the building material primarily by his choice of proportions and profiling. Seen in this way, we can regard him as a faithful servant of Semper's theory of evolution.

Besides the unusual combination of early Christian architectural elements with the art of Beuron, an extraordinarily modern industrial aesthetic, the Wagnerian engineering system and a love of ancient Egypt, Plečnik's constant wish to associate with the tradition of his homeland must not be forgotten. This expresses itself in the 'harsh taste for the Karst, uncongenial to the Viennese'[289] as well as in his personal, sometimes incredibly conservative devotionalism. The emotionally charged iconographic programme of the Ottakring crypt contradicts the cool clarity of the church area above it. Plečnik's brother Andrej and Unterhofer visited Palestine at almost the same time, and he wanted to evoke the memory of the Holy Land for their sakes with the chapels of the Nativity, the Mount of Olives and the Holy Sepulchre. In the very first draft of the Holy Sepulchre Plečnik had already moved away from the idea of the altar which he had realized for the Leo Society competition, and set against it a relatively faithful copy of the original in Palestine with an exaggeratedly realistic figure of the Saviour. On the other hand, the coloured glass lamps of the chandelier before the sepulchre were also meant to be linked to the tradition of his native land.[290] The combination of all these disparate elements can appear totally inexplicable to the unprepared visitor.

In view of the complicated situation with the building committee, the architect reported to his brother on 1 October 1910:

With this letter I will give another letter to Unterhofer, announcing that I refuse to work on the church – it is not to begin until the spring – and that with the aid of the programme based on my ground plans they can have the affair concluded by someone more qualified, and should begin to put it into effect. It is now that hunt for money begins: who is cheaper – all this is so alien to me – so

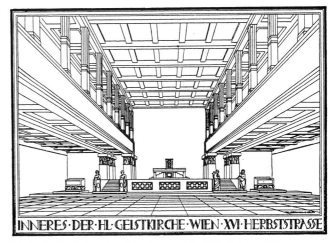

84. Study for the interior of the church of the Holy Spirit, 1910

boundlessly antipathetic – that I am sick in soul and body. That is why I am breaking off the connection and beginning a new life . . . In the church there are three things for which someone like myself – I stress this – should not ask: time, money and practicability. The church is outside these three premises.[291]

The work to which he had dedicated himself with great effort and love did not let him go, however, and later on, when he was already in Prague, he designed the interior fittings free of charge and used up his savings by advancing the payment for articles prepared in Prague. Since the church could be built only with the help of a considerable subsidy from the state, the application by the building committee became enmeshed in the wheels of the administrative apparatus. At the beginning of 1911 Plečnik had to send the plans to the Crown Prince at Konopiště Castle in Bohemia for approval. The verdict was devastating: 'A mishmash of the Russian bath + stables (instead of stables we might also put hayloft) + a temple to Venus.'[292] Francis Ferdinand wanted to persuade Plečnik to transform the church into a traditional columned basilica. Plečnik courageously rejected this suggestion, but consequently had all the people responsible for the project against him except for Unterhofer, who remained loyal. Since the end of his collaboration with Swoboda, even the idea of exhibiting the works of the religious artists at the Viennese Eucharistic Congress of 1912 in the church, could not be pursued. This would have enabled them to furnish the church by way of state purchases of these artist's works.

Plečnik was now planning his move to Prague and he was afraid that the anger of the Crown Prince would follow him to the Czech capital. To Kotěra, who was smoothing the way for him in Prague, he wrote: 'You can be quite calm – I am quite calm – I know that I have not made a stable . . . And do not reproach yourself either – if everything should burst like a soap bubble.'[293] He received a little comfort only from Wagner's offer to obtain the support of the Austrian Architects Society for the church of the Holy Spirit.[294]

The consequence of this shattering verdict from the highest authority was a state subsidy far below the expectations of the building committee. Salvation for the church was to be found only in the fact that the contract with the building firm was already agreed and could not be broken. The search for new funding spoiled Plečnik's pleasure in the work: 'As far as the church of the Holy Spirit is concerned, my integrated design has been thrown out – what remains is a poisoned compromise without a head. Only the crypt, insofar as it is completed at this stage, is the fruit of an honest and direct agreement between me and the initiator of the building. Let this be a warning that committees and the interventions of highly-placed gentlemen in such matters can almost without exception be compared to worms in the mightiest tree trunk.'[295]

While building on the church had already started Plečnik, now moving frequently between Vienna and Prague, did Unterhofer the favour of sacrificing the narthex for the sake of a larger organ loft. The alteration of the facade meant the removal of some parts already built. Since this meant that he also had to relinquish the idea of a porch standing higher than the wall, he found himself forced to look for a new correlation between the facade and the lateral links with the planned parish house and the apartment block. The result of these studies was a relatively conservative facade in the form of an ancient Greek temple with proto-Doric columns, a triangular gable, openings for the bells such as are typical of the Karst region, and a modest architectural sculpture, but this was never executed. He found a substitute for the abandoned theme by bringing forward the facade, which emphasized the central part of the building.

The building of the parish house and the apartment block then also had to be abandoned for lack of funds. In 1912 matters seemed to be sufficiently settled for Plečnik to begin on the planning of a high bell-tower.[296] On the main facade he tried to modify the impression of the unrendered concrete by means of stone cladding, thus giving the church more external brightness. But in the event everything stayed as it was and even the bell-tower was never to rise above the foundations already built.

PRAGUE AND CUBISM

Although from the financial viewpoint leaving Vienna was the only possible solution for him, Plečnik left the capital with a heavy heart at the beginning of 1911. He was hoping at least to find artists for the interior of the Holy Spirit church among the Benedictine artists from Beuron working at that time on the embellishments of the Emmaus monastery in Prague. He was about to realize his youthful dreams by going to Prague, but suddenly he was afraid that he did not speak Czech or know the Czech people well enough. The prospect of a professorship also worried him because he lacked the necessary experience. 'I have been trying for years to escape from the decorative – now that I am older, am I to go back to a school that is primarily dedicated to that?'[297] This was his complaint early in the autumn of 1910, after his first discussions with the Director of the Prague College of Arts and Crafts, the architect Jiří Štibral, and secretly he hoped the offer would never materialize. But Kotěra made sure that his friend could not change his mind by presenting him with a frock coat and everything else he needed for the audience with the Minister of Culture.[298]

Plečnik was not a stranger in Prague cultural circles. Thanks to Kotěra his reputation as a talented Slovenian architect, at the forefront of his age, had preceded him. A careful study of Czech pre-Cubist architecture would probably reveal the influence of the Zacherl House in more than one work. Of Kotěra's students, Pavel Janák showed the greatest respect for Plečnik. He had been a member of the Wagner School for two years, and always had words of praise for Plečnik, even when he took over from him at the School in 1922 and in the restoration of Prague Castle in 1936, and in both cases moved in a different direction. Janák's efforts to promote arts and crafts, and his emphasis on creativity over pure functionality, show his sympathy with Semper, and it was this that enabled him to understand Plečnik's work. On his return from his study tour of Italy he sent Plečnik some photographs of old monuments, as a sign of his admiration, knowing that the professor loved them and 'understood them better than anyone in the world'.[299] Even before Plečnik arrived in Prague Janák tried to familiarize him with some of the issues the city faced over its historical monuments, in the hope of winning his support.[300] Janák was also the first to draw attention to Plečnik's extraordinary talent for sculptural form,[301] and this was why he wanted to bring him closer to the Cubist movement. Janák's close associate, Josef Gočár, looked forward to Plečnik's arrival with similar enthusiasm.

The younger generation in Prague welcomed Plečnik

85. Plečnik in the Zacherl factory, around 1910

86. Competition model for the Jan Žižka monument, 1913

with open arms, seeing in him a counterweight to the late generation of historicist architects who had built Prague's National Theatre in the second half of the nineteenth century. Plečnik was less hostile to the Czech Neo-Renaissance; since his early youth it had been for him, as for all the Slovenian intellectuals, a symbol of Slav awakening. Moreover, in Vienna he had developed a feeling for the traditional formal language, in which the younger generation showed no interest. He would actually say to his students occasionally that he was a pupil of both Wagner and Zítek.[302] This deliberate playing down of the stature of Wagner, who was not a Slav, can only have come from an upsurge of national feeling, even if Wagner and the architect of the Czech National Theatre, Josef Zítek were both educated in the school which was based on Semper's theories.

Plečnik won the sympathy of the young generation of Czech architects primarily through his interest in folk art, which was an important element in Cubism, and particularly in the early 1920s when the search for a national expression prevailed in architecture. If Janák, Gočar and their associates looked to Czech late Gothic art and the Gothic reminiscences in the Baroque for confirmation of their adoption of Cubism, Plečnik acquired his knowledge of the mentality of the Czechs, Moravians and Slovaks mainly from their anonymous architecture. The death throes of the Danube monarchy forced him and Kotěra's students to an accelerated search for their own identity. As Plečnik held to his belief in the continuous development of architecture and restrained the younger generation's wish for revolutionary changes, he had manoeuvred himself to the outer fringe of the Czech architectural scene by the end of the 1920s. The Czechs always looked to Paris, but after Kotěra visited the Netherlands in 1905 they also developed some sympathy for the north of Europe. Plečnik's horizon was very much more limited. He remained caught in a kind of love-hate relationship with Vienna, and he always judged what was going on around him from that perspective.

In the year of his arrival in Prague, some of the younger members left the Mánes Artists Association (named after the painter Josef Mánes) and set up the Fine Artists Group (Skupinaumělců výtvarných). This was the official birth of Czech Cubism. Although Plečnik had come closer to Cubism stylistically by around 1907, he had remained anchored firmly in the plastic expression from which this movement proceeded, and was largely uninterested in fashionable slogans. In his well-known article 'Od moderní architektuřy – k architektuře' ('From Modern Architecture to Architecture') Janák echoes Plečnik in some of his formulations, confirming the view that the theoretical side of

Czech Cubism did in part derive from admiration for the Slovenian architect. Plečnik's influence is apparent in Janák's references to the rejection of Wagner's handling of flat surfaces, his practical views on church architecture and the tasks of art.[303] The same applies to some of the articles in the periodical *Umělecký měsíčník* (*Art Monthly*). As well as Janák Vlastislav Hofman also energetically propounded the doctrine of creativity over pure functionality.

In his manifesto 'Hranol a pyramida' ('The Prism and the Pyramid') Janák attempted to provide a historical legitimation for the new movement,[304] using the dialectics of the two basic Semper styles, Mediterranean Antiquity and French Gothic, each of which, he argued, was a response to the tectonic forces of nature. Janák saw the pyramid as the supreme achievement in intellectually abstracted mass, and it became the favourite motif of the Czech Cubists. Semper's belief in the organic growth of Greek architecture helped Janák to move beyond the strictly tectonic view of architecture.

The ideas on the psychology of form that found their way into Cubism from German art theory[305] corresponded to Plečnik's art to a certain extent; however, he was closer to Semper's view that folk art was dead and could not be revived.[306]

Even if the theoretical approach of the members of the Fine Artists Group was reconcilable with Plečnik's ideas, this cannot be said of his practical work. The facade of the Zacherl House is the result of a well-considered intensification of the dynamic of forces, and hence it differs from the Cubist attempts to fill the body of the building with movement on principle. Plečnik held on to the classical concept of eurhythmics. The ideal of the victory of the mind over matter must have greatly alienated him, as it negates the natural qualities of the material. This was drastically revealed in cubist furniture design, where certain structural connections could only be achieved using concealed metal supports. The issue was that raised by Semper, namely the moral quality of art, and here Plečnik was not prepared to make any compromises at all. So he was bound to take a rather reserved attitude to Cubism, which was then immensely popular. Nevertheless, he could not escape external influences altogether, and we do find the pyramid, for instance, in his work from this date, if in widely differing lengths and heights. He had, in fact, always had an inclination towards geometry and tapering forms, but the way he used them links him more with the revolutionary French Neo-Classicism of Boullée and Ledoux than the Cubist doctrine of dynamized material.

The competition for the monument to the Hussite General Jan Žižka held in 1913 was the grand finale of Czech

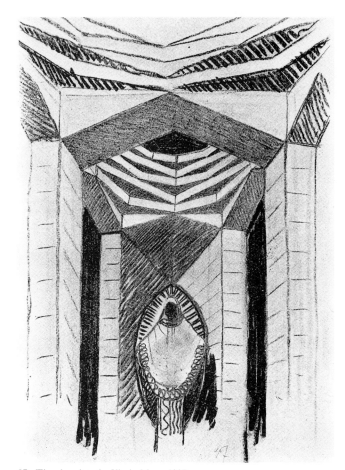

87. The chapel to the Virgin Mary, 1907

Cubism. Plečnik intended to enter jointly with the sculptor Stanislav Sucharda, and he worked out three different variants; however, he does not appear to have submitted them.[307] One was in the shape of a monumental pyramid with a figural relief (see fig. 36). In the second he used the metaphor of Hussite symbolism, and this cannot in any way be seen as related to Cubism (fig. 86). The proposal was for an equestrian statue set against a great spherical background of concrete, which was to lead down from the divided bowl of a chalice. With his brother in mind, Plečnik's intensive preoccupation with ecclesiastical vessels made for his brother gave rise to one of the most original designs for a monument, and it was to be echoed in the work of his pupils in Prague for many years.[308]

The publication of the work of Plečnik's Prague School, *Výběr prací školy pro dekorativní architekturu v Praze z roku 1911–1921*, published in 1927 is an unreliable guide in the search for Cubist references. There can be no doubt that modern currents crept into the students' work, although

88. Plečnik in the College of Arts and Crafts in Prague, 1912

89. Monumental building on a mountain, 1919

90. Monumental building on a mountain, 1919

91. Prague Castle, flagpole in the First Courtyard, 1925

92

92. Prague Castle, obelisk in the Third Courtyard, erected 1928

93. Sketch for the obelisk in the Paradise Garden,
1920

94. Prague Castle, the Paradise Garden with the granite bowl, 1923–5

95. Prague Castle, diorite bowl on the steps of the Paradise Garden, 1926

96. Prague Castle, baldachin before the entrance from the Third Courtyard to the Rampart Garden, 1929–31

97. Prague Castle, steps leading from the Third Courtyard to the Rampart Garden, 1929–31

98. Prague Castle, stairway and lift to the President's apartment, 1923–4

99. Prague Castle, stairway to the president's apartments, 1923–4

100. Prague Castle, vestibule before the president's stairs, 1923–4

101. Prague Castle, impluvium, 1923–4

102. Prague Castle, Golden Salon, entrance with D. Pešan's sculpture, 1924

103. Prague Castle, niche in the stairway to the Rampart Garden, 1929–31

104. Prague Castle, teak table in the White Tower, 1923–4

105. Prague Castle, the 'Plečnik Hall', 1927–30

106. Prague Castle, window by the president's stairs to the Paradise Garden, 1922

106

107. Prague Castle, chair in Alice Masaryk's salon, 1925–6

108. The fountain in the wall of the park at Lány, 1929–30

108

109. The church of the Sacred Heart in Prague, 1928–32

110. The church of the Sacred Heart in Prague, 1928–32

111. The church of the Sacred Heart in Prague, 1928–32

112. The church of the Sacred Heart in Prague, main altar, 1932–9

113. The church of the Sacred Heart in Prague, interior of the tower, 1929–32

114. The church of the Sacred Heart in Prague, crypt, 1928–32

their curriculum was based on a study of Antiquity. But the design for a memorial chapel by Faulhammer in 1912 shows that the crystalline and pyramidal forms were often only modest accompaniments to designs that were basically still historicist.[309] Only the most gifted had the courage to cut loose from the bonds of the School. One was Josef Štěpánek; his sketch of a christening chapel is very closely related to Vlastislav Hofman's design for the entrance to the cemetery in Prague-Ďáblice.[310] Bedřich Feuerstein concerned himself most intensively with Cubism. He only attended Plečnik's School for a year. His restless nature took him round the world by devious routes, until he committed suicide in the Vltava. Some of his drawings are in the architectural collection of the National Technical Museum in Prague,[311] and they show his great admiration for Plečnik's Mediterranean sculptural quality, from which it was only a step to the crystalline transmutation of form. Feuerstein's postcards of Moscow,[312] or Jiří Kroha's recollections of the time he came to Plečnik in despair after a devastating assessment by his professors,[313] are brief glimpses, yet they show us that the Slovenian architect was more than just an episode in Czech art.[314]

PROFESSOR IN PRAGUE

Plečnik only slowly settled into the life of a professor. He moved from the noisy city centre at the end of 1911, into a villa owned by Kotěra's mother in Vinohrady, but he often complained to his brother of his new life. He longed for his old freedom, and he missed the Museum of Fine Arts in Vienna with its collections of Egyptian and Greek art. He also disliked the liberal climate in Prague and the general antipathy to the Catholic priesthood. Most of all, he missed the big workspace he had enjoyed in Vienna. 'I have no real ties or friends here – the people are strange – they are gentle and kindly, but they are strange', he laments in one of his early letters from Prague.[315]

Ill at ease and tied to his School he longed to get back to Vienna. After a year of this isolation he received the tempting offer of a professorship at the Academy of Fine Arts in Berlin, but he decided to remain faithful to his students. He was less tempted by Balkan Belgrade, where the sculptor Ivan Meštrović and the critic Kosta Strajnić were trying to set up a Yugoslav college of art.[316] In fact, around 1910 Plečnik had been involved in the idea of a Dalmatian college of art in Split or Zadar which was not really practical, and he knew nothing of this plan to set up a college of arts and crafts outside the borders of the monar-

chy with himself as head. Meštrović and Strajnić had not expected him to turn the offer down.

More than the orthodox creed, Plečnik feared to be cut off from Western European culture in Serbia. In the tense political atmosphere filled with hatred for the Serbs before the outbreak of the First World War the mere mention of his name as honorary chairman of the Committee for the Organization of Artistic Affairs in Serbia and with the Southern Slavs could have had serious consequences. Fortunately, this was overlooked in Vienna, and none of his competitors in the later affair of Wagner's succession exploited it to his own advantage.

How highly Wagner regarded his former pupil right to the end is evident from his own final project, the *Artists' Court*,[317] where he inscribed the names of his models and pupils on the facade. They are: van der Nüll, Siccardsburg, Schinkel, Olbrich, Hoffmann, Plečnik. When Wagner reached retirement age at the end of the 1911/12 academic year the professors at the Academy of Art in Vienna unanimously agreed to his request for Plečnik to become his successor in his architectural school class.[318] But the Ministry of Education and Religion turned down the proposal and postponed Wagner's retirement for a year. The directors of the Academy again put forward Plečnik's name, but again were unsuccessful, and although the professors held to their original decision, when a third selection was required they bowed to the ministry's demand and proposed Leopold Bauer as well as Plečnik. Bauer was then appointed to succeed Wagner.

Initially Plečnik was devastated, but he abandoned his hopes before the media campaign built up. The final discussion over the fate of the Vienna Municipal Museum to do with the final arrangement of Karlsplatz had been going on fruitlessly since the beginning of the century and had opened his eyes to the changing political climate in Austria which was turning increasingly to Germany. He commented on Wagner's failure in the competition: 'He failed primarily – as far as one can judge – because they wanted a design not in the Classical spirit but in the spirit of German Romanticism. Goldemund, the Director of Municipal Building, shouted during the debate that Austria and Germany are one, we just have a different dialect.'[319]

Although Plečnik could not be sure of the real reason, he remained convinced for the rest of his life that the Crown Prince had blocked his appointment to a professorship in Vienna on nationality grounds. Even when the architect August Kirstein, who knew the background because he was a pupil of Friedrich von Schmidt, told him how conservative the Crown Prince's views on the visual arts were, Plečnik continued to believe that his appointment had been

115. Chalice for Mass, 1914

opponents were trying to evade his authority by having Plečnik's appointment confirmed directly by the Emperor, he was forced to act quickly. Bauer only suited his requirements in that, while he was once a pupil and admirer of Wagner, he had later become his bitter enemy. The Crown Prince did not know what direction Bauer would take as a university professor. The issue aroused vehement protests from the students, and actually led to questioning in Parliament. But Plečnik forbade the Czech members of the Parliament – who were of course ready to support him as a Slav – to make a political scandal of the issue, and the whole affair simply remained a bad memory. His standing in Prague was largely unaffected by it.

Plečnik maintained the proper contacts with his colleagues in Prague, and as he was determined not to take work away from anyone he was able to win their confidence. Up to 1913 he was still busy with his church in Vienna. Moreover, Zacherl approached him again, wanting to arrange a family chapel [322] in the Carmelite monastery church in Döbling and to enlarge his villa. Occasionally he also gave Plečnik smaller commissions, like the flag for the Association of Austrian Christian Youth,[323] and similar work. The work on the design for the chapel brought his friend Verkade from Beuron to the school as a guest for a week. Lacking major commissions, Plečnik concentrated on liturgical vessels. Initially this was only to help his brother, but later the work came to occupy him fully, and he designed chalices, jugs and other objects with passionate delight. The work was disrupted during the First World War, however, owing to the lack of material.

Plečnik's greatest achievement in the applied arts at this time is an ensemble of candleholders in dark bronze and crystal for the Zacherl chapel in Vienna. Symbolically it combines the motif of the chalice and that of the rosary. Disappointed by the poor artistic quality of Beuron work in Prague he sought inspiration in mediaeval Czech art, which stimulated him to experiment with new combinations of metal, semi-precious stones, marble and glass.

In his School he endeavoured primarily to build up contacts with the sculptors. In addition to Jan Kastner, who helped him with the commission for the Zacherl family in Vienna, his closest friends were Stanislav Sucharda, the central figure in the Czech art scene around the turn of the century, the religious symbolist František Bílek, although he was not connected with the College of Arts and Crafts, Josef Drahoňovský, Otakar Španiel and Celda Klouček, a highly cultured decoration designer of the older generation. From the fragmentary documents that have survived it is not possible to see how close these contacts were, we only know that of the architects Ladislav Skřívánek,[324] Professor of

blocked because he was a Slav. Kirstein's explanation accords with the following passage in the memoirs of Max von Hussarek, who was then Minister of Education and Religion. He recalls Francis Ferdinand pointing through the window of the Hofburg at the Loos House on Michaelerplatz when Plečnik's candidature was being considered, and saying: 'Are you asking me to appoint a man to teach architecture here who might hold up buildings like that to his students as a model?'[320]

The records in the Vienna War Archives confirm that the Wagner School had always been an eyesore to Crown Prince Francis Ferdinand.[321] As no suitable candidate was available among the pupils of the Ringstrasse architects, Hansen and Schmidt and because it was not likely that any of them would continue in an historicist manner, the Crown Prince's favourite style, and also because the latter had heard that his

Descriptive Geometry, who joined the college a year after Plečnik, was particularly close to him. They had known each other in Vienna, where Skřívánek had attended Friedrich Ohmann's class in the Academy with Meštrović. Of marked ascetic appearance, Skřívánek had little contact with society owing to his dislike of modern art, and like Plečnik he was isolated by his natural reserve. The rented apartment building erected between 1913 and 1915 on the corner of Platnéřská and Žatecká Streets in Prague is a testimony to their cooperation.[325] Plečnik's soft drawing of the facade is stiffened under Skřívánek's hand into a decorative scheme. But it is not likely that the Slovenian architect should have left no further traces in Bohemia before the First World War, apart from the monument to the factory owner Schroll in Broumov,[326] a commission he had received as early as 1901, the tombstone for E. Kratochvíl, director of an iron works, in Křivoklád cemetery of 1912,[327] and a lost sketch for the design of the environment of the Emmaus monastery in Prague.[328] A few other works were planned with S. Sucharda but they were never executed, like the decoration of the new bridge over the Vltava (1913; now Mánes Bridge) and a sketch (1916), barely identifiable, for a monument to Jan Hus.[329]

The College of Arts and Crafts in Prague had been modelled on the Vienna institution, which was seventeen years older, and so it continued the tradition of the English technical college, now reorganized to Semper's principles. When Kotěra left in 1910 to take up his teaching post at the Prague Academy of Fine Arts his post had been offered to Plečnik, and so he also took on Kotěra's students. For a long time there was excellent accord between the two institutions in Prague, and many of Plečnik's graduates went on to postgraduate work under Kotěra. However, the students at the College of Arts and Crafts came from less cultured back-grounds than those at the Academy, mostly technical schools where they received no education in humanities.

> I have 18 lads again this year – most of them new – some have been labouring for a few years in workshops – they are unskilled at drawing – and too docile etc. It's hard work setting them on the right path – the one I know I am on – but it is a charitable exercise as well, for often these young souls are full of faith and ideals. What a hand that has laboured and is exhausted cannot do – the heart can provide.[330]

Plečnik first took his students to Berlin, Dresden and Leipzig, as he had himself been longing to see the works of Schinkel and Semper for some time. Although the official excursion programme did not directly include tours of the Altes Museum in Berlin or the Opera House in Dresden, he studied them both carefully. Like Kotěra, Plečnik allowed some of his experience in Wagner's School to filter into his teaching, and chief among these was the motivation of the students. He was totally involved in his teaching, and in this actually outdid his own teacher. In fact, with their more profound study of Antiquity Kotěra and Plečnik were going back to the teaching practice at the Vienna Academy before Wagner's time.

Plečnik saw it as the teacher's task to promote his students' independent development. He felt himself to be primarily a mentor, but he could not entirely reconcile this with his teaching method. 'It is my task as your teacher to awaken in you a feeling for beauty, with the best will in the world I cannot give you mine', he would say to his students later.[331] In his loyalty to Semper's theories he directed his students away from the routine problems of architecture far back into the past, where, whether they wanted to or not, they had to trust to their tutor for guidance. This brought Plečnik's School a reputation for exclusivity, an accusation levelled at him later particularly by the Functionalists.

Plečnik was well aware of the limits to his teaching method, and in the unstable political climate before the First World War he encouraged his students to study anonymous folk art. As long as circumstances permitted, he took them on trips through Bohemia, Moravia and Slovakia. To a certain extent this took them away from current trends and prepared them for the period after the collapse of the monarchy, when national architecture replaced the more internationally oriented movement towards Cubism which was also an attempt in turn to move away culturally from Vienna and towards Paris. In the early 1920s most of his students did in fact easily settle down in the decorative style and they won nearly all the competitions.

Although Plečnik always remained faithful to classical architecture and warned his students not just to copy folk ornamentation, in practice he often had to compromise.

> I get to the College early every Friday – and give the lads the exercise they must complete the same day. I call it composition day – the lads quite like it, because they can compete with each other – then they get the practical exercise and so on. Today I set them a very particular task, and told them they could do it if they wished or leave it, if they didn't – by way of exception it is not a decorative or structural exercise, it is really a job for the heart – a Nativity scene – I had bought a few Russian dolls – they set to work eagerly – it is 11 now – and I already have quite a number of interesting results . . . for I told them that between the Christmas tree and the Nativity scene

there must be something that is Slav – now let the seed germinate – something may well come of it.[332]

Much of the work in the College was devoted to exercises like this. Religious subjects, which were particularly close to Plečnik's heart, or useful objects, often commissioned by companies,[333] were frequent.

Plečnik could only hold the balance between arts and crafts and monumental architecture with difficulty. Semper's doctrine was highly relevant for interiors, baldachins, triumphal arches and facade decoration, but it proved very much more difficult to teach the application of the classical principles to urban design. The great historical distance prevented the students from responding more creatively to antique models. Moreover, Plečnik rarely entered into discussion of the great Utopian projects that had dominated the teaching in Wagner's School. The study for a royal residence by Alois Mezera[334] is an isolated example among the works that are known, and it dates from right at the start of Plečnik's teaching. Plečnik was more successful with projects for churches and chapels, where the impressions of wooden buildings in the villages at the foot of the Carpathians he had seen on visits to the area are also evident. The single family home occupied a particular place in his curriculum. This combination of traditional and modern problems linked Plečnik's School to contemporary trends in architecture.

The Czech art scene was very lively; Plečnik looked to Kotěra, and remained loyal to the Mánes Artists Association. *Style* the official publication of the architectural section of the Association, came to have a similar importance for him and his School as *The Architect* had had for Wagner and his students. His sympathy with the Mánes artists – and most of the architects among them were graduates of the Vienna Academy of Fine Art or Kotěra's former students – finally brought Plečnik into contact with the Association of Czech Architects (Spolek českých architektů), which was reorganized after the collapse of the monarchy and renamed the Architects Society (Společnost architektů).

This took Plečnik into the mainstream of modern Czech architecture. The members increasingly felt drawn away from Classicism and the national tradition and attracted to Functionalism. Unlike some of the more radical movements, however, the Architects Society was able to hold the balance between Functionalism and artistic demands. Plečnik was highly regarded in the Society, not least because some of his former students were members. This was particularly evident over the commission for the church in Vinohrady in Prague when a number of renowned Czech architects proposed that he should be entrusted with the execution of the plans, and during the heated controversies in the early 1930s over the renovation work in Prague Castle. The commission for the work on the Castle was partly due to his colleagues in the Mánes Association.

THE SITULA OF VAČE

The war years were a violent disruption to the development of modern Czech architecture, and the Prague College of Arts and Crafts, too, had to pay a heavy tribute in human life to the international slaughter. The old world was falling down in ruins before Plečnik's eyes, and this strengthened his conviction that modern urban civilization would not bring the salvation of mankind. Towards the end of the war teaching at the College had to stop, there was no heating and the building was full of wounded civilians and soldiers. Plečnik saw the war as a great injustice to the Slavs. He buried himself with even greater intensity in Russian literature, and devoured everything he could find about Serbia. He would often spend the whole night with his dictionaries, learning the two languages. He pondered much on the culture and the past of his own people, of which he had become more aware since coming to Prague. A regular income and the College vacations had given him the chance to travel through Slovenia with his brother Andrej, and he also visited Dalmatia and Slavonia, and some nearby north Italian towns. He was most strongly drawn to the Karst region and the sea, seeking his own tradition in the Mediterranean architecture.

He sought refuge in the well-stocked College library, spending many hours there. This was also partly due to a bigger teaching load, for when the architect Alois Dryák left the College in 1913 Plečnik took over his technical drawing class in the metalwork specialization course, and in 1918 he took on the drawing class in the advanced course on styles. As he taught these classes voluntarily and on an unpaid basis, and also struggled for the erection of the exhibition pavilion for the Jedlička Foundation (fig. 117), where the war disabled could sell their products and so ease their circumstances a little, the College proposed him for promotion.[335] However, before the title of Imperial and Royal Councillor (k. k. Hofrat) could be conferred upon him the monarchy collapsed.

Plečnik then found himself professor of metal technology a good sixty years after Semper had held the same post. He had brought some basic knowledge with him from Graz, but he acquired much of what he needed only while assisting the conscientious College technician František Novotný, who made chalices for his brother.[336] Semper's *Stil* had drawn his attention to the Etruscans, who were regarded as the most skilful metalworkers among the ancient western Mediterranean peoples. Plečnik felt a boundless affinity with Etruscan art, and he studied the available literature on that secretive people with the greatest interest. The introductory chapter in Semper's work made a lasting impression on him in this context. Semper maintains that the development of civilization need not necessarily be regarded as altogether positive. The material culture of the individual peoples, in his view, shows that they were on a very much higher level before the descent into barbarism:

> The Finns, the Celts, the Teutons, the Scandinavians and Slavs all brought remnants of earlier culture and the corresponding architectural traditions into western culture; and when society regenerated after the collapse of the Roman empire these were active elements in the new social form, and the new art that emerged from it. This is a fact whose full importance and significance has not yet, as I believe, received the recognition it deserves.[337]

Plečnik held the view that there was a close relation between his own pictorial expression and Etruscan art, and from this he deduced an affinity between the Slovenians and their Etruscan ancestors, who must therefore also, he believed, have been Slav by origin.

The Slav people were facing historic decisions, and the pressures of the time and their sense of impotence during the war gave rise to ideas that could sometimes be quite unrealistic. Plečnik was not alone in his views on Slavic origins: some Slovenian etymologists put forward similar hypotheses, drawing on the fact that the few written records of the Etruscan language are indecipherable.[338] Plečnik, however, relied entirely on his pictorial sense, and from the standpoint of contemporary archaeology he was not entirely wrong. The central factor in his considerations appears to have been a bronze situla dating from the sixth century BC,[339] that had been found in 1882 not far from Ljubljana, in the village of Vače, above the Sava river. The Director of the Carniolan Provincial Museum, Karel Deschmann, showed the situla shortly after it was found as an example of ancient Etruscan metalwork.[340] The excavations uncovered more finds, and it appeared that Slovenia was one of the centres of situla art that stretched along the Alps to South Tyrol and down to Bologna. The oriental figural motifs reminded Plečnik of the archaic art of Greece, and this has also been noted by modern scholars, although they do not now ascribe the situlas to the Etruscans, regarding them as products of the Alpine Illyrians and Veneti, peoples about whom even less is known. The Etruscans are

116. Jože Plečnik, 1916

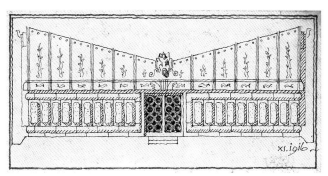

117. Study for the Sales Pavilion for the Jedlička Foundation in Prague, 1916

119

now regarded as having only transmitted the eastern influence.

In itself, the theory on the Etruscans was irrelevant, but it gave Plečnik's work a new dimension by enabling him to evade the dubious dialogue with folk art which – in Semper's eyes – was too recent. The result was to give Classical Greek and Eastern antique forms legitimate historical significance for the Slovenian area. Plečnik also included in his considerations Venetian architecture, with its Palladian view of Antiquity. His conviction that the population of large areas of northern Italy was of Slav descent actually played a major part in the conversion work on Prague Castle, where Plečnik attacked the Habsburg architectural heritage in the name of the new Czech democracy.

One of the first projects he completed inside the castle was the wall fountain with an old lion's head on the ground level of the south wing, in 1923. It bears the inscription SEMPER, which obviously has a double meaning (fig. 1). The base is adorned with an antique scale pattern, and the granite bowl, with two strap-like handles indicated in the stone, is simply laid upon this. It is a clear reference to Semper's characteristic metamorphosis. Plečnik's message did not lie in the bohemian heraldic lion's head, although contemporaries probably interpreted it as such, but in homage to the German architect. Plečnik celebrated his memory by transferring the archaic ceramic patterns into a more durable granite thus symbolically paraphrasing the essence of Semper's theory.

THE PRAGUE SCHOOL AFTER THE FIRST WORLD WAR

In October 1918, the Austro-Hungarian monarchy fell apart. Among the states that followed from it, the Czechoslovakian Republic, guided by the statesman and classically educated philopher, TG Masaryk, was the one which prospered best.

With the establishment of the Republic national euphoria reached a peak in Prague. The Cubist movement that had predominated before the war was replaced by a new decorative style, which included strong folk elements. Competition followed competition for monuments in honour of the war dead and similar themes. This suited the direction taken by the Plečnik School and it strengthened confidence in it. The classes were overcrowded, and in 1919 the college considered setting up an additional department of architecture.[341] The periodicals *Styl* (*Style*) and *Stavitel* (*The Builder*) strongly supported Plečnik and were full of work by his students.

In the competition for the new church in Vinohrady, a district of Prague, Plečnik enjoyed a real triumph even though he himself did not in fact enter. This was the first representative religious project by the new state and the number of entries for the competition was very high.[342] Thirty-one proposals were put forward, and the two top prizes went to former students of Plečnik, Jindřich Merganc and Alois Mezera. The decision was certainly not solely a result of the very positive attitude taken towards Plečnik by the jury, which included Kotěra and the future Archbishop of Prague, Antonín Podlaha, a highly regarded scholar of the history of religious art. In the broad field of Historicism, Cubism and the emergent Functionalism the work of the Plečnik School stood out with its wealth of ideas, clear ground plans and balanced facades. No one criticized the winner of the competition for inclining strongly to Plečnik's type of church placed on a transverse axis.

The housing shortage in Ljubljana after the First World War turned Plečnik's attention to social housing. He experimented with designs for clay buildings to make them durable and well insulated, drawing on the book by his friend Alfred Castelliz, *Einfache Bauwerke* (*Simple Buildings*), published in 1912. Half a century later we find the same idea in Le Corbusier's work.

He achieved more definite results with wood structures. At the same time as Loos (1921), but apparently entirely independently of him, Plečnik designed what he called a 'house with one wall'. This is a double house in wood, but it differs from Loos's version in its spatial division. As the side supporting walls are further apart Plečnik could not lay roof beams right across from one to the other, and so the facade is not suspended on these, as it is in Loos's version, where this method is used to lower the building costs. Nevertheless, Plečnik's design has certain advantages. He distributed the spaces in the ground plan in such a way that he could join the neighbouring houses' sanitary installations in the dividing wall between the two, thus bringing down the cost of the construction. Loos needed two interspaces for these even in the broadest variant, making the arrangement of the staircase and the partition walls more complicated. These terraced houses in the Dejvice district of Prague have not survived. The plans were drawn in the College by Václav Ložek and František Novák,[343] and they had a highly original facade, with visible beam heads. Unlike Loos, Plečnik was aiming to show that even the cheapest buildings could be made rather more humane with ornamentation. The roof, with its emphatic overhang, again shows Wagner's influence; he had designed facades held between two higher side pylons.

This concern with the economic aspects of social housing after the First World War left its traces in Plečnik's later work, where often only extraordinary inventiveness enabled him to realize his ideas. The St Michael church in Ljubljana Moor (Barje) (fig. 241), for instance, and the design for a mountain lodge in Upper Carniola for the Prelovšek family[344] are both indebted to the 'house with one wall'. And we find a transmutation of the theme in the ideal plan for 'social housing estate' of 1943, where the main feature is not the wall but a common roof (see fig. 342). The small front gardens to the houses in Dejvice also inspired Plečnik when he was designing the northern part of Ljubljana. He could be as rational as Loos in subdividing tiny living space, but later he preferred to leave such work to his competitor Ivan Vurnik.

The situation in Prague after the war, which had seemed so favourable for Plečnik, began to deteriorate rapidly when the new Republic was founded. The Director of the College of Arts and Crafts, Jiří Štibral, was accused of being pro-Austrian and had to vacate his post. Things had also changed in the Prague architectural scene. Rondo-Cubism, as it had come to be called, had to give way to other trends, principally the purism of Le Corbusier, which the critic Karel Teige strongly supported. The Architects Club (Klub architektů) formed in 1913 took Czech architecture in the direction of French and Dutch rationalism, with their social orientation, and this also lessened interest in Plečnik's architecture. While Kotěra could adapt to Functionalism with the help of his students, Plečnik was too loyal to Semper to be able to follow this trend which was also gaining ground rapidly in his own School. Many of his best graduates had taken teaching posts at rural technical colleges during the war, when they could find no other work, and the issue of the status of the graduates fuelled antagonism towards the graduates of the Prague Academy. The hostility was such that the merger of the College of Arts and Crafts with the Academy of Fine Arts, which had been the aim and would have given the College university status, failed to materi-

alize. For a time it actually looked as if Kotěra's first graduates and all Plečnik's former students would be forbidden to use the title 'Architect'. There were also differences of opinion in the Architects Society, where Janák and Gočár, who had quickly risen to prominence, were the main sources of the campaign against Plečnik's students, who had gathered around the periodical *The Builder*.[345]

So Plečnik had good grounds to reconsider his position. However, there was probably a particular reason for his decision to return to Ljubljana in 1921 despite the offer of a professorship at the Prague Academy of Fine Arts. He did not feel that he could continue his relationship with Pepínka Kolářova, the College caretaker who was also keeping house for him,[346] indefinitely and without concern for the future. But he was afraid that marriage would cost him his freedom and the personal position which he had so carefully built up with his consistent asceticism. His departure from Prague was more like panic-stricken flight from himself back to his homeland, although he expected to gain nothing by it. Again it was Kotěra who instigated the offer of an Academy post. The rector, Max Švabinsky, agreed to set up an extraordinary chair in architecture for Plečnik without delay,[347] and although he had made up his mind to go back to Ljubljana Plečnik was still torn by doubt:

If I am appointed – I shall be thinking of the chink in the door and looking to it for escape – I am longing to be home. I think Janez and all of you love our homeland more than I do – but my situation, like myself, is so confused and odd – it is true that others get used to being away from home and would profit from it – I stand there dreaming like a child and stretching out my hands for our blessed and unique land beyond the misty hills – last week I got a chest big enough to hold everything I own and it's off and away – home![348]

4 ARCHITECT IN PRAGUE CASTLE

Plečnik went through the year 1920 torn by inner conflict. He admitted later to Alice Masaryk, the Czech President's daughter, that in returning to Ljubljana he was going into 'an artistic death'.[349] He attempted to carry on teaching in Prague as usual, but his thoughts were often in Ljubljana, which had become the official Slovenian capital after the collapse of the Austro-Hungarian monarchy. As he had no one there, except his brother Janez, who might have helped him obtain a suitable post, and as it was impossible to earn a living as an independent architect with conditions as they were, he wavered in his resolve.

The founders of the Slovenian university were equally unresolved towards Plečnik. The technical faculty had commissioned the architect Ivan Vurnik to appoint a professor of architecture from abroad, and although Plečnik expressed his willingness to move to Ljubljana shortly after the end of the war he had to wait until the spring of 1920 for a reply. Only when Max Fabiani turned the offer of the post down did the faculty start to negotiate on Plečnik's candidature, despite Vurnik's efforts. Plečnik was virtually unknown in Ljubljana and he would in all probability have remained so if the periodical *Slovenski narod* (*The Slovenian Nation*) had not reprinted the short article from the journal *Styl* on the proposal to set up a special chair of architecture for Plečnik at the Prague Academy of Fine Arts.[350] This was enough to override any objections that he had no formal qualifications. But until 16 June 1920, when his appointment as full Professor of Architecture in Ljubljana was confirmed, Plečnik remained in considerable uncertainty about his future.

In the summer of 1920 he took his students to Slovakia for the last time. The Czechs had tried by various means to keep him living in Prague; they had raised his salary and they also invited him to join the jury of architectural competitions. So in February 1920 we find Plečnik as the official representative of Prague's College of Arts and Crafts on the jury for the gardens under the south wing of the Castle, together with Antonín Balšánek, an architect of the older historicist generation whose membership had caused Kotěra to decline to participate in the jury.[351]

The beginnings of Prague Castle date to the early Middle Ages. It had enjoyed periods of great splendour under the Czech King Charles IV in the fourteenth century, and later in the time of the Hapsburg ruler Rudolf II at the beginning of the seventeenth century, who had kept a luxurious court with a number of famous artists and scholars. The Czechs always regarded the Castle as a kind of national shrine. With the establishment of the Czechoslovakian state after World

War I, they tried to restore it from the neglect it had suffered as the Austro-Hungarian monarchy fell apart.

Archaeological excavations on the Castle, which in the next few years were to yield evidence of the oldest period of Czech history, had already indicated significant finds, and they dictated the main lines of the conversion work. Under the direction of the Castle Architect, Karel Fiala, the ground under the section between the Second and Third Castle Courtyards and in the former royal palace was surveyed in 1920 and 1921. In the Third Courtyard the foundations of a chapel were discovered. At the same time work continued on St Vitus's cathedral in the Castle and did so until 1929. The work on the interior of the chapels, in which Plečnik's colleagues and students from the College of Arts and Crafts were involved, went on almost throughout the entire conversion work on the Castle.

Kotěra undertook the design of the presidential residence on the second floor of the south wing. Together with Fiala he planned separate apartments for the President and his children. Each was to have a living room, a bedroom and a bathroom, while the family dining room was to be in the octagonal tower. The main concern was with the technical facilities, like heating, lighting, lifts and other installations. Such renovation as these required was highly undesirable to the President's daughter, who believed that her father needed not so much a conventional as a refined, intellectual working environment.

Thomas Garrigue Masaryk was a generation older than Plečnik and came, like the latter, from a similarly modest background. As a philosopher, sociologist and politician he uncompromisingly fought for democracy and humanitarian ideals in the Viennese Parliament; so he was held in high regard by the Slavs. His marriage to the American, Charlotte Garrigue, bought him closer to the Anglo-Saxon way of thinking. He spent World War I in exile, dedicating his efforts to the creation of a new independent state of the Czechs and Slovaks. As a president of great moral authority, he achieved much in the socio-economic sphere.

Plečnik found a statesman of elevated taste with identical views to his own on the moral task for art. To a certain extent Zacherl had shown similar qualities, but unlike Zacherl's Christian Socialist ideology, Masaryk's national philosophy opened whole new worlds for Plečnik.[352] The Czech President had a great love of Antiquity, as we see from his daughter's letters when the family visited Pompeii and Paestum in the spring of 1921. Masaryk returned from Italy with a number of books on art history, having expressed regret at the interior of the Czech embassy in Rome, in which, as Alice said, he could find nothing of originality.[353]

118. Masaryk in Pompeii, 1921 (his daughter Alice wrote on the photograph: 'Blue sky, marble, upwards!')

Plečnik was the only architect in the new Republic of Czechoslovakia who was capable of giving artistic expression to the President's philosophical ideas. Unlike some of the younger Czech architects from Wagner's School, such as Antonín Engel and Bohumil Hübschmann, he avoided the elevation and severity of Neo-Classicism. It was his desire to demonstrate the intellectual affinity of Masaryk's age with the democracy of Ancient Greece by stressing the formal variety of art in Antiquity, as Semper described it.

At the beginning of March 1920 Masaryk stated publicly that he intended to make Prague Castle a national monument.

> I frequently observe with what reverence and loving devotion people come to the castle to see the thousand years of our architectural history. So immediately after my return from abroad, I made arrangements for the necessary repairs to be carried out and for the various parts of the castle to be properly surveyed. My aim is to make the castle a worthy monument to our past. On the Letná, as on the northern and south-western part of the Petřín, I wish to lay out parks. I hope that all the parkland will be preserved in future, and that only the most select examples of our architecture will be placed there. I myself wish to have a glyptotheca. Man does not live on bread alone. To avoid continuing the irregular communication network of the old city without a plan and for the future, I believe it is necessary, to solve the problem of the regulation of and communications in this venerable part of Prague with due regard for general needs. We will only achieve an independent style if we pay proper respect to our rich cultural heritage, and learn to understand it and conscientiously preserve it.[354]

123

The President's words made a deep impression on Plečnik, and in his eyes no one could have put the obligations of the young Republic to its historical heritage more clearly. He was also surprised by Masaryk's farsightedness in including the Hradčany (the area around the Castle) in the problems of urban planning; finally, the President's desire for a glyptotheca said much about his humanist views. Plečnik felt that the Castle could benefit from some Mediterranean influences. Although Masaryk's ideas derived from antique scholarship rather than art – his study held the busts of Socrates, Plato and Aristotle even before the war – the result was essentially the same. Plečnik later recalled the start of his work on the Castle in these words:

> Do you want to know when I went to the castle – I was still at the School in Prague – I vehemently resisted the idea of touching it – but I could not get out of it. I do not regret it now – I was able to profit greatly. God knows what would have become of me without it – God knows how grateful I am to him for it.[355]

While the members of the Mánes Artists Association had stressed right from the start that the castle needed a high profile artist, who should be given a free hand but also be expected to bear sole responsibility for his decisions, the Chancellor Přemysl Šámal was trying to obtain Plečnik for the work, independently of this and at the instigation of Kotěra and the painter Karl V. Mašek. The energy with which the Slovenian artist initially declined the prestigious commission won over the members of the Association as well, and it was clear to them that it was only possible to avoid further differences within the domestic art scene by inviting a neutral artistic personality. So on 5 November 1920 Plečnik was officially appointed Castle Architect by President Masaryk.

The artist and the statesman agreed on the very first point of the programme. Masaryk was delighted by the proposal to set up a lofty monument to the Czech legionaries who had fallen in the war in the southern Paradise Garden (Rajská zahrada) in the form of an Eternal Flame that would be visible from afar.[356] Plečnik had taken the idea from Viollet-le-Duc's description of the lamps for the dead in the Middle Ages.

By now Plečnik was also under contract to the University of Ljubljana, but he promised the President that his most gifted and loyal pupil, Otto Rothmayer, would deputize for him in his absence from Prague. A short time later Plečnik was offered the post of professor in Zagreb,[357] where Strajnić's monograph had made a deep impact on the governing body. But Plečnik was too involved in his work in Prague to accept this, so much so, in fact, that for the first semester in Ljubljana he asked his colleague Ivan Vurnik to give his lectures for him there.

Much as Plečnik appreciated his commission on the Castle he was well aware that he was working in the midst of a large circle of observers who were not prepared to condone the slightest error by a foreigner. He also knew how fragile the friendly ties with the Old Prague Club (Za starou Prahu) who had supported his appointment as Castle Architect, were. However, he put up with the difficulties, as the commission from Masaryk promised to be more than the prestigious task of modernizing the presidential quarters; it offered Plečnik the chance to give permanent expression through his art to the ideals from which the young Czech democracy had sprung. Plečnik was laying the foundations for a new style.

The Hapsburgs had left the castle in a fairly desolate state, and in converting it to its new function Plečnik initially had to deal with much that was mundane. The statues in the attic zone above the Matthias Gate needed restoring, a position was needed for the new state arms, the sgraffito decoration in the ancient Ball-game House needed restoring, a decision had to be taken on access to the Spanish Hall, and on the future of the Old Provost's Lodge in the Third Courtyard and on what should be done with the gardens. There were many other similar questions.

The first published concept for the conversion was still relatively incomplete, and it was limited to the most important parts of the Castle.[358] Plečnik promised the Czechs that he would handle the historical heritage with due respect. He wanted to start with the paving of the First Courtyard. To ensure that the Matthias Gate, with its reconstructed painted decoration, was not too reminiscent of the Habsburgs, he wanted to add a figure of the victorious Czech lion by the sculptor Jan Štursa. In addition to the late Gothic Vladislav Hall and the Ballgame House (it was to be decorated by the painter Max Švabinský) above the Deer Moat (Jelení příkop), the Riding School beside the Gunpowder Bridge was to be converted into a glyptotheca. This appears to be all that was then envisaged, but fundamental additions were made as the work progressed.

Plečnik's operations for Masaryk began in the Palace of Lány, the President's favourite retreat in the country. The architect responded to Masaryk's wishes in regard to the residence and the park with simple means and great sensitivity. His work consisted mainly of setting up the President's library, a music salon and the dining room, where he was able to use some of the old traditional furniture from the store in Prague Castle.

As time went on he also gained the confidence of the President's daughter, Alice, who, owing to erroneous comments by others, had originally believed him to be a Neo-Gothic architect. Later she confessed how greatly she had feared that he too would praise a particular salon that had met with general approval. 'I keep feeling so relieved that you did not', she says in one of her letters.[359]

Masaryk, a platonic, enlightened and philosophical ruler, who set up an ethical social doctrine founded on religion to counter Marxism, agreed entirely with Plečnik's ideas. Alice personified all her father's intellectual virtues, but she expressed them more emotionally. Highly cultured and devoted to the Slav idea (her brothers and sisters, educated in the English manner were often irritated by this when they were young) she soon became the First Lady of the Republic. Burdened with affairs of state, the President left the matter of the Castle to her, and this brought her closer to Plečnik, who was five years older than she. While her father restrained his platonic idealism with David Hume's rational attitude to religion, Alice was more open to Plečnik's elementary forms of belief. She was influenced by the ideas of St Augustine's Christian love and the simplicity of St Francis of Assisi. Her marked sense of beauty made her a fitting partner in discussion for Plečnik. She admired the architect as an unequalled master of form, and she adopted his view that religious art must rank supreme. Alice's trust in Plečnik was also nourished by her conviction that the architect could give expression to the Slav idea in his work.[360]

As she become better acquainted with him and saw how greatly he revered their historical heritage she gave him her unconditional support, protecting him from an uncomprehending environment. Her task was not easy, and Plečnik was well aware of his own timidity. He hated any kind of carelessness in work, but lacked the courage to direct his anger to the right quarters. In such cases he would sometimes disappear altogether from Prague, leaving the difficult task of persuading the workmen to Alice or his assistant Otto Rothmayer.[361]

In what an idealistic atmosphere the discussion on the renovation of Prague Castle was going on can also be seen in Alice's belief that art could solve national and Pan-Slav issues. Secretly she was hoping that the use of Slovakian elements in the Castle would help soften Czech materialism: she always stressed the original and unspoilt cultural heritage of the Slovaks, who had a similarly unhappy history to the Slovenians. Alice regarded Slovakia south of the Carpathians as 'the Crete of Slav art'.[362] The idea of balancing Czech and Slovakian symbolism played an important

119. The Paradise Garden around 1919

part in the renovation work on the Castle; some actually went so far as to protest vigorously when the sculptor Jan Štursa used the Czech lion to crown the obelisk in the Paradise Garden, since it showed the lion bending over the double cross of Slovakia. A new version had to be made, with the cross on the lion's back, which, in turn, was not approved by the Czechs.

Although the new state arms had already been officially approved in three sizes in March 1920, Plečnik continued to work on it and he achieved several interesting solutions. One is the Czech heraldic lion with lightning (fig. 106), illustrating the verse of the national anthem that is dedicated to the Slovaks with the words: 'Lightning strikes over Tatra, wild roars the thunder . . .'.[363]

The arms included the symbols of the five historic provinces from which the new democratic state had grown, and so Plečnik also worked on the symbols of these provinces. He designed five columns, originally intending to install them on the garden facade of the southern wing of the Castle; later they were erected near the fountain in the park at Lány (see fig. 154). He often went back to old Czech legends, and he also drew inspiration from Christian symbolism (the surroundings of St George's Fountain are shaped as a huge halo, the motif of the Good Shepherd is used in references to Masaryk as the leader of his people, and so on). Plečnik's artistic greatness lay in his ability to use these ideas without recourse to cheap metaphor; as his work progressed his confidence grew, and he ceased to worry that the public in general would never be able to comprehend the philosophy on which his interventions were based.

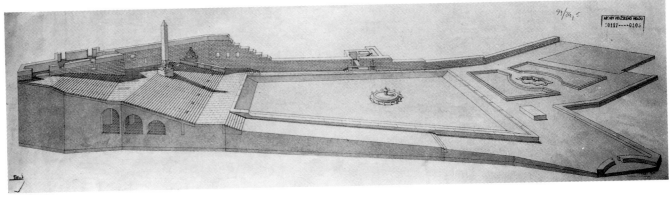

120

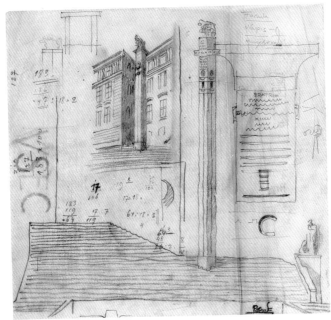

121

122

The Paradise Garden and the Obelisk

120. The perspectival view, 1920
121–2. Plečnik's sketch and Rothmayer's perspective, 1921
123–5. The sketches and the plan of the obelisk, 1921
126. Preparing the obelisk for transportation, 1923

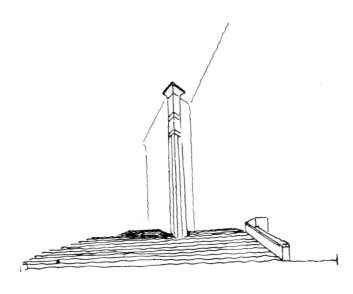

123

126

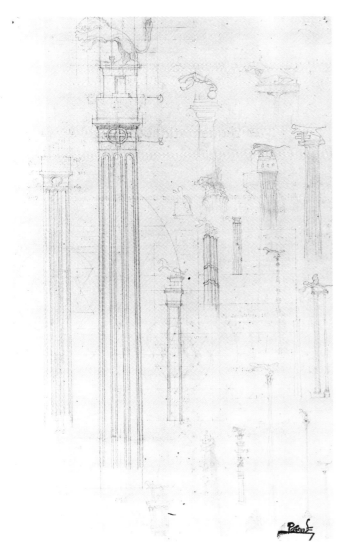

124

125

126

127

His discussions with Alice Masaryk at the end of 1920 and in early 1921 brought the full significance of the term 'Castle Architect' home to Plečnik. As mentioned, one of the main issues on which he enjoyed the unqualified support of the President was the erection of a monument to the legionaries who had fallen in the war. Plečnik wanted to combine this with his plans for an obelisk on the steps in the Paradise Garden. Like all his proposals, an obelisk was not out of character with the castle complex. Plečnik modelled his concept on two Baroque obelisks to the Defenestration of Prague in the Rampart Garden (zahrada Na Valech). The position of the new set of steps, with the fountain beneath, was not unlike that of the Spanish Steps in Rome.[364] Nevertheless, Plečnik took a long time to find an appropriate paraphrase of his historical model. The first variant was designed during the summer of 1920, and it was in the spirit of Roman Baroque (fig. 120).

As Plečnik envisaged the monument, it was to consist of several parts joined together, so that the mechanism bearing the Eternal Light could be supported inside (fig. 125). The obelisk was to be 20 metres high, thus reaching to the cornice on the Castle facade. This raised several complicated questions of a technical nature. Moreover, the figure of the lion mentioned earlier which the sculptor Štursa had produced to crown the obelisk did not satisfy Plečnik's artistic requirements. So the architect returned to the idea of a monolithic obelisk without an Eternal Flame. When the geologist J. Pantoflíček reported with some surprise that a stone 34 metres long had been extricated from the Mrákotín quarry Plečnik was inspired to make new designs. It would have been the largest monolith ever quarried.

In May 1922, angered and depressed by the threatened closure of the technical faculty in Ljubljana, although it had only just been opened, Plečnik set off for Moravia to see the stone. He was overwhelmed by the size of the block, but doubted that it could be quarried successfully.[365] And in fact, the unwelcome news from the quarry was not long in coming: efforts to remove the obelisk were being discontinued because the stone was cracking. Nevertheless, the episode fundamentally changed Plečnik's approach to the task:

I want to work the stone so as to preserve its natural quality. My designs to date have been the reverse of this. I was trying to show that the obelisk is made of a number of parts joined together. I hope I am thinking logically – that is, correctly. I promise to try and release the soul of the stone, and not give it a soul of stone.[366]

At first, Alice could not understand why Plečnik wanted the obelisk to 'fly'. Then, as she gained a deeper understanding of geology she saw the granite monument in a new light: 'It burned in the fire of the primeval mountains – terrible – in the centre of the glowing earth, which the God of Michelangelo and Haydn, with His great powers, has set in the universe. – You want to break the stone out and cast it into eternal flight.'[367] Plečnik had mystified granite in a similar way before, in a desire to overcome the temporal element, when he used it to cover the facade of the Zacherl House.[368]

Independently of the engineers from the Skoda works and the army, whom the President had commissioned to transport the block of granite, Plečnik proposed a simpler procedure, which in his view was less risky. Two beams were to be fitted under the stone, which was then to be rolled along about half a metre above the ground. He actually designed a vehicle to transport it from the station to the Castle that would have delighted any Renaissance architect.[369] He also concerned himself with the question of the installation of the monolith, proposing an interesting idea that involved tipping the huge stone on to the steps. Plečnik had lived so long with his thoughts on Antiquity that he no longer trusted modern technology.

Although an offer of a new monolith, 16 to 18 metres long, immediately came from Mrákotín, Plečnik continued to look for an alternative solution to the war memorial. For a time he contemplated a huge mast with the lion sculpture on top, and a core of concrete or oak clad in metal. In order not to diminish the President's enthusiasm he finally decided on a monolith 19 metres high (fig. 126), although the quality was not of the best. This time he intended to postpone his decision on the shape until he knew the exact dimensions of the block that had been quarried.

At the end of August 1923 the monolith was successfully loaded on to the transport vehicle and the journey to the railway station in Telč began. Initially, an engineer from the Ministry of Public Works, M. Klement, was instructed to take charge of the work, and all went smoothly. But when the military intervened and took over, misfortune struck. The chain began to break, and enveloped in a cloud of burning engine oil the men pulling the vehicle did not see the desperate efforts their captain was making to stop them. It was Saturday, and on Sunday a visit by high ranking military officials was to take place, and the team were working at top speed. The stone slipped down the steep slope and broke in two against a half-finished huge bowl for the Paradise Garden that was to be transported to Prague at the same time.[370] Plečnik was in despair, but according to Meštrović, a Croat sculptor who was working on the portraits of the

President and his daughter at that time, Masaryk took the news stoically.[371]

Offers of two new stones came from the quarry straight away. Plečnik chose the one with a more homogeneous structure, and changed the shape, making it broad enough at the bottom to stand alone, without additional iron supports. This time the stone broke while it was being quarried. Masaryk wanted to order a new one, but as none of the Czech quarries could provide a suitable stone within the foreseeable future Plečnik decided to use the longer part of the broken stone, which was, after all, 15.5 metres in length (see fig. 92). He also decided on a new position, in the Third Castle Courtyard.

This proposal caused an outcry. Of the group who had until then always supported him Bohumil Hübschmann, editor of *Styl* and chairman of the Architects Society, now opposed the idea of an obelisk.[372] However, Plečnik stuck to his decision, aiming at the same time to mark the coming thousand-year anniversary of St Wenceslas. He wanted to set the obelisk on a stylobate, with three inscriptions invoking God, while giving it a Classical Egyptian form with a golden pyramidal top.[373] He also envisaged a pyramid in polished glass with semiprecious stones to recall the great age of Charles IV. The obelisk was finally erected in haste at the end of 1928, to mark the tenth anniversary of the Republic; it had no decoration, but a technically interesting idea put forward by Plečnik was used. The stone was set on a partially raised concrete base, and for a time Masaryk wanted this to house the tomb of the Unknown Soldier.[374]

Small compensation for the failure to erect a monument on the steps in the Paradise Garden was the slender obelisk with a heavy Ionic capital in the Moravian Bastion (fig. 127). But although it is scarcely 10 metres high it is a powerful testimony to the static qualities of granite.

To a certain extent, the monument to the First World War dead which was erected between 1926 and 1928 before the entrance to the Palace of Lány was a side product of the obelisk for Prague Castle (fig. 128). It is a slender, roughly worked sliver and extremely elegant. From the way Plečnik has attached the granite to a stable background it is evident that he had in mind the flag poles in front of the Ancient Egyptian or Minoan temples. The double gold shaft ring is adorned with Karel Štipl's heraldic lion, which is taken from one of the designs for the top of the obelisk in the Paradise Garden. The monument is built up on the contrast between the squat, firmly anchored column and the mobile stone mast. After his disappointments with the Prague obelisks Plečnik would have had every reason to adorn the monu-

127. The obelisk on the Moravian Bastion, 1923

ment in Lány, as was in fact originally planned, with the inscription 'I am as fragile as freedom itself'.[375]

The last and probably most radical variant of the classical obelisk is certainly the 'recumbant' version beside the Slavata monument in the Rampart Garden (fig. 136). It is 8 metres long and oval in shape. It consists of two parts, with the joint skilfully hidden by two rings. These also mark the strap which binds the obelisk to the monument behind, symbolizing the arm of a cross, for the Defenestration of Prague in 1618, when the Protestants threw the two staunchest Catholic members of the Council, Slavata and Martinic, out of the window and into the castle moat, marking the start of the Thirty Years War, and proving indeed to be the commencement of a long path of sorrows for the Czech people.[376]

Contrary to all expectations, the episode of the Egyptian obelisk above the city left visible traces on Czech architecture. While the broken block of granite was waiting to be put in place, Gočar set up an obelisk on the steps in front of his grammar school in Hradec Králové, with a figure of Victory

128. The war memorial in Lány, 1926–8

The gardens of Prague Castle opened a new chapter in Plečnik's oeuvre. The irregular terrain below the Castle did not permit a repetition of the park that had been laid out during the Renaissance above the Deer Moat (Jelení příkop), although Plečnik did incorporate the leitmotif of the balustrade with stone balls and the parapet wall with a rounded upper edge. In the mid-sixteenth century, at the time of Archduke Ferdinand, only the Paradise Garden had been created here.[378] It had been a garden enclosed by a fortified wall and covered the extreme western part of this half-a-kilometre-long site. Of its later architectural decoration, however, only a low Baroque fountain and the Matthias Pavilion at a projecting corner had survived. During Nicolo Pacassi's conversion work on the Castle in the second half of the eighteenth century the remaining part of the site was made more regular. After the March revolution of 1848 part of the terrain was levelled for fear of new unrest, and fortified. When the monarchy collapsed in 1918 the Paradise Garden and the adjoining Rampart Garden, through which a small promenade was later cut, were in a very neglected state.

Plečnik came to be involved in the castle gardens through the competition mentioned earlier, which was held after a fragment of the monumental stairway was discovered in the northwest corner of the Paradise Garden in 1919 (fig. 119). As none of the proposals from the competition was felt to be satisfactory, Plečnik was asked to take on the work in the summer of 1920. Initially he limited his input to designing the steps, taking account of the plan, which had won second prize and been chosen for the realization of Paradise Garden, designed by the garden architect Josef Kumpán. Plečnik soon realized that a radical solution would be needed if the result was to be aesthetically correct, and he proposed a great flight of steps which would rest on brick arches and would lead in a huge curving sweep above them down to the grass carpet below (figs 120 and 130). Beneath the presidential residence he laid out a lawn, similar to the one which had delighted Masaryk and his daughter in Lány. He also left the healthy trees standing, carefully taking the stone border of his lawn around an old yew. He was not interested in horticultural elements alone, and when the Castle administration presented their own designs to him he crossed out all the hedges and metal pergolas, fearing these would reduce the impact of a concept that was essentially architectural. The gardener Leonhard Juklíček taught him how to use steep patches of turf, so enabling him to stress the linearity of the whole. Plečnik experimented with these again, but with less success, in Ljubljana, when he erected earthen pyramids

by the sculptor Štursa. After the Second World War it was intended to set a cast of the same sculpture, that had already adorned the Czech pavilion in Paris in 1925, on top of Plečnik's obelisk. A few years later than Gočár, Bohumil Hübschmann also worked on the theme of the obelisk when the environs of the Emmaus monastery in Prague were being designed, and he made use of the bigger section of the broken obelisk originally intended for the staircase of the Paradise Garden in the Castle.

All of which suggests that the Czech architects followed what was happening at the castle with admiration for the artist, who was struggling to achieve his ideal of eternal beauty in isolation and often in self-doubt. Even Plečnik's successor in the role of castle architect and an advocate of functionalist architecture P. Janák, too, held steadfastly to his belief in a timeless beauty.[377]

130

along the Roman wall, and later again with his grass-covered barrow-like chapel in Žale (see figs 307 and 335).

The Art Commission set up by the President's office to offer additional support to Plečnik recommended that the sculptor Jan Štursa be involved in the work again. But as his lion for the obelisk had proved disappointing, while the statue of the Good Shepherd by Alois Kalvoda had no classical features[379] Plečnik decided to decorate the gardens exclusively with metamorphoses of antique ceramics. The series starts with the balustrade on the platform at the entrance, which consists of rounded Greek craters, or large bowls, on high bases. In the niche directly after the entrance he placed an elegant ointment jug (which was also one of the first tasks he set his students in Ljubljana).[380] This was followed by a shallow Neo-Classical square vessel with a columned base (see fig. 95), both in hard black diorite, set beside the steps. The use of monolithic decorative elements in the presidential gardens was a moral issue for Plečnik, for a noble form should be made of the best material and should not be composed of more than one piece. A few metres lower down, where the steps reach the entrance to the 'crypt', Plečnik set a wall fountain with a stylized Greek crater. For a time, Masaryk envisaged an altar here beside the obelisk foundations. Before the entrance to the presidential residence Plečnik wanted an amphora on a stone base, but finally two metal lekythi with heraldic lions were set on the inside of the stairway.

The existing, relatively modest, Baroque fountain in the middle of the Paradise Garden was difficult to integrate into the ambience of the garden after these changes. Plečnik first tried to raise its height, but any attempt to elevate it was bound to fail because of the proximity of the proposed colossal monolith that would demand an equally monumental architectural counterpart. The granite bowl finally realized was placed on the site of the fountain and was certainly modelled on Schinkel's stone bowl in front of the Altes Museum in Berlin.[381] This was nearly 7 metres in diameter, and was a real miracle of stone masonry for the first half of the nineteenth century. Schinkel had originally wanted a smaller bowl so that he could place it under the cupola in the museum, but the stone mason chose a very much bigger block and worked it very carefully on the underside as well. In 1832 he proudly set it provisionally on a rather higher base, thus displaying the brilliant underside.

Plečnik had all this in mind in the summer of 1923 when he returned to Mrákotín and was shown a block of granite more than 8 metres long for the fountain in the Paradise Garden. Although he was enthralled, he soon revised his idea, returning to the plan for a round bowl of 4.3 metres in diameter. Not knowing how high the stone would be he

129. Quarrying the granite block for the great bowl in Mrákotín, 1923

initially contemplated a higher stand. When quarried, the block far exceeded his expectations, and Plečnik decided to leave it almost in its natural state, making only minimal alterations and placing it on two granite blocks (see fig. 94). This allowed the careful profiling of the vessel to be fully displayed. Plečnik could not envisage a really massive bowl beside the elegant obelisk, and by positioning it so as to give the impression that it was only provisional or better, so that it appeared to be suspended, he also gave the carefully chosen individual forms much greater impact.

Although the bowl is only 4.2 metres in diameter, and so very much smaller than the one in Berlin, working it was not an easy task in the twentieth century either. The dates show how difficult the project was. In August 1923, after extensive preparations, a stone was quarried in Mrákotín and roughly worked (fig. 129). At the end of April the following year it was loaded on to a specially converted railway waggon and reached Prague after a journey of two weeks. The work on the stone on site took until the beginning of 1925.

When the monumental bowl was in place the Baroque fountain was moved to the Rampart Garden. So the flowing spring of water was exchanged for a huge bowl in the antique manner, which did not need a fountain. Alice could not at first understand this. It is tempting to think, though difficult to prove, that the baths of Ferdinand, which once stood on this spot, played a part in the decision.[382] Plečnik's retrospective approach to the conversion work in the Castle would support the argument.

The views of the city from the gardens encouraged Plečnik to open the wall and create a number of terraces (figs 131–2). There was much public opposition to this project, and Plečnik was accused of destroying historical substance. In fact, he took the decision to open the wall, which was not

130. The Paradise Garden, 1922–5, photographed in the 1930s

of any particular architectural significance, in full awareness of the moral responsibility he bore. His sequence of prospects starts with the balustraded platform at the highest point of the Paradise Garden, where the new castle steps reach the castle.

Access to the Paradise Garden – completed in 1925 – is not through a monumental portal but an opening in the wall with a stone lintel above a massive central pillar. The solution is basically very radical, but clothed in classical ornamentation, with an architrave with fascia, consoles and a monolithic fluted half-column. The column is in the middle of the opening and so it introduces a new theme in Plečnik's architecture, one we shall encounter frequently in future. It looks classical, but actually owes much to the spirit of Minoan art.

In his discussions with Alice, Plečnik liked to raise the

question of the origins of European art. Alice often drew his attention to the English literature on the subject, with which he was unfamiliar. The two-part monograph on the excavations at Knossos on Crete by Sir Arthur Evans was published during the conversion work on the castle, and it was certainly a key work. If one may judge from Plečnik's shaping of door handles as jackals' heads and his use of motifs from Egyptian furniture, the sensational discovery of the tomb of Tutankhamen is 1922–3 did not fail to have its effect.

The wealth of hitherto totally unknown material on the origins of classical European civilization was a true revelation for Plečnik. The central column in the access to the Paradise Garden can be associated with the Lion Gate in Mycenae, or it could be a reference to Minoan or archaic origins, like the Temple of Apollo in Bassai or the basilica in

132

131

132

131–3. The Rampart Garden: viewing terrace (1924–5) with the pyramid (1925) and the Small Bellevue (1925–7), contemporary photographs

133

134. The Rampart Garden, photographed around 1926, shortly before completion

Paestum. It is a symbolic introduction to the Path of Meditation on Antiquity in the shade of central European vegetation, which extends below the Castle for half a kilometre.

The next prospect was at the Matthias Pavilion, at the end of the Paradise Garden. Plečnik designed this in 1922 on the rather lower terrace of the supporting wall, and he matched the height of the existing wall with a new balustrade looking on to the city. The black and white mosaic of the paving[383] imitates the dynamic twisted rectangles we are already familiar with from the decorative veneers on his Viennese furniture. The bollards indicate the imaginary axis to the presidential residence, and also delineate the space.

Plečnik distributed the stone balls which he had found already there but simplified their bases, in a rhythmic sequence along the entire garden wall (fig. 134), and he also used them to decorate the entrance to the bellevue in the upper part of the Deer Moat. Later he also liked to use them in various architectural and symbolic contexts (St James's Square, the stadium and the Three Bridges in Ljubljana (see figs 290 and 205)). How receptive the architect was to stimulus from the environs of Prague Castle is evident from

the little figure of a cockerel above the side entrance to the park in Lány; its historical model is attached to the roof ridge in the transept in the cathedral of St Vitus. At the junction with the Rampart Garden, which is barely half as wide as the Paradise Garden, Plečnik replaced the stone bollards with cypresses. Part of the wall dating from the second half of the eighteenth century was retained, and given greater importance with Alois Kalvoda's figure of the Good Shepherd. In laying down the axes Plečnik did not create specifically optical lines, as Wagner, for instance, recommended. Plečnik's approach is also clear from one of his comments: 'Monuments that are set up like a point de vue – Paris – have a deadening effect on me. I prefer the surprises in Italian cities.'[384]

The main axis is firstly shifted to the middle landing of the steps, the bend in which is necessitated by the irregular facade of the castle, and it runs finally into a void. The symmetry of the lawn in the Paradise Gardens evaporates in the east. The new and longest axis in the Rampart Garden begins with the fountain in its new position in the middle of the Baroque parterre, which plays the part of a kind of compositional joint below the bend in the castle wing. As orientation Plečnik used the old path beneath the castle, along which an English garden had been laid out in the 1860s. The geometric correction of the existing features necessitated extensive earthwork and the terrain had to be anchored (fig. 135). Part of the additional earth needed was to be taken from the excavations for the foundations of the steps in the Paradise Garden. 'In Prague I have just started laying out the Rampart Garden below the castle – a steep slope hitherto almost impassable . . . all in all it is a dangerous experiment – as it is all supported by built up earthwork. Large numbers of workmen are employed bringing up huge masses of soil to be deposited here', he said in a letter to his brother Andrej in the middle of September 1924, after his return home to Ljubljana.[385]

In the spring of 1926 the entire eastern part of the Rampart Garden started to slip, and there was threat of a real catastrophe. Extensive reparation work was needed, and it was two years before the garden was restored. This unforeseen event reduced the funds available for the renovation work. Plečnik's work was also affected and completion delayed.

His gardens in Prague combined a number of compositional themes. The paths were covered with snow white kaolin sand, and between them he laid out large lawns in varying sizes. He thinned out the old trees somewhat, but left most of them, disregarding the geometry of the rectangular ground plan. He enlivened the garden promenade rhythmically with various architectural additions, which were inventive variations of the historical remains found on the site, or a result of the desire to open up panoramas of the city.

The park axis is interrupted by three cross axes, the first at the Ludvak wing, where the southern entrance tower once stood. This historical reference was taken up by Plečnik relatively late, but it was something he had always had in mind. In 1925 he surprised the Art Commission by designing a monumental colonnade, which was to fill the bend in the Ludvak wing. As we saw earlier, five colossal columns were to stand as symbols of the most important historical lands of Czechoslovakia. Seen from the viewing terrace the cathedral would stand above a classical arrangement, giving even clearer expression to the idea that Prague Castle was like the Greek Acropolis. Behind the row of columns was to be the actual stairway connecting the Third Castle Courtyard with the Rampart Garden. However, the idea proved untenable because the foundation and renovation work needed on the Rampart Garden would have been too complicated and costly. Here it should be added that although sufficient funds always appeared to be available, in reality none of the great architectural ideas was realized. That was the case with the broad avenue in the northern

135. The Rampart Garden, levelling the terrain in the lower part, 1923

136. Recumbant monolith before the Slavata monument, 1925

137. Portal to the Alpine Garden, 1924–5

138. The Large Bellevue in the Rampart Garden, 1924–5, photographed after completion

139. Decorative metal vessels for the Bellevue, around 1926

part of the castle area, as well as the obelisk in the Paradise Garden and the colonnade.

Opposite this colonnade Plečnik opened one of the most beautiful views of Prague. He had part of the defence wall pulled down and surrounded the former bastion with a new wall, gaining ground for the Winter Garden in the meantime (1923–4); above the bastion he arranged a terrace as a vantage point. This was paved with a stone mosaic, the kind that can still be seen on the pavements of Prague's streets (figs 131–2). East of the Winter Garden, ie. below the remaining part of the defence wall, a terraced alpine garden was arranged, boasting some two hundred species of alpine plants.

In 1925 he placed a slender pyramid on the edge of the terrace, which takes up the dialogue with the towers and cupolas of the town. The pyramid imitating the outline of one of the roofs on the bell-towers of the nearby Romanesque church of St George also connects the garden with the castle and the cathedral, giving Plečnik's architecture historical legitimation. In the spirit of Wagner he was thus quietly marking out a space that opens up new aesthetic experiences. However, the symbolic contents were never clear to the Czechs. As the pyramid stands on the wall, like the Cestius Pyramid in Rome, it should probably also to be understood as a reference to Semper, who is buried in the Protestant cemetery at the Porta San Paolo or, in Plečnik's words, 'in the shade of the Cestius Pyramid'.[386]

Not far away, Plečnik placed a small gazebo on the walls (fig. 133); it has archaic Ionic columns with projecting ribs instead of fluting, while the capitals only have an egg-and-dart decoration on their echinus and have no volutes. Instead of an architrave bearing a roof, there are massive granite plates with rounded edges lying on them – a metaphor of a textile canopy. The rhythmically distributed empty spaces between the columns, the railings and the ceiling give an impression of stone-framed pictures with silhouettes of Prague's churches.

On the foundations of the bastion under the Theresian wing that dated from the time of Přemysl Ottokar II, Plečnik repeated the theme of the semicircular conservatory in the aviary (1924), creating a modest building with an elegant brick stairway inside that no longer exists. The small, one-storied building dating from the early nineteenth century served as the beginning of a second, less dominant cross axis in the form of two parallel paths leading towards the steps to the terraces below the wall (fig. 137). Together with the opening from the Third Castle Courtyard to the Rampart Garden that was made a few years later it symbolizes the opening of the Castle to the district of Vyšehrad. Whether the sculpture of a crowned female head that decorates the

136

arch over the steps leading to the terraces below the walls is the legendary prophetess Libussa must remain an open question, but the position of the head is certainly a reference to the legendary etymology of the name Prague, which is connected with the saga of Libussa, as it is said to be derived from the word for 'threshold', 'práh' in Czech.[387]

The portal to the steps of 1924/5 consists of a walled arch and a replica of the stone lintel at the entrance to the Paradise Garden that was made at almost the same time. The columns clearly show the effect of the tectonic forces. The shafts have one or two rings at their ends, which are modelled on Ancient Egyptian art. The optical effect is seemingly to preserve time from further deformation. In the combination of brick and stone the arch and the beam are deliberately presented as examples of the two oldest forms of building with which architecture has always been concerned.

The larger bellevue, in the shape of the letter L, is above the level of the garden path (fig. 138). It was built to provide the necessary border to the convent's garden next door. The slender columns bear a high architrave, the lower part of which is Ionic while the upper half consists of an encircling cornice in roof tiles. True to Semper, Plečnik regarded a similar feature on the university library in Ljubljana as an inherent part of the ornamentation on the building (see fig. 187); however, comparing this with the Zacherl House we can see it as a metaphorical relict of the tiled roof (see fig. 24). The echinus bends under the weight of the architrave, and so recalls Ancient Egyptian palm capitals. The gilt nails and cartouches of the wooden ceiling also point in that direction, although it is not entirely clear where the border should be drawn between pure form and its symbolic significance. The capitals on the half columns on the wall are even more unusual. On the double ring at the neck rests a square plate, above which a kind of little cloth is laid, and only then does the abacus follow. Without an exact idea of the genesis of the classical forms an architect would hardly have dared so masterly an infringement of the accepted rules of style. Plečnik was determined to prove the inexhaustible vitality of the column. The tectonic role of the column remains untouched, and Plečnik cannot therefore be regarded either as a Neo-Classicist or as one of the forerunners of the Postmodern movement.

Under the large bellevue, where the garden narrows again, he laid a third cross axis, and this accords with the difference in the level of the terrain. The patch of sand, from where there is an uninterrupted view of the city, is adorned with some Baroque sculptures that were found in the castle store. Plečnik spent a lot of time and much thought on the height of the base of the Hercules Fountain (1923), and

140. Studies for the granite table on the Moravian Bastion, 1922

finally decided to allow its shape to be determined by the meandering curve of the massive granite table which surrounds it. The stone bench (1924) beside the path looks back to Antiquity, but its soft forms also evoke the comfort of a Biedermeier sofa.

The Moravian Bastion is at the end of this path (fig. 127), and in 1922/3 the architect transformed this for the President by removing some of the high, historicist crenellated surround and making a kind of country seat, with a pergola and a granite table (fig. 140). He had Czech folk sayings inscribed into the table, and Alice also chose some for the copper vases beside the large bellevue (fig. 139). Plečnik thought these folk sayings were entirely original and so to a certain extent in keeping with the spirit of Antiquity.

In his designs for the southern gardens he again took up a number of antique themes. The gardens have suffered much, particularly in the 1960s,[388] yet they are the only surviving and representative example of their kind from the 'heroic modern' period.[389] It should also briefly be mentioned here that Plečnik became so deeply involved in his work in Prague that he was inclined to lose sight of the problems in Ljubljana, and this did not exactly strengthen his position at the Technical Department at the University.

141. Aerial photograph of Prague Castle, 1932

THE FIRST CASTLE COURTYARD

Plečnik's conversion work on Prague Castle recalls the universal approach of Fischer von Erlach. But while the Austrian architect aimed to legitimate Habsburg Absolutism by using historical models, Plečnik was trying to eliminate the last memories of this by orienting to Antiquity; he also wanted to create a link with the democratic tradition of the Classical age. Between the years 1755 and 1775, during the reign of Maria Theresa the castle had lost much of its former historical significance when the masses of the buildings and the roofs were homogenized. The imperial architect, Nicolaus Pacassi, not only altered the First Castle Courtyard, he also wiped out the traces of the pre-Theresian architecture. As this was an issue of national importance, Plečnik found himself facing a dilemma as to how far, if at all, the original state ought to be restored.

His solution for the paving in the First Courtyard was the most original (fig. 141). Although he had enriched the gardens with various combinations of stone and brick paving, he chose unusually large granite slabs for the representative entrance area. Starting at the entrance, he laid two paths across the courtyard which avoid the main entrance to the Second Courtyard. They are paved with a pattern in imitation of rustication. It gives the impression of two rhythmically edged official carpets, with a texture reminiscent of an old monumental wall.

The design for the First Courtyard accorded with the general concept of the Castle as the seat of the head of state. Until the Third Courtyard was reconstructed the first functioned as a kind of great antechamber for the entire Castle. It gave access on one side to the President's living quarters in the southern wing and on another side to the Spanish Hall which was to be a great reception or meeting room. Plečnik's proposal was to close the Matthias Gate in the First Courtyard; this gate had been built in the beginning of the seventeenth century as a free-standing triumphal arch and was later changed into a castle gate. In this way, Plečnik could

138

have obtained some space behind it for a kind of ante-chamber in front of the monumental Baroque staircase leading to the reception rooms on the first floor of the southern wing. He was probably encouraged to do so by the Czech aversion to anything that was Hapsburgian; the Matthias Gate was a symbol of such times of bad fortune, so Plečnik wanted to eliminate it from the castle's communication system. After careful study of the problems involved he reached the conclusion that an opening should be created through the cross section on both sides of the Gate. The President ought to have a separate way to his own apartments. This was identical to the route of the medieval Czech kings, known as the Coronation Way, while the wider opening north of Matthias Gate was intended for a public route to the Second Courtyard and on to the cathedral. These proposals were the result of Plečnik's conviction that more access to the compact mass of the building was needed, and he always paid due regard to the historical past, the only exception being his idea to double the Gunpowder Bridge in order to make the cathedral directly accessible from the north. However, the proposal to close Matthias Gate aroused such public opposition that the idea was dropped. Access to the Spanish Hall, one of the key elements to an understanding of his design for the paving in the First Courtyard, was only carried out in the early 1950s by Otto Rothmayer, and twenty years later it was again greatly altered.

Interestingly, Plečnik placed the rainwater drains at the edges of the courtyard, so making the ground slightly convex. This architectural refinement gave even greater prominence to the surrounding buildings. Symbolically, the courtyard could be envisaged as a segment of the globe, recalling the time when Prague Castle was regarded as the navel of the world. The state symbol was to be placed in the middle of the courtyard, with the purpose of directing visitors to the left and right of Matthias Gate. Because Plečnik did not succeed in finding a satisfying solution for this symbol, he later abandoned the idea.

Of iconographic importance are the two flagpoles, 25 metres high and originally made of two straight pines (see fig. 91). The preserved model is painted from top to bottom with the colours of the Czech tricolour and looks as if it could consist of several pieces of wood glued together; it was probably created as an alternative, as the work was technically very challenging.[390] The motif of masts with gilt tops before an entrance is of Egyptian origin, although in his first sketches Plečnik had in mind the huge flagpoles on St Mark's Square in Venice. The Matthias Gate, before which they were to stand, was then erroneously ascribed to the Venetian architect Vincenzo Scamozzi. The pronounced

semicircular moulding (torus) on the two granite bases is executed as 'softly' as some of the stone capitals and walls in the southern castle garden. The forms of the granite plinths recall the two gilt shaft rings with visible screwheads which are a literal adaptation of Semper's thesis that the columns in archaic Antiquity were wood clad in metal.

Last but not least we need briefly to consider the lighting of the courtyard. Plečnik avoided freestanding lights by using bulbs placed beneath the cornices and console-shaped lights on the walls. The lighting system in the First Courtyard enhances the grandeur of the castle; the lamps in the Third Courtyard are placed very much lower, so creating a more intimate atmosphere.

The paving of the First Courtyard (1922–3) relates to the historical urbanism in Italian cities; this can also be found on the former Congress Square (Kongresni trg see fig. 294) in Ljubljana (1926/7), which in turn prepared the way for the radical solution in the Third Castle Courtyard in Prague (1927–32) (fig. 147). Plečnik used models to try out his ideas, but he was only able to judge their true effect when they were actually realized.

THE WAY TO PERFECTION

In his work Plečnik always tried to remain totally independent. Despite the support of the President and his daughter frequent differences of opinion arose which Masaryk could often only smooth over with difficulty. It was some time, for instance, before he finally succeeded in clarifying the financial situation and giving Plečnik the staff he needed. The architect Karel Fiala, who saw his role as that of a conservationist, tried to brake Plečnik's creative energy, and this caused Plečnik to leave Prague at the beginning of August 1922. The following spring Masaryk wanted to pay Plečnik for the plans for the interior of the library; this provoked further misunderstanding and again Plečnik's temporary removal to Ljubljana.[391] Although Plečnik was then embarking on the conversion of his own house and did not know whether he would ever be able to complete it, he feared that the President's offer of financial support might destroy the idealistic nature of the work. When Masaryk did later instruct a large sum of money to be transferred to him, he kept only a fraction to cover his own expenses and returned the rest.[392] With regard to Plečnik's attitude to money it should be noted that he paid for the two college publications of the work of his students in Prague and Ljubljana in 1927 out of his own pocket.

On 17 April 1923 Kotěra died. A delegation of students immediately approached Plečnik, asking him to take over

142. Masaryk and his daughter Alice, 1931

Academy of Sciences and Arts, he made him a member of his Academy of Labour; two years later he awarded him the title 'Castle Architect', so giving him the rank of university professor and legalizing his claim to a Czech pension from the start of his teaching at the College of Arts and Crafts.

Further testimony to the President's unconditional affection is his will, which was signed in Lány on 20 April 1925.[394] In it he expressly states his wish that Plečnik be entrusted with the design of the entire castle complex and that this should be linked with the city. The work was to be 'well considered and carried out gradually, in the appropriate material and with the greatest care'. This is clear evidence of Masaryk's moral approach to architecture. Masaryk tried to impose an obligation upon his political successors to complete the conversion work, and this meant all the issues that were then under discussion, like the monument to the legionaries, the design of the state apartments and the Third Courtyard, right through to the glyptotheca. Finally Masaryk entrusted Plečnik with the task of designing a modest family grave.[395]

So, like Plečnik, who was often on the verge of despair over his own abilities, Masaryk also feared that the conversion work would never be finished. Alice, the only person who knew Plečnik well, tried to argue away his scepticism. With her boundless admiration for him she protected him from any unpleasantness to do with the work on the castle so that he could work in peace. 'I pray on my knees every day for your spiritual victory', she wrote to him at the end of 1924.[396] However, she did not expect to become more emotionally involved with him. This, she felt, would have put an end to their 'strong, religious and unsentimental friendship'.[397] When she became aware of her attraction to him which she had hitherto denied, she was afraid this might have repercussions on the work on the Castle, and on her father, and jeopardize her ability to continue the task she had undertaken. Plečnik must have put forward similar considerations in his letters to her, destroyed during the Second World War. Relations between the architect and Alice reached a critical point; personal feelings had to be suppressed, as both were convinced that a great task must not be disrupted by personal concerns. They maintained the formal and respectful mode of address throughout their correspondence. Indeed, Plečnik never did use the more familiar mode as an expression of affection, addressing people who were very close to him in the formal mode as well.

The roots of Plečnik's self-denial went back to his family and conditions around the turn of the century, of which we have already spoken. His frequent references to Ruskin's views on the moral basis of art were a reflection of his

the position held by his deceased friend at the Prague Academy of Arts. Masaryk also used this opportunity to attempt to bind the architect more closely to the Castle. Plečnik could have returned to Czechoslovakia, sure of the highest political support; however, at the same time he was in fact beginning to lose his elevated position in the modern architectural scene there, although, as will be explained, the Czechs were generous in their public recognition of him.

In the end, he took the occasion of his refusal of the offer for a moral lecture to his students: 'I am firmly resolved not to draw a salary from two sources. Nevertheless, one cannot simply avoid these issues – there are people who bind one, through the heart, reason and duty to one's homeland, and I have to take this into account.'[393]

The many titles which the Czechs awarded Plečnik in the 1920s were certainly a mark of recognition, but they were also a form of moral pressure to continue with his work in Prague; they were also an attempt to flatter Plečnik's protector. In 1922 Plečnik was made an honorary member of the Architects Society, and two years later he was given the same honour by the Society of the School of Architecture at Prague Technical University. When the oldest Czech artists' association, 'Umělecká beseda', added their name to the list, we can see that by 1925 Plečnik was enjoying the support of both the traditionalists and the modernists in Prague. Nor was Masaryk himself sparing in the honours he bestowed: in 1925 when Plečnik was appointed a member of the Czech

140

143. Otto Rothmayer, around 1938

brother Andrej's intransigent morality and his mother's ambitions. In Prague Plečnik had come very close to his ideal in life, and this strengthened his conviction that true art can only spring from pain. He said to his students: 'My prophecy to you is that as architects you will suffer until you go to your graves. I am not speaking from personal experience but the experience of great men. The sculptor and the painter fare better.'[398]

THE INTERIORS

In 1921, at the President's request, Plečnik's pupil Otto Rothmayer was asked to mark out on an illustration of the Castle the places of archaeological significance and the current use of the rooms. This was because the government had decided to vacate the Castle by the coming spring and leave it entirely to the President of the Republic.[399] The state apartments were to be on the second floor of the south wing. Although Kotěra had been working on the plans since the summer of 1920, Alice wanted Plečnik to be given this commission, with responsibility for the entire Castle:

> Nothing has remained of the cruel age of feudalism. But there is a danger that the spirit of the Habsburgs will remain in the castle and be taken over by the bourgeoisie. One can only overcome vicious aristocratic self-interest through the aristocratic democracy of love. It is terrible to live with a lie. As you see, I spend a lot of time with my father. I see, believe and feel that he suffers greatly from the pettiness and the vulgar environment.[400]

She wanted a self-contained residence, but this was not an easy task given the Baroque ground plan with suites of interconnecting rooms along a long corridor. Already in the

summer of 1921 she had determined that her father's library was to be the centre of the residence, and later she said that it must remain a 'national relic' even when all traces of herself had gone from the Castle and another president lived there.[401] The library was also made the central theme of Plečnik's work on the palace in Lány.

We find an interesting parallel to Alice's ideas in Plečnik's words to his students at this time. After his return to Ljubljana from Prague in December 1923 he set the design of the University Council Hall as an examination project. In the outline, beside the practical instructions, he laid particular emphasis on the didactic function of architecture, and the references to his experiences with Prague Castle are very evident:

> . . . Whatever you do, never forget the artistic significance of the hall! A hall dedicated to the flower of the nation, the finest representatives of scholarship, must be a sight worth seeing! The money that is spent on monumental tasks is not lost, it is returned with high interest. That is particularly necessary here, because the people who meet here are very one-sided, they are immersed in their scholarship. We need to make them aware that there are other things as well . . . I would not put anything else in the hall, neither a smoking room nor a cloakroom (the hall must be like a church, gowns should not be stored there). The room should always make the people in it aware of what they represent and what duties they have to perform![402]

His final words are also informative: 'You are not tied to any particular style, as I am in Prague. If I were not, I would greatly love to incorporate some of my Slovenian soul!'[403]

The grand staircase in the western part of the southern section of Prague Castle was quite a distance from the rooms around the corridor at the joint with the cross-section, where the presidential residence was to be. Nearby was only a small, round stairway, but this was not suitable as a main entrance. The new entrance (see figs 98–9), which Plečnik fitted with a lift, was made from the Second Courtyard, between the chapel and the cross-section. Owing to the slightly eliptical shape of the stairway the extension fits on to the old building without the irregularities on the ground-plan with the contact between old and new being noticeable. The same can be said of the placing of the four Minoan columns in the vestibule (fig. 100); they do not follow the ground plan of the entrance but the irregular disposition of the passage to the Third Courtyard. The basic concept is similar to that of the Zacherl House, except that this is closer to historical models. Plečnik supplemented the Minoan columns with Tuscan columns at the rear and less frequented side of the stairway. As this was a private area, he exercised greater restraint in the use of expensive materials. For the floors he laid out a 'carpet' of varying brick patterns, and visible brickwork dominates the walls of the stairway as well. A new feature, but one that was to recur frequently in his work in future, was the use of white joints as a decorative element (see fig. 99). It had been regarded as a specific characteristic of the castle since the renovation of the defence walls of the Paradise Garden by Kamil Hilbert shortly before Plečnik's arrival in the castle. The glazed lift doors can certainly be compared with Expressionist or Functionalist work, but Plečnik has deliberately kept the visual impact timeless. The convex glass surfaces are in no way less elegant than the attic windows of the Zacherl House and Loos's shop frontages.

Again on the antique model, Plečnik installed an impluvium in the centre of the presidential residence in 1923/4 (fig. 101). He opened up the room with wide arches and placed an oval window above. The soft daylight, replaced by artificial light at night, is caught in the flat bowl of the fountain (1923/4) that stands in the centre of the polished granite floor, which is slightly sunk like a basin. The ensemble of light and gently playing water was framed by three old vases on high plinths. Under the fourth arch Plečnik placed a low stone bench. In this part of the residence he was able to demonstrate his great love of stone. As he said, he would have liked best to cover the entire castle with it, including all the doors and their leaves.[404] The impluvium was also intended to recall the President's visit to Pompeii and southern Italy.

The fountain in the impluvium is one of a series with the granite basin in the Paradise Garden, and formally it is one of Plečnik's most perfect creations. He has balanced the height and size of the bowl, used the base to create a logical form and stressed the admirably elegant curve with two rectangular additions. He would often relate how he and Masaryk literally crawled round the fountain on hands and knees feeling the underside.[405]

Plečnik's students in Ljubljana could not, apparently, see the point of such considerations. Later they often quoted the comments by Plečnik which they had noted down to show how traditional their training had been. As an example we can take part of the dialogue with his assistant France Tomažič on Antiquity, when Plečnik was explaining his theory of the eternal laws of architecture: 'The classical materials torn from the earth are also part of these laws. They too embody the idea of eternity which you cannot find in concrete. I am not saying this in arrogance, what I say is drawn from my own experience.'[406]

Historically the most important part of the presidential residence was the White Tower at the start of the cross-section of the southern and tranverse wings; it is the only part of the original Romanesque fortification that had remained. Around 1580 Bartholomäus Spranger had decorated the vault with a medallion showing Hermes and Athena. Hence, Plečnik attached particular importance to this room, and he designated it for the signing of state documents (see fig. 104). He carefully cleaned the shell of the building, but for all his respect for history he unhesitatingly installed modern central heating radiators. In such cases he was always a faithful pupil of Wagner. When a new heating system was being installed in the castle he purchased the three heavy cast iron stoves that had been concealed in the marble fireplaces of the Tapestry Room for his house in Ljubljana. He recounted this unexpected acquisition to his brother Andrej in words that could be by Le Corbusier:

> The stoves look utterly practical, they have no decoration whatever, they are like machines, and that is why no-one ever allows them to be seen. The people would be angry – but I like them as they are – I shall just coat them with powdered graphite when I have time. They look like huge monsters – better than the noblest Doric.[407]

In the middle of the White Tower he placed a teak table; it stands on four massive legs on a granite floor, like the fountain in the impluvium. The quality of the hard, dense wood forms a fitting counterpart to the crystalline structure of the granite. The contrast between the materials is made even more effective by the motif of an inverted white marble table beneath. That Plečnik was concerned to achieve more than just a formally effective solution is evident from the following significant text: 'OBCI STAROSTI SVÉ OSOBNÍ PODROB' (Subordinate private to public concerns), which Masaryk had taken from an old inscription before the entrance to the Council Chamber in the Italian Court in Kutná Hora.[408] The inscription is chiselled into a slightly convex medallion in the floor beneath the table, and it is to a certain extent a counterpart to the ceiling medallion with Spranger's fresco. However, as the centrepoint of the solemn place it also has a deeper meaning, as this is where the destiny of the state is decided. Despite the difference in their formal laws Plečnik has united stone and wood in one and the same stylistic modality, possibly more perfectly than he was ever to do again. The wreaths of live plants with which Plečnik encircled the arms of the historical lands of Czechoslovakia are an interesting feature. This is a return to the starting point of Semper's ornamentation.

The library, now partly restored,[409] consists of two rooms beside the staircase to the Third Courtyard. Alice and

Plečnik were aware that there were certainly risks in borrowing from folk art. Nevertheless, and probably for that very reason, she compared her father's library to a farm living room, where apart from the polished wooden floor and the soft light that spreads through the room nothing is rural.[410] Only the mahogany book shelves, with their gilt consoles to match the old Empire candelabra, show that this is not a purely utilitarian interior. In the corner by the window stood a small fountain in Silesian marble. Besides its more prosaic function of increasing the air humidity, it symbolized the source of knowledge and purity.

Alice was delighted, and the architect told his students when he returned from Prague in 1924: 'When I saw my rooms in Bohemia, I was enraptured. The white, the simple but noble form, I exclaimed: That is entirely modern! Others will come and destroy it, but a residence of this quality is not a common thing!'[411]

In the course of his teaching in Prague Plečnik's views on the interior changed greatly. Owing to the lack of actual commissions he had buried himself in the history of the applied arts, tracing Semper's views. He combined his love of Antiquity with the familiar Biedermeier craftsmanship, although in almost all his seating he had to adapt to the Empire style used in the castle. With his extensive technological knowledge he was able to translate Egyptian, Greek, Etruscan and Roman work in stone, ceramics and bronze into highly imaginative work in wood. In the process metal played an important role as a material appropriate for the finest furniture design. Semper, as already mentioned, had believed that metal could not, as yet, yield a new monumental style, as it tended to produce an extremely light architecture. As he said: 'The thinner the metal structure, the more perfect is it in its way.'[412] He saw metal as playing a different role in the applied arts:

> The less suitable the metal rod is as a material for architecture, the more is it suitable for what, visually, we have recognized as the opposite of the monumental, it will create tools and household appliances of the utmost delicacy and lightness, and that is where it will find its most appropriate application.[413]

Plečnik therefore frequently designed wooden tables and chairs as if they were made of metal. Again he was following Semper's recommendation: 'The material should not be regarded merely as a passive mass, it should be used as a means, as an element to stimulate invention'.[414] Plečnik used extraordinarily bold constructions to exploit the advantages of the models he had chosen for his furniture. He was capable of giving wood an elasticity that equalled that of wrought iron, or of working it in very thin strengths like

144

145

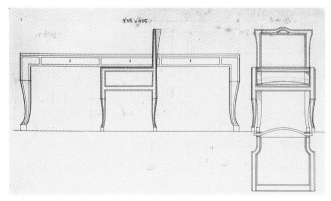

146

The interiors in Prague Castle:
144. The salon with the embroideries, 1925/26
145. The large salon, 1926/27
146. Writing desk and chair, drawing around 1921

sheet iron. He held consistently to Semper's ideas on the mobile nature of furniture, and the stylization of his chair legs frequently recalls the animal paws on antique seats.

His second source of inspiration was textiles, or what Semper meant by textile art. In his chapter on antique tapestry work Semper says that the upholstery was originally simply laid on the furniture, only much later was it fixed with nails.[415] That induced Plečnik to create a number of variations with loose, half-fixed and fixed upholstery. He also transferred textile forms to wood, as on the armchair in the President's daughter's salon of 1925–6 (figs 107 and 144). Originally a dark cushion was placed on the chair; it had a light embroidered stripe in the middle and this was a reference to the 'straps' attached to 'metal' frames. This formal superfluity, that is, doubling, of the motifs from different materials on one product or monument, is characteristic of Plečnik's translation of Semper's theories. It was a matter of a simultaneous use of the different stages of metamorphosing the original form was supposed to have gone through in its historical development. In this case he worked the seat of the chair as if it were fabric or leather, and he 'protected' the parts of the arm rests that would be most rubbed and worn by gluing on straps of wood, in the Wagner manner.

In this armchair Plečnik came very close to Marcel Breuer's well-known and contemporary chrome-plated tubular steel chair, the basic concept of which is a metal frame covered with upholstery. This shows that he was well aware of the avantgarde movements of his time, intuitively, even if he always concealed their application with historical exteriors.

Plečnik filled the other rooms of the presidential residence with nineteenth-century furniture, and at Alice's express request he made the rooms open and free. She had in mind Japanese interiors, with their sparse furnishing. We should mention the two ṣalons beside the impluvium, fitted out in 1925 and 1927. The smaller, which no longer exists, came to be called the 'Slovak Salon', owing to the embroidery hung on the walls (fig. 144); Alice had been purchasing folk handicraft work for it from the so-called Kretz collection, including Moravian and Slovakian embroideries, since the beginning of 1924. Plečnik arranged the embroideries and a number of items of peasant clothing on the walls in ornamental groups, using a direct application of the cladding theory. The elegant seating arrangement, the Persian carpet and dark mahogany walls took away any suggestion of folklore from the embroideries and the traditional ceramics on the shelves. Plečnik proved that with the appropriate measure of taste folk art could also be incorporated into high art. 'A pastoral without pastorality', said Alice of her new salon.[416]

The large salon next door was to radiate 'calm and monumentality', at the request of Alice (fig. 145).[417] She proposed decorating it with prints, blossoms, vases and carpets. The work on the design of the salon became protracted, and the plans for the columned hall were already taking shape. Rothmayer advised Plečnik to tackle the salon in the same antique manner. He then created a truly Neo-Classical canopied room, using the tectonic structure of thin wooden columns with architraves and green silk rep. In the calm atmosphere the gilt Empire candelabra on the ceiling look like decorative ornaments. The light polished chairs, designed to Greek models, deserve special mention: they are extremely bold constructions and can bear comparison with the best achievements of English furniture. Plečnik proved a master here, and his designs can stand beside those of Classical Antiquity.

In 1923/4 Plečnik displayed great inventiveness in solving the problem of the irregular space between the White Tower and the impluvium. He opened the disruptive partition wall with an arch and gilded the walls (fig. 102). He was motivated either by the chapel of St Wenceslas in the nearby cathedral or, more probably, the golden ceiling in the chapel of the Holy Cross in the castle at Karlštejn. The salon was named after the harp that once stood there. Particularly remarkable are the three noble wooden portals bearing sculptures by Damian Pešan, Plečnik's later associate on the church of the Sacred Heart in Prague. He also worked on the wardrobe with Pešan; this has not survived. It was a small, wedge-shaped room, which he panelled in a light wood and adorned with gilt busts of the representatives of various nations by Pešan.

THE THIRD CASTLE COURTYARD

The new paving for the courtyards was of particular importance in the conversion work on the Castle. When completed, the Third Courtyard was to function as the official 'antechamber', that is, the official route to the President's office and the gardens in the south. The building committee had initially considered this as early as 1920. As well as the courtyard paving the question of the equestrian statue of St George had to be considered. This is a valuable Gothic work by the brothers George and Martin of Cluj and dates from 1373. Plečnik undertook to design a number of variants, but was prevented from doing so by more urgent tasks although in the summer of 1924 he proposed restoring the monument and protecting it with a roof and a railing.[418] In the following spring the plan to erect the broken piece of the obelisk revived the issue of the paving in the Third Courtyard, but more archaeological explorations had to be carried out first, and these lasted from 1925 to 1929 (fig. 148).

In the course of his work on the Castle Plečnik suffered some bitter disappointments. The two gardens in the south were finished by 1927, but just before the work of paving the third courtyard commenced they became the subject of criticism that was not always well-intentioned. The paving work was extremely complicated, as not only were the remains of the oldest buildings to be preserved, with the new sewerage running between them, but the members of the Association for the Completion of St Vitus' cathedral also insisted on retaining the original levels of the ground around the cathedral. The decision to leave what the archaeologists had unearthed in position and protect the remains with a concrete roof convinced Plečnik that the courtyard should be radically levelled. The only problem was the Pacassi Portal in front of Vladislav Hall in the eastern part of the courtyard the original height of which could not be preserved. After much thought and tough negotiations with the art commission Plečnik succeeded in having his idea accepted (fig. 147). He saved the old entrance to the Royal Palace by using a ramp and skirting the Eagle Fountain, which he left on its original level; he then lowered the start of the steps to the Rampart Garden. Originally he wanted to preserve the unity of the irregular courtyard by including a semi-circular ditch on the ground. Finally, he proposed positioning the obelisk so that it immediately confronted anyone coming in from the Second Courtyard and St George's Square. Plečnik appears to have had in mind the similar arrangement in Venice,[419] where the Campanile of St Mark's acts as a link between two squares.

In this design he moved the equestrian statue of St George, which until the mid-eighteenth century had stood beside the south wing of the castle and later at the end of the ramp beside the church, on to the axis of the castle portal. This was the only part of the plan retained when it was actually carried out. The obelisk had to be moved to the corner of the Old Provost's Lodge when it became evident that it would not have the desired effect so close to the mighty bell-tower. Plečnik placed the obelisk exactly on an imaginary line between the two fountains in the Third Courtyard (fig. 141). It should not be forgotten when comparing Plečnik's work with Venice that the paving in the Italian city is one of the most outstanding historical examples of a monumental solution for a great public place.

In the early thirties Plečnik experimented with a number of public places that had two or more different levels. For example, the flower market beside the cathedral in Ljubljana, the square by the church in Komenda, the square in front of the church in Hotedršica, the square by the cathedral and Castle Square (Dvorni trg) in Ljubljana; the latter was not, in fact, realized. They are all variants of the Prague theme. His main experience came with the paving of Congress Square (Kongresni trg) in Ljubljana in 1926 and 1927 (fig. 294), where he drew on his solution for the First Courtyard. The result convinced him of the monumental effect of a great uniform area.

In 1928 Plečnik displayed the archaeological remains from the Third Courtyard near the cathedral under a separate roof. It had not been possible to treat them in the same way as the others owing to the difference in the level of the ground. He decorated the roof with stylized lime leaves, the symbolism recommended to him by Alice to evoke the Slav idea. Bohemian history could not have been respected with more sensitivity. Plečnik even piously took some stones that were not needed into the crypt of his Prague church, and used them for a symbolic triumphal arch behind the altar.

The square granite slabs of the courtyard paving have a side one metre in length, and they seemed more suitable to Plečnik than the traditional Prague mosaic paving. He took the check pattern from the existing ornamentation on the ground in the Third Courtyard and the neighbouring St George's Square. As the courtyard had a totally irregular shape, Plečnik oriented to the axis of the portal of the south wing. The work of laying the paving began in 1927 and it lasted for a full five years, as the excavations were not finished. The Castle administration decided to use eight different quarries in Bohemia and Moravia, and the slabs they provided were carefully distributed all over the courtyard, in order to add colour to the severe pattern. The desire to have a number of different types of Czech granite represented in the castle will also have played a part here, as this was traditional practice in Bohemia.[420] The same practice had been used for the National Theatre in Prague, where the foundations had been drawn from various parts of the country.[421] Masaryk also originally wanted to commission a quarry from each land in the state to provide stone for the First World War memorial. There were, moreover, entirely practical reasons for doing this in Prague Castle, for no single quarry could have executed so large an order within such a short time as stated in the contract.

While the paving was being laid Plečnik placed the figure of St George[422] on a dark diorite base, and beneath it, instead of the Baroque fountain basin, he placed a flat square bowl. Like the base of the obelisk it fills one of the fields in the paving. The encircling railing is covered in metal and it surrounds the fountain like a great swaying halo. Plečnik also used the motif of the circle, with its neutral direction,

147. The Castle Third Courtyard, 1927–32

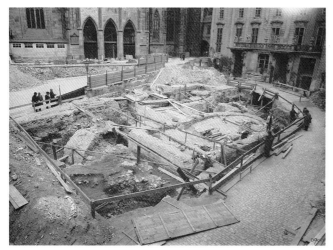

148. Archaeological excavations in the Third Courtyard, around 1926

146

on the Eagle Fountain, on the steps to the Old Provost's Lodge and at the entrance to the former chapel between the south wing and the cross section.

The ramp to the Royal Palace (1928–9) corresponds in its lower part to the width of the gothic portal, while it narrows upwards. Its axis leads just past the obelisk. Along the centre of the axis Plečnik laid a curving 'runner' in granite, to facilitate walking in this steep part of the courtyard. Originally he intended to place two crowned columns with twisted shafts at the end to mark the entrance to the royal part of the Castle. Again, he found the motif in the Castle itself, on the portal of the Johann Nepomuk chapel, which was added to the basilica of St George during the Baroque period. The granite lattice bearing the date of the tenth anniversary of the founding of the Czechoslovakian Republic has Plečnik's favourite plaited pattern, and this occurs again on the bronze manhole lids.

THE STEPS TO THE RAMPART GARDEN

The design of the way from the Third Courtyard to the gardens in the south was carried out between 1927 and 1931, and it is closely related to Plečnik's work on the stairway in the former Chamber of Trade, Commerce and Industry in Ljubljana, which began at almost the same time but was finished earlier (fig. 180). The idea had a historical foundation in the old south entrance from the Rampart Garden, which was lost in the Baroque conversion work, but it also provided a symbolic link to the old city and the district of Vyšehrad, which was the former and oldest seat of the Czech kings. In his will of 1925 Masaryk expressly mentions Plečnik's first project for the garden portal, with its five columns, and in the following four years this went through a number of development phases. As mentioned, the architect designed several variants of stairways, each arranged differently. Behind the temple frontage to the stairs he originally wanted a serpentine ramp leading to the Third Courtyard. In a later variant he drew the columned hall on a high stereobate, from which the steps would have led in a semicircle towards the viewing terrace in the garden. In his most radical solution Plečnik proposed access to the gardens in a straight line. Owing to the big difference in the levels the steps would have descended steeply to the sandy area beneath, and so given even greater prominence to its cross direction. The very much more modest solution which he presented to the art commission in 1927 was greeted with enthusiasm (fig. 149). He now placed the steps entirely in the south part to reinforce the castle walls, and endeavoured to compensate for the monumentality of his unrealized initial idea with the quality of the material, proposing granite for the steps and consoles, diorite for the columns and sandstone to face the walls (fig. 197). It was agreed that the stone should be polished wherever it was visible. As Plečnik had the niches very elaborately worked, instead of placing sculptures in them as originally agreed, the project became rather more expensive (fig. 103). Expensive capitals were also needed, as the order of the columns was changed, for Plečnik turned the shafts of the Doric columns around, creating a Minoan order. It is hard to say why he did this. Directly or indirectly the stylistic change must have been influenced by the publication of the second volume of Evans' monograph on the palace at Knossos. Plečnik, by now well settled in Ljubljana, was starting to transfer ideas he had conceived for his home town to Prague, rather than vice versa, as had originally been the case. So this could be a variant of the stairway he designed for the Chamber of Trade, Commerce and Industry in Ljubljana, which was Minoan. There are, indeed, many architectural similarities. The architectural decoration of the staircase facade is a metaphor for building in wood and so further underlines the archaic concept of the whole. Plečnik also used the detail of steps with under supports, a structural necessity in the Ljubljana Chamber, to reinforce the balconies in Prague (figs 183 and 199).

The design of the staircase facade is based on Semper's speculation on the intermediate metal phase between wood and stone building practice. Plečnik achieves this through the contrast between the rustication of the facade, which calls to mind beams, and the copper cladding of the architrave above the stairway.[423] He was able to hide the iron crossbars which supported the opening in the facade with tin. He also imitated wood in the plaster on the court facade of the Chamber of Commerce in Ljubljana, and on the People's Lending Bank in Celje, which dates from the same time (fig. 254).[424]

He canopied the access from the Third Courtyard to the stairway (see fig. 96). If such a fundamentally provisional arrangement is translated into a permanent material, it can, according to Semper, be used in monumental architecture, particularly if all the components are adapted to the new technology and combined into an organic whole. Plečnik proves here, too, that he was an unequalled master in Semper's metamorphoses. He could give stone the appearance of wood, but still endow it with profiles that only a stonemason's tools could produce. Between the metal canopy and the wood that supports it lie some metal straps so that the roof does not rest directly on wooden beams, but there is a decorative element in between which softens the contact between the support and the crome elements. The copper plates are made to look like fabric and they are riveted together, as Plečnik paid homage to one of the oldest techniques in metal working, and one which, according to Semper, also has a high decorative value.[425]

Plečnik could not have found a better way to stress that this entrance was only a provisional arrangement than with the four bronze bulls that bear the four beams. They are a direct paraphrase of the contrast between the mobile and the rigid architectural elements, as Semper understood it. As Plečnik needed a roof over the entrance, but did not want to change the historically defined space, he decided to use a feature that had solemn or celebratory connotations in Antiquity. In his *Stil* Semper comments in detail on the role of the *Vestiarius*, for instance, who would cover the walls with textiles on special occasions.[426]

While Pešan's carvings on the beams do not convey any particular symbolic message, the bulls can be interpreted in a number of ways. The legend that they are the oxen of prophetess Libussa's bridegroom is credible, and for a time there was discussion of a monument to Přemysl near the castle; however, when the model proved a failure the project was abandoned:[427] It is certain that Plečnik saw the bull as a characteristic beast of Minoan culture. In the spring of 1927 he had sent Rothmayer a postcard from Athens showing a sculpture of a bull from the suburb of Kerameikos, and written: 'Prague castle keeps faith with the Acropolis'.[428] The sculptures here are very similar to those on the postcard. It is evident from sketches that have survived that Plečnik wanted to cover the bodies of the animals with double circles (fig. 151), as he had seen on fragments of panthers dating from the 6th century B.C. in the museum on the Acropolis.[429] This ornamentation is also to be found right beside the canopy, on the horse of the equestrian statue of St George, and this example will show how careful one has to be in imputing what look like motifs from folklore to Plečnik, as they almost always prove to be part of the Classical Antique repertoire. He himself contributed much to the double meaning of his symbols; he liked to identify Czech legends with Antiquity, regarding both as the elementary expression of the human soul.

THE PLEČNIK HALL

In May 1927 Plečnik took his students to Dalmatia and Greece. In his major work in the parts of the castle accessible to public, the problem of the transition from the First to the Second Courtyards, north of Matthias Gate, was still unresolved, as was the access to the Spanish Hall, which needed to be restored concurrently. It is not surprising that he

wanted to make careful preparations for his work of designing both these tasks as the general public were still watching his interventions on the Castle with great distrust.

In the first plans for the hall Plečnik oriented strongly to the existing buildings, but he soon realized that only a fundamental change could achieve the desired effect. He did not hesitate to remove the inside walls and ceilings in the part of the castle north of Matthias Gate, transforming the space thus gained into a solemn entrance to the staircase that was to lead up to the Spanish Hall.

He compensated for the irregularity of the existing window axes by placing rows of columns before them inside the hall (1927–30) (fig. 152). The semi-circular steps, the portal, the balcony and the column in front of the round window are very definitely facade elements and they give the interior the grandeur of a Greek temple. By arranging his columns in rows one above the other Plečnik also recalled the Baroque, while the regular intervals between the columns provide the uniformity required in a great hall. His visit to Athens and Delphi had filled him with enthusiasm for the mature Classical period, and this was probably another reason why the two lower rows of columns have Doric capitals. Because it would be difficult to clean or whitewash such a high ceiling he covered it entirely with riveted copper plates.[430] This method of covering a large area is derived from Semper's tubular principle and it also takes the whole room back into an archaic time.[431] Plečnik avoided any difficult direct contact between the columns and the metal by using capitals with Ionic volutes for the top row; they are like rolls of textile fitted between the abacus and the echinus. In view of the intention to glaze Matthias Gate and create a new main entrance, the south door into what came to be known as the Plečnik Hall ceased to be of importance, and the architect contented himself with a small wrought iron door, after his desire to have the leaves cast in bronze like those on the Pantheon proved too complicated and costly.[432]

THE BASTION GARDEN

The Bastion Garden (zahrada Na baště) is a component to Plečnik's idea to have a walking path surrounding the Castle. The plans for the garden were made in 1927 but only implemented five years later. It was to create a transition between the First Courtyard and the representative courtyard on the one hand or the Deer Moat on the other, which lies north of the Castle and was then difficult to access. No further archaeological finds of any significance were to be expected in this part of the Castle, and the old arsenal, that had been

149. Steps to the Third Courtyard, 1929–31, contemporary photograph

150. Plečnik on the Acropolis, 1927

151. Study for the bulls bearing the baldachin in the Third Courtyard, 1928-9

situated on the southern portion of the garden, had already been partially removed in the mid-eighteenth century and incorporated in the middle section. A hundred years later a large part of the area beside the Spanish Hall had been made into a rather modest English park, similar to the southern gardens, so that the entire area was divided into the garden position on a higher level and a smaller – fourth – courtyard to the south; the two were separated by a masonry wall. Plečnik first had the courtyard cleaned and covered with gravel between strips of granite (fig. 153). However, the pattern here is not neutral, as in the central Third Court-yard, but follows the direction of the path which is already indicated by the position of the slabs in the first courtyard. The access to the garden area was enabled by a circular staircase in the middle, similar to that designed by Bramante for the Belvedere Court in the Vatican, and later also by Loos for the Villa Karma on Lake Geneva. Such a solution made it possible to focus several of the accesses to the courtyard and redirect them towards the Deer Moat in the north.

On the upper, sanded part Plečnik had several rows of cypress trees planted, no doubt to recall the classical south-ern Mediterranean. The gradual transition from the stone paving to the green of the castle moat is indicated by a stretch of lawn, edged with granite, before the entrance to the Spanish Hall. With its irregular stone slabs and bushes it recalls traditional Japanese gardens. Plečnik repeated this idea at almost the same time in the garden of the Villa Prelovšek in Ljubljana. The remains of the small watch-tower dating from the time of Přemysl Ottokar II, which were only discovered during the work under the entrance to the hall, were more of a hindrance than a help to a consistent realization of the design for the garden.[433] Plečnik concealed them under a wooden pergola with climbing plants. The 'Japanese' garden is simply a prelude to the green area that extends behind the Bastion Garden balustrade. Basically the theme is a continuous transition from the urban into open green nature, and Plečnik used it at the same time, in a slightly altered form, with the sand path in the Tivoli Park in Ljubljana (see fig. 302).

Two paths leading in different directions follow the symmetry of the lawn. One corresponds to the ramp leading up to the Spanish Hall and dating from the nineteenth century. Plečnik greatly shortened the start of the ramp, and extended it symmetrically on the other side of the en-trance portal. The short, steep ramp gives the impression of a Venetian bridge which has its logical continuation in what is known as the Plečnik Bridge down to the Gunpowder Bridge. The second sand path leads to a roughly worked flight of stone steps to the Deer Moat. These winding steps

152. The 'Plečnik Hall' between the First and Second Courtyards, 1927–30, contemporary photograph

look very archaic in comparison with the steps leading to the Plečnik Bridge which is opposite, and indeed they are a purely Minoan invention, so they do act as a transition to a natural park. In order to link the garden with the Gunpowder Bridge, thus continuing the walking path, Plečnik had to extend the garden northwards and provide walled arches as supports. Originally he wanted unplastered arcades on columns, but he changed this when the foundation work proved too difficult.

Of interest is the relation between the ceramic vases in the Tuscan manner on the granite wall beside the circular staircase and their metamorphoses in stone at the end of the garden. Plečnik only later used these as a balustrade.

Plečnik was also concerned with the area north of the Deer Moat, but with the exception of the viewing terrace around a big lime-tree (1922–4) he left no major traces there. He had the earth, removed from archaeological excavations in the Third Courtyard, heaped by the Deer Moat to create a walking path, leading across the Gunpowder Bridge, and continuing along the edge of the so-called Royal Garden to the Renaissance Queen Anna Palace. From this path, there would be a beautiful panoramic view of the Castle and St Vitus' cathedral.[434] It was partially realized only long after Plečnik had left Prague for good. Another the Plečnik's ideas was to rebuild the Riding School north of the Gunpowder Bridge and change it into a library for the President (1931). Despite the fact that the project had already been approved, the plan was not realized because of finanacial and legal difficulties.

LÁNY

Parallel to the adaptation of Prague Castle, work on the castle at Lány was also going on. This castle was bought in 1920 by the presidential office from the family Fürstenberg, to serve as a summer residence for Masaryk and his family. The edifice was rebuilt at the end of the previous century in the neo-Baroque style, but its condition was very poor when the Hapsburg monarchy came to its end in 1918. Plečnik first started to renovate the President's working rooms (1921). He furnished the library with simple shelves made of soft wood, and for Masaryk's study he made, among other things, a round table inlaid with the motif of three lightning bolts which symbolize, as mentioned before, the Slovakian stanza of the then anthem. On the walls of the dining room, immediately below the ceiling, he fastened a richly profiled stucco cornice, and he furnished the place with old furniture brought over from Prague Castle. The interiors are mostly of the Empire style.

Because the works at Lány were relatively small-scale interventions, mainly the rearrangement of the existing inventory, the interiors of Masaryk's summer residence do not reach the quality of Plečnik's interventions in the castle at Prague. Besides, the purpose of individual rooms was often changed. On the occasion of one such a rearrangement, Plečnik had a room on the second floor painted with a geometric pattern, after the model of ancient Roman fashion, which he later reused on his farewell chapels at the Ljubljana cemetery Žale.

Plečnik's interventions in the castle park were more radical. When the village waterworks were constructed after World War I, there was a chance to arrange fountains. In 1923 Plečnik placed one in front of the entrance to the park, opposite his already mentioned memorial to the victims of the war. He had the earth, collected while channels were being dug for water pipes, heaped in front of the southern castle façade thus creating a level ground from which a view was opened into the English section of the park. He had this ground planted with grass plots arranged in a geometric pattern. He spanned the brook that meanders below it, flowing into the pond, with several bridges with massive stone fences. To enable the villagers to attend the services in the castle chapel, in 1923 he opened a new gate in the park wall between the chapel and the castle. The part of the wall by the pond was so ruined that it had to be replaced. So in 1926 Plečnik designed a new one of 200 metres in length, composed of visible brick (figs 108, 154). He made it look more frail by including windows and decorating it with stone vases. Later on he designed several brickwork walls in Ljubljana in a similar way (the stadium of the gym association 'Orel'; the garden by the parish house at St Peter's; the summer athletics grounds; the Teutonic Order monastery). At Lány he placed five granite columns into the wall by the pond; their state-forming symbolism has already been mentioned. From bronze lion heads, made by the sculptor D. Pešan, streams of water pour down into a stone basin from where they drain off into the pond. Because the construction of the brick wall was expensive, it lasted until 1930. The presidential office also invited Plečnik to arrange the castle outbuildings; so, for example, he designed an excellent timber hen-house, an apiary, and the like. He also designed several more facilities for Lány which, however, were not realized (a swimming-pool, a pavilion on the isle in the middle of the pond).

VIALE

As soon as he began to work on Prague Castle Plečnik also had to consider its surroundings since, as we have said, the

153. The Rampart Garden, 1929–32, contemporary photograph

President wanted a closer link between his new residence and the old part of Prague. Apart from his diploma work, which was still entirely theoretical, and a few unrealized experiments for Ljubljana, Plečnik had until then no experience at all in town planning.

Between 1920[435] and 1922[436] he devised a number of ways of reaching the castle more easily from St Wenceslas Square, either over a new diagonal bridge, or across Mánes Bridge, which would be widened. He also wanted to restore the historical Coronation Way taken by the Czech kings, which had once led across Charles Bridge and the Mala Strana; however, under the impact of the recurring competitions for the redevelopment of the large area of Letná Plateau, east of the narrower castle area, he realized that the solution to this would have to determine the new access routes. It became increasingly clear to him how necessary a broad avenue

north of the castle was. Alice called a serpentine, intended to join the avenue, a 'viale', on the Italian model. Plečnik recognized that this whole communication was essential if the presidential seat was to function properly. The avenue was to be free of tram lines and used for state occasions. Otherwise Plečnik wanted to leave the Castle, as far as possible, in its 'splendid isolation'.

Inevitably, this idea led to conflict with the State Commission for the Regulation of the Capital City of Prague and its environs, whose members approached the problem from quite a different angle. As Masaryk supported Plečnik, the members of the commission could not simply bypass him, although they were not able to finish the communication network around the Castle. Plečnik saw the greatest problem in the road links with the suburb of Dejvice in the north, which Antonín Engel was rebuilding and extending.

154. The fountain in the wall of the park at Lány, 1929/30, contemporary photograph

Engel wanted the north-south link with the Old City to run across the new Deer Moat Bridge, right beside the Castle, while Plečnik resolutely opposed this idea, which in his view was most unfortunate. On the other hand, the Regulation Commission was not satisfied with Plečnik's idea for an avenue which would follow the old fortifications in a straight line and end on the square. For the latter, the President's daughter was willing to donate her own plot of land where Plečnik could have built a structure similar to the Roman Pantheon to house Masaryk's Academy of Labour. However, the idea never progressed beyond rough sketches. It was argued that the earth work for such an avenue would be very costly, and that it could hardly be satisfactory, owing to its extreme length. The world slump actually gave Plečnik rather more grounds for hope in this connection, as the funds made available in Ljubljana to help the unemployed enabled him to carry out some regulatory work which was similar, although not nearly so extensive. He was convinced that the only proper access to the castle was through the

Klárov district south-east from it, not least in order to keep the supply route separate from the official access in the north. Hence he worked out a number of variants for this. As in Ljubljana, he proposed a panorama way, which would lead past the steep Baroque gardens to the eastern entrance to the castle. Instead of the bridge proposed by Engel, which would have affected the castle at its most vulnerable point, he proposed a new bridge in the lower Deer Moat near the Queen Anna Palace.

Plečnik nurtured his plans for a long time, but he never had the courage to make definitive drawings of them, although the Castle administration repeatedly requested him to do so. Not until early 1927 was he ready. Almost at the same time Engel completed his plan for Klárov, and Plečnik thought it was a disaster. As there was no room for compromise, Plečnik published what he thought was the proper solution for the Castle the following year (fig. 155). A new element in his plan was the road to link the Smichov district along the Vltava with Klárov, and rise from there in a broad sweep to the Castle and the avenue behind. However, the Regulation Commission dismissed the idea as utopian, as it failed to resolve the problem of the differences in height and would have involved demolishing a number of old houses.

Although the question of the general access remained unresolved, the congestion on Chotek Street east of the lower Deer Moat made a speedy decision essential. In reaction to the proposal from the Regulation Commission in 1930 to widen the existing road, Plečnik sent a sketch to Prague showing that the difference in height could be overcome by curving the road. The critical intersection was resolved in this plan in a similar way to the 1928 project, where the access route was to pass under the arches of Charles Bridge.

Plečnik's last major project for Prague was the regulation of the environs of the castle in 1934. It was also the synthesis of many years of work. This time he decided to take the road up a gentler slope, behind the Straka Academy, and he wanted to have the access to Klárov Street for pedestrians only. Chotek Street was left out again, and instead a huge Smetana concert hall planned. The avenue north of the Castle remained the backbone of Plečnik's composition, and it was to be 40 metres wide. This time it was also to end in the west in a square but on the opposite side be integrated in the road network of Letná plateau. The Castle was to be reached from the north through the triumphal arch before the proposed new Riding School Square, from where the double Gunpowder Bridge was to lead to the Second Castle Courtyard, or directly to the cathedral. Plečnik also proposed two large pools, one near the Queen Anna Palace

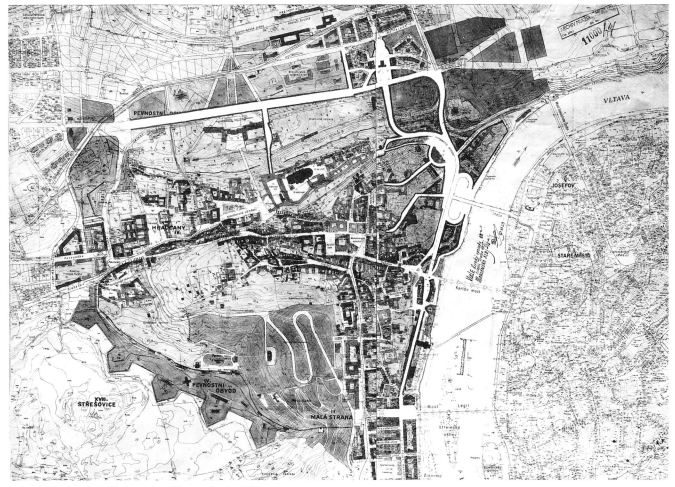

155. Project to regulate the environs of Prague Castle, 1928

and the second in front of the Riding School. He also wanted a pool in the upper Deer Moat. The new residence for the head of state, the White House, was to stand north of the Riding School where the pheasantry had once stood.

When the project was published it aroused almost unanimous public opposition, which developed into a kind of witchhunt against Plečnik. This time not even Masaryk's support could help him, and the campaign reached its height with a petition from 245 women 'To save the castle from interference by a foreigner who is ruthlessly destroying Bohemian monuments'.[437] In 1935 Plečnik was again opposed by some of his former students over the issue of regulating the Square of the Virgin Mary in Ljubljana. On 26 November 1934 the architect officially ended his residence in Prague, and he never visited Bohemia again.

Officially, he continued to keep the title of Castle Architect for another year,[438] but after Masaryk resigned circumstances greatly changed, although the new President Beneš assured him that he intended to continue the regulatory work as his predecessor had wished. Plečnik replied to Beneš' invitation to continue to work on the conversion of the Castle in these words: 'A man needs to be sensitive to the voice and hints of Providence, and always keep an ear open. I have heard her voice and taken the hint – you no longer need expect me.'[439] In 1936 Janák took Plečnik's place. So again Rothmayer had the unenviable task of playing second fiddle. Despite differences of opinion with Janák he remained faithful to his former teacher, and he completed the conversion of the Theresian wing of the Castle as Plečnik would have wished, continued the construction of the panoramic path on the northern ride of the Deer Moat, and built the monumental stairway before the Spanish Hall.

5 PROFESSORSHIP IN LJUBLJANA

Plečnik's position as professor in Ljubljana was not fully comparable with that in Prague, although his teaching methods did not vary greatly. Conditions in Plečnik's home town were extremely provincial. The new university had neither the premises for a technical faculty nor sufficient funds for a new building, and as soon as his appointment as professor was finalized at the end of 1920, Plečnik found himself confronted with the need to design a modest building in Aškerc Street. It was ready for use by the autumn of 1921. Although it was only intended as a provisional arrangement, he dynamized the mass of the building by making two bends in it and laid out a small park before the entrance, with a row of poplar trees creating a diaphanous veil in front of the recessed half of the facade. A cornice separating the ground floor from the first is a rudimentary indication of the theme of the building's double 'skin' facade cladding.

As Plečnik was also asked to build up the library, he set about buying a number of standard works of art history, periodicals and reference books in Prague, works he was familiar with from Wagner's office or the College of Arts and Crafts. Besides Viollet-le-Duc, who was almost obligatory, his list also contained Letarouilly's collection of Roman Renaissance monuments. This had been an indispensable aid for Semper, as it was later for Wagner too.[440] As most of the works could only be obtained secondhand, he asked Strajnić, who was then in Paris, to help him in his search.

Very few of the prospective architectural students had a clear idea of their future profession, and even less of their professor. While awaiting his arrival they had eagerly discussed the modern currents in art, imagining that he would immediately confront them with the things they found in periodicals. However, no one seemed too put out when this did not prove to be the case, for Masaryk's esteem secured Plečnik a special position in his home town as well. His striking, ascetic appearance and the strict principles to which he lived had a charismatic effect on his students. They began to believe dogmatically that his pictorial sense was unerring, and they imitated not only his handwriting but even his manner of speaking and his gait. Some actually grew a beard and cut it in the same way as his, they wore dark clothes and his typical shapeless hat with the broad brim. Nevertheless, Plečnik remained a mystery to them. He could win over his students with kindness and kindle great enthusiasm in them for their work. He always quietly rewarded their efforts at drawing for his projects with money, and he helped the most gifted to find work when they had qualified. In spite of this, he would have his way when they were too carried away with enthusiasm. On one such occasion he said: 'As far as the teaching is concerned, let it be understood that I am the only one who teaches here.'[441]

Plečnik could be so cutting that some of the students began to doubt the objectives of his School. But as there were always more applicants than the relatively small rooms could take, he had no difficulty in inducing the students to follow his own example and use the drawing room every day, regardless of the examination requirements of their other subjects. Those who did not, more or less voluntarily excluded themselves, and lost their right to a drawing table, as he took their drawing boards outside the room and left them by the door.

Plečnik tried to teach his students that architecture is the supreme form of art. It was his aim to prepare them for a selfless existence, dedicated to art, and this was very far from their idea of a carefree bohemian life. As a teacher, Plečnik showed much understanding for young people, and he would often comment that he had been young and full of high spirits himself; but he could say from his own experience: 'First one must suppress nature and then she will serve you loyally'.[442] Instead of expressive modern forms, he began by teaching the students to design objects of applied arts, signposts, monuments, dolls houses and so on, placing most emphasis on the development of the decorative and insisting on extremely pedantic, correctly shaded drawing.

For Plečnik the art of graphic expression was the basis of the architect's profession. He himself was a master at sketching in different scales, and he often illustrated his ideas with what is known as the 'cavalier's perspective'. When the shading needed to be more elaborate and in colour he helped the students with examples of work from the École des Beaux Arts, and this shows how much the Viennese manner of architectural drawing, as adopted and transferred to Ljubljana, owed to the French tradition. The particular feature of Plečnik's pictorial expression was a rather nervous but always controlled line, and the students diligently imitated this, convinced that it was an invention of their master. In the exercises on Antiquity Plečnik based his teaching mainly on Vitruvius and Vignola. His student Lenarčič says that he would explain the profiles and proportions in an exaggerated way, using caricature, to make the students aware of mistakes they could not see themselves. On such occasions he would say that architecture was entirely a matter of feeling, and no canon could help. Plečnik was frequently dissatisfied with his students' work. His habit of reaching for a pencil himself and then letting the

156. The classroom in the School of Architecture at Ljubljana Technical University, contemporary photograph

157. Plečnik's students around 1925: Vinko Glanz, Boris Kobe, Miroslav Oražem, Janko Valentinčič, Marjan Mušič, Emil Navinšek

157

student carry out his ideas made many of them realize that he had imagined architectural studies quite differently. Their biggest disappointment came at the end of the academic year, when Plečnik announced that he expected to see his students in the drawing room during the vacation as well. But in this way he trained them to be diligent draughtsmen, and they were eager to earn his praise.[443]

In order to bind his students even more closely to their work, Plečnik founded a club, soon after he arrived, and as a tribute to one of Semper's basic moral categories he named it the 'Hearth of Academic Architects' (Ognjišče arhitektov akademikov).[444] The club adopted Semper's belief that public taste must be educated, adapting this to their native tradition. Plečnik's efforts to popularize architecture with excursions, competitions, school publications and lectures were almost a literal interpretation of Semper's words of 1851: 'Here, of course, example and practical instruction are the essentials, oral teaching is secondary. Hence, above all we need *collections* and *studios*, possibly united around a hearth or centre, where the prizes for the competitions between the artists can be presented and the art judged by the people.'[445]

The publications of the Hearth club that have survived show with what respect the first generation of Slovenian architecture students noted every word spoken by their professor and coped with his often contradictory aphorisms. The Saturday discussions in the drawing room were almost ritualistic. As with Wagner and Loos, formal questions were discussed, and Plečnik would often say that the architect 'has to stick his nose into everything'.[446]

Plečnik was convinced that he had to start at the very beginning, that is, with Antiquity, if he was to liberate his people of their dependence on Romanesque and Germanic culture. 'There is nothing greater than Classical form and proportion, and you will not go further than that either', he would say to his students, adding: 'You will work differently, as you will have no choice. It is impossible to work like the classics; but your work will never be finer or better.'[447] In the lectures on architectural history for the students in the first two terms he discussed the art of ancient people, devoting special attention to the Romans, whose tradition was still, in his view, 'in the bones and the spirit' of the Slovenians.[448] This historical approach, which did not, in fact, come very naturally to him, shifted his attention, in contrast to his time in Prague, from the genesis of form to form itself. So the Slovenian students had no access to their teacher's basic formal grammar, which would have served as a support.

Plečnik initially gave his lectures mainly in order to avoid accusations from his colleagues that he was neglecting his teaching duties. However, he soon ceased to do so and instead introduced studio work in the tradition of the Viennese masterclasses. He discussed his views on aesthetics with his students, often using illustrations in books on art history, and the students listened with amazement to his comment that Michelangelo's *Moses* was the supreme achievement of sculpture, while the figure of the slave, which was also intended for the tomb of Pope Julius II, could not be regarded as art.[449] With their ignorance of the visual arts they had no choice but to accept this and similar judgements and make them their own.

The first publication of students' work appeared in the spring of 1923.[450] It is still full of hesitant confrontation with the past, as is also evident from Plečnik's encouraging foreword. Two years later the members of the Hearth club produced a more extensive publication.[451] The stylistic disorientation is very evident, and there is no lack of attempts to approximate Plečnik's work in Prague. Dušan Grabrijan, for example, varies the motif of the stone vase at the entrance to the Paradise Garden, which was then a current issue. His diploma work and that of his colleague France Tomažič primarily reflects Plečnik's ideas on the Tivoli Park and the castle in Ljubljana, two central issues which were to occupy their teacher all his life.

With the school publications of 1925 the period in which Plečnik's attention was mainly absorbed by Prague came to an end. Moreover, the doors were slowly beginning to open for him in Ljubljana as well. As a consequence, his students could be occupied on specific projects. This cooled the fire of the Hearth a little, and their contact with the teacher lost some of its spontaneity. In addition, in 1924 the atmosphere in the school had been poisoned somewhat by Vurnik's conflict with Plečnik. Vurnik had been court architect to the bishopric of Ljubljana but was well aware that if it came to open competition with Plečnik he would lose. Hence, a conflict with Plečnik's brother Janez over the establishment of the Anatomical Institute in Ljubljana came at an apposite moment for him. The outcome was the establishment of a parallel school of architecture with Vurnik as director. The students took sides in the personal dispute, and Plečnik took the opportunity to pass on to Vurnik all the students who seemed to him insufficiently talented, or who were not prepared to accede to his demands.

As early as 1915 Plečnik had helped his brother Andrej buy a single-storey house behind the church in the suburb of Trnovo in Ljubljana. The two were hoping that if they could offer their sister a home, she would be able to escape her unhappy marriage. However, Andrej was only able to enjoy his long-desired return from Idirija for a short time; two years after the end of the First World War a disciplinary procedure was opened against him at the Modern School in Ljubljana, because of his conflict with one of the pupils,[452] and he had to move to Kočevje, where he had commenced his professional career. From there he went as a priest to the convent in Repnje near Ljubljana, where he remained until his death. So Plečnik's hopes of seeing the family united were thwarted. Fearing that someone might prevent him, which was very possible with the legal situation at the time, he began to build an extension in his brother's absence, regardless of their uncertain financial situation. However, a brief period of living with his brother Janez had shown him again how different their temperaments were. Nor did he seem to have any luck with his housekeepers, who changed frequently.

The narrow-minded, provincial atmosphere in the small town added to Plečnik's unease. No one was willing to believe that he had not made a fortune in Prague. He was able to find a refuge of sorts in the outskirts of Ljubljana, which had retained their rural character. In his isolation he complained to his brother: 'My predecessor in Prague, Professor Ohmann, is said to have exclaimed that he would rather be a porter in Vienna than a professor in Prague'. He went on:

> Now that everything is decided, I am quite calm. My only regret is that I do not have a fifth of the millions of Czech crowns I am supposed to have, for I wish I could build in a really beautiful place – a great vaulted hall – full of exotic flowers. Senseless to wait, empty dreams – I shall continue to live among the suffocating bourgeoisie, running back and forth between small houses – until death sticks out a foot and trips me up.[453]

Plečnik did not find it easy to escape from the envy and malice around him, and still uphold the high moral tenets of his school.

The Kingdom of the Serbs, Croats and Slovenians – as the new Balkan state was called at first – had been established after World War I by uniting the Slovenians and the Croats, who had previously been ruled by the Austro-Hungarian monarchy, to the Serbian kingdom under the rule of the Karadjordjević dynasty. Within this, the Serbs played the leading political role. Unwelcome initiatives repeatedly came from the state authorities in Belgrade. Over the technical faculty in Ljubljana, the Damocles sword of university reform hung permanently, with Belgrade threatening to close some of the Slovenian faculties. Another depressing development was the introduction of fees for the acquisition of the licentiateship of architecture. In this context Plečnik wrote to his brother in April 1925:

158. Plečnik outside his house, 1926

I told the Dean's office – that, if I work, I work without a fee – I work from my duty as a teacher, in order not to stagnate. That I work like a mathematician – a philosopher – a physicist – at my problems, driven by inner compulsion. It is an impulse like that which makes a flower grow. But if this kind of work and donation is not permitted I am ready to work just for my own portfolio in future – and occasionally for foreign commissions.[454]

At the start of his teaching work in Ljubljana Plečnik was probably surprised himself to see how willingly the students followed him, as the atmosphere in Prague had been totally different. He waited for the moment when avantgarde ideas would arrive and unsettle his students, here, too; however, only sporadic information on trends in Europe reached Ljubljana. The French Cultural Institute, which had been set up when the Balkan kingdom was pro-French, certainly played a part in transmitting these ideas. Only Plečnik's pupil and assistant France Tomažič was slightly better informed, but he did not venture to speak openly about modern architecture. Once he deliberately left a monograph on

159

Auguste Perret lying on the table, and was surprised to find an unmistakeable message from Plečnik in it: 'I can't do what Perret can do – but he can't do what I can do'. After this the naive Viennese saying was added, which the students regarded as evidence of Plečnik's failure as a teacher: 'No drop-outs here – and this applies to everyone – so shut up and continue to serve'.[455]

In the early 1920s Perret personified modern architecture for Ljubljana, soon to be followed by Le Corbusier. Plečnik respected Perret as an excellent engineer, and he actually sent him some of his publications; in Le Corbusier, however, he saw primarily a Protestant and an engineer responding to social needs. Although neither Perret nor Le Corbusier could be a 'danger' to his art, he saw the excursion organized by Hearth - to the International Exhibition of Modern Decorative and Industrial Arts in Paris in the summer of 1925 as a particular test.[456] At the last moment he drew back and let the students go without him.

They came back unsettled by the experience, which for almost all of them was their first contact with the 'big wide world'. The classical monuments of northern Italy, the busy life of the great city, Le Corbusier, Melnikov and the play of the fountains on the exhibition grounds illuminated in rainbow colours left lasting impressions on his students, and it took them some time to digest it all. Then there was quiet in the school for a few years, although Plečnik could never entirely eliminate the doubts to his approach and method. But he was content with the assurance from his assistant that a 'new gospel' had not become established, and the architecture shown in the exhibition had already been fully illustrated in the architectural periodicals.[457] The feeling that art was at a fateful turning point pushed him even more into the role of a passive observer, and this was certainly one of his reasons for declining the official invitation from Belgrade to visit the Paris Exhibition and compile a report on it. A year before he had been invited to participate in a restricted competition for the pavilion of the Kingdom of Serbs, Croats and Slovenians in Paris, but he handed the offer on to Vurnik. Had time not been so short, Plečnik would have erected a prefabricated oak structure on a marble stereobate.[458] Vurnik made use of Plečnik's dislike of the modern movement to absorb the latest German influence into his school, although he himself had studied in Vienna, indeed under Wagner for a short time, and initially at least his artistic aims did not differ greatly from those of his rival.

Plečnik never enjoyed good relations with the Yugoslav King Alexander I, who was, as Masaryk had said, too much the soldier and too uncultured.[459] The king only learned of Plečnik in 1922 when he paid a state visit to Czechoslovakia. Then he tried to persuade him to take charge of his new residence and his villa in the Belgrade suburb of Dedinje, but the work had already progressed so far that Plečnik was not interested. The contact between them was more or less limited to a brief visit paid by Plečnik to Belgrade in April 1927, of which many anecdotes are related. They all show that the architect and the king did not get on well. 'I did actually enter the residence – and I was accommodated, of all places, in that hemicyclical building that I would have pulled down at the first opportunity. I spoke to the King on one single occasion – for a good five minutes – clearly I got thoroughly on his nerves,'[460] he wrote after his return to his colleague, the Serbian architect Nikola Dobrović, whom he knew from Prague.

Belgrade, however, made a strong impression on Plečnik, particularly in connection with Masaryk's accounts of the city and Serbian politicians. Dušan Sernec, the Minister of Building, came from Slovenia; he wanted Plečnik to handle the new parliament building and took him to the old Belgrade fortress, Kalemegdan.[461] Plečnik was so impressed by the position of the fortress, high above the junction of the Save and the Danube, that he proposed a new royal residence and the preservation of all the historical parts of the fortification walls. But as the government soon changed the plans were dropped. Plečnik only worked for the court in Slovenia, where he built a hunting lodge in Kamniška Bistrica in 1933/4.[462] Of the Villa Suvobor in Bled, intended as a gift to the king, only the supports above the lake had been completed when the king met his violent death, at the hands of Croatian nationalists in October 1934 while he was officially visiting Marseilles.

Plečnik expected more from the Church than from the secular rulers. Even before he started teaching in Ljubljana, in 1921, he tried to obtain contact with the Bishop of Ljubljana, Anton Bonaventura Jeglič, who was energetic but not particularly interested in the fine arts. In Vienna, Plečnik had once tried in vain to win over the court chaplain, Swoboda, to his ideas, and he did not meet with any real understanding on the part of the bishop for the idea of setting up a Christian Academy of the Fine Arts, either. He was encouraged by an offer from Canon Kimovec to rebuild the bombed pilgrimage church in Sveta gora north of Gorica, but the plans were never carried out, as Slovenia had to hand over a considerable part of this territory to Italy after the war. As early as 1919 Plečnik proposed converting some of the churches in Ljubljana when new parishes were being formed or existing ones enlarged, explaining to the bishop that the work could be done at relatively low cost.[463] In regard to the prospective changes in the urban design, for instance, he argued that the position of the old church of St Bartholomew (sv. Jernej) in the district of Šiška was better than the new site that was envisaged, which was on a road bearing heavy traffic. As he had proposed before World War I in his study for the enlargement of the church at Trsat, Plečnik wanted to keep the old church and add a priest's dwelling and a high bell-tower along the line of the building (figs 159–60), with a new building on the opposite side of the street, under the slope of the hill. Should this proposal prove too expensive, he put forward three other variants.

However, Plečnik was soon disappointed by the church authorities. He wrote: 'Ljubljana is full of affairs like this. They don't work here, they engage in politics, it's all intrigues and mudslinging. It is depressing, it drains your strength and empties your mind.'[464] Among the few cultured priests he initially esteemed Alojzij Merhar most highly; he is best known by the pseudonym Silvin Sardenko, under which he wrote poetry. Plečnik developed a warm and more lasting friendship with his neighbour in Trnovo, the priest and writer Fran Saleški Finžgar; he was a tough character, like an Upper Carniolan peasant, and proved a great support to Plečnik as he watched the daily disputes in the Slovenian Church destroying people's faith. As he could not engage the bishop's attention he sought allies among the brethren. The agile Jesuit Franc Tomc was perhaps most like the Prague chaplain Alexander Titl in the enthusiasm with which he realized Plečnik's plans. It was for Tomc that

Plečnik built a meditation centre (1923/4), and gradually fitted out the church of St Joseph in Ljubljana, which he would otherwise certainly not have touched, for its architecture was poor, in the historicist style.

When preparations started in Prague in 1922 for the construction of Plečnik's church in Vinohrady no one in Ljubljana envisaged a similar possibility arising there. Only the conservationist France Stele tried to involve Plečnik in every church project he learned of. This was how Plečnik came to be involved in the enlargement of the church in Laško in 1922 and one year later the parish church of St Magdalen in Maribor. In both cases it was apparent that the Slovenians were totally unprepared for his architectural reforms. As Plečnik was still preoccupied with Prague at this time, he left the Maribor project to his assistant Tomažič, after giving him instructions on the main features. The old church was of relatively short length and stood on an irregular site; even if the long side were opened and arched it could only have been linked functionally with the new building with difficulty, and so Plečnik decided to enclose part of it. He attempted to solve the question of the broken axis with a sequence of circular areas or a bent nave, which opened an interesting and dynamic view of the altar. Tomažič worked out four variants, but was finally dismissed by the Dean very abruptly.[465]

Plečnik tried to obtain at least a modest fee for his assistant, but soon had to give up, deeply hurt by such inhuman behaviour. In Vienna and Prague he could have reckoned on acknowledgement of his unconventional approach, but achieving the same recognition in the tradition-bound Slovenian environment seemed more like the labours of Sisyphus.

Pregled komplexa šišpuskega svetišča v approximativni obliki

159. Proposal for the enlargement of the church of St Bartholemew in Ljubljana, 1919

162

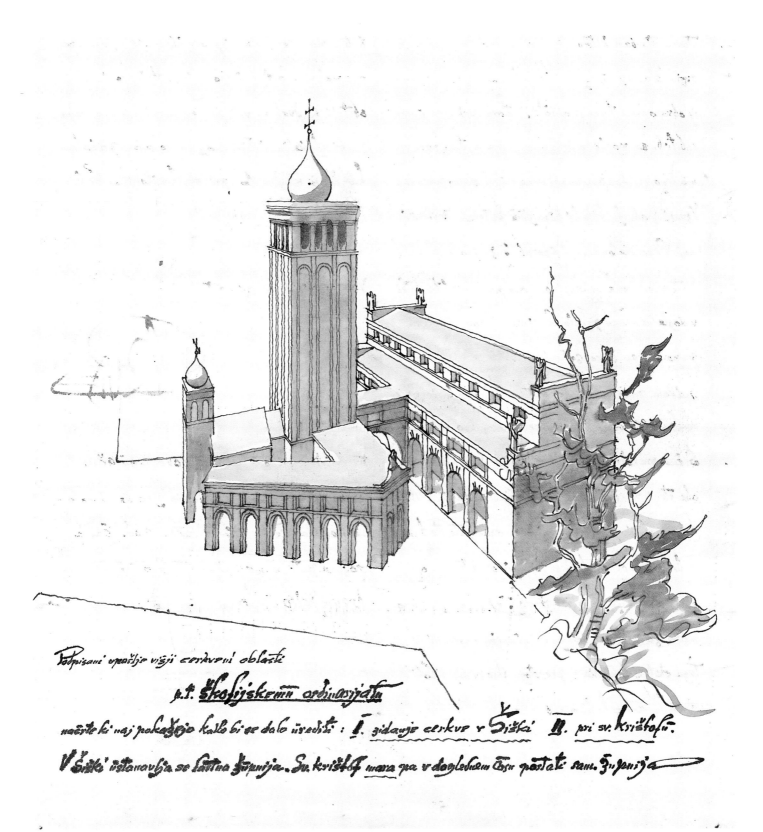

160. Proposal for the enlargement of the church of St Bartholemew in Ljubljana, 1919

161. The tower of the church of St Francis in Ljubljana, 1930/1

164

162. The church of St Francis in Ljubljana, 1925–7, interior to original designs by Plečnik not completed till the 1970s

163. The church of St Francis in Ljubljana, tabernacle on the altar to St Anthony, 1937

164. The church of St Francis in Ljubljana, the great chandelier, designed in 1939, executed in 1963

165

166

167

The church in Bogojina, 1925–7:
165. The rear facade
166. Columns in the interior
167. Wooden ceiling, 1950

168

168. The church in Bogojina 1925–7

169. The church of St Anthony in Belgrade, 1929–32, view to the main altar (fitted in the 1930s and 1950s)

170. The church of St Anthony in Belgrade, 1929–32, view to the entrance

171. The church of St Anthony in Belgrade, door to the sacristy

172

172. The church of St Anthony in Belgrade, 1929–32, upper gallery

173. The church of St Michael in Ljubljana Moor, 1937/8

174

174. The church of St Michael in Ljubljana Moor, presbytery, fitted in 1940

175. The church of St Michael in Ljubljana Moor, 1937/8, fitted in 1940, some parts in the 1950s

176

177

The church of St Michael in Ljubljana Moor:
176. The lights, 1940
177. The entrance to the choir gallery, 1950
178. The bell

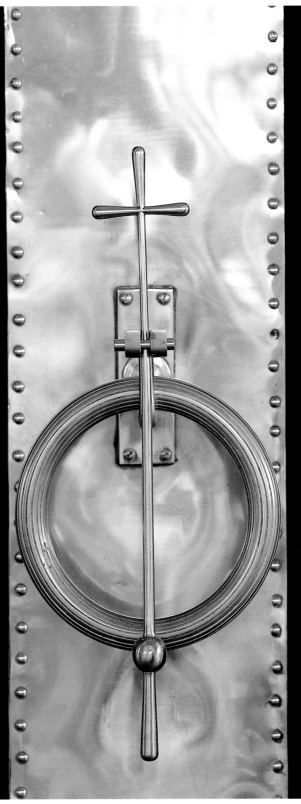

178

179. The Chamber of Trade, Industry and Commerce in Ljubljana, staircase, 1925–7

180. The Chamber of Trade, Industry and Commerce in Ljubljana, stairs, 1925–7

181. The Chamber of Trade, Industry and Commerce in Ljubljana, vestibule outside the conference hall, 1925–7

182

183

The Chamber of Trade, Industry and Commerce in Ljubljana:
182. Door handle on the ground floor
183. Detail of the stairs
184. Detail of the ceiling in the conference room

184

185. The Vzajemna Insurance Company offices in Ljubljana, 1928–30

182

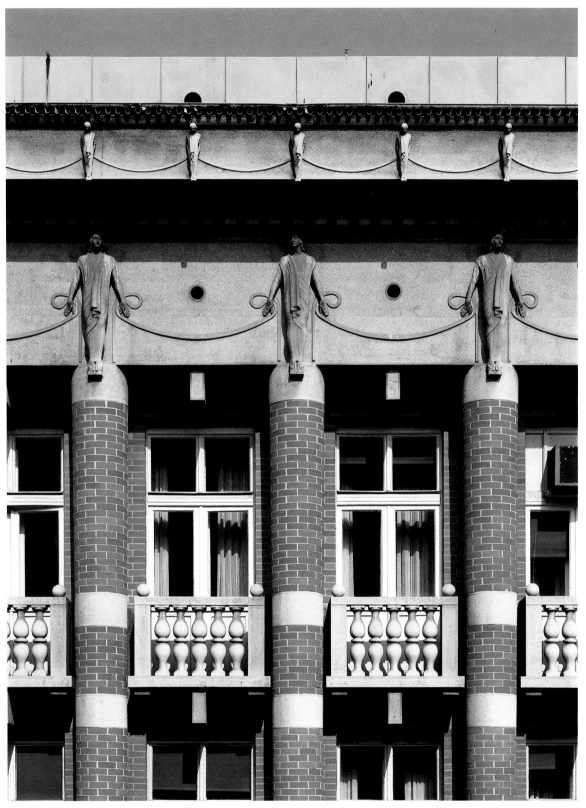

186. The Vzajemna Insurance Company offices in Ljubljana, 1928–30

187. The university library in Ljubljana, 1936–41

184

188. The university library in Ljubljana, 1936–41

189. The university library in Ljubljana, stairs, 1936–41

186

190. The university library in Ljubljana, stairs, 1936–41

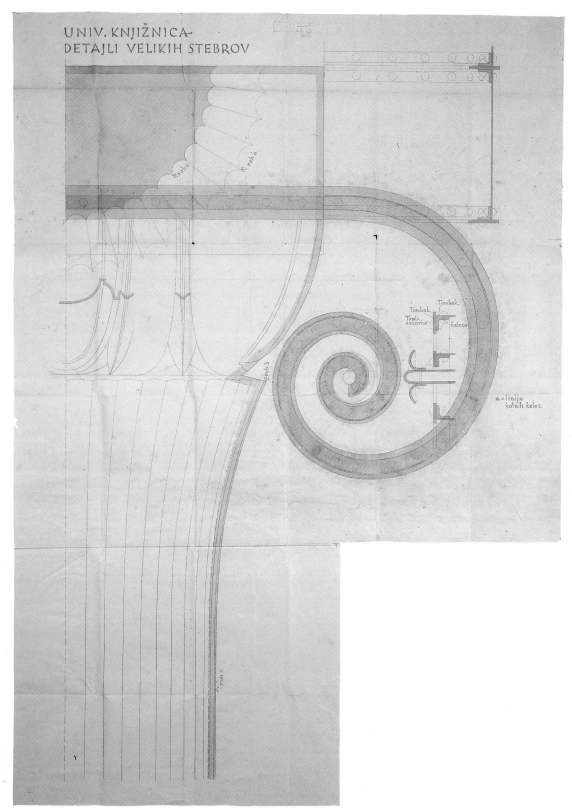

191. Capital before the reading room window, university library, Ljubljana, 1939 (drawn by Zdenek Sila)

188

192. University library, Ljubljana, light in the reading room, 1946/7

193. University library in Ljubljana, reading room, 1936–41, partly changed during renovation, 1946/7

194. University library in Ljubljana, reading room

195. University library in Ljubljana, entrance to the exhibition room, 1940/1

196. University library in Ljubljana, ceiling over the stairway

197. Perspective drawing of the 'Flat-Iron House', 1933

194

198. The 'Flat-Iron House' in Ljubljana, 1933/4

199. Conversion of the Prelovšek Villa in Ljubljana, 1931–3, salon

200. Conversion of the Prelovšek Villa in Ljubljana, 1931–3, library

201. The column of the Virgin Mary on St James's Square in Ljubljana, 1938

198

202. The Illyrian Provinces monument in Ljubljana, 1929

203. Candelabrum near the Philharmonic Society building in Ljubljana, 1932/3

204. Candelabrum on Cobblers Bridge in Ljubljana, 1931/2

205. The Three Bridges in Ljubljana, 1930/1

206. The market by the river Ljubljanica, 1940–2

207. The tobacconist's kiosk by the Three Bridges in Ljubljana, around 1934

208. The flower shop by Ljubljana market, 1941/2

209. The first design for the sluices on the river Ljubljanica, 1933 (drawn by Edvard Ravnikar)

210. The sluices on the river Ljubljanica, 1940–4

211. Entrance to Žale in Ljubljana, 1938/9

212. The main chapel with the catafalque, 1939/40

213. The entrance to Žale, 1938/9

214. The entrance to Žale

215. Žale, chapel of St Peter, 1939–40

216. Žale, chapel of St John, 1939/40

213

217. Žale, interior of the chapel of St Nicholas, 1939/40

218. The workshop building at Žale, 1939/40

215

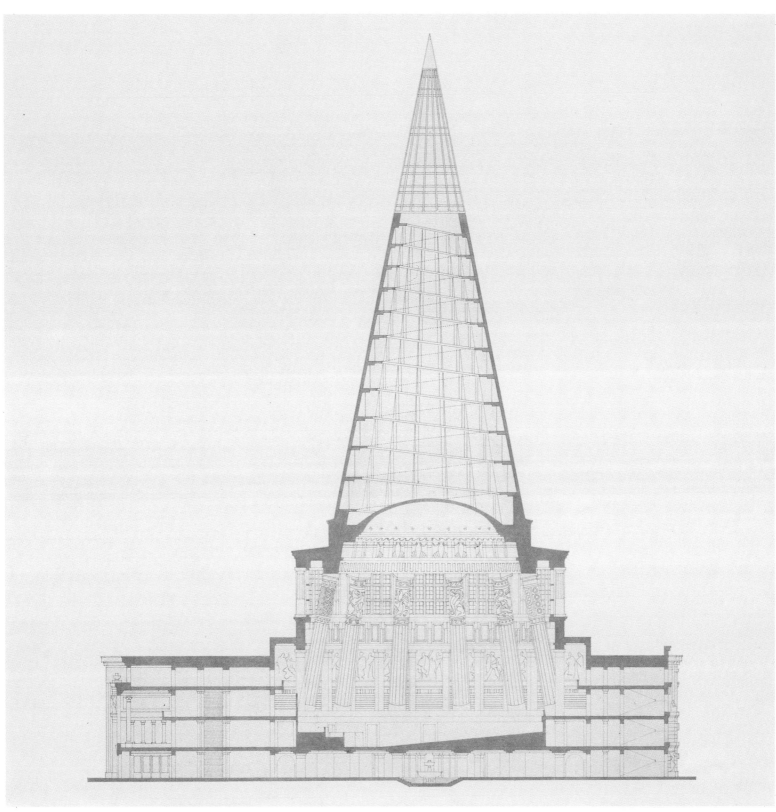

219. The Slovenian Parliament building, 1947

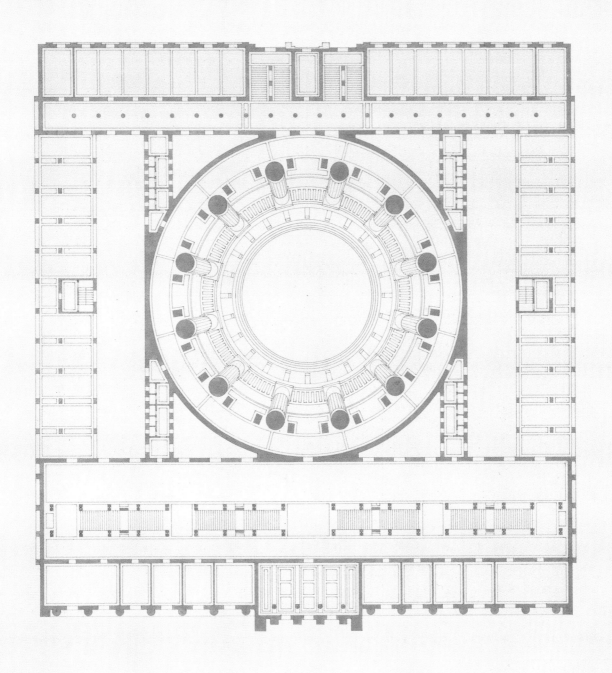

220. The Slovenian Parliament building, 1947

221. 'Devil's Court', in the former monastery of the Teutonic Knights in Ljubljana, 1953–6

218

THE CHURCH OF ST FRANCIS OF ASSISI

The new Franciscan church in the Šiška suburb of Ljubljana had been under discussion for some time.[466] The first plans were designed in 1914 by Anselm Werner, a Benedictine monk highly regarded in Carniola, but the First World War prevented their realization. The immediate reasons for building a new church was that the old provisional wooden church was in an extremely bad condition. Plečnik could offer the Franciscans a modification of his Prague project in Vinohrady, as the question of the position for this was still not resolved. This justifies a more detailed discussion of the Prague project, for the history of the design and construction of the church in Ljubljana will then be better understood.

As already mentioned, the competition for the second Catholic parish church in the Prague suburb of Vinohrady brought a number of interesting proposals. On 4 April 1919, immediately before the competition was announced, the Architects Society sent the building committee a letter of recommendation, signed by the leading Czech architects, suggesting that Plečnik should be directly commissioned to design the church.[467] It was too late to cancel the competition, but the committee later went straight to Plečnik, and by the end of 1922 he had produced sketches for a church with a free-standing Venetian bell-tower (fig. 226).[468] In comparison with the Church of the Holy Spirit in Vienna, which has only a main facade subdivided in the Neo-Classical manner, the Prague church would have resembled a Doric temple. If we recall that Plečnik was then in the middle of designing the castle gardens, was intensively studying antique ceramics in that connection and was also giving lectures in Ljubljana on the architecture of Antiquity, his proposal is hardly surprising. The secretary of the building committee who was responsible for the project, Alexander Titl, used Plečnik's words to explain to his parishioners the Neo-Classical forms: according to the architect, the church was to reflect modern collective sensibilities. But as the age had not yet found its own style, one had to choose between the Egyptian and the Greek, the only two original tectonic styles in Antiquity.[469] It hardly need be said that these assertions owe much to Wagner, and even more to Semper.

So in this design Plečnik moved away from early Christian models and turned to Classical Antiquity, and the Greek temple in particular. The most outstanding new feature is the ambulatory which goes right round the church, but is blocked in some places. It is doubled by a columned walk in the cella. Using a modular net of 2.5 metres – which he had been using ever since he began to work with columns

222. Making the artificial stone capitals for the church of St Francis, 1925

– Plečnik created a clear, symmetrical ground plan. He closed the ambulatory along the long sides with two lower ceilinged chapels leading into the sacristy and the area for the choir before the altar. Plečnik believed that the latter would suit the mentality of the musically gifted Czechs. The nave of the church has two major features, which also play a significant part in the church in Ljubljana as it was later built. As the presbytery is not spatially delimited, the altar is, so to speak, in the midst of the congregation. To ensure that it could be seen, Plečnik raised it in his plans by a few steps. The second feature is the colonnaded ambulatory, which was to serve for processions, for practising their devotion to the Stations of the Cross and for persons wishing to hear Mass but remain unseen. On the transverse axis the height of the building is carefully raised towards the centre, where it is raised again by a columned storey with a gallery. The design for the Prague church is based on the contrast between the different volumes of the building, held by a flat saddleback roof supported on columns. The columns on the facade were to be of bare brick, while the walls behind would be yellow plaster.

Unlike the Prague church, however, the church in Ljubljana would not be a monumental parish church in the middle of the city. For a long time the Franciscan monks did not know which site they would be able to acquire, and Plečnik must have found it hard to conceal his disappointment, when, instead of the majestic position on Šiška hill, they offered him an ugly site near the railway line. In the early stages he concerned himself with the project more out of interest, and only when he got to know some of the monks better did he take the commission seriously.

Although the Ljubljana project was more or less idealistic, and the need was for a rather smaller and less expensive church, Plečnik did not try simply to reduce his Prague version in scale, but adapted the plan to the *genius loci*. For him this was best represented in the monochrome severity of the baroque Ursuline church, which had Palladian overtones. In his mature years he regarded this most highly of all the Ljubljana churches. He attempted to achieve a similar spiritual concentration in Šiška, and he admitted openly to his students that he had borrowed the high base of the columns from the Ursuline church.[470]

However, it is less clear why he replaced the Doric columns in the Prague project with Tuscan. Could it be a reference to the imagined Etruscan heritage? Whatever the reason may have been, the columns had to be unfluted since they were to be in brick. As Plečnik did not have a very flattering opinion of contemporary Slovenian artists and feared that someone might change the character of the church, he did not provide any areas specifically for decoration. The extreme shortage of funds also affected the design. In view of the unfavourable climate with its long winters, Plečnik made the ceilings relatively low. This reduced the building costs and also made the building easier to heat; it would also make for better accoustics.

He first removed the entire external colonnade from the Prague design, retaining the core of the building but enlarging this slightly. He indicated the ecclesiastical character of the building simply with the portal before the main facade (fig. 223), making this the leitmotif of the exterior, which is in itself modest. He subdivided the long side with pilaster strips, repeating the triangular gable on the lower part of the bell-tower. To ensure that the portal, which was based on the square,[471] would stand out sufficiently from the broad facade he shortened it optically with darker vertical strips at the corners of the building. This also proved an original solution to the Palladian theme of the integration of one portal with a second. As the basic concept of the church was the hall, he retained the uniform height of the architrave, and actually lowered the central tympanon, including this in the triangular roof gable. The Venetian white is emphatically Baroque and stands out from the rest of the plaster, which is ochre-grey; so the use of colour also reflects Plečnik's endeavour to achieve a certain synthesis with the other ecclesiastical buildings in Ljubljana.

He made more important changes to the ground plan. The impressive long room with the colonnaded ambulatory was greatly shortened and widened with two extra columns, so giving it a transverse direction. Later he used the same idea to suggest a more rural character in the church of St Michael in Ljubljana Moor, which is to a certain extent a derivation of the church in Šiška. Immediately before building started, in the spring of 1925, he extended the design by 5 metres and again gave the room a square shape (fig. 224). He also raised the ambulatory around the main nave by three steps, so strengthening the impression that the altar is in the middle of the room (see fig. 162). In the first Prague project the side chapels had taken over the role of the crypt, but in Ljubljana the Winter Chapel, as it is called, behind the altar, was sufficient for this need. Its barrel vault may actually have influenced the changes to the ceiling of the crypt in Prague later.

Initially Plečnik particularly wanted a free-standing bell-tower, linked to the church by a passage. Eventually he placed the tower on the building, rising behind the altar. Although he had always been content with the Venetian campanile, in Ljubljana he immersed himself in the theme of the bell-tower on a square ground plan. He decided to make this lower, not least to save costs, and conclude it with a narrower tempietto and a pyramidal roof. However, during the building work he decided on a round bell-tower with a columned drum in two storeys. As on the plan for the church of St Bartholomew in Šiška he first wanted to crown this with a 'Slav' onion roof, but finally decided on a steep conical roof (see figs 159–60), and in the version as built (1930/1) this gives the building as a whole the suggestion of English Baroque. The round bell-tower was later to play an important part in the extension to the church in Bogojina (see fig. 165), and in using it in Šiška Plečnik was taking a new theme from Le Corbusier's 'promenade architecturale'. From then on the bell-towers were spatially the most dynamic elements in his ecclesiastical architecture, and in some cases they were actually an indirect acceptance of the avantgarde tendencies of his time. We find the initial stages of this in the two observation towers in his diploma work of 1898 (see fig. 21).

The question of the lighting is also resolved more simply in Ljubljana than in the Prague version. In Šiška the daylight enters only through the rectangular windows at the sides, and despite their high position these give an almost secular impression, although they are to be understood as

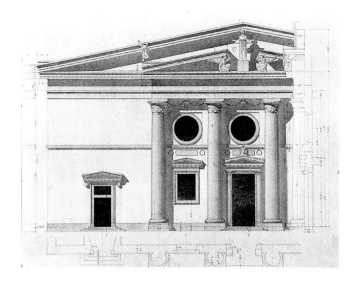

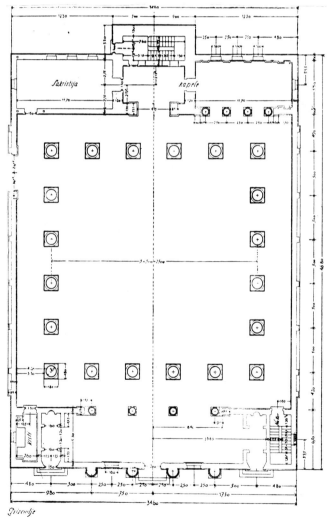

223–4. The facade and ground plan of the church of St Francis, 1925

the final stage of clerestory lighting. In analogy, however, one can hardly say that the orthogonal network of beams which forms the wooden ceiling is an imitation of the Classical coffered ceiling. But the early Christian spirit is evident in the concept, for we find an evocation of a Renaissance depiction of the lowered nave in the primitive St Peter's Basilica in Rome.

The artificial light, which creates a more intimate atmosphere, helps to soften the Neo-Classical severity of the interior. Plečnik inscribed the name of the donor on each candelabrum, and so included the parish in the interior decoration of the church. With the help of these donors he was able to create one of the most valuable collections of candelabra in modern Slovenian art. The electric light filters through the coloured glass and spreads over the metal lampshades, creating the rich fairytale atmosphere that was characteristic of the period of early Carniolan Baroque known for its 'golden altars'.

As in Prague, Plečnik intended to have plastered columns in the interior of the Franciscan church in Ljubljana. Under the watchful supervision of the young engineer Anton Suhadolc, however, they were so carefully executed that Plečnik decided to leave the bricks visible. The columns stand on mighty cubic concrete bases, behind which one can follow the service unobserved. The harmony of the white plaster and the warm red of the bricks is only interrupted by the fresco that was created by one of the Franciscan monks shortly after the church was completed.

The new church was officially consecrated at the beginning of October 1926, after some initial difficulties with the building enterprise. Owing to the shortage of funds, however, some of the work had not been finished by then. Right from the start, Plečnik had never hesitated to adopt emergency solutions, as when he replaced the rotten wooden floor with asphalt, placing one altar after the other on this profane ground. Holding in high esteem his colleagues in Prague, he first obtained Pešan's statue of the Virgin with Child for the space above the portal. Initially he clearly avoided native sculptors, with the exception of the precise stone masonry work of the renowned stonecutter Alojzij Vodnik, of Ljubljana.

The altars of St Theresa of the Child Jesus (1927) and the Virgin Mary of Sveta gora (1929) had great stone retables. While he skilfully combined the modest image of St Theresa with the altar, surrounding her with a restrained frame in reddish Hotavlje stone, he surrounded the more important Venetian Madonna from the pilgrimage church of Sveta gora that had been demolished with a very much richer frame in grey polished Podpeč stone. With reference to Semper's principle of cladding the correct framing of the

wooden sculpture in the marble retable was important. Plečnik monumentalized the statue of St Elizabeth by gilding it and only then laying it horizontally beneath the image of the Virgin Mary (see fig. 162), no doubt borrowing the idea from old Bohemian art. He actually retained the base, but added another in the shape of a cylindrical cushion at the head. Any other positioning of the two saints to whom the altar is dedicated would have destroyed the symmetry of the composition, or required a very much higher retable.

The counterpart to the altar to the Virgin Mary was the slightly later altar to St Antony, with its mighty concave background in Podpeč marble. The figure of the saint is in wood and gilt, with ivory face and hands, a combination taken from descriptions of the deities in Greek temples. It is by Božo Pengov, who later became Plečnik's constant associate, or, as he jokingly said, his 'home sculptor'. Most striking is the tabernacle, with the asymmetrical inlay of marble and coloured glass (see fig. 163); the influence of Bohemian craftsmanship of the time of Charles IV is not difficult to recognize here. For the main altar, which initially was provisionally fitted with older pieces from the Franciscan church in Ljubljana, Plečnik proposed a stone tabernacle with a pyramidal crown. In his design he attempted to go back to the origins of the liturgy, by, for example, indicating that the altar originated in a table. In Šiška he placed the thin white marble plate on a massive table in dark Podpeč marble (see fig. 162). In the tabernacle, too, he was anxious to retain some Biblical symbolism. So, for instance, in 1922 he designed a tabernacle covered with fabric in the form resembling a Jewish tent with the ark of the covenant for the church of Sts Peter and Paul at Vyšehrad in Prague.[472] Originally he had similar ideas for Šiška. He spoke of the slender pyramid, which he had taken from his urban design projects of the same period in Prague and Ljubljana, in a letter to his brother in the spring of 1927: 'The tabernacle will be about 5 metres high – to put it simply, it will be a monument – the centrepiece of the church. Behind are the columns with the lights: the four gospels – the net etc.'[473] In 1939 he drew a plan to complete the altar area. It contained a pulpit in the form of an early Christian reading desk, or ambo, to which a stone canopy on columns led.[474] He intended to make the background in the form of a triumphal arch with a balustrade and the figure of St Francis at the tip, but a new variant of this design was only realized after his death. There were other parts of the church in Šiška which Plečnik was not able to finish, like the Winter Chapel, the baptistery and the great candelabrum, which he had designed in 1939 (see fig. 164).

The design of the church of St Francis was so new for Slovenia, where all the buildings had been on traditional lines until the 1920s, that some of the monks could not refrain from biting remarks. The church authorities showed even less understanding. Josip Dostal, the bishop's secretary responsible for ecclesiastical art, actually induced the bishop to put a stop to the building work for a time. The church also met with a negative response from some of Plečnik's students. Dušan Grabrijan later tried to find reasons to justify his dislike of the columnar structure, which he regarded from the functional viewpoint as a mistake.[475] He called the subsequent attachment of the capitals to the columns, as they had been overlooked during the building work, ridiculous. In the early 1940s no one could see that Perret's church in Raincy and Plečnik's church in Ljubljana were only two variants of one and the same modern current.

THE CHURCH OF THE SACRED HEART OF THE LORD
IN VINOHRADY, PRAGUE

Plečnik could not understand how the district of Vinohrady that was as big as the whole of Ljubljana could have two parishes and only one church. The authorities wanted him to build a church there immediately after the end of the First World War, but Plečnik declined, on the grounds that he was not familiar enough with 'the religious spirit of the people of Prague'.[476] When the project was held up owing to problems over the site, the building committee again approached Plečnik. However, he proposed to the priest in Vinohrady that a number of provisional churches be erected gradually, each attached to the existing buildings, pointing out that there were few free-standing churches in Rome, either.[477] 'I do not want to see a fine new church in Prague at the moment; I would like to show that the real issue is pastoral', he wrote after his first meeting with the priest František Škarda.[478] Plečnik was distressed to see that he had a novel open on his desk, not a breviary. The architect was equally disappointed by his later meeting with the priest Ivan Baša in Bogojina. Plečnik tended to judge the clergy by the example of his elder brother, but in both these cases he had to revise his opinion very thoroughly.

In the summer of 1921 Plečnik put forward a few proposals, including one for a round extension to the Aloisius School chapel on the Square of King George of Poděbrady (fig. 225)[479] (which had until then been used as a temporary church for the second Vinohrady parish), thus avoiding the problem of the site for a new one. The big rotunda would have had rented housing on both sides, similar to the arrangement on the plan for the Church of the Holy Spirit in Vienna. The idea recalls Plečnik's plan for Trsat; the only

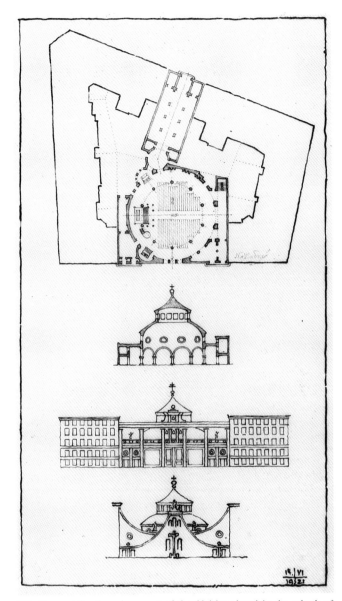

225. Proposal for the enlargement of the Aloisius chapel in the suburb of Vinohrady in Prague, 1921

223

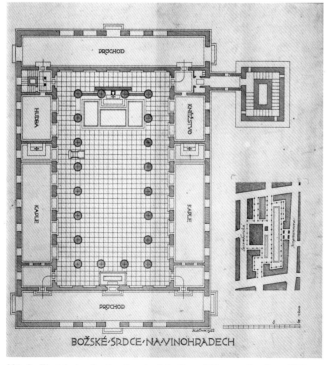

BOŽSKÉ·SRDCE·NA·VINOHRADECH

226–8. First design for the church of the Sacred Heart and variant, 1922

difference was that the church would have been lower, and like the early Christian sanctuary of Sta. Costanza in Rome, surrounded by an arcaded ambulatory.

The planning for the church in Prague extended over six years, and it proved a similarly stony path to the construction of the church of the Holy Spirit in Vienna. Plečnik made several designs with different variants. The first – dated 8 December 1922[480] – was in response to the request from the building committee for a monumental parish centre (fig. 226). Plečnik wanted an exemplary church, that could stand out against the high apartment blocks around it. For this reason he concentrated on Palladio's theme of the double facade. The variant of the plan of 1922 (fig. 227), which we have already discussed in the previous chapter, no longer has any particular external similarity with an antique temple. The great arches would have given a clear view of the centre of the building. Plečnik also intended rich decoration with the figures of saints. He wanted to adorn the roof cornice with antique band ornamentation; however, he also considered a frieze with angels, a feature he had liked to use in his drawings of churches before the First World War, and which he did realize later, on the office building for the Vzajemna insurance company in Ljubljana (see fig. 186).

On this plan the church is 25 metres high, and it was intended to dominate its block, which contained two schools, a presbytery, and several rented apartment blocks (fig. 228). The bell-tower was to dominate the central area. Work on this variant was broken off owing to lack of funds, and to the uncertainty over the site, for the urban planners wanted to make the entire square an open park. Arguments went on between the politicians over the location for the church, and Masaryk had to intervene. The disputes were finally only settled by the Faculty of Law of the Charles University in Prague, and in the meantime Plečnik had changed his idea fundamentally. Although the Archbishop, Antonín Podlaha, gave the architect his wholehearted support, Plečnik himself had realized that a church of the size proposed could hardly be financed. He reduced the height by almost half, and made the ground plan smaller. Consequently, he later added an underground crypt and used a wide bell-tower to give the church the impression of monumentality.

In 1925 an interesting development for this project evolved for a low church with an extremely wide bell-tower at the side (fig. 229).[481] With the motif of rows of interlaced arches on the facade, the bell-tower and in the nave of the church, which recalled Czech Rondo-Cubism, and above all with the five columns, one of which stands free in the middle of the church, he endeavoured to continue the concept of the church in Bogojina. He wanted to give the building a big, easily accessible gallery for the choir, and provide a symbolic indication of the dedication of the church to the Sacred Heart through the Stations of the Cross. Above the sacristy he provided a room for the catechesis and above this again a large hall.[482]

In January 1927 he decided on the following:

I have suffered long over the Vinohrady project – finally I realized that I will have to give up and go back to the old project. The new idea would have required new surveyance work – and I did not want to risk that. Now I am letting the old project stand, that is, the plans I made last year. The church will be expensive – so let it be, in God's name. I don't think the people of Prague like it and so it can hardly be feasible.[483]

The interior of the new church was roughly the same size as in the first proposal, but externally, despite the extension to include the bell-tower and the sacristy, it was shorter than the 1922 design (fig. 231). As Plečnik was forced to cut out the arcaded ambulatory for financial reasons, he created a balanced and open, but secular interior and had to 'give it an ecclesiastical character' afterwards. So he again moved closer to the solution of the single nave that he had already built in Vienna, however, this time the asymmetrical placing of the side altars is new. This idea was revolutionary in the liturgical sense, but again it was not, after all, realized. It was probably derived from an illustration of the canopied altars on the sarcophagi in Ravenna. It also shows the desire to add a number of isolated 'sacred places' where the believers could gather during the celebration of mass. The altar beside the entrance would actually have concealed the view of the high altar. This would have corresponded to Plečnik's view of the religious ceremonial, but certainly not met Wagner's requirement that the interior of a church should be open. So the role of this altar is comparable with the function of the great column bases in the church at Šiška. Nevertheless, all the seats face the presbytery in the traditional way, regardless of the side altars.

Unlike the church of the Holy Spirit in Vienna, there is no change in floor level with the transition from the nave to the presbytery, and the windows of the crypt are set into the floor of the church above. Plečnik's belief in the importance of music to the Czechs is again evident from his intention to create a special area for the choir beside the high altar. Concealed from sight, they would have had to sing 'seriously and calmly here, without a loud accompaniment'.[484]

The brick walls inside, probably intended to represent the

229. The church of the Sacred Heart, variant, 1925

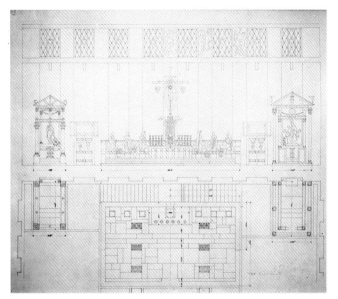

230. The church of the Sacred Heart, area around the altar, around 1933

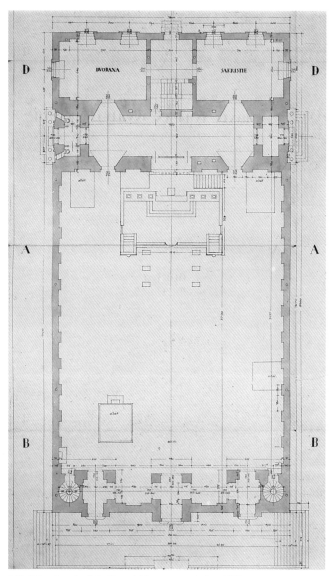

231. The church of the Sacred Heart, ground plan, 1928

biblical temple in Jerusalem, are articulated with lisenes in a simple rhythm which, according to Semper, was one of the basic characteristics of the ancient peoples (fig. 234).[485] Between the pilasters are rectangular windows. They are separated from the lower part of the wall by a narrow gallery intended for cleaning the windows. This white strip of light between the wall and the ceiling, gives an impression that the great wooden coffered ceiling literally sways above the room. Unlike the design for Ljubljana, here Plečnik took as his basic theme Semper's correlation between ceiling and floor, two extremely 'textile' architectural elements.[486] As the ornamentation was to come from carpet weaving, Semper recommended schematic patterns that were neutral in direction. Plečnik used the square for the coffered ceiling and the circle for the terrazzo floor. Convinced that this would improve the accoustics, he wanted to have a large number of lights of different shapes hanging low from the ceiling, as in the church in Šiška, and for these he designed special horizontal supports to be attached to the metal structure of the roof. They could also be used to hold provisional scaffolding to paint the walls, for cleaning purposes and any repairs that might be needed.

The exterior of the church is determined by its position in the urban design and the symbolic significance of the double facade (figs 109–11). It should be mentioned that the State Commission for the Regulation of the Capital City of Prague asked Plečnik to propose a design for the square as well. Hence he moved the church from the edge of the park to the centre of the square, and put the main entrance on the axis of Mánes Street. To provide the appropriate monumentality for so prominant a site he placed the bell-tower, which occupied almost the entire width of the church, between the nave and the sacristy. The height of the tower is the same as the length of the nave. The unusually broad elevation, which is a paraphrase of a Gothic cathedral front, draws the gaze, and it is intended to form a focal point for the former Vilímova Street. This was also a major consideration in some of the other variants of the plan. Plečnik later corrected the elongated body of the building by raising the iron construction of the wooden ceiling and so raising the roof by a few metres.

In the project as it was finally executed, instead of the dual facade originally planned, he merely indicated its textile character. Relying on Semper's statement that in Antiquity textiles had been used on special occasions to lend the architecture greater significance, Plečnik 'dressed' the church, from the windows downwards, in an 'ermine cloak',[487] imitated by bricks burnt twice (klinker), between which are inserted brighter squares of granite and artificial stone. The upper part of the cladding has the function of a protec-

226

tive cornice; the hanging 'ermine tails' are also intended to symbolize the collar of the sovereign's cloak, and this is a clear reference to Christ the King, as the building committee said, 'the most Sacred Heart rules in Bohemia'. Plečnik further underlined this reference with a huge imperial globe on the tip of the tower, and originally this was to have been gold. The windows and doors in this part of the building also give the impression of being fitted with elegant white curtains.

As the foundations of the church had to be very much more extensive than had been expected, Plečnik simplified the ornamentation of the upper part of the facade a little in the summer of 1930; he abandoned the costly figures of angels and replaced the original design for stone surrounds to the portal and windows with less costly plaster. He decorated the upper part of the church with Secessionist frames and stylized garlands, and their textile metaphor almost insistently proclaims a robe of white linen beneath the festive cloak. Plečnik used the same ornamental system on the bell-tower. The original plan for a campanile is recalled by two slender pyramids that are citations of Venice, as they resemble those on the roofs of many of the elegant palazzi on the Grand Canal. The two big round windows with which he opened the wall in the final variant, look like Cyclops' eyes towards Prague Castle. Plečnik felt particularly drawn to the Venetians, not least owing to his speculative belief that the inhabitants of the lagoon city could be of Slav descent as well, as has already been mentioned.

The interior of the bell-tower is one of the most expressive solutions in modern art to the 'promenade architecturale' (see figs 113 and 232). Convinced that a Functionalist form would lessen the monumental impact, Plečnik hid this in shame behind a 'timeless' mantle, as his personal way of measuring up to the avantgarde of his age. The roomy interior of the bell-tower enabled him to build an easy ramp instead of a staircase, and it winds past the two round windows with their clock faces, which add the dimension of time to that of space. The windows helped him to avoid too large an undivided mass of building, and they also help to make the tower lighter.

The relatively small crypt is the opposite of the big light nave (see fig. 114). As Plečnik did not include side chapels, he needed a quiet contemplative room elsewhere. Although he himself warned that the costs might be too high and created a number of alternatives, he was glad when his recommendations on saving costs went unheeded in Prague and the crypt was realized in full. The brick barrel vault lets indirect daylight through two rows of windows surrounded with textile metaphors. Plečnik did not decorate the vault, as, according to Semper, this was not an independent art

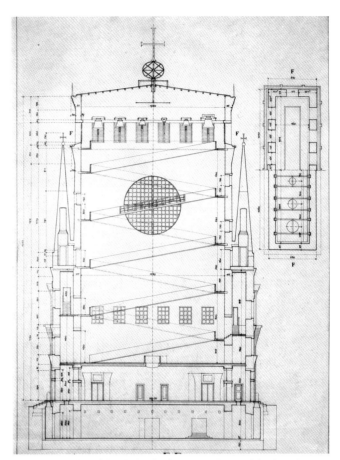

232. Final version of the design for the tower, church of the Sacred Heart, 1930

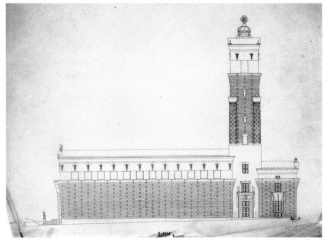

233. Design for the facade before final reworking, 1928

234. The church of the Sacred Heart, interior, fitted 1932–9

form but only a curved roof or simple ceiling for the room, without inherent structural symbolism.[488] The well-proportioned altar table stands out advantageously against the white background. The historical continuity of the sacred room is indicated by the symbolic arch. As the position of the church was not originally determined by the existence of an earlier historical building, Plečnik helped to elevate and legitimate it by using some items from the oldest Prague churches out of the Castle.

At the end of October 1928, after protracted efforts by the chaplain, Titl, Monsignore Podlaha was finally able to bless the foundation stone, although almost another year was to pass before work on the foundations could start. During the building work Plečnik designed the interior from Ljubljana. At first he wanted to place three figures of Bohemian saints on each side of the presbytery, symbolic assistants at the Mass, with a high tabernacle beside the altar, as in the church in Šiška. To link the high altar with the rich Czech ecclesiastical tradition, he decorated the doors of the tabernacle with precious and semiprecious stones, in the style of Charles IV (see fig. 112). He intended to embellish the walls of the presbytery in a similar way, using stone slabs and semi-precious stones, and gild the joints, but in the final version of 1933 he dropped that idea again. For the candelabrum over the altar he used the design he had made before the First World War for the Zacherl chapel in Döbling. A few details, like the balustrade in the choir or the small columns beside the altar recall the balustrades on the Three Bridges, that are of the same date, and Cobblers Bridge (Čevljarski most) in Ljubljana. Plečnik was slightly disappointed by Pešan's altar figures, finding them 'not very aristocratic', but it must be said that at that time he had only seen photographs of them. The church was finished in skeletal form in 1930, and it was dedicated in May 1932, although the interior was still almost totally empty.

Although Plečnik was firmly convinced that art could not develop any further qualitatively, it could only change, he had to admit of his church in Prague that 'no one, from the Ancients to the moderns, has been able to build halls like these; this is real progress'.[489] As he was in Prague for the last time in 1934, only the altar area could be fitted out under his direct supervision, all the other work was undertaken by his selfless associate Otto Rothmayer, who designed the two altars to the right and left of the presbytery, using his teacher's formal vocabulary; later he also designed the other two side altars. To ensure that things were going correctly, he visited his teacher in Ljubljana a few times. The main altar was finished by 1939, apart from a few details. Plečnik decided for metal lights, which are like candelabra of Pompeian origin, no doubt inspired by Semper's description of the development of tectonic techniques in Antiquity.[490] Work only started on the sculptures for the facade and the interior of the crypt and the sacristy during the Second World War, but the church was never entirely finished. Much was also done later against Rothmayer's will. One of the last works of art from Plečnik's hand was the free-standing lavabo with the figure of St Wenceslas, which was donated by Alexander Titl and added in 1937.

Originally a house for the priest was to be built behind the church, but Plečnik refused to draw up the plans for this, and he actually protested at the request to make the front similar to the facade of the church.

THE CHURCH IN BOGOJINA

The most interesting feature of the church of the Ascension of Christ in Bogojina is the combination of folk, rural and classical elements, concepts that are generally interpreted arbitrarily, if not altogether wrongly.

It must be stressed that Plečnik hardly knew the Mura river district (Prekmurje) before he received this commission. But in the course of time he came to love the area, and its strong-minded priest, Ivan Baša, with his 'immaculate,

holy congregation'.[491] The low-lying plain of Pannonia on the ethnically mixed Slovenian-Hungarian border was at first very strange to him, accustomed as he was to the Karst landscape. As an aid to understand the local layout better Plečnik could only rely on Stele's comment that the characteristic feature of the medieval architecture of this district was the combination of a porch under the bell-tower with a portal and a group of buttresses on the western part of the church.[492] All the rest was the result of his own ideals and his experience to date with church architecture. He expected the church in Bogojina to be rather more modest, but he still oriented to Classical Antiquity. The folk element, or, perhaps it would be better to say the non-urban element, is evident in the modification of the monumental scale, but not in any imitation of regional peculiarities. The steep saddleback roof is the only visible concession to the local heritage, and this is not least because the plain required stronger vertical architectural accent.

Plečnik's brother Andrej knew the priest Ivan Baša slightly, but Plečnik was offered the commission through one of his students who came from the Upper Mura district. The architect accepted the offer from the parish to design a new church in the spring of 1924, although he had not as yet had any opportunity to inspect the site personally. As he was on principle opposed to the removal of old buildings he offered two variants,[493] as ways of saving at least part of the existing church. In the first he opened up the building to two side extensions with big arches, so creating a three-aisled interior which recalls an early sketch of 1910 (fig. 79). The spatial concept itself, however, has little in common with the Vienna design, and the ideas for the monumental church in Prague with its external ambulatory, the mighty bell-tower placed behind the presbytery, the uniform ceiling and the windows placed high beneath it are very evident. In this variant only four corners of the old church would have remained.

In the second variant Plečnik proposed a round church with three apses, which he presented to the priest as a symbol of the crucified. In this variant the semicircular presbytery of the old church would have remained intact, and Plečnik wanted to place the new, larger bell-tower in front of the old. This reconsideration of the Pantheon in Rome resulted in a number of designs for round churches, although most were lower than the antique model and had little in common with the basic theme of the semidome.

Plečnik sent both variants to Bogojina, although, under the impact of the initial disappointment with the church of St Magdalen in Maribor mentioned above he was not expecting a positive outcome. When Baša again invited him to Bogojina he went, at the beginning of September 1924, on

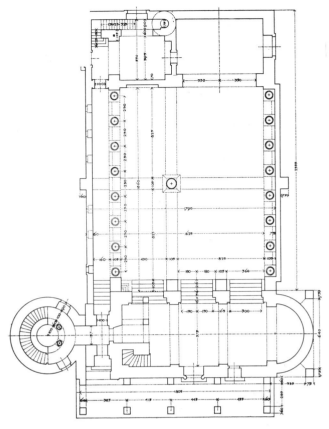

235. The church in Bogojina, ground plan, 1925

his way back from Prague. He agreed immediately to his brother Andrej's proposal to preserve the old church and add the new one to it. As little money was available, he had to be economical in his building. As the interior had supporting elements, including columns, the external walls could be made thinner. The motif of the Antique column had grown in importance for Plečnik with the advance of Functionalism; beyond its structural value it had become the symbol of his humanist philosophy. For the village church in Bogojina he chose much lower and cheaper brick columns than those in Šiška. However, when the local people began to grow enthusiastic over the grander effect of granite from Pohorje, he proposed octagonal columns, clad in Podpeč marble, although he was sure that this variant would also prove too costly. To his amazement the congregation were not satisfied with this idea either, and decided on columns in solid Podpeč stone (see fig. 166). Overwhelmed by the news Plečnik wrote to his assistant and associate France Tomažič: 'Let me know how the columns are progressing – they will be Baša's monument. Who would

have thought the little village of Bogojina would have so grandiose an idea!'[494]

Plečnik retained the simple spatial proportions in Bogojina as well (fig. 235). He changed the old church into an entrance area placed crossways and developed a highly respectful dialogue between the old and the new building. Unlike the high columns in the Franciscan church in Ljubljana, across which straight beams could be laid, the low squat columns here required arches, and Plečnik used these to continue the belt of late Baroque arcading in the old church. He may also have had in mind Roman or – at least as he saw it – Etruscan models. Semper's influence had so far withheld him from contact with Baroque architecture, although it was widespread in Slovenia.

Following the model of the Pantheon he designed the larger arches as if they were around a 'ball touching the floor' (fig. 238).[495] In choosing local pottery to decorate the wooden ceiling he might have been inspired by Semper's description of early Antique terra cotta cladding (see fig. 167).[496] Plečnik made his ceiling of beams, rafters and boards; arranged in a highly imaginative way they recall archaic workmanship. The spatial concept with the central pillar recalls some early Antique architectural monuments. Plečnik borrowed the motif of the columned ambulatory from the first variant of the church of the Sacred Heart in Prague.

The church in Bogojina as it was finally built is slightly reminiscent of the ground plan of the church of the Holy Spirit in Vienna (see figs 82–3). The porch and the square shape, surrounded symmetrically by the old church with the new bell-tower and the presbytery and sacristy, correspond to the arrangement in Vienna of priest's house–church–rented apartments. To put it simply, one could say that Plečnik used the longitudinal dimension of the old nave of the church and the bell-tower for his square addition. The north wall, opened with arcading, would suggest a three-aisled interior, but Plečnik has merely indicated this by continuing the western belt of arches, creating an asymmetrical composition with two aisles of different width. The length of the new church is determined by two squares, each side of which is the width of two arcades, that is, two bays of the old church. The minimal deviations are the result of corrections to the proportions, owing to the difference of the new measurement system. To perfect the adaptation, the shorter side of the presbytery is the same as the bay of the old triumphal arch. The number of such coincidences could be multiplied, and we could conclude from this that the particular features of the old church gave Plečnik a sense of moral responsibility towards the past. 'I have never yet pulled down a good building by our fore-

236. The church in Bogojina, 1925–7

237. The church in Bogojina while the new tower was under construction, 1925. In the centre the priest Baša, left his half-brother Ignac, right the foreman Horvat.

the old church and the increasing vertical accentuation (fig. 236). Plečnik turned the church from a longitudinal to a transverse direction, and gave it a new facade, but we can still trace the body of the original building behind the arches around the apse of the presbytery. The heightened presbytery, like the rounded corner of the Zacherl House, gives the impression of an upright cylinder behind the mantle of the building, and creates a balanced relationship to the new bell-tower. His respect for the old building is also reflected in the almost complete preservation of the old bell-tower. It seems as if Plečnik, in his efforts to achieve a symmetrical facade, has derived the round bell-tower from the semicircular apse (fig. 237). A short time later he used the same motif in the Franciscan church in Ljubljana (see fig. 161), but in a more monumental and 'urban' way, in a version enriched with classical ornamentation. The cylindrical bell-tower with the onion tower, which is also indicated in Bogojina, is one of the constant themes in his 'Slavonic' flirtation with Russian art. In doubling the tower motif he skilfully relaxed the emphasis on the body of the building and created a constellation of vertical accents that is interesting for the viewer from a number of positions (see fig. 165). As he had used a small attached pier on the column of the Virgin Mary in Ljubljana to suggest historical legitimation (fig. 201), he finished off the bell-tower in Bogojina with a small cylinder placed asymmetrically. The theme of dynamic architecture, which is illustrated in so masterly a way in Prague (see fig. 113), was continued in Bogojina. The only difference is that the way to the tower platform in the village church is much steeper and less easy to ascend, but then the surprise is all the greater at the top.

Work on the church in Bogojina started in the spring of 1925, as did that of the Franciscan church in Ljubljana, and the church was finished two years later. As the money began to run out towards the end an interior design was out of the question. The priest, Ivan Baša, died in February 1931. Franc Bajlec, who had been the mediator right from the start, did induce Plečnik to draw up a few plans for the interior, but the work could only be resumed in the late 1940s. In the postwar years Plečnik had to make do with cheaper building materials. Instead of wood or stone carving he suggested clay sculptures and instead of costly metalwork, wood. The high altar was erected between 1950 and 1952 in natural oak, and the altar of St Joseph (1955/6) and the pulpit, which was inspired by an early Christian ciborium, were in Podpeč stone. Although he had carefully supervised the stonework in Ljubljana, Plečnik was to have no opportunity of seeing the interior here in its rightful form.

fathers', he commented to Baša, on his very first visit to Bogojina.[497]

Parallel to the spatial hierarchy – the level of the new church is higher than the old – is the arrangement of the columns and the arches that were built or those that were only planned, but not executed, for the roof. The higher level of the floor in the new building made it possible to erect a gallery for the choir above the arch of the old church. Within this consistent compositional scheme Plecnik would admit no compromises, and he was extremely annoyed when Tomažič changed the upper access to the bell-tower without his knowledge.

The interior of the church has two focal points, a spiritual centre in the presbytery and a physical centre in the broad central column, which focusses the eye most strongly. According to Plečnik this column symbolizes the priest supporting the congregation on his shoulders. The outside of the building is dominated by two themes – the cladding of

232

The church in Bogojina, 1925–7, interior, fitted in 1960

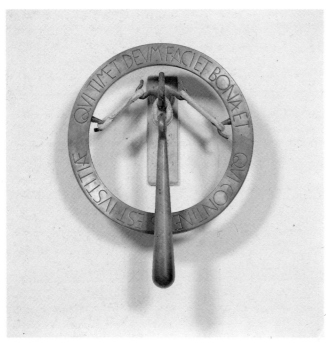

239. Bell in the presbytery of the church in Bogojina, around 1955

THE CHURCH OF ST ANTHONY OF PADUA IN BELGRADE

Parallel to the theme of the rectangular building, Plečnik also worked intensively on that of the rotunda, deriving this not from Wagner's economical standpoint but the classical examples in Mediterranean architecture. His favourite models were the Pantheon in Rome and the mausoleum of Theoderich in Ravenna, whose monolithic cupola in the stone from Aurisina by Irieste fascinated him. Plečnik designed numerous variations of both monuments, but the local architectural tradition discouraged him from choosing a monumental rotunda. It was not until he had contact with the Byzantine and Moslem culture of Serbia and Bosnia that he was induced to take this step. The close relation between the Slovenian Franciscan monks and their Bosnian brethren brought him a commission for a church in Belgrade to be built in the Serbian filial of the Bosnian province of the Order. In 1928 the Belgrade Guardian of the order, Fra Arhandjeo Grgić, went to see Plečnik, and literally lay down across the threshold of his studio until Plečnik agreed to his request.[498]

A church in the Balkans was a particular challenge to Plečnik.[499] He had visited Belgrade shortly before and was overwhelmed by its non-European appearance. He was only too willing to agree with Masaryk, who had maintained that Belgrade had no bell-towers.[500] Plečnik greatly admired medieval Serbian architecture, but with the exception of

Fruška gora in southern Vojvodina, which had visited, he lacked the detailed knowledge to be able to take up a direct dialogue with it. Hence, he oriented his design for Belgrade to some early Christian churches of the Byzantine type, and also drew on his own variation of the Pantheon for Bogojina of 1924, which he had later rejected. From this design he took the arrangement of the masses of the building, giving greater emphasis to the long axis (fig. 240). He intended to position the bell-tower on one of the two apses that were envisaged.

Parallel to this project in Begrade Plečnik was working on a round chapel in the Logar valley in Slovenia,[501] where the facade was to extend uninterrupted above the vault into a bell-tower of the same width. Later he wanted to use the design for this building, which, to his great disappointment, the local people executed in an absolutely arbitrary way, for the church at Žale cemetery in Ljubljana.[502]

The Franciscans had only limited funds for their church in Belgrade, and this soon brought Plečnik back to reality. The great classical cupola would have made the building very much more expensive. Moreover, he was not sure whether the builders, whose work he did not know, would ever have been capable of realizing it. So he decided on a simple concrete slab, covering this with a wooden ceiling. This made the building lower, and took him away from the basic proportions of the Pantheon. So that the imaginary height which would be the same as the width of the building is only marked by the cross on the roof. Also designed after the example of the Pantheon are the chapels with their apses recessed into the depths of the massive wall, whereas the interchange between the reddish brickwork and the lighter concrete strips is inspired by the Byzantine architecture of medieval Serbia (fig. 170). This combination of colours, which he also used on the facade of the Vzajemna insurance company office building in Ljubljana, which is of the same date, was intended to give the Franciscan church the appearance of 'extreme severity and asceticism'.[503] Plečnik did suggest changing the brickwork, should this prove too expensive, and plastering the walls instead,[504] but the Franciscans finally agreed to his initial proposal. Inside, the church is encircled by four concrete strips, which also delineate the spatial hierarchy. The chapels are dominated by the presbytery, which is a storey higher. Above the chapels runs a gallery with a stone balustrade, while a clerestory with rectangular windows concludes the subdivisions (fig. 172).

Like the nave, the presbytery and the chapels have flat roofs. Although Plečnik tried to avoid using classical ornamentation – the chapels are like folds in the mantle of the building rather than tectonically defined side rooms – bal-

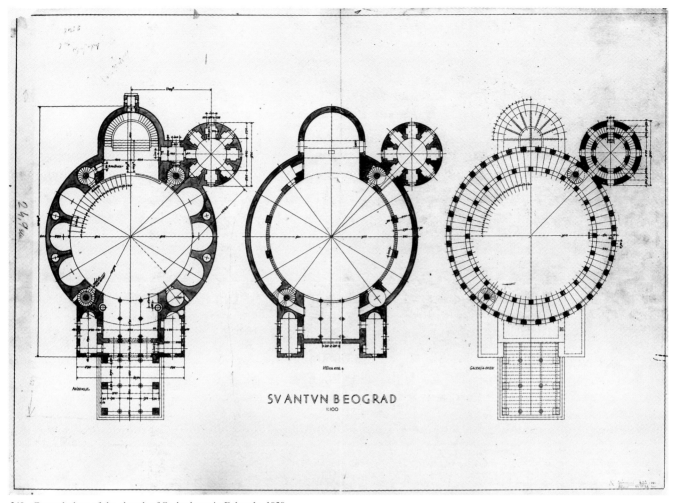

240. Ground plans of the church of St Anthony in Belgrade, 1929

SV ANTVN BEOGRAD
1:100

ance in the Antique sense is very evident. The round bell-tower with the sacristy on the ground floor is twice the height of the church. It was only completed after Plečnik's death,[505] while the church itself was built by 1930, and dedicated two years later.

For his work on the interior Plečnik found a creative associate in Fra Josip Markušić, who had already rejected plans by another architect in favour of designs by Plečnik when he was a still the head of the Bosniar Franciscan Province in the mother monastery at Jajce. Between 1931 and 1939 he headed the Franciscan monastery in Belgrade, and was thus also the parish priest at the church of St Anthony. Markušić was highly cultured and liberal in his views, and he was also a great reader, but despite his wide-ranging interests he maintained a strict discipline in his monastery. He was soon to become one of Plečnik's closest friends. After the death of his brother Andrej in 1931

Plečnik often went to Markušić with liturgical questions. The design for the interior of the church of St Anthony dates from 1936; it was the fruit of joint considerations, and Markušić carried it out conscientiously. Plečnik owed it to Markušić that the interior of the church in Belgrade outshines all his other churches. That the concrete bands strips on the walls in the interior finally remained unpainted was due more to the lack of suitable painters than a lack of funds.

Even in the planning phase Plečnik had envisaged a concrete beam, adorned with a cross, in the presbytery to support the ceiling, and to hold the light. Later he added brackets and partly covered the beam with copper. The figure of Christ crucified and the candelabrum beneath were in the Romanesque spirit. The main altar was raised by a few steps and had a high pyramidal tabernacle. When Ivan Meštrović's figure of St Anthony was installed on the taber-

235

nacle in the early 1950s, throwing the concept of the presbytery off balance rather to Plečnik's dismay, the pyramid was also abbreviated (see fig. 169). The architect had originally envisaged a perfectly antique figure with the face and hands in onyx.

Plečnik marked the altar off from the brickwork behind with a solid semicircular screen in Podpeč marble. As he only trusted the craftsmen he knew, all the more demanding parts of the interior were made in Ljubljana. The rich use of different metal cladding with visible studs in the presbytery shows his intention to give the most sacred part of the building a solemn, archaic character in accordance with Semper's tubular principle (see fig. 171).

For the chapels Plečnik agreed to a Franciscan iconography which is closer to folk art and expressly didactic in its aims. The sculptor Božo Pengov carved over-lifesize figures of the Virgin Mary and Christ to Plečnik's instructions, and these correspond to the hieratic art of the Beuron artist monks. In the side altars Plečnik tried to avoid the traditional retable architecturally: he surrounded the sculpture of Christ with columns of differing size, but placed a wall of polished Podpeč marble behind the Virgin Mary; the handling of the joints here is like a quotation from the facade of the Zacherl House. The funnel-shaped capitals of the columns under the organ gallery and the porch also recall his Viennese designs. They point downwards and are similar to the ones Plečnik had designed in 1905 for the exhibition of religious art in the Secession. Beside the entrance and on the axis of the presbytery Plečnik placed a praying desk with a depiction of the Saviour bending down from the cross. He had seen the motif in 1901 in the Easter issue of the periodical *Jugend* (*Youth*),[506] and found it again in the famous group of St Luitgard by M.B. Braun on Charles Bridge in Prague. Clearly it meant a great deal to him, as he used it again in an enlarged version for the priests' grave in Ljubljana cemetery. In Belgrade Pengov's figure represents a pastoral supplement to the majestic figure of Christ crucified in the presbytery.

A peculiarity in the Belgrade church would have been an altar of the Garden of Gethsamane. This was not executed. Here Plečnik imitated popular devotion and tried to unify the whole way of the cross with the holy grave; over this would have stood a column showing Christ's passion, with the cock as the symbol of the betrayal by Peter; the altar would have been a symbol of mercy and a warning.

Markušić often stimulated Plečnik's imagination and his contribution to the narrative appearance of the altars is evident. Only the Franciscan Martin Perc was to play a comparable role later, in the conversion of the church in Stranje. In the years immediately before his death the architect fitted

out the other chapels as the changed circumstances permitted. On the altar of St Francis he placed two candelabra in Podpeč marble with hanging oil vessels; these were influenced by Pompeian art, and he later had similar vessels made for the Greek Catholic church in Ruski Krstur in Vojvodina; for the table and the canopy of the altar of St Joseph he was content to use wood.

THE CHURCH OF ST MICHAEL AT LJUBLJANA MOOR

Throughout his life Plečnik was drawn to the problems of smaller churches, which needed to be representational in character while funds were limited. It was not a matter of building purely practical, technically interesting provisional structures, as Otto Wagner had proposed before the First World War in Vienna, Plečnik designed rectangular or round churches that were in their way were monumental. He often went to the borders of folk art in these designs, but he always remained faithful to his principle of the reinterpretation of Antiquity. A typical example is the church of St Michael, for which the first plans were made in 1922 at the request of Plečnik's neighbour in Trnovo, the priest Finžgar.[507] Difficulties arose over the site and price increases during the slump delayed the building work, and in the meantime Plečnik's earlier idea of close contact between the priest and the congregation began to take concrete shape. When his nephew, who was chaplain in Trnovo, took the initiative with the building after Finžgar retired in 1935, Plečnik decided for a relatively low church, its body turned crossways to the entrance axis, with a porch, a low bell-tower and an extension for the priest's house.[508] He took the basic idea for the interior from the design with the altar on the long side which he had tried in vain to realize in Vienna in 1906. The row of windows in the higher entrance wall would have given sufficient light for the interior. The main feature which this plan had in common with what was later executed was the church's orientation along the street. Owing to the frequent flooding in the moorland Plečnik intended raising the church upon a slight embankment.

The fruitless meetings of the church's building committee would probably have gone on for a long time, had a major landowner, Josip Kosler, not left part of his fortune for the construction of the church.[509] Negotiations on the bequest, however, revealed that the amount was very much smaller than had at first been expected. This meant a completely new design, for the church now had to be built in the cheapest possible way. Only after protracted efforts by his nephew, the priest Karl Matkovič, to persuade him to carry on, did Plečnik agree to continue. He was only able to use wood that had been donated and building material from the nearby Podpeč quarry, as it could be taken almost up to the site on boats. In order to avoid the law that made the Ministry in Belgrade responsible for all public buildings, which at best would have very considerably delayed the granting of a building licence (as did in fact happen over the university library) Plečnik called the church an interim solution, and with the help of determined intervention by the Municipal Building Director Matko Prelovšek, he saved it from the grip of state bureaucracy.

The question of the site remained open to the last. The City Council was willing to allocate a large field free of charge, in exchange for the smaller site originally envisaged, beside the school and an inn. When Plečnik saw the site he agreed immediately, and so avoided any further urban planning problems. He did not know that in making this choice he had given his nephew new problems, as the innkeeper, who felt deprived of the neighbourhood he had hoped for, vehemently opposed the construction of the church.

Based on his experience in Prague with cheap terraced housing, where he had used the principle of 'one wall', Plečnik designed individual walled sections as the main supports for the church in the Moor with wooden partition walls (fig. 241). In order to make the building even more economical he planned to use the priest's apartment as a substructure (see fig. 173). However he opposed any further simplification of the original plan with regard to the bell-tower, which he placed boldly before the church instead of a portal. In view of the soft ground this was also structurally preferable to a tower rising from the nave. Plečnik retained the monumental width of the tower, but reduced its depth severely, which entailed shifting access to the bells to the outside. The tower, its weight reduced by many arched openings, is the most striking feature of the church, and it has a similarity with the bell gables in the facade towers of many churches in the Karst region. Judging from a number of preliminary studies, the similarity was very definitely more than coincidence, as Plečnik loved the Karst land. The 'promenade architecturale' is concealed in the bell-tower of the church in Prague, but here it is visible. The movement starts on the steps and the staircase divides before the entrance of the church into a horizontal and a vertical component, as the visitor can either enter the nave or ascend the stairs. The latter could also be interpreted as a symbol of Jacob's ladder into heaven.[510] With this dynamic element Plečnik again moved in time with the avantgarde of his age. Sure of the support of the municipal building department he could actually permit himself a convincing formal solution in a stairway inadequately

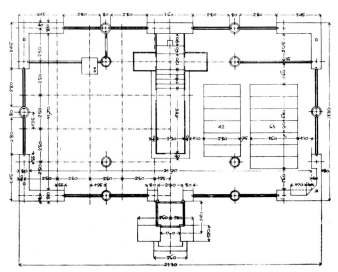

241. Ground plan of the upper floor of the church of St Michael in Ljubljana Moor, 1936/7

secured by a balustrade, which would hardly have been allowed anywhere else.

As there could be no question of stone columns owing to the shortage of funds, he used 'secular' concrete pipes from the municipal sewerage works, which he joined together and set upright. Before the carpenters arrived on the site he had these polished and later they were adorned with paintings. The columns on the facade, on the other hand, were merely plastered. Four of these internally reinforced 'columns' mark out the centre of the interior, as in the church in Šiška, and they also support the wooden frame on which the ridge purlin rests (see fig. 175). The unusual timber work shows that the architect did not have a conventional ceiling in mind, he wanted a solution that would be definitely archaic (although he also had his students draw an alternative design for a round church with an interesting wooden ceiling structure). He found his model, which was basically very primitive, in the reconstruction of the roof of the armory in Piraeus by A. Choisy,[511] who maintained that the Etruscans had roofed their buildings in this way. Plečnik was similarly inspired by Choisy in the church in Zgornja Rečica near Laško in Slovenia, which he built in 1935–9 with his assistant Valentinčič. To cover the gently sloping saddleback roof, which is not typical of this part of Slovenia, Plečnik used cheap concrete tiles on the Roman model for the first time, a solution he was frequently to return to later in order to avoid the heavy costs of lead roofing.

Owing to the soft moorland ground the church had to stand on supports. When the work started, in the summer of 1937, Plečnik wrote in delight to his old friend Alfred

Castelliz, and described the old Venetian method of ramming these supports into the ground;[512] he clearly enjoyed sharing an experience with the builders of past centuries. While the foundations were being prepared he completed his plans with an apsidal extension behind the altar, which contained a spiral staircase to the priest's dwelling. The stone walls were to have unplastered rough hewn stones inside and out, as in cyclopean masonry. However, the masons built the wall of stones laid together far too regularly, and Plečnik used brick in the upper half of the facade between the stones, as he had done on the facade of the university library, which is of the same date and from which the church ultimately derived its entire spatial disposition.

He compensated for the total lack of expensive material in the interior with polished metal covering for the stipes, the pulpit and the sacristy wall behind the altar (see fig. 174). The last in particular is a true apotheosis of Semper's tubular style, with its arches and velvet curtains. The comparison with the Greek orthodox iconostasis would appear inappropriate, in view of Plečnik's strict Catholicism, and it would have been more apt to see here a reference to the arcades in the early Christian churches.[513] The presbytery is entirely incorporated in the rectangular ground plan, and with the communion benches it constitutes an enclosed area in the middle of the church following through the axis of the entrance.

The ornamentations of the beams and columns look like folk art at first glance, but on a closer inspection it can be seen that they are more or less free variations of paleo-Christian patterns. The *genius loci* or the local mentality has played a part in the symbolism of the interior. Outside the immediate area of the altar Plečnik has incorporated the folk tradition very much more strongly than in his urban churches, and in places he has combined this with very personal liturgical views. Not only the chandelier before the altar, which bears the scales and sword of St Michael, or the figure of St Anthony with the unavoidable swine on his offertory, but even more, the lights, made of Turkish coffee mills, coloured glass and an ox horn that was found by chance, the supports for the organ loft, which are like a grape press, and the wall clock above the entrance show his concern to bring the archaic closer to the spirit of the people (see figs 176–7). Plečnik also found confirmation of all this in the symbols in the Gospels; for instance, there are twelve supports for the roof, symbolizing the twelve apostles, there is the horn of redemption, the Holy Trinity, the two depictions of Christ, the beads of the rosary and similar items. How concerned Plečnik was to take account of the local, largely peasant population, who could not make any very

great financial contribution, is evident from the table placed near the altar for gifts of food.

The interior was only completed in the 1950s. Initially Plečnik had to use fitments from other places, like the folding winged altar in the shape of a chest,[514] which he had designed in 1935 for religious classes in the neighbouring school. As well as his own work, which was unpaid, he sacrificed his brother's savings for the church and a considerable part of his own money and works of art. But the shortage of funds also led to some highly inventive details, and these include a substitute bell consisting of a hanging metal ring and stick, and the candleholders made of standard rods of iron (see figs 174 and 178); Plečnik has given these an entasis that looks genuinely antique, simply by using interim pieces.

CHURCH COMMISSIONS FOR BOSNIA AND CROATIA

Kosta Strajnić, painter and art critic, had buried any illusions he might have entertained about the emergence of a common south Slav culture, especially while he had been a teacher in Zagreb and Belgrade before and during World War I, and later during his stay in Prague (1918–20). In 1927 he took over as head of the Historical Preservation Office in Dubrovnik and made intensive efforts to persuade Plečnik, or at least some of his students, to work in Dalmatia. Plečnik was attracted by the rich Latin cultural heritage of the coastal towns, but he lacked the time to devote himself exclusively to such work. He recommended to Strajnić a graduate of his School, Vinko Glanz, who was born in Kotor, but he was soon called up for military service and then returned to Ljubljana. The only testimony to Plečnik's presence in Dalmatia is the summer house for the Ljubljana dentist Verčon in Lapad near Dubrovnik. It was built in 1933/4 but sadly underwent conversion work in the 1950s that has made it almost unrecognizable.[515]

Markušić made similar efforts to obtain a major commission for Plečnik in Bosnia, but he was unsuccessful with both projects for Sarajevo: the cathedral in Vrhbosna and the priests' seminary. The first of these in particular, the Catholic cathedral of St Joseph of 1935 (figs 242–3), had an impact on Plečnik's later work.[516]

Plečnik chose to draw his inspiration for this alien Moslem environment from the greatest of the old Byzantine churches, Hagia Sophia in Istanbul. The main compositional problem was the dome, and he adapted this to the round ground plan of his church. The span he wanted for the dome gave him the idea of providing better support with tilted arches, which would also give a greater space beneath.

Later, in his design for the Slovenian parliament building of 1947,[517] he developed the same idea further on (figs 219–20). He roofed the hall with a low vault, placing above this a high cone in reinforced concrete. In using these severe geometric forms he took up the theme of the double dome in Wagner's church Am Steinhof. In practice, Plečnik shared Le Corbusier's view that the problems of modern monumental construction could be solved with geometry. The design for the Franciscan church of the Holy Cross in Zagreb, which dates from the same time but was never built, is a variation of the same theme.[518]

The cathedral of St Joseph was to have a wide bell-tower like that of the Prague church, and a spacious crypt. Owing to the round ground plan the altar in the crypt would face in a different direction from that in the nave. This idea was much too unusual for the Bosnian congregation, and Markušić could never win any support for it. In 1941 Plečnik gave the rejected plans to the Zagreb parish of St Joseph in Trešnjevka, but the war put an end to the project.

The interesting project for the priests' seminary of Mary of the Angels in Sarajevo of 1938/9 met with the same fate (fig. 244). The seminary was designed as a triangular structure surrounding the church.[519] As with the Baragas priests' seminary in Ljubljana Plečnik reached for his compass (see fig. 330), as it was always his wish to base monastic work on an ideal geometric plan. In this he was no different from the architects of revolutionary Neo-Classicism. Plečnik had enjoyed the support of Sarajevo's Provincial but when a new one was appointed, all monumental work for the town ceased. The pyramidal stone chapel in the mining town of Vareš of 1937 – it was moved in 1953/4 to a new but unsuitable location – and a few unimportant conversions on the Franciscan monastery in Jajce were Plečnik's only architectural testimonies in Bosnia.[520]

Markušić also recommended Plečnik to Canon Ivan Delalle in Trogir near Split. The priest was highly artistic, and he enthusiastically supported the idea of building some new churches in Dalmatia. This brought Plečnik into contact with stone Romanesque church architecture, and he endeavoured to combine this with his experience in Slovenia. However, as almost all these commissions were offered to him in the difficult economic times just after the Second World War, and Plečnik, who was now advanced in years, disliked travelling, none of the plans came to fruition.

Thus, most of the stimuli from the Slavic South were not destined to bear fruit right from the start. Nevertheless, Plečnik did succeed not only in building the church in Belgrade but also the crypt of the Franciscan sanctuary in Zagreb between 1934 and 1937.[521] This was planned as a

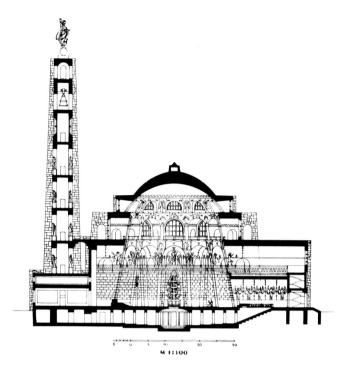

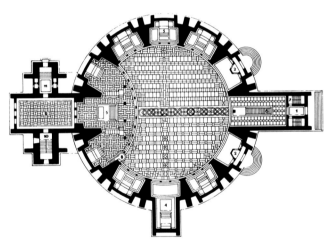

242–3. The Catholic cathedral of St Joseph for Sarajevo, 1935

239

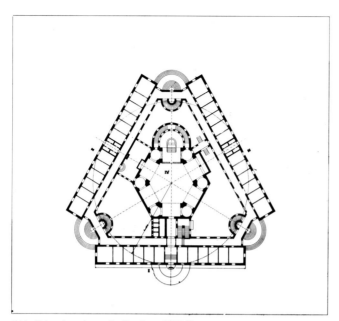

244. Priests' seminary for Sarajevo, 1938/9

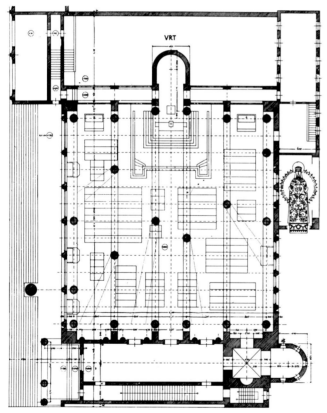

245. The church of Mary of Lourdes for Zagreb, 1934

monumental structure dedicated to Mary of Lourdes (figs 245–6). With its almost square ground plan its debt to the churches in Šiška and Bogojina is not difficult to see (fig. 235), and the narthex shaped like a church placed crossways, with a bell-tower and an apse, also links this design with the latter. Nevertheless, Plečnik introduced an entirely new theme in Zagreb with the irregular arrangement of the columns inside. At first glance these appear to be set unsystematically, but in fact it is just a matter of the variations in recesses of the columns, running parallel to the axis of the space. Also as they would have obscured the view of the altar Plečnik tried to avoid the blind areas with larger or smaller groups of benches. On both sides of the narrow apse he wanted windows that would reach down to the floor, opening a view to the fenced *hortus conclusus* behind the altar, which would reinforce the impression that the columns personified the idea of a holy forest.

The mantle of the building is in several layers and adorned with columns, and we can trace it back to the first 'temple-like' design for the Prague church. Plečnik made intensive studies of differently proportioned columns, which can be seen in his design for the gateway to South Square (Južni trg) in Ljubljana, which dates from the same time (fig. 296). In the interior of the crypt at Zagreb we should also note the brass rods fencing the altar, which look back to Wagner's glass case for the silverware producer J.C. Klinkosch in Vienna.

In 1937 the Jesuits in Osijek in Slavonia asked Plečnik to design a new monastery for them. In their initial enthusiasm they wanted a complex that would include a church, a monastery and a seminary.[522] Plečnik aimed to fill the wide angle of the big site with the church, and his elliptical ground plan suits the position far better than the attempt of the previous unknown architect. He made the long monastery building behind the church concave, in order to create an open space. The entire ensemble was to be dominated by a tower in the centre of the curve of the monastery, 50 metres high. But before building work started in 1940 Plečnik shortened the original length of the church from 56 to 42 metres and instead of a flat roof gave it a pitched roof supported on columns above an elliptical central nave. This was reminiscent of early Christian round buildings. At the same time he abandoned the original accentuation of the facade, replacing this with a calmer rhythm of colossal half-columns set between the windows. Apparently dissatisfied with the bell-tower he reworked this several times, broadening it as he had done in Prague, to create a more monumental background for his church.

The building work was very much slowed down by the war, and finally it stopped altogether. The Jesuits saw that they would never be able to complete their monastery to the original plan and so in 1940 Plečnik again reworked the bell-tower (figs 248–9), the design for which was now 90 metres high, placing in it the monks' cells, the refectory, the main hall and all the ancillary rooms.[523] Probably he never expected the design to be realized, but he was attracted by the idea of crowning the five-storey living quarters with an even higher tower. To take the weight of the heavy tower he had to provide appropriate foundations, and these are vaulted aisles in the core of the building. The tower was also supported by a separate framing balustrade on solid corner pillars and columns.

Similarly, the slender pyramid at the top of the tower was treated as a monolithic structure. Plečnik wanted to embed part of this in the body of the tower. He gradually found convincing formal answers to the complicated problems of statics, revealing great sensitivity for the balance of the masses of the building, and producing a masterly solution to the relationship between solid and open forms. The bell-tower for the Jesuit church in Osijek is one of the last skyscrapers, after Loos' Chicago Tribune Column, to be conceived in the Classical spirit, and formally it has an unintentional intellectual relationship with English Baroque towers. Nothing has remained of Plečnik's efforts in Osijek today. After the end of the World War II the Jesuits were expelled or imprisoned, and the church, that had been built up to the windows, was blown up.

The second major project in Croatia with which Plečnik attempted to free himself of the restrictions imposed by the war years, at least for a time, was the enlargement of the church and pilgrim complex in Marija Bistrica (1942/3).[524] It would appear that this design was conceived right from the start as an ideal, as Plečnik showed it to the Archbishop of Zagreb, Stepinac, in a richly worked drawing, presenting it as an intellectual concept not bound by the constraints of implementation. With regard to the removal of some of the old buildings which would have been in the way of the new grandiose design, his main concern appears to have been to give greater prominence to one of the most important national monuments in Croatia. Plečnik had regarded projects of this nature as a challenge even while he was still studying under Wagner, and it was unimportant to him whether the project was for his own people or another na-tion. Here he wanted to build a large church on to the existing nave with the main altar on the long side, so return-ing to the theme he had already tackled in Vienna. A novelty was the spacious semi-circular apse with the double ambula-tory around the choir. The lighting inside was to come from a pitched roof rising steeply towards the altar, with a row of windows with semi-circular tops beneath it. The same

246. The church of Mary of Lourdes in Zagreb, crypt, 1936/7

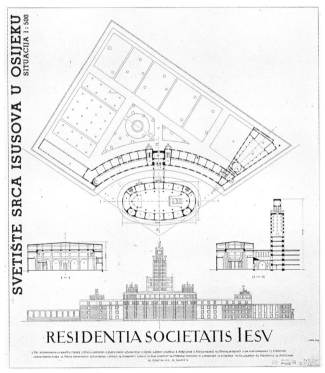

247. The Jesuit monastery for Osijek, first variant, 1937

241

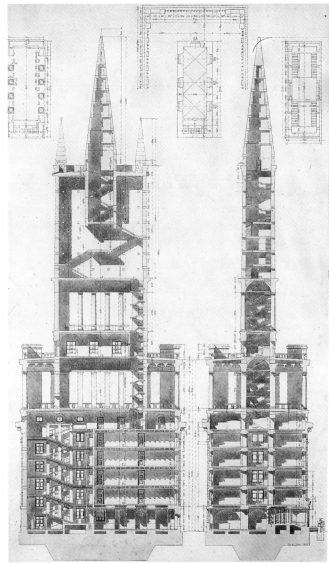

248–9. The Jesuit monastery located in the church tower at Osijek, 1944

windows on the entrance facade would have lit the choir gallery. The church would have had buttresses of differing height, and been divided into three aisles. It was to be built in stone with a brick superstructure.

After the war Plečnik took up his work on some churches for Croatia and Bosnia again. He well knew that they could never be built, so he used the designs to try out some new architectural themes. In the design for a church for Dolina in Bosanska Gradiška he moved away from the shape of the Pantheon and developed the 'three-sided' church (1948) on a round ground plan[525] with a dynamic relationship between the outer and inner shells (fig. 250). The latter would have followed the model of an entrance to the World Exhibition in Paris in 1900, which had consisted of three interlinked arches.

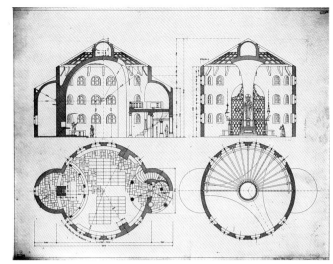

250. The 'three-sided' church for Bosnia, 1948

Plečnik met with much understanding in his conversion work on the Ljubljana Chamber of Trade, Industry and Commerce from 1925 to 1927, as the members of the Chamber had supported the new Slovenian School of Architecture right from the start. So he made good use of the opportunity, reminding his clients that they had an intellectual and moral responsibility to promote art and to represent it. Plečnik was becoming increasingly and painfully aware that his fellow countrymen lacked imagination and had no desire for lasting artistic values. He poured out his feelings in a letter to Alfred Castelliz:

> The Slovene is a great rationalist by nature – he loves science and is less favourably disposed towards art. He certainly has good taste, he understands and appreciates high art (he is incapable of ornamentation), but he does not need it. His nature is fine but tough and biting, and this has made him the most democratic being in Europe – he wants to be prosperous – but he does not want to be rich. There have never really been any political assassinations, revolutions etc. here. The aristocracy has never felt at ease here – the Jews have not risen to prominence – so far – but the future is in God's hands. A strange people – probably a lot of slave blood – undeveloped land, Carniolan soil earth – the word says it all – for Carniola, for all the coastal area and Carinthia – what pain to think of all that![526]

So in this respect the task was not so very different from the work in Prague. Nevertheless, the cultural and economic conditions in his homeland were less promising. The commencement of work on this project coincided with his students' visit to Paris to see the exhibition of decorative and industrial arts in 1925, and it ended two years later when they went on their excursion to Greece. During these years great progress was being made in European architecture, not only in France but in Germany too, not least as the Bauhaus moved to Dessau. Gropius' ideas also reached Ljubljana, and they were eagerly taken up, particularly in Vurnik's class. However, Plečnik reacted to the challenges of his time with a categorical and demonstrative return to the beginnings of the European humanist tradition. He embarked upon the conversion work at the Chamber as if he were designing for an antique royal palace and not a modern office block.

His gifted assistant France Tomažič was initially very devoted to him, and Plečnik tried to further his career by naming him on the plaque as the architect of the conversion. Could this have been due to a guilty conscience over the

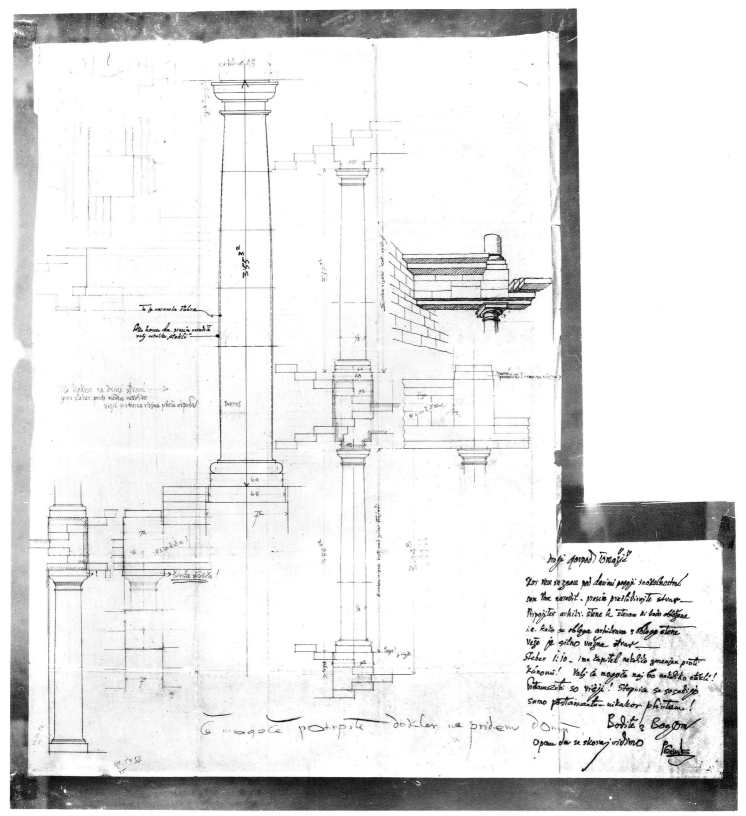

251. The first variant of the stairway for the Chamber of Trade, Industry and Commerce in Ljubljana, drawn by F. Tomažič with Plečnik's corrections, 1925

252. The small meeting room in the Chamber of Trade, Industry and Commerce in Ljubljana, 1927, contemporary photograph

unfortunate episode of the church of St Magdalen in Maribor, where Tomažič had deputized for Plečnik and never received a fee as the plans were rejected, or was the final result simply not what Plečnik had wanted? Tomažič certainly invested a lot of work in the Chamber, and he deputized for Plečnik while he was in Prague. However, the complexities of aesthetic solutions exceeds by far the capabilities of the assistant and proves that Plečnik supervised all the work on the building to smallest detail. There are some drawings by Tomažič which survive and which Plečnik corrected and commented upon while he was staying in Prague (fig. 251).

Plečnik's absences nearly had fatal consequences; the builder Ogrin had ordered the stone in the summer of 1925 from a company in Celje but from sketches, and before Plečnik had decided on his final version. In great agitation, Plečnik demanded that the work be stopped. [527] The second disappointment came when the building inspectorate declared the stairs, that were already completed and only attached at one side, to be unstable. The stone had come from the quarry in Aurisina. Plečnik had to attach each stair individually to a concealed steel crossbar,[528] and he skilfully incorporated these into the railing (fig. 183). In spite of this his brief reports to his brother on the progress of the work are full of varying assessments of his own capabilities.

The execution of the project was of great importance, both for Plečnik's students, who were able to follow every phase of the work, and the education of the local builders, who first had to get used to Plečnik's precise way of working. Plečnik rightly called the conversion 'a stage in the development of our craft'.[529] All the work, with the exception of the great bronze candelabrum, which was cast in Prague, shows that Plečnik had indeed ushered in new times for Ljubljana.

For the new requirements of the Chamber some rooms were to be added and more office space created on the attic floor. Plečnik reserved to himself the design of the larger stairway and the official rooms. He created a true *parcours narratif* in the antique Greek manner, using as the leitmotif columns, which had almost ceased to play a part in European architecture at this time (see fig. 180). The 'route' commences with a colossal column, passes a monument bearing folk sayings and ends in an extreme mannerist transformation of the theme. Although Plečnik initially chose the Tuscan order, he finally gave the columns Minoan form. Up to the upper floor they are granite from Pohorje in northeastern Slovenia, and only where the columns have to bear the wooden roof purlins is wood used instead of stone (fig. 253). Plečnik made use of the wealth of domestic stone quarries, as he had done in Prague. The stairway walls are

253. Sketch for the wooden column on the top floor of the Chamber of Trade, Industry and Commerce, around 1926

clad in the dark marble-like limestone from Podpeč, creating a rather dim but stately atmosphere.

The stairs are lit on the long axis through the glazed walls of the landings and the round windows (see fig. 179), which Plečnik was then using frequently. No chandeliers were hung in the official rooms, light bulbs are set into the centre of each coffer in the ceiling. The stairway is lit by metal candelabra in the shape of columns or slender vases, and we can also interpret these as a translation of Semper's speculation on the metal interim phase in Greek architecture. Smaller versions of these stand in the middle of the round windows, so that the artificial light comes from the same direction as the daylight.

The interior of the Chamber corresponds to the ideas Plečnik was developing in Prague and his discussions with Alice Masaryk. Early Aegean culture seemed to him, through its subsequent influence in the Mediterranean area, a legitimate basis for his new national art, that was to be free of the taint of ethnography. The entrance, the stairway and the main hall are full of unconventional details, and these

cannot be Tomažič's work, for this deliberate overstepping of Classical norms displays a sovereign familiarity with Antiquity.

The entire composition follows a strict grammatical system, which leaves nothing to chance but still allows a certain amount of freedom. The more aware Plečnik was of the etymology of the individual architectural elements the freer he was of stylistic constraints, as Semper would have understood this. Although he insisted that his students study Antiquity, they did not have enough historical experience to be able to recognize Greek art as the point of departure for the new architecture. He explained to them the characteristics of the various styles, like the 'rhythm of forms, colours, lines and motifs',[530] and how he used these to establish the syntax of the traditional ornamental elements. His method was not based on an adaptation of Antiquity to the academic rules of the nineteenth century, but on Wagner's free attempt to carry on from Semper's non-formalistic view of ancient art. Instead of the Neo-Classical hierarchy and symmetry, Plečnik introduced in Ljubljana a democratic wealth of formal variety.

With the polychrome coffered ceiling outside the main hall Plečnik was citing Semper literally (see fig. 181). His wealth of ideas is reflected in the textile metaphors of the stone 'carpets', the gently twisted hand rails of the banisters, the use of stylized 'woven' or 'plaited' ornaments instead of the usual consoles above the doors, and similar details. The finest example is without doubt the ceiling of the main hall, which suggests a 'three-aisled' room along a long axis (see fig. 184). It derived from Semper's description of stretching sails or woven read mats.[531] Plečnik's gilt wooden loops are only an addition with respect to the principle of cladding, they have no structural value. The 'ceiling sheets' are 'stretched' on a frame that encircles the room, and the gilt bolts indicate their derivation from metal. Like the ceilings, the wall panelling also derives from textile metaphors. The success of the whole is due to Plečnik's wealth of ideas and the extraordinarily high quality of the workmanship, which is equal to that of the Prague carpenters. The bronze chandelier before the entrance to the hall (see fig. 181) recalls the twisted columns of Bernini's baldachin in St Peter's, although it is basically a literal translation of Semper's dynamic antique hollow column.[532] Visually the chandelier articulates the change in direction of the flow of movement and so prevents the stairs from appearing to end in the wall. The solution is based on the functional use of an ornament, a technique that Plečnik had learned from Wagner in Vienna and which he perfected in Ljubljana in fully plastic form. Indeed, the hall in particular breathes something of the spirit of Wagner.

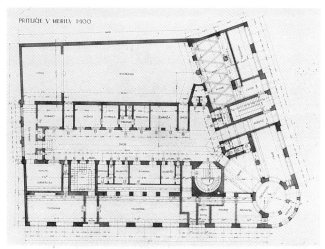

254–5. The People's Lending Bank in Celje, 1928/9, facade and ground plan of the ground floor

In the furniture, too, we can find similarities with his Prague designs. The monumental shape of the armchairs derives from Egyptian models. This is a development of the type which Plečnik designed in 1926 for Masaryk's dressing room, and later perfected for the library in the Prelovšek House in Ljubljana (fig. 203). The chairs and tables from the small meeting room beside the big hall have not survived (fig. 252). They had fluting to match the richly articulated wall panelling. Despite the formal differences the arms had the same dynamic as the 'strap' armchair in Alice Masaryk's salon in Prague Castle (fig. 107). The legs widened towards the floor and tapered again at their ends, giving the impression of only lightly touching the floor, thus according with Semper's definition of the mobile nature of furniture.[533] During the Second World War the seating arrangements on the attic floor also disappeared; these had been equally dynamic, but more comfortable, the shapes appearing to be perfectly adapted to the human spine.

THE OFFICE BUILDING FOR THE VZAJEMNA INSURANCE COMPANY

At the end of 1927 Plečnik began to work on buildings for two financial institutions that were closely connected with the Catholic People's Party – the Vzajemna Insurance Company in Ljubljana[534] and the Cooperative Lending Bank in Celje. Apart from some studies for facades made after he left Vienna, like the Skřivánek House in Platnéřska Street in Prague, which we have already mentioned, Plečnik had no opportunity to build a large town house until the late 1920s. Occasionally he made a few sketches, but as there was no chance of realizing them these did not progress beyond the initial idea, and would no doubt have been subject to fundamental compositional considerations had they been taken further. In these sketches Plečnik invented a wide variety of architectural ornamentation, as well as using columns, plant decoration and figural wall paintings. He was always in search of new ways of creating rich facades in one or two layers, but when he was actually building he was able to limit himself to the most essential.

The bank in Celje was given to one of his favourite students, Vinko Lenarčič, as a diploma subject, and he designed it under Plečnik's supervision (figs 254–5). As the two projects were very similar, Plečnik regarded the work for Celje as a kind of preparation for the facade of the insurance building in Ljubljana, and as the work on the bank progressed faster than that in Ljubljana under the direction of Anton Suhadolc, he was able to make the necessary

256–7. Studies for the facade and vestibule of the Vzajemna Insurance Company offices, 1928

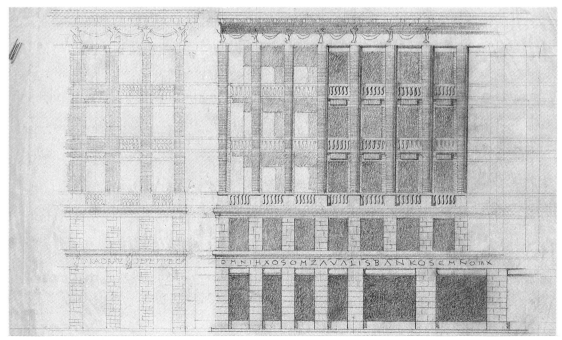

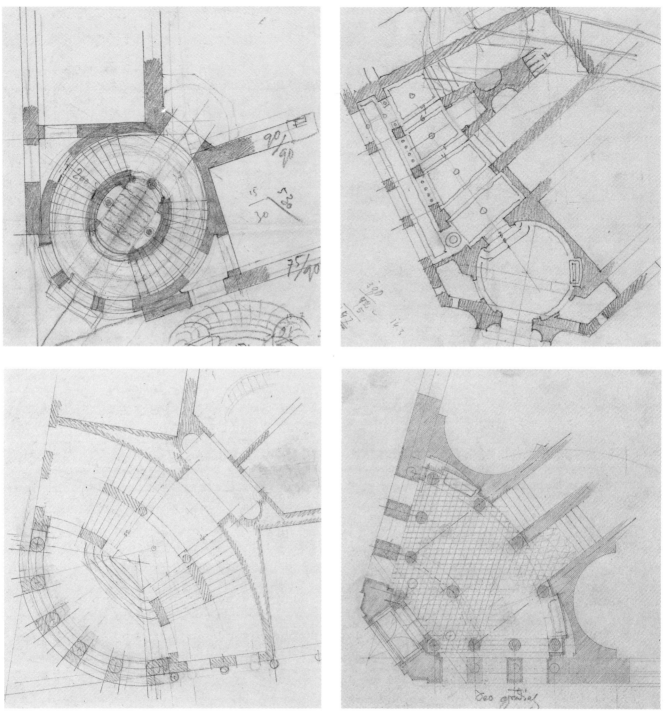

258–61. Variants for the entrance to the Vzajemna Insurance Company offices, 1928

modifications to the Ljubljana plans in good time. The basic compositional problem for both buildings was an exposed corner on an irregular bend between two streets (figs 254 and 262). In Ljubljana the building had to have doors facing the railway station, because most of the insurance company's customers came from the country and arrived in the city by train.

In Celje Plečnik followed the solution he had used for the Zacherl House in Vienna, that is, a cylinder enclosed in a facade. This was one of the greatest achievements of his early period; it has since often been copied in Vienna, and Plečnik himself used it with growing frequency as he grew older; however, here the flat Secessionist surfaces give way to Mediterranean plasticity. The dual texture of the facade covering and the structural core, only fleetingly indicated in Vienna, becomes a play of volumes in Celje, and the cylindrical insert that joins the wings of the building is not merely hinted at behind the balconies, it is visible. On the upper floors the cylinder is divided into several layers, and it ends at the top with an almost Baroque semi-circular recessed structure. This solution bears a strong resemblance to Wagner's corner house on Wienzeile, to which the Celje bank certainly bears some resemblance. A frequent practice of the Wagner circle was to erect a glass frontage right up the two lower floors; however, like the court facade of the Chamber of Commerce in Ljubljana and parts of the castle in Prague (see fig. 149), the bank in Celje has imitation wooden beams on the first and second floors. Wagner imitated a similar motif in rusticating the outside walls of his Postal Savings Bank in Vienna, but there is a difference in that he was endeavouring to keep pace with contemporary developments, while Plečnik was looking back to the beginnings of European culture.

After exploring a number of alternatives for the facade in Ljubljana Plečnik went back to a similar solution to that in Celje, namely the insertion of a corner cylinder (fig. 254). The first variant of the facade which was to include a monotonous repetition of columns between the windows in each floor did not satisfy him; so he was forced to look for a more monumental form of expression, although the building work had already started. Finally he decided that the columns would have to be taken over all three upper floors (see fig. 185). This fundamentally changed the composition, and brought it much closer to the Zacherl House. In Ljubljana, too, the functions of the upper and lower parts of the building differed, and Plečnik marked them off strictly from each other, contrasting the lower business premises, which are covered in Podpeč stone, with the upper residential floors, where the brickwork is left visible. In order to soften the vertical articulation somewhat he gave the col-

262. The Vzajemna Insurance Company offices, 1928–30

umns stone shaft rings, again recalling the initial version of the façade with accentuated horizontal caesurae between the floors. The local stone and the bricks could not of course create the dynamic tension he could have achieved with granite slabs, but they do increase the plasticity of the facade. The tectonics of the building were so clearly defined that the muscular telamons of the Zacherl House could be replaced by a decorative frieze of figures in the antique manner (see fig. 186). Plečnik placed them on consoles, as Josef Hoffmann had done on his Skywa-Primavesi House in Vienna, and gave them clear symbolic significance. The bands on the wall, which link their out-stretched arms, suggest that they should be interpreted on the one hand as an allegory of mutuality, thus taking up the name of the insurance company, and on the other as a translation of one of the basic textile elements in Semper's sense. The band is repeated twice more on the facade, firstly on the upper cornice, where it is held by smaller figures, and secondly beneath the gutter, where it is in the form of a wavy copper line.

According to Janko Valentinčič, who drew the detailed plans with his colleague France Tomažič and directed the building operations, some problems arose with the slight tapering of the columns downwards,[535] the means Plečnik used to achieve optical correction of the perspective distortion of the high columns. What influence Minoan architecture had on this idea may remain open. As he did not give

263–4. Main stairs in the Vzajemna Insurance Company office building, 1928–30

his columns capitals, the figures carry the vertical forces on upwards over the architrave. The façade of the insurance company's building in Ljubljana is markedly ambivalent. On the side views, which predominate, we see the building foreshortened, so that the windows are hidden behind the columns and the wall appears as a unified, windowless curtain in alternating red and grey. Only when we approach the building can we see its other, 'true' façade.

A specifically Viennese compositional theme Plečnik employed again in Ljubljana was the richer treatment of the exposed corner. While Wagner always treated this as an autonomous surface, Plečnik has attempted to integrate it in the facade as a whole. On the insurance company building he has solved the problem by changing the rhythm of the balconies and widening the gap between the columns and the wall. This gives emphasis to the corner facade, but incorporates it convincingly in the texture of the exterior as a whole.

The plastered court facade is the opposite of the monumental street facade. The long corridors with their metal balustrades look Biedermeier, but they are historically fully justified by the long tradition of this style in Ljubljana. Behind the deliberate contrast between the two facades is the idea of the ceremonious and workaday nature of the architecture.

The location of the stairs proved to be a particular problem (figs 258–61). Plečnik considered both the corner cylinder, which would have given this feature an additional functional justification, and a position outside the corner area. The triangular stairway which was finally chosen had the advantage of compensating for the irregularity of the site and making better use of the ground plan (figs 263–4). Nevertheless, Plečnik could not immediately decide in which of the sections to place his stairway or how to design the entrance. The round shape of the vestibule is a classic example of how the problem of the change in spatial direction, can be solved, the problem that was familiar to Plečnik from Wagner's Länderbank in Vienna.

The main stairway differs from the two others in having a more classical design. The mantle of columns is arranged around the light shaft, and is rich in dynamic. The mighty columns in Podpeč limestone can be seen as prerunners of the peristyle of the university library. Plečnik was aware of the difficulty of fluting the dark stone with its white veins, and, for this reason following Semper's instructions, he chose only the Roman Doric or Tuscan order here.[536]

We also need to mention the interiors, and at least some of these have survived the postwar era. Plečnik designed three types of chairs. In the waiting room of the fire insurance department he used natural wood and carved legs for the chairs, so coming slightly closer to folk art; however, the seats and arm rests are clearly metaphors of textile forms, and some of the details recall Wagner's table in the waiting room of the municipal railway station in Hütteldorf of 1898.[537] The 'aristocratic' counterpart to this ensemble are the veneered chairs upholstered in red leather for the large meeting room. They are a combination of the shapes of antique metal furniture and Egpytian wood furniture in an extremely bold design.

In October 1930 the office building for the Vzajemna Insurance Company was completed, and as the project came to an end Tomažič also ended his association with his teacher. The insurance company immediately offered him further work: the construction of an addition to the south side of the building and the construction of terrace houses in the suburb Bežigrad. He took over this lucrative commission on his own, thus evading Plečnik's control. He also broke off all connections with the School. After this disappointment Plečnik was more cautious. As his new assistant he chose Janko Valentinčič, who remained loyal to him to the end, and with his help he built what was known as the 'tourist chapel' in the basement of the building in 1933, where visitors could attend Sunday morning mass before departing.

THE UNIVERSITY LIBRARY

Few of Plečnik's works offered the Functionalists so much scope for criticizing his architecture as the building of what is now the National and University Library in Ljubljana. Vurnik disparagingly called it a 'Baroque palace', and tried to prove he could have done the work better and at less cost.[538] By the early 1930s the new movements in art had become so established in Europe that from the perspective of a big city the library building did indeed appear an anachronism. As the critics have sought – in vain – in this building for what Plečnik deliberately refrained from putting into it, they were bound to overlook what makes it one of the classic works of the modern age in a formal respect, and from the standpoint of today. There was complete misunderstanding, and Plečnik, caught in the crossfire of opinions, tried in vain to clarify his position: 'I am well aware of the importance of a good library – I am even more aware of the need for large, fine rooms.'[539] In a letter to the rector of the University of Ljubljana he wrote, confident of his abilities, that the building would be an honour to the town 'even after it may no longer be serving its original purpose'.[540]

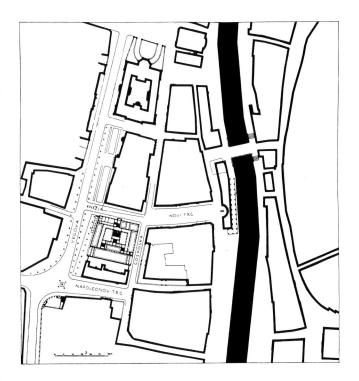

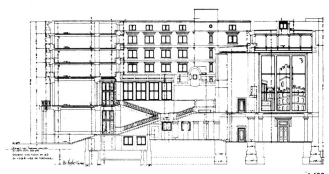

265–6. Project for the university library, 1932, site and section along the stairway.

After his experience with the library for Masaryk in Prague Castle Plečnik equated his task with the creation of a temple of learning and human wisdom, essential for the healthy development of his people and their independence. The question of a central library had become acute in Ljubljana after the First World War, when the Slovenian university was founded. As early as 1927 Aleksander Dev, in Plečnik's School, had been working on a building for the new library.[541] But for tactical reasons Plečnik did not immediately want to offer his assistance to the university authorities and he preferred to wait and see how the engineers of the public administration would tackle the work, expecting them to fail miserably.[542] He accepted the invitation to join the project in the spring of 1930. The Slavists Franc Kidrič

253

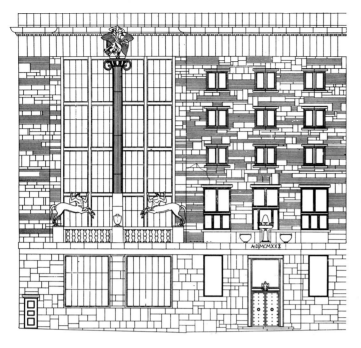

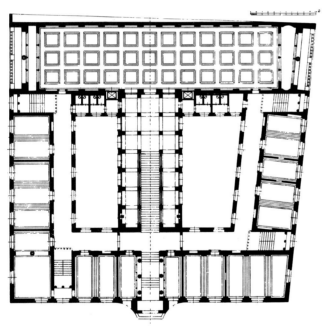

267–8. Final version of the university library project of 1936, part of the facade and ground plan of the first floor

and Ivan Prijatelj outlined the programme, which was still rather vague, to him on behalf of the rector, explaining the university's vision of the building, which was to take a million books and be sufficient for the demands of the next hundred years. So it could be better controlled it was also to contain the living quarters of an administrator, who was to have a separate entrance.

The site envisaged for the new library was that of the old Palais Auersperg, which sadly had been demolished after the earthquake of 1895. It lay between Vega Street (Vegova ulica) and Gentlemen's Street (Gosposka ulica) (fig. 265). It was a prime site, next to the New Square (Novi trg), and hence it formed part of a dialogue with the old urban network. Plečnik's main aim was to heal the wound in the urban fabric and he was only secondly concerned with the functional part of the project. As we see from the lifts, and his placing of the books in concrete cells that were easily accessible but fireproof, he adapted the functional parts almost literally from Wagner's project for the Vienna University Library of 1910.[543] Wagner's internal arrangement seemed to him so appropriate that he evidently saw no need to study other modern libraries, as Kidrič and Prijatelj had envisaged when outlining the project. Plečnik only moved away from the principles of his teacher in the reading room, which Wagner maintained should not exceed 4.7 metres in height, as a higher ceiling would have an unfortunate effect on the users.

Plečnik, in fact, monumetalized his reading room by making it 10 metres high; he also opened it on the narrow sides with two full-length windows. These had been requested by the university authorities, who believed that the view of the city would help to relax eyes tired from reading. As the clients could never entirely agree, major and minor alterations were introduced during the planning phase, not always to the advantage of the building. The lecture room below the reading room, for instance, is inadequately lit, because of the need to give slide talks there, and this is one example of the short-sighted arguments Plečnik had to cope with during the work.

Where Wagner had added a book museum to his second variant of the Vienna library of 1914,[544] Plečnik went a step further in his interpretation and designed the entrance to the reading room as a mental preparation for the encounter with scholarship. In accordance with this symbolism he divided the ground plan of the building with a stairway in the inner court which was to end under a smaller cupola before the reading room (fig. 266), which was placed crossway to the main axis of the entrance hall. The arrangement of the broad tripartite stairway resulted in floors of different heights. From the outside this is evident from the higher ground and

254

first storeys and the lower storeys above, which house the books. As the site was on a slight slope this subdivision could not be taken consistently around all three facades, and the front on Vega Street, which lies on a slightly higher level, has one floor less. The more spacious rooms in the lower part of the building were for offices, catalogues and card indices, exhibitions and the curator's apartment. As it did not seem likely that the building would be filled with books within the foreseeable future, the authorities initially allowed the Arts Faculty to use the lower floors. Plečnik then suggested that some of the ceilings here could be installed later on the concrete supports that would already be in place.[545]

On the first version of the facade Plečnik emphasized the *piano nobile* and he also framed the two windows of the reading room with rustication and balustrades. He skilfully compensated for the unparallel course of the two main roads by forming a triangular inter-space between the outer and inner windows of the big reading room facing Vega Street. In itself, the project was rational, but the representative parts, i.e. the facade, the staircase and the reading room, owed much to historicism, the grandiose finale of which he had experienced in Vienna. Inspiration for the theme of the processional route, which Plečnik had investigated thoroughly already in the staircase of the Zacherl House and now developed further in the library in Ljubljana, can also be found in the Burgtheater in Vienna and the Bavarian State Library in Munich, although they cannot be cited as direct models.

The work on the library was held up by numerous obstacles. The short term deliberately allowed by the authorities for the utilization of the government loan had already expired before the plans could be submitted for approval. Some of the plans were then actually lost in the State Ministry of Building in Belgrade, causing considerable anger and several petitions were presented by Slovene politicians to the capital. The students particularly, who had united in the Academic Action for the construction of a university library, put pressure on the local politicians not to give in to Belgrade, as Slovenia ought to be given back at least part of the money from the state budget it had paid into the joint fund. Then in 1934, when the Ministry approved the project, difficulties unexpectedly arose in Ljubljana. The management of the neighbouring Slavija Bank objected to the siting of the library on the northern line of the old palace. Plečnik vainly tried to show that the New Square would then simply be restored to the coherent shape it had lost in the earthquake of 1895. The bank, however, was successful in its protests, and this in turn brought protests from other neighbours and ultimately caused planning per-

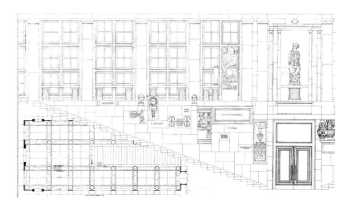

269. Plan of the stairway in the university library, 1938

mission to be withdrawn. Finally, it became apparent that the university was not a suitable counterpart in the discussions with Belgrade and that this was a task for the regional administration. Its technical department, where a former pupil of Plečnik, Vinko Glanz, was employed, undertook the implementation of the project and the supervision of the building. This change was particularly painful for Plečnik's assistant Janko Valentinčič, who had executed many of the drawings; now, from mid-December 1935 Edvard Ravnikar, as a friend of Glanz, took over this work, and he worked with Plečnik on the library for nearly three years. The association later came to an end, when he took over some of Plečnik's other projects.

While Plečnik was waiting for the answer from the Ministry he put the project on public display, with an accompanying study by France Stele, in the summer of 1933.[546] The following year Ivan Vurnik put forward a rival study,[547] and this started a polemical dispute which penetrated as far as Belgrade and again threatened to delay the start of the building work. Although the budget for the Slovenian library was approved by Parliament in the summer of 1935, Plečnik had one final obstacle to overcome. During the lengthy dispute, the standard format for bricks had been changed by law in the Kingdom of Yugoslavia. The new regulations meant that the project had to be reworked. Resignedly Plečnik wrote to the president of the regional administration:

Since I started to design the university library, I have developed further with the help of God. I do not wish to think about past events, and I have no comment to make on the wisdom of the engineers in changing the format of the small bricks and its terrific importance for the country's economy, especially at this present time, etc. My days may well be numbered now, and I have other, greater tasks in mind, as I am already climbing the hill to

270. Building the stairs, 1937

colder and clearer air. For that reason I ask you to be so very kind as to refuse to deal with my project any further. You must know that I have no ulterior motives or designs in saying this. So that I do not have to do it in public, I ask you to cut through the thread that binds me to this unappetizing affair, energetically and ruthlessly.[548]

Although this would cause further problems with the calculations and the building permit, Plečnik altered the plans at the beginning of 1936, while the tender for the building work was actually being held. This was not, as might be thought, in reaction to comments by the new rector, who, in an effort to calm the dispute, sent both projects to Switzerland. The architect O.R. Salvisberg in Zurich had made some very negative remarks about Plečnik's spatial concept, and efforts were being made in Ljubljana to persuade him to work with Vurnik whose project found more favour with Salvisberg; the absurd suggestion was put forward that he should only be responsible for the facade. Nevertheless, this episode was not the reason for Plečnik's final remaking of the plan. Moreover, he had recognized that in spite of everything the project was actually starting to move. He wished to reappraise his original concept since the first solution he had worked out under the impact of the designs for the insurance company and the People's Lending Bank now seemed to him to have lost so much of its directness that it was no longer sufficiently convincing.

When he left Prague for good in 1934 Plečnik also moved away from his concern with the formal problems of Antiquity which had preoccupied him for nearly fifteen years, and returned to the dialogue with Semper's cladding theory that had led him to the radical solution of the Zacherl House in his youthful conflict with Wagner. In his mature years he attempted to continue this boldness with the help of local building materials. The grey Podpeč stone and the visible bricks on the facade of the university library (figs 187–8) produced a decorative combination like those in some of his Secessionist sketches. But he may also have been inspired by elements in West European and Byzantine art. It is probably going too far to say that the Zuccari House in Rome is the inspiration here,[549] particularly as we know that Plečnik mentioned the monumentalization of the typical Karst house, which is made of stone and brick, to his assistant Valentinčič in connection with the university library.[550]

But this explanation also needs to be treated with caution. It is certainly right that Plečnik initially intended more of the wall to be of stone,[551] but this proved too costly. Curk, the builder, used various kinds of granite and marble, as well as Podpeč stone, and stones which he found when digging the foundations. Thus he incorporated remnants of the old Palais Auersperg and the Roman and medieval city walls in the facade, completing the whole with concrete blocks. The stones are all differently worked – under the contract the projecting stones were paid for only to a maximum of five centimetres from the façade wall – and this created a dynamic on the facade that accords with Semper's account of the foundations of the Wall in Jerusalem, which he took from Viollet-le-Duc.[552]

The architect liked to stress that the corner of his library on the New Square radiated a monumentality similar to that of the Palazzo Medici-Riccardi in Florence.[553] To accord with the dominant position he included profiled stone in the wall; this also retained the historical reference to the old Palais Auersperg. Whether the stones were genuine remnants or imitation was of secondary importance to him. To display his wishful thinking that Slovenian culture had Mediterranean roots on the library building as well he placed above the portal round ceramic vessels, cast in concrete, and based on Etruscan models.

Plečnik's instruction that all the stones were to be built in horizontal rows without caesurae is evidence of his 'textile' approach to the facade. He moved away from the classical arrangement dictated by tectonic laws and gave another demonstration of the richness that lies in the textural application of material. The facade of the library is like a great oriental carpet, with the coarse threads of stone 'worked' into the brick ground. The lower part is entirely in stone, and so corresponds to the traditional rustication. As in his first work, the Villa Langer in Vienna-Hietzing, Plečnik only left the brickwork visible up to a certain height, thus

271. Stairway in the university library, 1936–40

272–3. Portal of the Exhibition Room in the University Library, 1939–40; a detail and the whole

allowing the shadows from the wave-patterned cornice, which replaces the roof projection, to play on the smooth top strip. It is designed as a metaphor of the antique roof of Roman tiles with their ends concealed in ornaments known as *antefixa*, and so is thoroughly in keeping with a monumental building. The cornice is thus reduced to pure ornamentation. While Semper compared the ornamental parts of a building to the adornment of a woman,[554] Plečnik called them a necklace. His associate Ravnikar had to draw seven variants in full size before he could decide which one to use.[555]

Like those on Wagner's houses on the Wienzeile, the windows are treated as modest openings in the wall, without reference to the texture of the facade. The difference in size reflects the hierarchy of the rooms behind them. The smaller windows on the upper floors echo the English bay windows that were so popular in Vienna around the turn of the century and were also used on the Zacherl House; they not only enliven the facade, they also form an even structure of folds. The same also applies to the two entrances to the library. They are like organically projecting folds with no trace of classical tectonic ornamentation and so they are also subordinate to the textile mantle of the facade. Only the main entrance door and its frame are a consistent citation of Antiquity or, better, an archaic variant of Semper's depiction of the door to the Pantheon[556] with the central column and the door handles in the form of horses' heads. Initially Plečnik wanted to have these cast in bronze on the Roman model, but he ultimately had to be content with covering the wooden core with copper. He agreed to such a compromise after failing at Prague Castle to use bronze wings on the doors of the columned hall, such as once had decorated the Roman Pantheon.

The particular importance of the reading room is emphasized by a colossal column set in the archaic manner in the centre of each window. It can be thought of as the only visible element of the unclad core of the building, that is, an imaginary columned hall (see fig. 191). Its bronze volutes are made according to Choisy's explanation of original Corinth capitals which were supposed to have had tin frameworks, although Semper's speculation on the development of the Ionic capital from the Assyrian tree of life hammered in tin, must not be overlooked.[557] At the beginning of the nineteenth century, Neo-Classical columns, were often decorated with bronze capitals.

The creative recreation of Antiquity, which Max Fabiani, to cite one example, so greatly esteemed in Plečnik's work[558] is also evident in the entrance to the reading room. This part of the building also underwent fundamental changes from the original design (fig. 268). Plečnik put the reading room on the first floor, making it accessible from a direct flight of stairs with no interim landings (see fig. 189). It was an infringement of the building regulations, as was his renunciation of hand rails. He reduced the original width of the stairs to leave room for four additional stairways at the sides. In the new plan he incorporated the hall outside the reading room into the monumental columned room that extends right across the floor (see figs 190 and 271). Plečnik took heed of Semper's warning regarding the working of dark stone, and did not flute the massive Roman Doric columns;[559] however, he deliberately gave them shafts composed of differently veined drums of Podpeč stone. When the stone mason used a similar but unpatterned stone for the ceiling beams, he protested, arguing that it was 'as dead as Protestant philosophy',[560] a comparison which Plečnik, as an orthodox Catholic, no doubt thought was annihilating.

It was his desire to revive the spirit of the Acropolis in Athens in Ljubljana by incorporating epitaphs, allegories and hermae on the walls of the stairs (fig. 269), but he would have needed the appropriate assistant for the work, one possessing the same skill in antique stylization that Plečnik himself had displayed in the vases on the St Charles Borromeo Fountain in Vienna. As he could not find anyone with the appropriate skills among the local sculptors he dropped the idea, apart from the door handles and the female figure with the vase, the plaster model for which was ready when the war started. The centaurs which he wanted beside the windows of the reading room (fig. 267) and the figures of the athletes and scholars on the Roman wall before the library were not realized either. In contrast to the compositional severity of the peristyle, which has no figures, the balustrades have squat, freely designed Doric and Aeolian columns (see fig. 190). Instead of hanging lights he placed high metal candelbra near the windows. They recall torches and show that Plečnik's Secessionist organic designs and the classicism of his later recourse to Antiquity often sprang from the same roots. As a final adornment the building was given Lojze Dolinar's over-life size bronze figure of Moses (see fig. 187). It was a gift from the Regional Government to the City Council, but the Council could not find a suitable place for it. Placing the figure above the side entrance to the library was a provisional solution in Plečnik's eyes, and he looked for ways to provide a special support on a more suitable part of the facade.[561]

Plečnik perfected the symbolic path leading from darkness into light with numerous textile metaphors. Beginning with the 'doormat' in granite, he spread over the entire stairway an imaginary runner, which is only indicated by the spacing between the upper part of each stair and the point where it joins the wall, which gives an impression of something else lying over the stairs. Between the columns he laid light-edged 'carpets' in reddish Hotavlje stone, and these correspond with the square coffers in the ceiling in Semper's sense (fig. 271).

A peak in Plečnik's response to Semper's descriptions – in this case his account of the function of the Antique vestiarium – is the solemnly clad portal of the exhibition room (figs 195, 273).[562] Translating this into a more durable material Plečnik created a eulogy of the two local stones that he used most, grey Podpeč stone and the reddish stone from Hotavlje. With the latter he formed a two-part 'curtain', or portière, on the door, the 'folds' of which do not consistently reach to the floor.[563] The 'stitched' transition from one kind of stone to another and a band intended for lettering above the door are further illumination of this monumental metamorphosis of antique decoration. The door leaves are a combination of boldly inlaid wooden frames and stone infills, deriving from Semper's speculative considerations on the original technique of covering wood with metal.[564]

The decision of the university authorities not to place a book store above the reading room gave Plečnik the opportunity to raise the ceiling even higher (see figs 193–4). The long room stands at right angles to the entrance. The height is visually reduced by the inclined ends of the wall cupboards and shelving, which contain the hot air pipes, invisible to the library user. The central heating radiators are hidden behind the bookcase doors, which have open slats.

Of particular interest are the two metal paths between the galleries in the reference library, which cross the room beside the entrance. The supports for these, like all the other balustrades in the room, are gas pipes that have interim pieces in bronze at their joints. This elegant citation of nineteenth-century industrial aesthetics – originally more costly chrome plated pipes were to be used – borrows from Otto Wagner.[565] However, if we see the paths and balustrades in the light of Semper's speculations they lose their profane nature, as they can also be regarded as imitations of the metal tubular constructions of the early Asian peoples that are said to be modelled on bamboo and reed.[566] This is very evident with some of Wagner's furniture,[567] but it could also apply to Plečnik's metal installations in the university library in Ljubljana. First and foremost, however, this is the restrained use of functionally necessary constructions, and Plečnik probably did not attach any very great symbolic importance to them. He covered the underside of the two paths with wood parquet and so raised them from the functional to the ornamental level. In reconstructing the original significance of individual ornamental components Plečnik liked to draw on analogies and his experience of the local environment, and for this reason his metamorphoses are often difficult to penetrate, and it is not possible to interpret them with the help of classical iconography.

In January 1944 an Italian mail aircraft crashed on the library building, which was barely finished and not yet fitted out. The reading room was badly damaged, but the skeletal structure was restored during the war. However, the ceiling, lights and interior fittings could only be installed after the war.[568] Plečnik simplified the new ceiling slightly, bringing it closer to a large wooden carpet in appearance, with flat surfaces and a contrasting edging. To the two chandeliers that had originally been envisaged he added a third with a tectonic core and plant-like light vessels facing the convex metal mirror (see fig. 192). Following Semper's instruction, he hung it in the middle of the ceiling[569] and not on the entrance axis as a Neo-Classicist would have done.

More than a decade after Gunnar Asplund's municipal library in Stockholm Plečnik erected a similar work in the south of Europe, so drawing attention to the relativity of the concept modernity in architecture. He had an advantage over the Functionalists in his faith in Semper, and this enabled him to tackle all the classical formal problems of architecture without directly quoting the ancients.

VILLAS AND INTERIORS

There is a social element in Plečnik's designs for residential buildings; this was not due to the dictates of Functionalism, but reflected his concern to create comfortable living conditions for less prosperous social classes as well, with as much space as possible. He strenuously objected to the idea of minimalized housing. As he said: 'Utilitarianism, typology and standardization are the death of any art; art cannot be industrialized.'[570] His experiments with terraced housing in Prague and his interest in building in clay should be seen more as a form of intellectual exercise. While he was still in Vienna Plečnik had objected to designs for rented apartment blocks that did not provide for the needs of all their occupants equally. In his youth he had loved Dickens' novels, and there is an echo of Dickens rather than socialism in Plečnik's characteristic comment that every palace ought to contain a free apartment for a poor family, 'so that the wealthy ladies and gentlemen on the upper floors are reminded of poverty and need, while the poor can see that the lives of the rich are not all joy and fulfilment'.[571]

Plečnik's attitudes were socially oriented, but he was opposed to a violent change in social conditions. He always held the view that true art can only be secured by wealth.

That needs to be borne in mind particularly when considering his residential buildings and interiors, as he was primarily creating individualized architecture for wealthy clients. We find a similar situation, though under different conditions, among the representatives of the classical modern movement. Nothing could have been more alien to Plečnik than Le Corbusier's machines for living in. However, although he rejected the modern Functionalist achievements, he always demanded good lighting, ventilation and hygiene, which he saw as traditional architectural values. The glass walls of the contemporary avantgarde architects, for instance, merely caused him to enlarge his classical windows. He would say jokingly that the British Water Closet was the only true contribution made by the modern age to living culture.

Apart from the buildings of his time in Vienna Plečnik built relatively few private houses, as most prospective clients were frightened off by his reputation for disdaining comfort and the high costs his representative style would have involved. Beside the extension to his own house he designed two villas in 1936, on for the doctor Josip Bežek in Kranj, and the other for the manager of the royal hunting grounds, Ciril Dimnik in Belgrade. Only the villa for Bežek was actually built. Other projects included the grandiose summer house, mentioned above, for the dentist Verčon on Lapad near Dubrovnik in 1933/4, and designs for the Villa Freyer in Ljubljana in 1944. Plečnik's own house and that of Bežek were both bachelor establishments, and so they have little family living space.

For his own use, Plečnik would have liked a more representative dwelling with polished marble columns,[572] but he lacked the financial means for that. Nevertheless, the variant he did build is very convincing (fig. 274). In 1923 and 1924 he added a round two-storey tower to the suburban house he had purchased, confounding his students by adding a saddleback roof. Later he found confirmation of this idea in a book on old Spanish architecture.[573] His brothers Andrej and Janez were to live in the tower. Owing to his limited funds Plečnik had to content himself with materials left over from other sites, and he paved the path by the house with concrete slabs, which were slightly damaged and could not be used in the concurrent constrution of the stadium in Ljubljana for the gym association 'Orel', and he used old windows, left over from his adaptation of the Jesuit monastery in Ljubljana, for his conservatory.

For the Villa Bežek in Kranj Plečnik went back to the cubic concept of a building with tectonic ornamentation. He set a pent roof on the house, raising it on the street frontage and dropping it down on the lower garden side. The ground floor is clad in roughly worked stone, like the university

274. Plečnik's own house in Ljubljana, 1923/4, conservatory, 1930

275. His study on the first floor, set up in 1927. (The two photographs were taken shortly after the architect's death.)

276–7. Plečnik's living room and bedroom on the ground floor of his house, present state.

library building and St Michael's church in the Moor. The main door is also modelled on that of the university library, and is emphasised by the projecting mantle of the building. The pilasters, architrave and window heads are classical ornamental elements that had almost passed out of usage in European architecture at that time. The interior of the villa, which was partially destroyed in the 1970s, now gives little indication of the once spacious double wooden staircase (fig. 278) and the excellent design of the grand living room, which once held part of the owner's art collection.

The Villa Dimnik in Belgrade was on a much more liberal scale (fig. 279),[574] and here Plečnik took up Schinkel's theme of an open stairway set behind columns. His pupil Alois Metelák had handled this theme in 1920 for the Villa Kusa in Skuteč in eastern Bohemia,[575] and Plečnik would certainly have had a hand in the designs. Nevertheless, with the Villa Dimnik he was probably reminded of the theme by the great double window in the university library. The composition of this building, which was never executed, was enriched by some favourite motifs from Plečnik's time in Vienna, like the hall extended up through all the floors, balconies taken round the corner of the building and similar features.

The design for the Villa Freyer in the Poljane suburb of Ljubljana was similarly ambitious (fig. 280).[576] Its execution was prevented by the war. Plečnik wanted to enliven the facade by alternating two different textures, and he would probably have used plaster and brick. For the two narrower side facades he wanted Neo-Classical triangular gables. The Freyers admired Plečnik's art and they also asked him to make a number of small artefacts for them to sell in their souvenir and gingerbread shop on Congress Square, which the architect had fitted out for them some years earlier.

However, not all Plečnik's ideas were what the client wanted. He was never, for instance, able to accept Izidor Cankar's decision to leave the priesthood, and when asked to design a house for him, Plečnik drew a building for a cultured priest and not a family home, which was what Cankar wanted.[577]

The range of his views on the interior is particularly evident from his own home and the Prelovšek residence. While he himself refused to accept many of the achievements of twentieth-century civilization, like central heating, a modern bathroom and the radio, preferring to surround himself with the many 'objets à réaction poétique' which he had been given or found (figs 275–7), the Villa Prelovšek, which he rebuilt between 1931 and 1933, displays a very formal side of his nature. His own home was that of an artist, who needed a particular atmosphere, the second is a noble residence for the Director of the Municipal Building Department. The Prelovšek residence thus became a counterpart, adjusted to take account of local conditions, to the interiors in Prague Castle, and now that some of these no longer exist as he designed them it is all the more important a testimony to Plečnik's residential work (see figs 199–200, 281–5). For that reason it deserves a closer examination. It has in common with the salons in Prague its many metamorphoses of the antique in the Semper manner.

Matko Prelovšek was an engineer who had already built a villa to his own designs before the First World War. As buildings were required by law to be two-storey in this part of Ljubljana, but he and his wife only needed the ground floor of a detached house, he had to have very high ceilings – a fact that was later very welcome to Plečnik. The architect's interventions were limited to giving a more representative look to the whole. Instead of a modest entrance he added an external staircase to the building, beneath which he built a cellar in dialogue with folk art, using the remains of an oaken bridge that had once spanned the Ljubljanica. He christened the cellar after the Slovenian folk hero Martin Karpan. He gave the stairway a meandering ground plan, strengthening the impression of archaic Cretan art by placing concrete vases on cubic plinths and adding a metal balustrade influenced by the ornamentation on the clay vessels in the palace in Knossos.

Plečnik enlarged the antechamber by making a great arch, as he had in the Zacherl Villa in Döbling and later in the so-called salon with the harp in Prague Castle. The use of black for all the furniture adds to the atmosphere of the new room. He used the same method for the existing coffered ceiling in the salon, which he thus incorporated in the redesigned space. Where the loggia had been he had to extend the ceiling, but he changed the scale of the coffers in order to mark the old off clearly from the new.

He enlarged the spacious living room by knocking through to the adjacent room, which also gave him extra daylight. Plečnik had a particular ability to harmonize heterogeneous elements with minimal intervention, as he did for example, with the three doors in this room, by adding the same wooden lintels on gilt volutes, so distracting attention from their different design. The villa had a large window decorated in the Secessionist style; Plečnik disliked it, and he covered it with wooden shutters for the winter in the English manner. He suggested that the colourful chimneypiece should be screened with red woollen material in the summer, to match the armchairs beside the fireplace. The same Semper theme of textile covering and screening is

278. Stairs in the Bežek House in Kranj, 1936

to be found in the full-length white linen curtains to the glass balcony wall. In the dining room, he used a solemn, grandiose architectural vocabulary with grey Podpeč stone. Instead of the old partition wall Plečnik made three arches on two Tuscan columns (fig. 281).

His treatment of the library was quite different, for this was to be an intellectual environment for discussions that would be in the main official (see fig. 200). Following the model of the salon for the President's daughter in Prague Castle Plečnik fitted the library with Croatian folk embroidery collected by Prelovšek's wife Elsa. He panelled the walls with carefully selected pine wood, simply polishing this with natural wax, so that over the years it acquired a pleasant warm yellow colour.

He matched the furniture consistently to the function of the room. In the library he monumentalized the armchairs by combining Egyptian and Greek models, making use of the structural elements in a decorative design. The leather of the seats and backs extends over the edges, and this can be interpreted in Semper's sense as an interim stage between

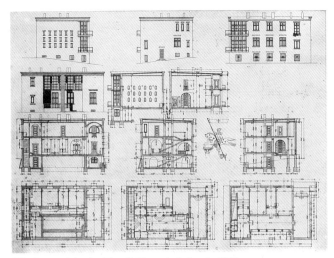

279. Proposal for the Dimnik House in Belgrade, 1936

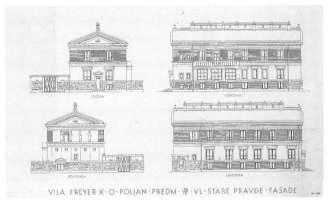

VILA FREYER K·O·POLJAN·PREDM·⚜·VL·STARE PRAVDE·FASADE

280. Proposal for the Freyer House in Ljubljana, 1944

upholstery laid upon the seats and fixed upholstery. The visitor may well feel honoured to be seated thus, but the chairs are not so comfortable as to induce him to linger. In contrast, the chairs at the long dining table are comfortable, but the shape of their backs forces the user to sit correctly upright. The architect's approach to designing furniture was diametrically opposed to the functionalist one. The prototypes of his chairs helped him to observe whether they allowed a dignified posture for the human body.

The furniture in the salon is certainly one of the Plečnik's greatest achievements in interior design, and we see him taking his skills as a carpenter to virtuoso performance. The basic concept is an ideal metal chair, which, according to Semper constituted the peak of furniture creation in Antiquity. Plečnik changed it into a modern one very convincingly, as he not only retained the black of the metal, but also allowed the elasticity of the original material to flow literally into the arm rests (see figs 199 and 285). The same applies to

the backs, which curve backwards slightly at the top, displaying the logic of sheet metal in wood. The suggestion of metal is further reinforced by the contrast between the 'soft' disc-shaped inlays of the arm rests, which are in lighter mahogany. The elegance of their shape transmits the Ionic spirit, and Plečnik actually imitates the capital of the order in the backs of the chairs.[578] The recollection of Wagner's favourite metamorphosis of the Greek tripod and the sacrificial altar gave rise to the matching round table and the walnut sideboard in the dining room (figs 281 and 284). Plečnik used solid wood tables on stylized Egyptian or Greek plinths again later, in the dining room of the Villa Šverljuga in Bled and in the reading room of the university library.

The stove in the salon is covered with tombac, and it clearly derives from Semper (see fig. 199). Plečnik handles the lights similarly. The gilt wooden lamp in the library, seen in conjunction with the embroideries, gives the impression of a decorative buckle (fig. 282). The upper part of the chandelier in the dining room is inspired by Etruscan metal lights, while the great round plate of this chandelier bears the Bohemian saying: 'A guest in the home is God in the home', although the client originally wanted: 'Two days are enough for any guest'. The chandelier in the salon is highly imaginative, consisting of a severe architectural core and arms inspired by vegetable forms; it is thus a forerunner of the great chandelier in the university library reading room (see fig. 192). Plečnik, faithfully following Semper's instructions, hung it in the middle of the uniformly designed pre-existent ceiling, disregarding the spatial axes. The two basic elements of textile art, the band and the knot, are to be found translated into more durable material on the candlestick in the corner of the salon. Some older metal objects, which Plečnik appreciated for their careful workmanship, are also characteristic of Semper's approach, being composed or 'elevated' into a new function.

Although such universal artistic themes predominate, Plečnik's endeavoured to create an interior with symbolic reference to his client. He incorporated the civic arms and included a bust of the daughter of the house, Tatjana, who had died young. He designed other items of personal significance for the family, like a candlestick for family celebrations or the washstand in Podpeč stone, which is like a font. They also reflect the architect's views on the social and cultural obligations of the national élite.

The garden of the Prelovšek residence (1930/1)[579] occupies an exceptional place among the works that Plečnik created for Ljubljana. It consists of a raised, geometric area with lawns, rose and juniper spaliers interspersed with sand or paved paths, and a lower part around the fishpond, which

264

281

282

283

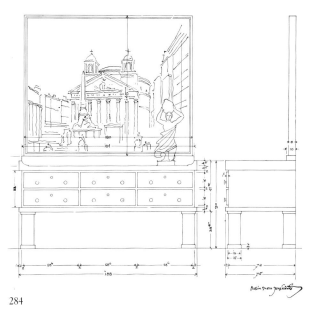

284

Converting the Prelovšek Villa in Ljubljana, 1931–3:
281–2. Dining room and Library.
283. Sketch for the library, around 1932.
284. Sideboard, 1932

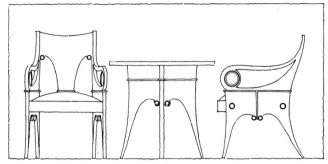

285. The Prelovšek Villa: salon furniture, around 1932

is more loosely planted in the Japanese style. The two levels of the garden are linked by a broad flight of steps, which marks the shorter cross axis. The point of intersection of the two axes is not given prominence. Plečnik used the columns and older stone masonry together with the trees in a purely architectural sense.

In his own house, he did not need so rich an environment, since, particularly after the death of Andrej in 1931, he had finally abandoned his hopes of anyone joining him in the house. For furniture he was content with a few prototypes of his own armchairs, which he selected from the carpenter's shop. Among other things he furnished a small room where he could entertain his rare guests in winter by a warm stove with black coffee and Cviček, a slightly sour red wine from Lower Carniola. In view of the importance which Semper attached to the ceiling he had a purely decorative beam attached in the ground floor of the extension thus linking the door of the bathroom visually with the wardrobe (fig. 276). A ridge beam over two characteristic door frames is typically Etruscan, found most frequently in the burial chambers of the necropolis in Tarquinia. In this way Plečnik manifested the speculation about the Etruscan origins of his own nation right in his room. On the second floor he covered the ceiling of his work room with wood, and the walls are clad in pine wood, out of which two cupboards protrude into the room. The ceiling is a dynamic combination of variously turned wooden coffers, which he explained to his nephew in the following words; 'For a man to invent so natural a construction he must go through a whole life full of experience.[580] He did not fence the garden behind the house. Only the part close to the house was to be planted with Alpine plants and flowering bushes, the remainder he left for his neighbour to use. In this suburban isolation he wanted quiet above all things. When the house next door was put up for sale he bought it for fear that a noisy business might be set up there. In 1930 he added a south facing conservatory to his house, which was pleasantly warmed by the sun even in winter.

8   DESIGNING HIS HOME TOWN

Plečnik always maintained that he had no feeling for large scale planning.[581] And in fact, at the time of his return to Ljubljana his experience in this field was limited to the gardens at Prague Castle and its parks. Alice Masaryk had tried to interest him in urban design by stressing that Prague was to be the national metropolis and showing him books on American cities. But Plečnik saw his task as primarily to ennoble and enhance the existing fabric of the city. He had already begun to concern himself with Ljubljana while still a student; he could still remember the Mediterranean city that had been destroyed in the earthquake in 1895, and he could never come to terms with its redesign to Austrian models.

He missed the late Renaissance Palais Auersperg in Gentlemen's Street, the Square of the Virgin Mary, once dominated by the Franciscan church, and not least the old course of the river, that had been turned into a concrete canal quite alien to the spirit of the town before the First World War. His love of his hometown was so great that he was actually jealous of Fabiani's regulation plan of 1895, and although it had undeniable qualities he regarded it as the work of an alien intruder. When the political map of central Europe changed radically after the First World War, Plečnik quickly realized Ljubljana's new role, which had changed overnight from a provincial Austro-Hungarian town into the capital of the Slovene people. Therefore, his town planning was not only meant to heal the wounds left by the renovation after the earthquake of 1895 which was carried out in imitation of Hapsburgian Vienna, but he strove to make it the nation's capital.

The politicians in Slovenia were not ready for Plečnik's visions, but in the engineer Matko Prelovšek and the art historian France Stele he found partners of like mind. Prelovšek was four years younger than Plečnik; he had studied architecture in Vienna and briefly made Plečnik's acquaintance there. His career was almost entirely in the Municipal Building Department in Ljubljana, which he headed, with a deep sense of responsibility, from 1914 to the spring of 1937. He displayed great skill in holding the balance between the liberals and the Catholic politicians without seriously disconcerting either side, although he was always being accused of giving Plečnik one-sided support. When he retired as Director of the Municipal Building Department one of the happiest periods in the history of building in Ljubljana came to an end, for Plečnik had enjoyed a free hand while Prelovšek was in office and did not have to fight with rivals.

France Stele was younger than Plečnik and Prelovšek, and he only went to Vienna some time later than they. He studied under professors who had already moved away from Semper's theories, and for this reason Plečnik entertained some reservations towards him. He regarded the art historian Izidor Cankar, by far the best-educated and the most cosmopolitan among the Slovene clergy, as more competent in technical matters. Plečnik only grew closer to Stele when Cankar, to Plečnik's bitter disappointment, resigned from the priesthood, but he never fully confided in him, indeed he did not to anyone in Ljubljana. Stele was one of the greatest living experts on Slovenian art, and he did much to make Plečnik known. From the mid-1920s he discussed Plečnik's work with great enthusiasm in the Catholic press, and this also strengthened Prelovšek's position.

When Prelovšek retired, Stele, who was then a member of the City Council and became chairman a few years before the outbreak of the Second World War, ensured that Plečnik continued to receive prestigious commissions from the Council. The friendship between the three men who were most concerned with the city's appearance proved ideal. In connection with the design of St James's Square (Šentjakobski trg) Plečnik wrote to his brother: 'They know me now in the Council – and I sometimes just jot an idea down on the back of a bill.'[582] Bureaucracy was often circumvented, and the architect would give the head of the Municipal Garden Department, Anton Lap, for instance, instructions on the spot. The discussions on current issues in Ljubljana would take place in the evening over a glass of wine in a local inn, and Prelovšek generally succeeded in squeezing a few extra dinars out of the tight municipal budget for one or other embellishment, which Plečnik then carried out with stones selected from masons' yards or retrieved from municipal stores. Prelovšek would also ask the architect about minor issues, like the design of parks, which, as in Austria, had public toilets and tobacco kiosks, or the paving for alleys and squares. In fact, Plečnik was involved in anything connected with town planning that came on to the Building Department's agenda in Ljubljana.

Plečnik worked at the monumental designs with his students in the School, and he had already established the main starting-points for the future development of Ljubljana before the State Building Act was passed in 1931. This envisaged making urban plans for the capitals of the units of the Yugoslav monarchy. This was followed by the preparation of the regulation plans. France Tomažič entered all the projects that had been designed in the School on this theme up to the appearance of the third School publication in 1928 in the old city plan,[583] and in 1929 Plečnik presented his views on the design of the city to the public in the regulation plans for Ljubljana and the northern part of the town, which

he published in the magazine *Dom in svet* (*Home and World*).[584] They differ fundamentally from the aims of the new avantgarde architects' organization CIAM, but the concepts are not really comparable, for Ljubljana was a very small town, not then expected to have more than 160,000 inhabitants before 1990. So unlike Le Corbusier and the other members of CIAM, Plečnik was not facing the urban explosion of modern civilization.

He named the plan for the regulation of the northern part of Ljubljana after the new cemetery by the church of the Holy Cross (fig. 287). The railway line was difficult to cross; it had cut off this area and created a miniature satellite town with its own vital functions. The shape, a segment of a circle, initially recalls the geometry of Ebenezer Howard's utopian garden city of 1898, but there is an essential difference in the course of the main road.[585] Howard saw this as playing the part of a concentric spine in his autonomous agrarian-industrial city, but he was unable to realize it owing to the extraordinarily schematic design. In Plečnik's plan the main road ran – opposite to Howard's scheme – in a radial direction. In fact, his ideals of a housing estate in a green belt were closer to Raymond Unwin's garden cities, which also drew on Camillo Sitte's ideas about a historically grown city, and were thus closer to life than Howard's bare urbanistic scheme.

Plečnik tried to avoid block edge building wherever possible, and he developed a broad typology that included freestanding villas, terraced housing and larger apartment blocks. He told his students, in a polemic against Le Corbusier's views: 'I am convinced that the sole salvation for Europe is now in the house; one must give the family a house!'[586] It may be assumed that Plečnik was familiar with Loos' efforts to reform the construction of the terraced housing estate in Vienna-Lainz in 1921, for he defended the long gardens on his houses with the same arguments, and during the Second World War, in his project known as the 'houses under a common roof', he pursued the idea of including the inhabitants in the planning. The emphatic individualization of the architecture was also an answer to the monotony of the new villa district in Ljubljana, and Plečnik always had a warning in the environs of his School in Mirje of what happened if the initiative was left entirely to the owners of the houses. On the other hand, it should not be forgotten how intensively he had devoted himself to the questions of individual and social housing with his students right from the start. In that respect Plečnik certainly did not lag behind Ivan Vurnik, his rival in the Ljubljana School of Architecture, and he no doubt had him in mind in the following instructive comments in his brief description of the Holy Cross district project: 'The division into lots for

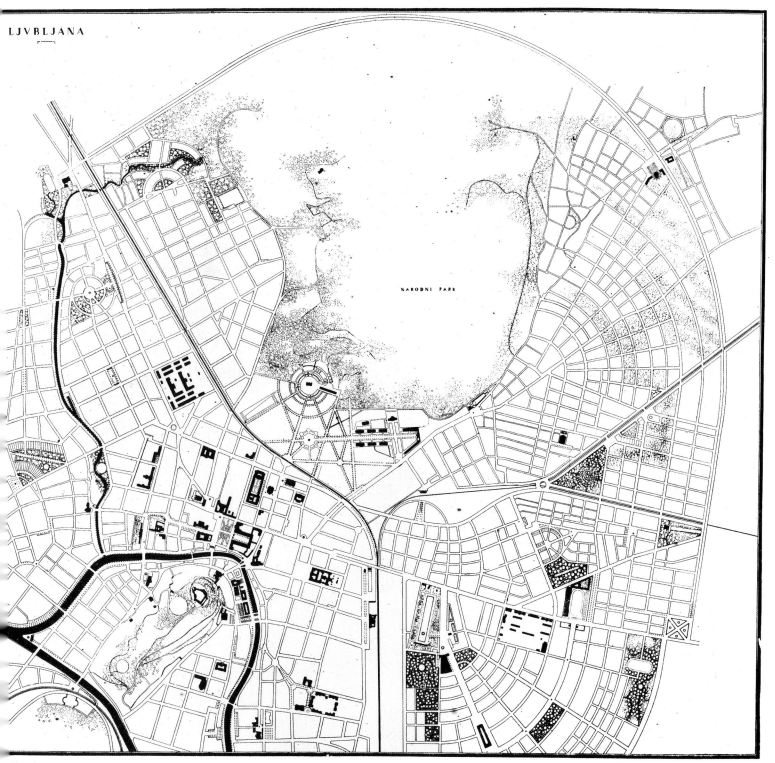

LJVBLJANA

NARODNI PARK

Plan for the regulation of Ljubljana, 1928/9

269

the single-family homes is simply the old autochthonous system that is applied in the Krakovo suburb, or better, the most modern English system. The plots are narrow and so they are long, in order to get the sun all day if possible, like the houses. The high buildings, that is, the apartment blocks, are not based on the block system, and this requires an extremely careful and clear solution to the ground plans and all the facades.'[587] He thus warded off any possible criticism or accusation that he had ignored the social aspects of modern urban design.

In this Plečnik agreed with Le Corbusier's ideal model of the 'ville radieuse' of 1930–5, although he never insisted on Le Corbusier's strict division into functional areas, and even less did he regard the tower block as the basic type of twentieth-century building. The Holy Cross district did not house a uniformly technocratic population, it formed the transition from an area still partly rural to one fully urban. The zig-zag groups of houses do recall Le Corbusier's utopian 'immeubles à redents', but they are on a totally different scale.

The railway line which we have already mentioned, and which was built in the mid-nineteenth century, was the line between Vienna and Trieste. After only a few decades it was already hampering growth in Ljubljana. Max Fabiani had constantly drawn attention to this problem.[588] When he designed the streets for the almost totally unpopulated area north of the railway line in 1899,[589] he also incorporated some of the field paths. In the middle of the road that was to be built to the cemetery he marked out 'Middle Square', which also plays a crucial role in Plečnik's Holy Cross district plan.

Twenty-five years later Plečnik was confronted with the same task.[590] The municipality tried to solve the issue in 1913 by holding an urbanistic competition for this part of Ljubljana. Despite this, circumstances had not greatly changed. The area was still full of gravel pits, and only a few scattered houses had been built in a north-south direction, along old Vienna Street. Plečnik also wanted to redesign the railway crossings, but the Railway Ministry in Belgrade refused to agree to put the railway underground because of the frightening experience of poison gas during the First World War. Plečnik devoted great attention to the main railway crossing on Vienna Street. This involved an underpass, and he was convinced that a smooth crossing could only be achieved by slightly sloping the street.

Unlike Fabiani, Plečnik used the ring road as the basis of his division of the area into lots. In the segment thus created he arranged the sites concentrically, and radially to the road network, with parks around the big gravel pits; in one case he created an amphitheatre. Only in the south east did he

not envisage mixed building; owing to its exposure to the wind this area was to be an industrial estate, separated from the houses by a green belt. He set the main road further in the east-west direction than Fabiani had done. It was to have the main offices and cultural facilities, a theatre, the district court, a new church and the appropriately large squares. At the old city cemetery, which was to be converted into a park dedicated to the memory of famous men, the main road turned off from Vienna Street and skirted two sides of the court building, to end on the other side of the ring road in the new cemetery. Plečnik described its position as 'extra muros',[591] and in giving the new main artery in the city this symbolic *memento mori* he preserved the memory of the district's former character. Instead of the anthropomorphic approach of the 'ville radieuse' he had centrally grouped monumental accents taken from historical urban design. These had also been starting-points for the two men to whom he looked in his work in this field, Camillo Sitte and Otto Wagner.

The plan for the Holy Cross district is like a colourful carpet. One could say that Plečnik's intentions were entirely decorative. J. Stabenow points out that Plečnik's geometric scheme, which is distinguished by a rich typological variety, is also full of contrasts.[592] That is even more evident in the plan for the regulation of the city as a whole, where we also find irrational ground plans that would have been very alien to Wagner, the symmetrical doubling of motifs and the retention of the fragmentary nature of the existing scheme. The variations or capriccios are, of course, closer to Sitte's deliberate inclusion of irregularities than to Wagner's General Plan for the Regulation of Vienna of 1893.

It is informative to compare Plečnik's plan with the building plan for the XXIInd district of Vienna which Wagner published in his study *The Big City* (*Die Großstadt*) in 1911. This is a similar organization of the city network with a broad avenue that is interrupted in the middle by offices and, as in the Holy Cross plan, ends with a church and a cemetery. The other city functions are either pushed to the fringe or combined on a cross axis that Plečnik's plan does not have. If we look back even further, we find the quintessence of Wagner's urban monumentality, the 'Artibus' plan of 1880. It shows a city dedicated solely to art and culture, in the Roman manner, and located on the Mediterranean. This ideal project is fundamental to all Wagner's work. Plečnik first encountered the idea in concrete form in the study for the new building for the Imperial and Royal Academy of Fine Arts in Vienna, and he varied it in his diploma work. Ljubljana was a small town and Plečnik could avoid the monotony of large tower blocks in the Wagnerian manner by building lower and less densely, but with greater variety. What Stabenow calls a mannerist polemic against his teacher's Neo-Classical perspective[593] is also an ideological shift from concern for the city as a whole to the main semantic feature of the centre of the new national capital.

The Holy Cross plan was approved by the City Council in the spring of 1929, and a year later by the Regional Administration.[594] However, it soon became clear that the plan would be extremely difficult to realize. Although Prelovšek had urged that the sites along the planned road should be bought in good time, the owners took matters into their own hands, encouraged by the rapid rise in prices. Some houses that had only just been finished but were in the way of the regulation proved to be an insuperable obstacle. So the planned street network had to be adapted to the existing situation in several places and the result was a gradual impoverishment in the variety of the building types. Plečnik initially tried to meet some owners halfway, but by the late 1930s he could only watch while decisions were taken in Council meetings to shift streets and change lines of building. The plan did remain basically valid until the Second World War, but in practice all its real features had been eliminated before that.

As part of the preparations for the regulation of so-called 'Greater Ljubljana' some suburbs were incorporated in the city in 1935. Although Plečnik's plan was also intended specifically to achieve this objective (fig. 286), only part of the town was included, namely the centre and the usual subdivision in the north and south west. While Fabiani had thoroughly prepared for the technical and functional problems of the city traffic of the future after the earthquake of 1895, Plečnik restricted himself almost entirely to giving a monumental character to the existing architecture. Nevertheless, the plans supplemented each other with regard to two most important features of town planning: functionalism and formal perfection; so it would not be correct to interpret Plečnik's contribution in any other way. Plečnik may have found some more or less direct inspiration for his redesign of Ljubljana in some passages in Wagner's commentary on the General Plan for the Regulation of Vienna of 1893. Wagner says: 'Hardly anyone would deny the great importance of art for mankind. France, and above all Paris, have owed not the smallest part of their prosperity to the fine arts for two centuries.'[595] In the following passage he supports Semper in sublimating the influence of the urban scene on the aesthetic education of its citizens.

In functional questions to which he himself had not worked out answers Plečnik always relied on Wagner. He adopted Wagner's view that a city needed a new ring road every fifty years and that the new radial roads leading out

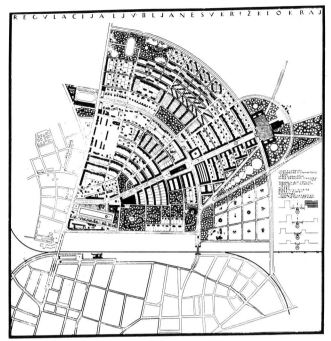

287. Plan for the regulation of the northern part of Ljubljana, 1928

from the centre would have to take account of this. Plečnik acknowledged this in his regulation plan by marking some as yet not urbanized suburbs along the ring road and leaving out others that were of less interest in this respect. The links between the 'restored' city and the new town that was planned on the north are the weaker part of the study. The ring road was intended for fast traffic but it encounters natural obstacles, like the curving course of the river Gradaščica; so it follows it and practically disappears where this tributary enters the Ljubljanica. Fabiani had been much more consistent in that regard, although his ring road encloses a smaller area.

There are some spiral-shaped alleyways on Plečnik's plan. He envisaged a big park in Trnovo, the main avenue of which would have given the visitor a view of Mount Krim. All this certainly helped to open up the traditional orthogonal street system, in which the Holy Cross district was also unhappily incorporated. From Fabiani Plečnik took the idea of some diagonal links in the city centre, such as Wagner had recommended for Vienna. His flexible adaptation of the plans to the existing situation made a positive reaction from the City Council likely, although the difficulties that would be caused, mainly at the intersections of the streets, were undeniable. Plečnik tried to solve some irregularities by using 'green curtains' of trees, bushes and other greenery.

271

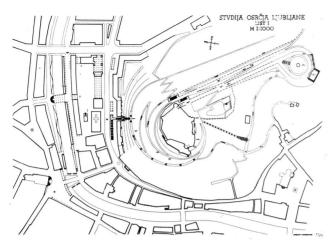

288. Plan for the regulation of the old part of Ljubljana, with the serpentine leading to Castle Hill, 1942

289. Plan for the regulation of Ljubljana, 1943/4

Ljubljana could not play the part of a national metropolis without new administration buildings and public squares. The question of bringing together the Council offices, that were scattered all over the town, had been a subject of constant discussion throughout the interwar years. When the University and the National Gallery were established immediately after the First World War the appropriate sites had to be found for them. A few years later the question of a site for a new office building also arose when the state administration was reorganized. For a long time the diocese had considered moving its headquarters to Holy Cross. Besides these, a number of other urgent works were considered, some of which dated back to the monarchy, like the need to complete the regulation of the Ljubljanica river bed, the museum on the castle hill, the indoor market, the mortuary and, when the state building regulations came into force, the need to work out partial regulation plans for some of the suburbs, a war memorial and a monument to the assassinated king, and other projects. The traffic on the central Square of the Virgin Mary caused particular problems, and in the mid-1930s this question grew into the central problem of town planning in Ljubljana; the younger generation of Slovene architects also began to address the issue.

Plečnik naturally took a more comprehensive view of the problems, and he felt the lack of monumental places particularly keenly. First and foremost he wanted a centre around which Greater Ljubljana could grow, as the medieval city had once grouped around the old Council building. Whatever the degree of urgency, he tried to utilize every part of the plan to stress existing and create new urban motifs. He fought persistently for the sites he had selected and was untiring in proposing new buildings or monuments.

The 1928/9 Regulation Plan for Greater Ljubljana was the finale of the optimistic overture to Slovenian municipal building before the sobering impact of the world slump. The economic crisis did not have such devastating effects in Ljubljana as in more highly industrialized towns, but it certainly affected the priority of municipal tasks. The big projects, like the conversion work on the castle, the university, the Council building and the national gallery, all of which would have ,required extensive funds, were postponed. However, the Council was able to utilize cheap labour paid out of the unemployment fund to carry out some of the major public works. Chief of these was the regulation of the river Ljubljanica and the redesign of the castle hill.

In the mid-1930s the situation in Ljubljana gradually began to improve. The new municipal administration, in which Catholic politicians headed by the Mayor Juro Adlešič were in the majority, began to tackle some of the municipal building work , but despite their good intentions they were held up by the growing self-management of individual municipal offices, which was the result of the building act mentioned above. The efforts to redesign the former Square of the Virgin Mary (fig. 299) showed that the problems were not only political, they were partly caused by graduates of the School of Architecture, who were no longer willing to leave all lucrative municipal commissions to their ex-teacher. After the completion of the Three Bridges (Tromostovje) in 1932 the issue became acute (fig. 300), and it was dominated by the conflict between Plečnik's vision of a monumental public place and the proposals from the engineers, who were solely concerned with the traffic problems. A new Mayer House at the start of Wolf Street became the key issue; as the owner had outmanoeuvred Plečnik, a competition was held in 1937 for the design of the square, at the same time giving a true picture of the tension in Slovenian urbanism.[596] Plečnik's students, or at least the most talented of them, adhered to their teacher's principles and remained loyal to him.

However, the situation changed subsequently when a public competition, open to the whole of Yugoslavia, was held for the regulation of Ljubljana, regardless of Plečnik's already existing plans. It was held in 1940 in accordance with the guidelines that the Municipal Building Department had worked out after the new building act was passed.[597] The radical proposals came mainly from Plečnik's graduates; some had now succeeded in working in Le Corbusier's studio for a time, and they came back full of new ideas.

Plečnik did not enter the competition, as on principle he tended to avoid such events. The younger generation of architects were international in orientation, and they had no understanding of the ideals of national urban building that were sacred to him. So the competition merely confirmed the gloomy forebodings which he had confided to his nephew Karl in 1929: 'I have had a quiet but unmistakeable family revolution in the School for some time now.'[598] Although he had been passed over for the urban planning of Ljubljana, he responded by designing the Žale mortuary, his miniature city, where he sublimated the architecture to his desire for pure form, separate from life.[599]

Plečnik's last plan for Ljubljana dates from 1943, and it was initially drawn up without his knowledge (fig. 289). It was started by his assistant Gizela Šuklje, who was appointed by the City Council to work with the professor on some projects.[600] Although the plan was entirely optional, and not in any way binding, as the official regulation would

be carried out by the technical department in the Council in accordance with the guidelines of the competition, it is certainly interesting to see what had remained of Plečnik's project after fifteen years. The plan only covers the centre of Ljubljana, between the castle and Šiška hill, and Holy Cross in the north. Gizela Šuklje included some of Plečnik's monumental constants, like the Tivoli Mansion, the university and Holy Cross district, from the original plans and incorporated them in the new plan, ignoring the fact that the situation had changed, at least in the last case, irreparably. However, she embellished the plan with later projects by Plečnik, like the City Council building, the Odeon, the theatre, the access to the castle and the 'houses under a common roof', some of which she drew in Plečnik's studio (figs 288 and 342). The plan is a mixture of reality and fiction, above all, it proposes far-reaching interventions in the road network and the creation of grandiose avenues. The plan is the fruit of the years lost through the war, and it was only of anthological value, for it could not influence the future development of the city. Plečnik's Ljubljana was largely complete; only some slight additions were to come in the 1950s.

PUBLIC PLACES AND SQUARES

Plečnik concluded one of his letters to his brother Andrej with a sigh: 'Your affectionate brother Jože – who would love to be travelling through Italy with its wealth of columns. There are no columns here – how can anyone live here?'[601] The columns in the Roman style in St James's Square, the balustrade of Cobblers Bridge (Čevljarski most) and the colonnade on the market are examples of Mediterranean architecture in different contexts. However, they are not only Mediterranean in origin, for Wagner also saw the column as an essential feature of urban architecture. In the commentary to the General Plan for the Regulation of Vienna of 1893 he lists other items as well as columns that should form classical purtenances in urban design: monuments, obelisks, triumphal arches, fountains, masts, candelabra and similar objects; the architect should use these together with open perspectives, the combination of street axes, the creation of observation points and park design.[602] Plečnik had concerned himself intensively with these items during his work on Prague Castle, and he applied the experience he had gained to his home town. The limited funds available for paving the streets and squares were measured by the standard size of stone slabs and granite blocks, but Plečnik proved highly inventive in replacing these with sand, gravel and concrete, thus saving

290. The column of the Virgin Mary on St James's Square, 1938

money which he could use for the arrangement of other parts of the area.

The Paradise Garden in Prague and St James's Square in Ljubljana are similar in composition as far as the decoration with an obelisk and fountain is concerned (fig. 290). The large square below the castle in Ljubljana once had the main road to Zagreb along one side. It was the result of historical development and not part of a deliberate urban design. Like Fabiani, Plečnik was also aware that the road would sooner or later have to be shifted to the eastern side of the square, which was lined with buildings, and the centre would have to be made free of traffic. The square had a slightly raised and elongated island of sand, on which stood a column bearing a statue of the Virgin Mary. He erected a stone fountain beside the column and lined the island with trees and concrete edging stones in the form of cubic bases surmounted by balls. This is a clear reference to the symbolism of the rosary, and it recalls Plečnik's associations with the church of St James, which faced on to the square, and memories of his mother, with whom he had attended this church. Plečnik may well have worked out this part of his design without any knowledge of Gaudi's stone balls in the Güell Park in Barcelona, where the same symbolism is evident. Plečnik used maple trees, weeping willows and tall slender poplars to define the square and conceal the ugly late historicist facade of the church.

At about the time Plečnik wrote the letter to his brother complaining of the lack of columns, Loos was proclaiming the revitalization of the classical column in 1923: 'The great Greek Doric column will be built. If not in Chicago, then in some other city. If not for *The Chicago Tribune*, then for some other client. If not by me, then by some other architect.'[603] The other twentieth-century classicist rooted in Antiquity was Plečnik, and in 1938 he set up a Tuscan column in honour of the Virgin Mary. It is freely drawn after Vignola, and Loos would no doubt have regarded it as small. For Ljubljana it was colossal. Plečnik used it to replace the monument dating from the second half of the nineteenth century; it was now derelict, but it had borne an original statue by the Salzburg sculptor Wolf Weißenkirchner. Plečnik removed the old column into the garden of the Prelovšek villa and provided it with an antique Corinthian capital and a Beuron statue of the Virgin, thus restoring to it all the insignia of its former glory. He then devoted himself to the new monument with the same piety. He reinstated the bronze figure of the Virgin on a repaired fragment of the original Baroque column, and surrounded her with more recent sculptures from the old monument.[604] On the new column the subsidiary figures are not on the corners of the capital, they are coordinated with the main view from the longitudinal axis of the square. The empty bases on the stereobate mark their original position. The textile metaphors are particularly imaginative, like the stone band with which a small Doric column is attached (see fig. 201). Plečnik's characteristically mannerist superfluity reflects the confused history of the monument. There is also a high degree of antique refinement in the contrast between the hard crepidona and the 'softer' stylobate, which has a bolster-like top. It is another example of the extreme sensitivity with which Plečnik could handle antique tectonics.

In 1927, at the same time as St James's Square, Plečnik also designed Zois Street on the opposite bank of the Ljubljanica (fig. 291). He used trees to combine the two sections of the street into one whole, and a few years later he continued this past the church of St Florian to Ljubljana Castle (fig. 292). This sequence of public places is based on the idea of the garden promenade around Prague Castle, but its origin is to be found in Sitte's doctrine regarding the classical rules of formation of town squares and their flowing into one another. Plečnik added the following comment to his plans in a letter to the director of the Municipal Building Department: 'I am sending you some more work – work executed with much loving care. I believe I have never done better work, within the narrow limits of what is reasonable and possible. But judge for yourself.'[605] In the same letter he

291. Zois Street, 1927

describes his vision of Zois Street: 'The sunlight flooding in', 'with ivy-covered walls on both sides', and 'a columnar arrangement of sixty trees'. To the dismay of the local population, who were not used to change, he felled the existing damp avenue of horse chestnuts and replaced them with smaller oaks and tall poplars. The new trees marked out the new urban area. At that time Zois Street still came to a dead end, and so was not part of the main traffic network, and Plečnik was able to emphasise its special appearance with added greenery.

Plečnik decided not to pave the pavements but to lay a less expensive strip of concrete in the sand. Where the street bends he set a pyramid, and its great solid shape acts as an optical correction to the slope of the terrain towards the river (fig. 291). It consists of roughly worked and decoratively jointed blocks of stone, and it is dedicated to Žiga Zois, who was a patron of the arts and lived in a nearby house. The shape of the monument, and its position here by the old city wall, relate the pyramid to that pyramid on the fortification wall of Prague Castle, but it would be wrong to deduce from this that the Ljubljana monument has the same symbolic function as the one in Prague, although the ear-shaped handles at the top of both recall the monolithic lids on Roman sarcophagi. In the same letter to Prelovšek Plečnik says: 'In Ljubljana there is no possibility, nor will there ever be one, of creating anything similar – so Zois Street would be unique, as you might say – no other city in central Europe would so easily equal it!' In another letter to Prelovšek we see that Plečnik originally wanted to cover the

pyramid with ivy and artificially give it the appearance of age. When the head municipal gardener took his idea too literally the architect felt bound to protest:

> As I am the creator of the pyramid, and as this kind of greenery is quite counter to the basic concept, nor do I want outsiders to be making fun of me and us, I ask you very firmly to remove the two troughs and the soil immediately. The pyramid should appear to grow out of the earth like the pyramids in the Sahara. As this is my last work for Ljubljana – and as I am not likely to cause any further trouble here – I ask you to do as I request.[606]

The last sentence is one of Plečnik's many threats to cease working for Ljubljana, forcing Prelovšek to defend the sensitive architect with even greater vehemence.

The pyramid, the column and the fountain divide the open urban spaces and create a fluid transition between them. In 1932 Plečnik transferred another item from his Prague repertoire to Ljubljana when he set a broad flight of steps at the corner of the church of St Florian (fig. 292).[607] The steps leading up to the main entrance to the church were in such bad condition that they needed to be replaced. They were also obstructing the entrance to Florian Street (Florijanska ulica). Plečnik took the opportunity to make the old side entrance the main one to the church, and in the now empty portal he placed the Baroque figure of St John Nepomuk, which had stood inside the church. As a few steps were left over from the redesign of the entrance to the Ursuline church he added these to the old St Florian steps

292. The way up to Castle Hill, past the church of St Florian, 1932

1929, when he concentrated all the views from the narrow streets on to the obelisk and so gave the square, which was too big, the centrepiece it lacked, without holding up the traffic (figs 202 and 293). The reason for initially limiting his intervention to the immediate proximity of the obelisk was the celebrations to mark the 120th anniversary of the foundation of the Illyrian provinces under French rule, which was very close to the culturally and politically francophile orientation of the kingdom itself. Plečnik made the monument of light Dalmatian stone, and underlined its elegant height with two sets of four corner pillars on both sides. If he had seen monolithic design as a moral obligation in Prague, he could not afford to take the same standpoint in Ljubljana, although he did not abandon certain ethical norms. When one of the blocks of stone was damaged during the work he allowed the addition to remain visible, in order to avoid the false impression of completeness. It was characteristic of Plečnik's pragmatism that he raised the obelisks by about 30 centimeters before the scaffold was removed.[608] He was similarly pragmatic in his approach to the corner pillars, of which the four outer ones are of artificial stone, because during the working process he realized that such a solution was architecturally more convincing. The inscription constituted a special problem. As the contours of the letters would have been irregular on the roughly worked surface, he had the text cut into the stone in a U profile rather than the usual V, and gilded. In the same way as he had carefully skirted the old yew tree in the Paradise Garden in Prague, he left room for the two weeping willows that grew on the corner of the monastery by making the line of the building containing the public toilets concave.

On the opposite side of the square Plečnik set up a monument to the poet Simon Gregorčič in 1937 (fig. 293). He had loved his poetry in his youth. Gregorčič came from the Soča river valley, which had been ceded to Italy after the First World War; hence the unveiling of the monument was of national importance. It was a bronze bust by Zdenko Kalin, and Plečnik provided it with a characteristic Karst pergola, which was initially covered with wild vine. He chose the stones quickly from the stonemason Vodnik, and in the 1950s, when the wooden beams on the pergola had rotted, he replaced them with concrete arches and added a vase, which, in his own words, was intended to represent the heart of the poet imprisoned.[609] This changed the original symbolism of the monument, which now stressed the tragic fate of the poet, restricted by the small-mindedness of his people; it was a fate which Plečnik believed he shared. Of particular interest is the endeavour to include part of the surrounding area in the architecture by placing the front columns over the edge of the pavement, as we have already seen in the

and made a new flight. He also used some old border stones to indicate an imaginary corner of the building by the steps. He added stone slabs to the lower part of the church to underline its key position on the street, which was regulated and paved at the same time. It has an elegant curving shape like a runner between the pebblestones, consisting of blocks of granite.

The second axis of Plečnik's Ljubljana starts modestly in the middle of the low buildings of the outer city, by the church of Trnovo. It crosses the start of Zois Street and changes at the Square of the French Revolution into a broad avenue. Fabiani had also worked on this square before Plečnik, and he had endeavoured to straighten the irregular shape with a monument at the corner of the monastery of the Teutonic Order. Plečnik arrived at a similar solution in

293. The Square of the French Revolution: the Illyrian monument, 1929, the Simon Gregorčič memorial, 1937, the university library, 1936–41, the city wall, 1940–1, the former monastery of the Teutonic Knights, 1951–6

plans for the vestibule of the church of the Holy Spirit in Vienna and the canopy in the Third Castle Courtyard in Prague.

The positioning of the two monuments on the Square of the French Revolution aroused heated public opposition, as the people's imagination did not appear to stretch beyond the core of the city and Tivoli Park. However, Plečnik handled the matter with great skill, ultimately placing the monuments in what were in his view the only proper places. In dedicating the obelisks to Napoleon and the Illyrian provinces the architect and Prelovšek were actually risking a diplomatic scandal, but in fact after the official unveiling, for which Plečnik had bedecked the square with masts and coloured flags, they were given an award by the French Government. Apart from the controversy then and later over the Gregorčič monument we should remember that Plečnik also solved the problem of the end of the Roman wall by placing it here, and any other monument for which there might have been occasion would for that reason have been just as welcome to him. He liked to combine ruins and the remains of historical walls with the pergola motif. Examples of this are to be found in the Rampart Garden in Prague, the variant of the restored Roman wall that was not executed and the pergola in Ljubljana Castle, that has not survived.

The obelisk formed the focul point of Vega Street, and before 1932 it was very evident that the street was the result of a number of different attempts at regulation that had never been completed. For the preparations for the 60th anniversary of the Music Association (Glasbena Matica) he laid out a raised park in front of the Association building, on the remains of the medieval city wall. He had this planted with birch trees and other varieties. To improve the visual appearance of the street he lined it with poplars and the lower growing maple trees. Border stones and hermae with the portrait heads of well known musicians were similar embellishments. For the hermae Plečnik was able to use blocks of Aurisina marble, and originally the members of the Association wanted to surround their building with these. Plečnik adopted the idea from Fabiani's monuments in front of the Technical University in Vienna, but he made the bases more archaic and adapted them to the poetic mood of the park. The Music Association building's façade had a balcony, supported by four high columns, but it was removed after World War II because their foundations were sinking. This façade originally formed part of the design. The steps in front of the houses, the tobacconist's kiosk at the bend in the road and similar small items helped to form the street scene.

Just before the outbreak of war Plečnik was working on the intersection of the Roman and the medieval city walls in front of the university library building (fig. 293). He had already had part of the wall covered with greenery

277

294. Congress Square, 1926–8, below the river facade of the Philharmonic Hall, 1936

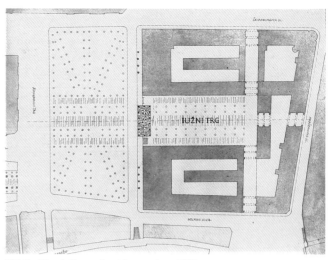

295–7. "South Square", with propylaea, 1937

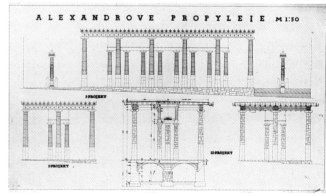

296

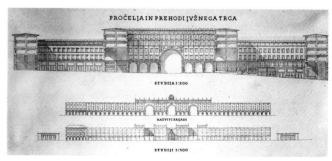

297

278

and edged with cubic stones for the unveiling of the Illyrian obelisk, and after the university library was finished he covered the wall, which he believed had once enclosed the Roman city of Emona, with Podpeč stone and finished it off with a denticulated cornice. By defining the different areas and levels he separated the pedestrians from the traffic and the visitors to the park. Between the standardized concrete benches on the wall he wanted to place several vases, stelae and hermae in the antique manner, but later two fairly academic sculptures were placed there, with his agreement.

Vega Street ends in the north without an evident conclusion, at Congress Square, which slopes down to the river, and Star Park (Zvezda). Plečnik applied himself to the long rectangular space between the Baroque Ursuline church and the Slovenian Philharmonic Hall building (fig. 294) at the same time as he was working on the paving of the Third Castle Courtyard in Prague. For that reason he first tried a solution on two levels in Ljubljana as well, but he finally decided for a levelled area in checkerboard paving pattern, impressed by the uniform appearance of the First Castle Courtyard. He exchanged the smaller pattern along the long axis while the work was in progress for square fields, which he edged with darker concrete strips. Regardless of the axes of the buildings and streets he treated the paving like a textile carpet, giving it its own ornamental logic. In order to place the series of old wrought iron lights along the central axis and so give them greater prominence, he chose an unequal number of fields for the cross axis. This was following Wagner's advice that large places need monuments and energetic divisions.[610] As well as balustrades, avenues and perrons, lights are a major means of providing the appropriate focal points and dividing such areas. Plečnik only treated the monumental Neo-Palladian Ursuline church of the Holy Trinity more individually, restoring the facade in Neo-Classical colouring. Before the entrance he placed the Baroque column of the Holy Trinity that had stood in Ajdovščina Square, where it had been in the way of the traffic. That gave the church its religious axis and the square a centre of vision. It also gave a fine view of the castle and shortened the distance from the Ursuline church, an architectural monument of Venetian origin which really needed a very much smaller space. As school masses were held in the church, Plečnik changed the shape of the steps leading up to the entrance in 1932 to make them safer, adding a balustrade on the street side.

Star Park had been marked out in 1821 on the site of the former Capuchin monastery, as part of the preparations for the Congress of the Holy Alliance which took place in that year in Ljubljana. As there was no real need for building

298. Sketch for the monument to King Peter I, before Ljubljana Town Hall, 1930

here later, it remained almost unchanged. At the end of the 1920s Plečnik straightened it in places and bordered it with cylindrical concrete stones with 'metal' caps. In the mid-1930s, when the question of a monument to the assassinated King Alexander I. Karadjordjević became urgent, Plečnik offered his propylaea design,[611] in which he had already proposed a figure of Janus, looking towards Congress Square and towards the South Square (Južni trg) that was planned. In 1937 he indicated the axis of Vega Street with a weather house, which has now been restored, at the side of Star Park (figs 295–6). The idea of the propylaea aroused vehement protests from the sculptors, who were afraid of losing commissions. The public disputes between the supporters of the architect and his opponents ultimately prevented Ljubljana from acquiring a new public place with Plečnik's propylaea in honour of the Yugoslav monarch. Neither Stele's assurances that the city really needed 'our St Mark's Square, a main square, which we do not have as yet',[612] nor the energetic support from some of Plečnik's students were of avail. Wearied by the everlasting party political disputes that blocked every far-sighted project in Ljubljana, Matko Prelovšek resigned from his office soon after the affair of the monument.

Owing to the pressure from the preservation office and the many vested interests involved an unsatisfactory compromise was reached, with an equestrian statue in the

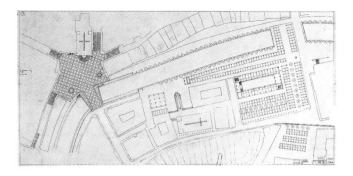

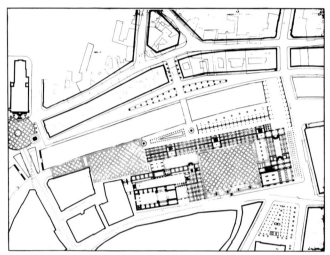

299–300. Proposal for the paving of the Square of the Virgin Mary, a new town hall building and the market, 1928 (above) and 1932 (below)

middle of Star Park.[613] Plečnik unburdened his feelings in the following letter to Prelovšek in the spring of 1940:

Tomorrow (Monday) the chestnut trees in Star Park are presumably to be felled, in accordance with the plan that has not been thought through or properly worked out. The committee sat round a table bargaining over the height of the base, and that was how they decided it, and the gentlemen of the Council probably used a ruler to decree that a place 45 metres wide is to be created in Star Park. Perhaps they also recorded in the minutes where the monument is to stand. No-one appears to have thought that the terrain slopes down there – that it is agreeable to the eye if the slope is along the long axis, but unpleasant if it is along the cross axis. The hind quarters are always a problem on a statue of a horse standing still (I know there are exceptions – in the Middle Ages). It is much easier if the horse is rearing up, if it is supported by the tail, for instance, etc. In our case the background

should be as close to the horse as possible, so a green or stone wall – or the beast should be placed so that its rear is really 'behind'.[614]

Between 1930 and 1931 Plečnik had shown how imaginatively this problem, that has preoccupied architects in every age, can be solved, with the equestrian statue of King Peter I. Karadjordjević on the steps before Ljubljana Town Hall (fig. 298). He designed several variants of the monument to the king. In one he wanted it to crown the converted fortress on Castle Hill. He created the propylaea in honour of King Alexander in 1937 at the request of the former mayor and chairman of the monument committee, Ivan Hribar. It was the perfected variant of the grand entrance to South Square, which lies rather higher, and which we have already encountered in his regulation plan for Ljubljana. In the middle of the propylaea he intended to set an equestrian monument to the king whose portrait head would be interchangeable – in accord with current political needs, which would have saved the city a lot of money in future. But he does not seem to have seriously defended the idea. South Square opens to the south – hence its name – and he designed it as an urban forum with arcades and passageways to neighbouring streets. He wanted to surround it with high buildings of similar design, like a kind of modern Uffizi. When the Italians occupied Slovenia at the beginning of World War II and demolished the monument a few months after it was officially opened, Plečnik began to consider taking Vega Street in a straight line across Star Park and past South Square to the Square of the Virgin Mary,[615] which was still not regulated.

In various plans he also considered the eastern end of Congress Square and Star Park. Before Cobblers Bridge was built he still wanted to demolish the Philharmonic Society building and build a bridge across to the other bank of the river. During the war he designed a monumental odeon, a large hall to be used for concerts and theatre performances[616] which would have eliminated the difficult street crossings in the east of Congress Square. This also raised the question of the nearby Castle Square (Dvorni trg). In 1935 he proposed an interesting solution with steps along the long axis,[617] but the city's traders objected to the proposal, arguing that the hand carts would no longer be able to cross the square on their way to market.

The same theme is evident in the broad flight of steps leading to Pagačar Square (Pogačarjev trg), near the cathedral, where once a supporting wall stood with a narrow passage. Plečnik was able to win over the municipal authorities to his idea to pave Dolničar Street (Dolničarjeva ulica) at the top of the steps, by using gravel, which cut down the

301. The colonnade of Ljubljana market, 1940–2

cost by half from the usual slabs of porphyry.[618] He transferred the characteristic mosaic pattern of paving from Prague to Ljubljana here.

However, the main problem remained the Square of the Virgin Mary beside the Three Bridges. The axes were as chaotic as those in the third castle courtyard in Prague. In the variant of 1928 (fig. 299), which included a new wide bridge, Plečnik chose a neutral check pattern for the paving, which did not match either the houses or the streets. Four years later he put forward a new study with a central five-cornered field facing the main entrance, but when the technical experts said they disliked it he quickly changed it to a circle with a traffic island in the middle (fig. 300).[619] He wanted to pave the circle in a uniform check pattern and use the same pattern for the entire surroundings, from the City Council offices to Dragon Bridge (Zmajski most).

The monument to the poet Prešeren, which in his opinion stood in an unsuitable place, posed a question of a particular kind. Plečnik had always wanted to move the monument to the opposite side of the Square of the Virgin Mary, where it would have more room,[620] but the owner of the new large department store at the end of Wolf Street refused to agree. A similar problem arose over the tobacconist's kiosk (see fig. 207). After several inspections by the authorities it was reduced in length and placed, contrary to Plečnik's intentions, beside the monument to the poet.

Although new municipal investment of any kind was virtually impossible in the summer of 1942, Plečnik once more turned his attention to the task of thoroughly reworking this central crossing point in the city, in connection with a possible redesign of the Franciscan monastery and its church. His proposals were collected in a study which he entitled 'An Attempt at Healing the Square of the Virgin Mary'. As the war had suspended all norms, he felt, at least in this respect, more free in his work. He no longer included the Prešeren monument in the plan, and this time intended the pattern of the paving, which was now to fill the entire square, to follow the main directions of the traffic. Another novelty was the double colonnade on the side facing the river. On a level stretch without pavements he marked out the traffic routes with a few larger border stones, and he also changed the awkward entrance to the church, using a round form to recall the 'hill' that had once marked the site.

A few years before his death Plečnik came back to the question of the Square of the Virgin Mary, that had been dear to his heart ever since the earthquake. This time he made a rapid sketch. As he could not redesign the facades that could have given the square the focus it needed, he again drew a circle and set three monuments beside it, in an attempt to draw the irregular shape together.[621]

Plečnik's regulation study of 1928/9 also provided for food markets in the suburbs. He worked out in more detail the indoor market beside the church of St Bartholemew in Šiška, with which he hoped to enliven the old local centre that was bypassed by the new main road. As already mentioned, he had vainly struggled immediately after the First World War to build a new parish centre in Šiška (see figs 159–60), and later was equally unsuccessful with his plans for a monumental square before the church. Between 1934 and 1936 he succeeded in at least renovating its immediate surroundings in two phases. Beside the church he set a broad flight of concrete steps facing the Bellevue Hotel, with a lamp post at their foot. The plump shape encircled by several belts looks like an abstract of a market woman bearing a basket on her head.

The church was built into a slope and the walls were damp. To let them dry out Plečnik had part of the earth removed and surrounded the building here with a columned vestibule. Stabenow described the ennoblement of the modest old building with the monumental mantle in these words: 'Plečnik's strategy is always the same: by adding new he reinterprets the existing structure, without affecting its substance. By changing a few elements he imbues an old building with his vision of a new Ljubljana.'[622]

THE PARKS

Apart from the relatively big green areas dating from the last century that gave Ljubljana the appearance of an idyllic administration centre, garden art in the town had long been limited to big horse chestnut trees and a few flower beds. Plečnik introduced a wide variety of trees and shrubs, climbing plants and flowers. His approach was very much closer to English park culture than to the customs of the municipal gardeners. We see from his correspondence that Plečnik always greatly loved to grow plants and liked receiving them as presents. He had great skill in decorating rooms with plants, and he certainly saw this, as did Semper, as part of the profession of the architect. Green, as we have seen, played a large part in Plečnik's vision of a new Ljubljana, and it is not surprising that in his commentary on the regulation study he says that a town of 100,000 inhabitants should have an army of gardeners, at least 500 strong, to look after its parks and gardens. He wanted to leave whole areas of Ljubljana unbuilt, and he declared Castle Hill and Rožnik Hill nature reserves. Beside the university in Tivoli he wanted a botanical garden, with an 'avenue of every tree'.[623]

Nature was sacred to him and this elevated it above the work of human hands. Wherever he encountered nature he did so with respect, allowing room for existing trees to stand and leaving them to grow wherever possible. By the portal of the church of St Bartholemew in Šiška, for instance, and at the Bežek Villa in Kranj he preferred to cut out a concrete slab or leave out part of the garden wall to avoid felling an old tree.

In selecting trees for a particular place he always paid heed to their manner of growth and the shape of their crowns. He spent a long time with the gardener Lap, looking for suitable trees for the Prelovšek residence garden, for instance.[624] He showed his love of the Mediterranean by introducing some more resistant conifers from that region. He also planted a number of climbing plants, including wild vine, for purely practical reasons, as they protect the walls from rain and also draw moisture out of them. He had learned this during his period in Prague.

This was a broad field of activity for Plečnik, and it has not, as yet, been adequately researched. More research would certainly reveal the extent of his knowledge and the wealth of his ideas, which was no less great. Here we shall discuss the architectural aspect of his work in parks and gardens, for Plečnik often used green to solve a problem in individual town areas, if not enough money was available to solve it by means of architecture itself. In such cases he used trees or climbing plants as a green curtain to cover up faults or give greater emphasis. In some cases he actually used them to add to an abundance of metamorphosed vegetable forms. In this context we also need to consider the two unusual earthen pyramids by the Roman wall in Ljubljana (fig. 307), and Plečnik's passion for covering primal architectural forms with turf, a question to which we shall return.

The Tivoli Park aroused Plečnik's interest as soon as he returned from Prague. Initially he tried to complete and restore to geometric order the network of horse chestnut avenues that had been planted after the collapse of the Napoleonic Illyrian provinces, and were more or less blurred in the second half of the nineteenth century by romantically branching paths and flower beds. He wanted to dedicate a large part of the park to the fine arts, which had already made their entrance in Fabiani's exhibition pavilion for the painter Rihard Jakopič (1908), and use the former Kosler property beside the Palace of Leopold's Rest (Cekinov grad) for university buildings.

The link between art and science, both of which were of

302. The promenade in Tivoli Park, 1931, from a photograph taken in the 1960s

303. The conversion of the fortress Entrenchment on Castle Hill, 1934/5

283

304. The canopied entrance to the sports ground in Tivoli Park, around 1934, contemporary photograph

crucial importance in the establishment of a national consciousness, and their separation from the busy everyday world in the quiet of a municipal park, was one of the fundamental premises in Plečnik's urban design. Up to the Second World War the architect showed great interest in the building of the university – the site plan was drawn in 1928 by Boris Kobe in his School[625] – although the great project was continually being cut down by the shortsightedness of the politicians, until it was finally reduced to the site between Vega Street and Gentlemen's Street.

This condemned the university to remain scattered throughout the town. Nor was there any real possibility of building the National Gallery near the Tivoli Mansion (Tivolski grad), which Dušan Grabrijan had designed as part of his diploma work in 1924.[626] As economic conditions deteriorated in the early 1930s the plans were laid aside for

an indeterminate period, and the two institutions had to be content with provisional arrangements. When the Modern Gallery was built later, at least the problem of a national exhibition centre for works of art was solved. After the Second World War Plečnik tried to bring up the question of the Tivoli Mansion again: the building was then used as a residential house of the lowest quality. He suggested converting it for official municipal occasions,[627] but the plan never progressed further than an exercise for the students in his School.

In Tivoli Plečnik had to be content with smaller tasks. In 1931 he laid out a sand path in continuation of the central promenade in the town (fig. 302), but it has now only survived in fragments. It was an elegant, straight line that ended after about 400 metres without a perspectival focal point in the green of Šiška Hill. The walker is accompanied

284

along the central stretch by concrete lamp posts with Ionic capitals, which Grabrijan has aptly called a 'necklace'.[628] Benches flank the path, and behind them Plečnik had trees and bushes planted. With his metamorphosis of the town road into a park path he preserved Tivoli from the disadvantages of a narrow, damp avenue and also created a link with the city centre. The concept not only recalls the monumentality of Congress Square, it also paraphrases the Bastion Garden in Prague, which dates from the same time, with its strong emphasis on unimpeded natural growth. Plečnik also laid out the broad parterre on the model of the Bastion Garden, with rows of low cypresses. However, this had to be changed when the Modern Gallery was built.

In 1933 several adjustments were made. Plečnik had an area levelled behind the Tivoli Mansion, and set up a summer theater there, but it never really prospered. Beside the railway line he transformed a three-cornered site into a children's playground, and set a round pool there. This part of his Tivoli has recently been restored, and it contains all the elements of the classical Baroque park, sand, grass lawns, trees, living hedges, border stones, candelabra, figural sculpture and water. Here they are combined in a completely non-baroque way.

Plečnik fenced the nearby sports ground and gave the entrance a big concrete canopy, translating the subtlety of its predecessor in Prague into monumental plasticity with the stone cladding (fig. 304). He made the textile origin of the roof evident with double curved concrete beams. Finally we should mention the idea of the promenade 'over open terrain' of 1937. It is connected with Tivoli and to a certain extent it is a Ljubljana parallel to the ideal axis between Prague Castle and Vyšehrad. It would have led in a straight line from the Castle Hill to Rožnik.

The renovation of the fortress Entrenchment (Šance), that had remained standing after the Napoleonic Wars, a relic of former fortifications in the east of the Castle Hill plateau, was carried out as part of a public employment creation programme. At the same time the avenue between the castle and the fortress was redesigned. Parts of the fortification walls were derelict, and in 1934, when these had been repaired, Plečnik proposed a more comprehensive solution (fig. 303). He consolidated the substance of the building and secured it at the top with cheap concrete blocks, sewerage pipes and iron balustrades, making it possible, as in Prague, for people to walk around on it in various directions and on various levels. This also integrated the structure, that had stood isolated until then, into the existing system of paths. With very modest means he had also made it one of the most attractive leisure spots in the town and avoided underlining its military character. In some places he

actually negated its historic function by adding new elements or covering the walls with stone buttresses.

His attitude to the past is even clearer from his handling of the walls of the ancient Roman settlement, Emona, that had stood on the site of the present Ljubljana. These relics were in the district of Mirje. Over the years these walls had become an obstacle to the organic growth of the town, because they blocked the course of two traffic-bearing roads heading south which the Council wanted to build. Before the First World War the archaeologist Walter Schmid had cleaned the ruins and given them a uniform height. But only when Plečnik and Stele initiated a joint action 'against public opinion'[629] was their future decided and Plečnik encouraged to restore the wall, which had meantime been greatly neglected. When the most badly damaged parts were restored at the end of 1932 he still did not have a definite idea what was to become of the wall.

The drawings made in the School at this time show that he was more concerned with the surroundings of the Roman wall than with the wall itself and only envisaged a walkway along the top of it. By redesigning the existing passages, and adding a lapidaria and pergolas, this park-like environment of the wall would still have stood as an intact testimony to the city's history. But there was no money available for the restoration, and Plečnik had to help himself by using the soil removed from the north part of the wall for the regulation of the Gradaščica. This made it possible to siphon off funds from other sources to restore the wall itself. Because the work was half finished the Council was forced to take a quick decision: the municipal building department approved Plečnik's proposal for reconstruction at the recommendation of Stele and the archaeologist Balduin Saria in the summer of 1934.[630] However, the final plan was only finished two years later, just before the work started.

Plečnik's reconstruction of the Roman monument combined two different objectives (fig. 305). His concern to display the wall as a concrete witness to a specific age accords with the manner of presentation he had used in Prague. The visitor was to have the opportunity to walk along the wall, cross it and in some places actually ascend it, and so be able to examine the particular qualities of Roman building. Plečnik carefully observed the scientific instructions with regard to the original and all the parts discovered during the excavations were marked. In the north, for instance, he had the abutments cleaned and the Roman sarcophagi that had been discovered nearby displayed.

He solved the archaeological and didactic problems imaginatively, adding later finds or even new creations to the original. He renewed the Roman hypocaust, allowing it to rear out of the ground as part of an aqueduct not yet exca-

305

306

The restoration of the Roman wall, 1934–7: 305. North side with lapidarium
306. South side with the old poplar trees   307. The earthen pyramids

vated, but in other places he created an entirely new architecture out of remnants. Plečnik's rich associative imagination was given full expression in the Roman wall. Memories of his childhood – when in his own words he played hide and seek here with his friends – mingled with memories of his encounter with Roman Antiquity in its Italian homeland and his later thoughts about the roots of his own people. So the Roman wall was a creative interpretation of Semper's rule according to which it was possible even change to the original function of a monument in the sense of its historical continuity.

Behind the surviving most easterly city gate two earthen pyramids erected over wooden scaffolds had once stood (fig. 307). They were covered in turf, like the pyramid at the entrance to Murnik Street (Murnikova ulica). Although Plečnik used the pyramid to symbolize not only Egypt but the whole of Antiquity, he was basically concerned with the association with the prehistoric earth mounds and Etruscan tumuli. The Etruscan element is also evident in the arches of two new passageways that do not have historical roots and are marked one with a pyramid and the other with a flight of steps that recalls Bramante's solution of a circular flight of steps in the Vatican. In this context we should also draw attention to the sensitive separation of the original and the new. The two old city gates in the east are marked either by Roman stones or by an indication of the function of the passage. The modern iron railing that no longer exists but which served as a gate was Plečnik's 'pious deception', while the columned spalier is an attribute of the past. His approach was different in Murnik Street and Snežniška Street, where there was no passage originally, or where the wall had only been opened in more recent times. In this case he felt more free and he visibly negated the historical elements which he combined with Renaissance motifs and more recent finds. The high concrete merlons that lent one of the ramparts the character of a castle display the same artistic freedom.

Plečnik found architectural similarities with his lapidarium (fig. 305) in the burial chambers on the Via Appia antica in Rome. The turf covering the pyramids is also a recollection of burial mounds. The way in which the wall, the pyramid and the city gate are combined recalls a similar situation at the Cestius Pyramid in Rome. Is there also some memory of Plečnik's great model Semper, whose remains – as mentioned earlier – rest in the Protestant cemetery in the Pyramid's close vicinity? More adventurous is the interpretation of the Etruscan features of the Roman wall, and this inevitably leads to speculation. The possibility cannot be excluded that the architect wanted to give the monument national significance by borrowing from

308–9. The upper reach of the river Ljublanica in the town, around 1912, and after regulation in 1935/6

Etruscan art. The row of poplars before the wall, which no longer stand, used to act like an imaginary mental filter, separating Plečnik's imaginative world from the bad taste of the adjoining villas (fig. 306). However that may be, the Roman wall is one of Plečnik's most complex aesthetic and philosophical statements, and it is not always easy to penetrate into his creative imagination.

THE CITY AND ITS RIVER

Until the mid-eighteenth century, when the Gruber Canal was dug between Castle Hill and Golovec Hill, the south of Ljubljana experienced frequent flooding. Before the First World War work started on deepening both the canal and the river bed, but only the work on the canal was completed. In drought periods, the water only ran in the canal behind the city; the empty river bed stank and it was feared that the foundations of the bridges were slowly crumbling. An architect from Graz, Alfred Keller, who had made a name in Vienna by covering the river Wien at the Naschmarkt and Karlsplatz, attempted to improve the monotony of the new concrete banks that had been built by adding emphatic architectural articulation. But the work stopped in 1915, and some new bridges, proposed already in the plan by Max Fabiani after the earthquake, were not built either.

Although all the authorities were determined to complete the regulation of the river Ljubljanica, between 1925 and 1928 only the upper part of the tributary, the Gradaščica, could be regulated. However, by 1930 the City Council had managed to raise the necessary funds to tender for some work on individual sections. The following year the world slump forced the Building Ministry in Belgrade to set up a special technical department to handle the regulation of the Ljubljanica, for work on the deepening of the river bed was to be accelerated as part of a programme to reduce unemployment.[631]

It is interesting in this context to see what Plečnik's ideas were on the dialogue between the city and its river. Matko Prelovšek had already succeeded in interesting him in the work. While the technical department took up its work where the Austrians had left off, Plečnik took a very much more comprehensive view of the regulation. In preserving the old Franciscan Bridge he *de facto* put paid to the desire to make the river navigable. Drawing on Wagner's ideas on the river Wien,[632] he even made a sketch of the river covered with a concrete roof, planning to place warehouses beneath, while transforming the surface into a central boulevard.[633] The idea to bridge the Ljubljanica in segments with very wide bridges was to some extent the result of Plečnik's considerations of this kind, since he saw the main problem as the alienation of the river from the city. For that reason Keller's cosmetic attempt to make the concrete banks more attractive with greenery was not convincing. While he sketched out numerous variants for regulation, Plečnik's thoughts went back to Venice and Florence. The view from one bank to the other and to Castle Hill should not be hidden by high buildings; he wanted to open up the buildings with arcaded passageways, so that the city could continue, as it has done for centuries, to live with its river. He had expressed similar ideas on water as early as 1905, when he said to the editor of the magazine *Naši zapiski* (*Our Notes*): 'A good week ago I was back in Ljubljana, enjoying

287

310–11. The bridge before the parish church of Trnovo, 1931

the wonderful architectural prospects along the river from some of the bridges there'.[634]

Plečnik first turned his attention to the central bridges. In his regulation study of 1928 he had sketched some new crossings over the river and proposed planting trees along the bank, in accordance with the tradition in the city. Before the regulation of the river bed became an acute issue, he had given his students the task of linking the Square of the Virgin Mary with the old city beneath Castle Hill. He proposed a solution with three bridges to the students,[635] as he wanted to preserve the old nineteenth-century stone Franciscan Bridge; moreover, this solution was very much cheaper than the proposal put forward by the city engineers.

The Three Bridges were built between 1930 and 1932 (see fig. 205). Plečnik apparently developed the idea in Prague, where the new Mánes concrete bridge was being built over the Vltava by the side of the old suspension bridge in front of his school. The fan-like shape of the Three Bridges creates a celebratory entrance to the old city, and also helps to organize the very irregular spatial axes of the Square of the Virgin Mary and redirect them to the passage across the river. The high poplars which conceal the differences in width between the new and the old river beds are also part of an imaginary triumphal arch, as in the more expensive walled version in the drawing by Dragontin Fatur in Plečnik's School.[636] Plečnik provided a path down to the lower promenade along the river, only part of which was finished, beside the two side bridges. They give the entire ensemble a very Venetian character, and this is further underlined by the typical rounded balustrades. Compared with the plan of 1929,[637] the historical appearance of the design as executed is surprising. In order to unify the bridges, Plečnik also replaced the old iron balustrade on the middle bridge with concrete. He articulated the edges of the triple crossing with lamp posts, which define the curve of the bank, the centre of the old bridge and the two outer bridge contours. The balustrade is also divided rhythmically by the mushroom-shaped tops of the supports. The plasticity of the whole presents a constant succession of new and dynamic prospects to the people crossing the bridges. Delighted with the success of the work, Plečnik said to his students; 'The line of the arches on Franciscan Bridge is wonderful, I feel I am looking at the eyebrows of a lovely girl.'[638]

According to Plečnik's sketch, the Mayer storehouse on the Square of the Virgin Mary was to have arcades leading down to a wall on the river bank.[639] He envisaged a similar arrangement for the new building of the Slovenian Academy of Science and Art on the New Square (Novi trg) and all the

312. Cobblers Bridge, 1931/2

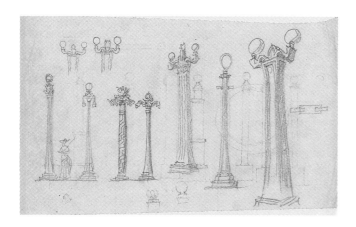

313–14. Sketches for the candelabrum outside the Philharmonic Hall, 1932

buildings along the river bank. In fact, only the complex of the indoor market was eventually built and it can truly be said to be Venetian architecture pure and simple. Plečnik first wanted the markets to have a picturesque river frontage, with differently jointed buildings opening with arcades and steps leading down to the river (fig. 315). The dynamic silhouette would have formed an appropriate foreground to the monumental new Council building.

The version of the market that was actually built between 1939 and 1941, however, bears the imprint of Palladian Classicism (see fig. 206). While the lower part of the long building is strongly rusticated, the upper part is plastered, while great arched windows give rhythm. The monochrome colouring reflects the heroic Baroque phase of Ljubljana, on which the white of Venice made a lasting impact in the early eighteenth century. An essential component of the market was the plan for a roofed Butchers Bridge[640] in the centre, with which Plečnik wanted to take the market across to the other side of the river as well. The idea is related to Palladio's project for the Rialto, as the facades of the two buildings in between, which reflex the rather monotonous perspective, are similar to the portico of the Villa Cornaro in Piombino Dese and similar buildings, albeit in a more severe Neo-Classical version. Plečnik wanted to give the impression of a Tuscan temple on a broad Doric substructure, and not a Palladian supraposition of an easily varied motif.

The point where the market joins the Three Bridges displays an extraordinary architectural sensitivity. Behind the flower shop with two façade porticos doubted in the Palladian manner (see fig. 208) Plečnik placed a long open columned hall. This was to be matched by a counterpart on the opposite bank, where the neighbouring houses are further away, that is to say by the much more compact body of the Prešeren Coffee House.[641] The columned hall is linked to the market in the Wagner manner (see fig. 206) with a higher fire wall. After experimenting with a straight flight of steps to the Fish Market, which is under the colonnade, Plečnik finally decided on a spiral staircase. The interplay of the dwarf columns inside is the only mannerist intervention in a whole that is exemplary Classicism.

Between the Three Bridges and Cobblers Bridge, where the architect Keller had redesigned the concrete bank before the end of the First World War, Plečnik was only able to plant a few weeping willows and other foliage, owing to a shortage of funds. He worked hard on the question of the concrete footbridge by Gerber Passage, which would have linked the Main square (Mestni trg) across Fish Market (Ribji trg) with Star Park and across Šubic Street (Šubičeva ulica), which was already planned, with the Tivoli Park and the Rožnik. Gerber Passage used to be a neglected corner at the start of Wolf Street (Wolfova ulica); Plečnik designed it *en passant*, so to speak, using stones left over from the wall on the bank after Cobblers Bridge was widened, and the old iron balustrade of Franciscan Bridge (fig. 316). The passage was also to lead to the landing stage planned below it, and Plečnik very skilfully resolved this with a 'promenade architecturale' that ends in a space with three arches leading to the river. Of thematic interest is the section of the steps that narrows perspectively in the Bernini manner, but the immediate model could have been Wagner's entrance to the rented apartment block in Stadiongasse in Vienna. Plečnik probably arrived at this solution through his work on parks and public places in Prague and Ljubljana, where he was often confronted with the question of perspective. He solved the narrow stairway of 'Flat-Iron House' (Peglezen) in a similar way.

In 1932 he created one of the most imaginative paraphrases of the Ionic column, setting it beside the Philharmonic Society building near the Ljubljanica. The lamps emerge directly from the centre of the capital and incline over the volutes, in an immediate expression of Semper's primal form (figs 203, 313–14). Like the lamp post on Gerber Passage, this column is also derived from the concept of the great obelisk in the Paradise Garden in Prague, but its scale is adapted to the nature and the character of its position.

The old wrought iron Cobblers Bridge was a technical masterpiece of the nineteenth century. Before building work on the new bridge started Plečnik shifted the old bridge to the former state hospital and used the oak from the bridge that had stood there to clad the Krpan cellar in the Prelovšek villa. As Cobblers Bridge (fig. 312) was financed from a different budget than the deepening of the river bed, the architect found himself in an unusual situation: he was forced to design the supports for the bridge in great haste, and only then could he concentrate on the top. It is true to say that this task reminded Plečnik of Wagner's viaducts for the city railway, but of course in totally different classical forms. Later he turned this to his advantage. The supporting wall was broken by two round openings which diminish its massive impression. He marked both sides with concrete lamp posts and strengthened the sides of the wall supports with 'buttress beams'. Upon these he laid the crossbeams of the bridge and the paving, concluding the whole with a columned balustrade. While the Three Bridges have Venetian balustrades, Cobblers Bridge, which is not arched, apostrophizes the theme of the Classical column. The three main antique column orders follow each other in

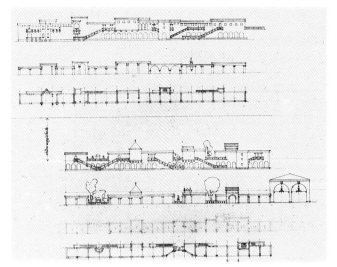

315. Variant of the market, around 1939

sequence from bottom to top; they are strongly stylized. In the balustrade we encounter the Doric, in the candelbra the Ionic and in the rows of six columns on the sides, the Corinthian order (see fig. 204). According to the plan, the columns should have borne horizontal beams for climbing plants. The unusually wide bridge was intended as a kind of public place above the water, its walls forming a green background between the columns. In the plan Plečnik wrote the words 'For economy' on the abacus of the Ionic capital, in an attempt to justify his work in advance.

In the early 1930s the balustrade of Cobblers Bridge must have looked very conservative. The studies that have survived show that Plečnik preferred the most historical variant. The theme of a public place above a river is a variant of the bridge in Trnovo, but the real counterpart to Cobblers Bridge would have been Butchers Bridge, with its roofed market. This was not executed. The motif of a covered bridge was familiar in Ljubljana in the Middle Ages and during the Baroque period. In the late 1930s Plečnik took up the subject again during the extension of the convent of the Sisters of Mercy in Stari dvor near Radeče, and after the war in his bold drawing for the Town Hall above the river Kokra in Kranj.

Between 1932 and 1933 Plečnik worked intensively on redesigning the idyllic but neglected course of the river Ljubljanica in the districts of Prule and Trnovo. Above the junction with the Gradaščica tributary he created walled terraced walks around the abandoned landing stages (fig. 309), adding benches and weeping willows and giving the whole a highly poetic atmosphere. In this way the town gradually entered a park, for the stretch of the river above

316. 'Gerber Steps', 1932/3

317. Building the Three Bridges, 1931

the bridge in Prule was also a favourite bathing place in summer. The elegant stone terraces beside the winding river recall the fluting of a Classical column.

Finally, Plečnik turned to the sluices by St Peter's Bridge (Šempeterski most), which kept the water level at the same depth and were also intended to prevent the Moor from drying out too quickly. Attempting to make the river navigable, Plečnik envisaged a landing stage by the nearby Vraz Square (Vrazov trg), to be accessed up a broad ramp. Similarly, he planned a small hydropower station beside the sluice,[642] but he dropped the idea later, as there would not have been any real need for it. Of the whole concept only the sluices with the pedestrian crossing were realized, and basically they recall Janák's dam in Předměřice. In his first plan of 1933 (see fig. 209) Plečnik approached the task with a definite sense of what would be useful, and despite the three high, rusticated pylons and their temple-like tops, which he had adopted from the tobacconist's kiosk on the Square of the Virgin Mary, and the mast, which he later placed in front of the 'Flat-Iron House', his design retained the character of a monumental engineering construction.

Six years later in 1939 we find in his final plan a fundamentally different formal language. Designing Žale mortuary had brought him closer to a more symbolic architecture, and the sluices now look like an antique apotheosis of the element water (figs 210 and 318); with their monumental pylons they recall the time of the early high cultures in Mesopotamia or on the Nile. With the architecture of Žale and the Roman wall they are a kind of review of the history of Ljubljana, going right back to the time before it was actually built. Nevertheless, the sluices are not a product of some irrational philosophy, resulting from the determination to shake off the burden of the recent past, they also again manifest Plečnik's deep debt to Egyptian, Greek and Etruscan art. On the mighty fluted columns stand Etruscan vases with gryphons – on the plan they are even more similar to the original vases[643] – a clear indication of the relationship he assumed to exist between the Slovenian people and the ancient settlers of northern Italy. Plečnik very deliberately used recognizable stylistic elements. He set the slender walkway, for instance, on a combination of column and caryatid that are an imaginative reworking of Etruscan capitals from Vulci (fig. 319). For the composition he used the same visual counterplay of supporting, load-creating and framing elements as on Cobblers Bridge. The only difference is in the wealth of historical pomp. The mixture of Egyptian and Greek architectural elements results in a strange effect in the architrave of the pylons. The motif of the corner capitals, that indicate a column that does not really exist, can be seen as an extraordinary reflection on Semper's genesis of monumental forms, with which Plečnik stubbornly set his face against the trends of his time.

In the late 1920s he again worked on the immediate neighbourhood of his house. As there was no room in front of the church in Trnovo he set a new bridge towards the entrance to the church and widened it to make a public place above the water (figs 310–11). He protected the pedestrians from the traffic with border stones and trees. First he had low cypresses planted, but later he replaced these with birch trees. In this way the bridge opened directly to the newly designed avenue along Emona Street (Emonska cesta). He put balustrades along the bridge, modelling these on Minoan *rhyta*. Plečnik spanned the bridge between two pyramids, and marked the tip of the arch with a slender pyramidal obelisk and the figure of St John the Baptist, the patron saint of the church in Trnovo. As this was also the border between two outlying districts, and the church in Trnovo had once been the responsibility of the City Council, the tip of the obelisk probably deliberately recalls the symbolic Robba Fountain on the Main square in Ljubljana.

What Plečnik had wanted to erect along the Ljublanica he was able to realize now, though on a smaller scale, along the river Gradaščica. He laid out paths along the bushy river banks, and created some broad steps for the washer women, who still washed in the river fifty years ago. On the right bank he extended the avenue of chestnuts with birch trees, built a concrete path, set a stone table in the new park, renovated a fountain he had discovered during the work, and provided the irregular square beside the church with a little rest area like an amphitheatre. He cleaned and enriched the neighbourhood as he had done in Prague Castle, if with incomparably more modest means.

THE CASTLE

Ljubljana Castle cannot be compared exactly with the seat of the Czechoslovakian President at the Hradčany. It never played any great part in history, and during the nineteenth century it was used as a gaol, mainly by the Austrians for their Italian prisoners of war. At the turn of the century the Mayor of Ljubljana, Ivan Hribar, proposed making the castle into a national museum. In 1905 the Council bought the building, but were at a loss to know how to realize their ambitious plans with their limited financial means. As a result the castle was preserved for this ideal purpose between the two world wars, while the old provincial

318–19. The sluices on the river Ljubljanica, 1940–4 (the head on the capital is by B. Pengov)

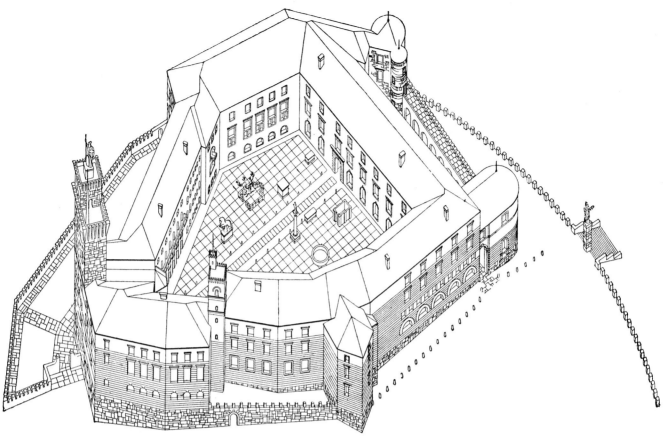

320. Proposal for the conversion of Ljubljana Castle, 1932

museum building became the subject of various speculations in connection with the new university or the enlargement of the building for the state government offices.

Plečnik was attracted by the picturesque position of the castle above the town. In various places in the town he opened up a view of the hill, or used it as a natural background when laying out public places. When in 1930–2 the architect Vladimir Šubic built his skyscraper in Ljubljana, Plečnik complained that 'Castle Hill has lost its function in providing a scale'.[644] Only in 1931 did he begin to consider redesigning the castle, and he gave the subject to his student Milan Sever for his diploma work (see fig. 320).[645] The heterogeneity and lack of artistic expression of the various wings of the castle induced Plečnik to try to unify the body of the building and dynamize it by achieving new focus points. He devoted particular attention to the courtyard and the immediate surroundings. By adding storeys, enlarging windows and enriching the building with sculptures he achieved, at least on the drawing board, the impression of a building that was also stylistically unified; however,

it still needed a stronger vertical accent, as the mid-nineteenth century tower was no longer sufficiently prominent. It needed to be made higher and designed on the model of the Town Hall in Florence. With two asymmetrical viewing terraces and a small tower in the bend of one of the wings he would have created a better balance, while also recalling the similar arrangement on the church in Bogojina. The Renaissance character would have been even more evident in the new stairways, the arcades and the redesigned court facades. In his plan Plečnik made use of the historic imbalance of the building for an imaginative enrichment of the monument.

This plan, which was drawn in 1932, reflects, though in very rough outlines, his original idea to raise the relatively modest architecture to the level of a 'Slovenian Acropolis'. The idea had to be abandoned, however, in the world slump, although the City Council supported it until the end of the Second World War, and the architect who adapted the south-eastern part of the castle in 1941, Boris Kobe, took part of it into account. It his plan Plečnik continued with certain ideas he had realized in Prague Castle. Had archaeological finds come to light during the building work the project would certainly have been changed fundamentally and enriched with symbolic accentuation.

For the link between the castle and the old city Plečnik also drew on his Prague experiences, as far as the modest funds would allow. However, the budget the City Council could approve only permitted a few paths to be improvised along the hill with extensive views over the picturesque roofs of the town. The city was not in a position to build a flight of steps linking the old city with the castle, similar to the one that had existed in Prague since the seventeenth century. Plečnik experimented with a number of different possibilities. Originally he envisaged access from Krek Square (Krekov trg) (Tomažič's diploma work),[646] but during the war he shifted it westward, closer to the cathedral (fig. 288).[647] Finally, in 1947, while working on the parliament project, he contemplated a monumental, roofed stairway leading from the Robba Fountain in front of the Town Hall (fig. 322).[648] This would be the most direct way to link the castle and the old city, and he was actually prepared to demolish a few houses beneath Castle Hill to realize it. Finally, however, he only succeeded in renovating the nearby fortress Entrenchment and Castle Avenue, work which was performed in the early 1930s.

Plečnik revealed the full extent of his ideal solution for the castle very much later, in his alternative study for the Slovenian Parliament building (fig. 321).[649] Here he eliminated the irregular sections of the castle and regrouped the building into a pure octagon, setting towers at the corners and erecting a great tower-like section to serve as the future symbol of the city. So in this proposal he was acting like a Renaissance architect. As he knew that he would never be able to persuade the new rulers to agree to his proposal, he decided to work out an entirely utopian idea to please himself. With so sweeping a concept it seems pointless to wonder what would have happened to the historical substance, it is more appropriate to admire unreservedly the extraordinary achievement of an architect who was now seventy-five, and giving free rein to his memories and his imagination after years of frustration during the war. This was the true 'Slovenian Acropolis', of which he had dreamed right at the beginning of the century, when he designed a monument to crown a city on the model of an Ancient Egyptian temple (see fig. 73). Time had banished from the architect's mind the mythical and picturesque elements the study had contained, and what remained was a clear architectural proposal by a classic oriented to the past.

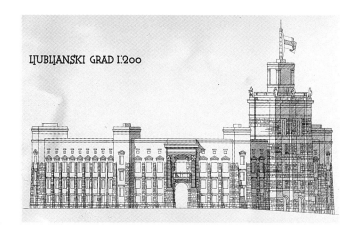

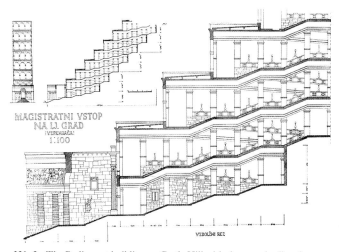

321–2. The Parliament building on Castle Hill with the steps leading down to the old part of the city, 1947

THE CITY COUNCIL BUILDING AND THE MARKET

Building new offices for the City Council was one of the essential elements in Plečnik's vision of the Ljubljana of the future. The architect approved of the proposed site – by the food market – which had been created by the destruction caused in the earthquake. In the diploma work by Tomažič of 1924, which we have already mentioned,[650] he had tried to solve the question of the City Council offices and the market while creating access to the castle. The City Council had already commissioned plans from some firm in Prague before the First World War, but they waited so long to realize them that in the end the planned big roofed market went out of fashion. Plečnik very much preferred the Mediterranean type of market in the open air or under arcades, an old tradition in Ljubljana, and he argued that this was a very much more hygienic way to sell food. As Tomažič's diploma

323–4. Proposals for the Dukič apartment blocks, around 1932

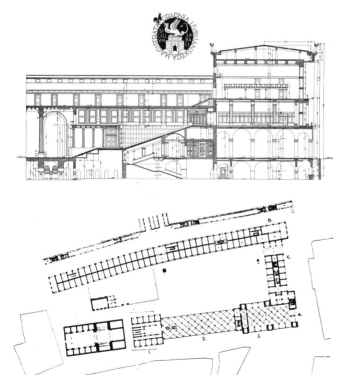

325–6. The new town hall for Ljubljana, section showing the grand staircase (1940) and site plan (1939)

work was not tied to a specific building programme, he added a music conservatory with two concert halls to the City Council building he designed on Vodnik Square (Vodnikov trg), something that had been desired by the Music Association for a long time. In this context Plečnik also worked on the odeon by Congress Square and Star Park during the war.[651] Immediately after the end of the war he took up the idea together with the project for the Music Association building in Gradišče suburb.[652]

After a brief interim phase, in which the City Council tried to find a site more to the west of the city centre where the so-called Dukič apartment blocks were later built, Plečnik was able to go back to the original site, to his great delight. His brief attempt to solve the building question of these apartment blocks is documented in three rapid sketches (figs 323–4).[653] He wanted to link the apartment blocks by bridges of varying height in the Venetian manner; the horizontal levels are skilfully incorporated in the facade cornices and result in a lively appearance.

Plečnik began work on the real building programme in 1932, at the insistence of Matko Prelovšek. The plan we have already mentioned in connection with the paving of the Square of the Virgin Mary[654] was drawn up in two variants (fig. 300). The more extensive also includes the link with the new seminary building beside the cathedral, while the less expensive variant only includes the building for the civic offices and the mayor's office. Of the existing Baroque seminary palace Plečnik intended to preserve only the richly decorated library and the valuable portal, wanting to replace all the rest, including the nearby priest's house, with a monumental new building. This would have surrounded the church on two sides with buildings in the shape of the letter L. Later, when the Baraga seminary was erected in Bežigrad this part of the project became superfluous. The City Council building was designed similarly to the priest's house beside the cathedral, but on a larger scale. The section looking towards the river was jointed at right angles to the mayor's office with a great hall on Kopitar Street (Kopitarjeva ulica). This would have created a big rectangular place between the church and the City Council offices; in shape it would have recalled the First Castle Courtyard in Prague, while its paving would have recalled the Third Courtyard, that was just finished. The ground floor of the surrounding section would have held shops and market stands, and the rent from these would have covered part of the building costs. The space between the river and the office buildings would have been filled with market stands, like that on the old Jubilee Bridge (now Dragon's Bridge – Zmajski most), that would have been widened. Hence Ljubljana would have had a sequence of interlinked paved public places, stretching from Krek Square to South Square, which was an equally ideal design.

With the start of the world slump the purchase of the Mahr House at the south-east corner of the market place, that had been released for demolition, was delayed, and this postponed the building of the Council offices for the foreseeable future. However, the unhygienic conditions in the food market demanded action, and in 1934 a special committee was set up under Prelovšek[655] to consider this part of the project and ensure that the new market stalls did not infringe the plans that had been approved. The committee only negotiated on the crucial question of a site for the meat stalls. Plečnik's idea of locating these inside the Council building aroused much criticism, as people argued that selling points of this kind ought to stand on the bank of the river. The architect thereupon proposed a cheaper variant, building over the concrete walls on the bank; however, some time was to elapse before the work could start.

Plečnik designed the meat market in the shape of a long columned hall (fig. 301), allowing it to follow the slightly curving river. He used the Classical elements in an admirably fluid way, and also added to them several formal neologisms in a very sovereign way.[656] He subtly marked the transition from one building type to another using Doric or Tuscan orders, varying the bases, adding or removing the abacus and varying the size and shape of the architrave. Wishing to avoid a major disruption of the curve of the market above the loggias, he only doubled the antefixa. (He chose a similar procedure above the two entrances to Baraga seminary, where they are simply marked with horizontal 'diadems'.) That this is nevertheless a metamorphosis of the Classical tympanon, which he used on the river side, is evident from the two stylized acroteria on the sides. The axes of the great arched windows on the two sides of the building correspond, giving the architecture maximum transparency. The combination of the doors and windows perfectly reflects the spirit of Antiquity. The window frames are in artificial stone, which is more durable than wood, the form of which they imitate.

With its wealth of forms the flower pavilion by the Three Bridges (see fig. 208), which we have already mentioned, introduces the free interpretation of architecture from the oldest times to the end of Imperial Rome. The space-within-a-space motif is accompanied by a variation on the Corinthian and Ionic styles. It is not clear why Plečnik rejected the idea of setting a smaller portal on four columns beneath the larger portal between 1941 and 1942, while the work was in progress. The half-capitals without column shafts suggest the same economy with architectural elements as do the pylons on the sluices on the river

327. Model of the new town hall, around 1940

Ljubljanica, which were designed at the same time. On the flower pavilion Plečnik suffered a setback, and one of which he had always warned his students to beware. As most planning is done in the summer, the architect can easily forget to allow for the winter. For this reason the flower pavilion could only be given a provisional chimney in the coldest part of the year.[657]

Plečnik continued to concern himself with the new City Council building only as part of his teaching programme, until Matko Prelovšek persuaded him to start on the definitive plans in 1939, as the situation with regard to the building work had changed (figs 326–7).[658] Plečnik extended the office section and adapted it to the slightly curving meat market; on the opposite side he added a new priest's house and the wing of the building department. The horseshoe space between the cathedral and the City Council building would have been very much larger in this design. In the west it would have ended with the seminary library, transformed into a temple with a pronaos. Plečnik wanted to mark the shorter axis of the planned square in the direction towards the railway station in the north of the towns, that was to lead across the projected Butchers Bridge into the square, with an obelisk bearing a statue of St George, the oldest patron saint of the town. Towards Kopitar Street, on the other hand, he wanted a flagpole. This symbolic urban inventory is almost exactly the same as that in the courtyards in Prague Castle.

The masses of the buildings surrounding the new square are carefully worked on the plan and with the arcades on the ground floor they would have given the impression of floating above their foundations. For the view from the opposite bank of the river Plečnik wanted to enliven the section before the cathedral with a high colonnade, in which he relied on his old idea about five monumental columns in front of the stairway reading to the southern gardens of

Prague Castle. As a counterpart to the cathedral itself he wanted a corner section with reception halls clad in stone (fig. 325). Its shorter, asymmetrically composed entrance facade on Kopitar Street would have been similar to the Town Hall in Florence, while the longer side took up the motif from one of the variants of Plečnik's first plan for the church in Prague (fig. 227): a double facade in the form of two great arches before a sheet of glass.

This Florentine and Venetian vision, created at the start of the Second World War, brought to an end Plečnik's long process of approximation to the urban models of his youth. He was aware that he was moving on the fringe of the trends of his time. For this reason he ironically added the current slogans 'Eclecticism – Corbusierism – Skeleticism – Urbanism & – Purism – Trafficism – Scientificism – Concretism – Economicism' to the plan for the facade of the Town Hall.[659]

In the spring of 1941 Ljubljana was occupied by the Italian army. Plečnik's design for the Town Hall, distinguished as it is by its consistency to the human scale and the restraint with which it draws on tradition, had nothing in common with the empty bombast of contemporary Italian architecture, despite the Italianate impression which it gives.

THE FLAT-IRON HOUSE

Apart from the market, the building known as the 'Flat-Iron House' (Peglezen)[660] is the only part of his grandiose idea for a new town hall and its immediate surroundings which Plečnik was able to realize (see fig. 198). Despite the regulation guidelines laid down after the earthquake, and which classified this extremely narrow triangular site at the start of one of the old streets, which was also on a slope, as not suitable for building, Plečnik ventured upon an interesting experiment.

The problem of a very narrow house was a challenge, particularly as a single-storey house had stood here in the nineteenth century. Owing to its unusual shape the local people had christened it 'Peglezen', a popular term borrowed from the German 'Bügeleisen'. Elsa and Matko Prelovšek fulfilled the architect's wishes, and although the country was still in the grip of the economic crisis, and they did not need the house for their own use, they bought the site and financed the building. However, the application for building permission at the end of 1932 marked the start of many difficulties. All the neighbours objected, and they succeeded in having the arch across the narrow Chapter Street (Kapiteljska ulica), with which Plečnik wanted to hide the muddled background, taken out of the plan.

The concept of the ground plan proved the main problem. Initially, Plečnik wanted to place the stairs in the narrowest part of the house, towards the street intersection. But in 1933 discussion over alterations to part of the building plan for the neighbourhood of the new Flat-Iron House forced him to revise this idea (fig. 329). He moved the stairs to the opposite side of the house and decided on a long rectangle shape instead of a round or semicircular one. The diagonal dividing the two flights one from the other made the stairs look longer, and created the illusion that they were easy to ascend. The feeling is rhythmically underlined by the vertical iron rods between the flights. Similar problems arose over the facades (fig. 328). Plečnik changed the window portals, such as were later used for the market buildings, into an arcaded shop frontage, which all the houses in the vicinity were to have to match the new City Council offices.

Meantime the Council had laid down the final building line for the street leading to the suburb of Poljane, and they pointed out that the Flat-Iron House, as the first in the row, would have to be of the appropriate height for all the others. This caused Plečnik to raise the building upon steps, accompanying these along Poljane Street (Poljanska cesta) with an ornamental division like a Palladian overlayering of the old Town Hall in Vicenza with the new facade. Each of the three levels has its own scale, and it is additionally individualized by the ornamentation. The contrast between the snow-white walls and the grey terrazzo of the masonry relates the Flat-Iron House to the monochrome handling of the market, as do other compositional similarities, like the cylindrical bollards of the arcades. Plečnik used ornamental artificial stone in a variety of ways, sometimes even to imitate wood or hanging fabric.

While the richer facade on the main road is more severe,[661] that on the narrow Chapter Street achieves its effect through the free functionalist composition of the fenestration. The seeming disharmony of the facades recalls the differences between the exterior and the interior of the bell-tower on the church of the Sacred Heart in Prague.

In the end the narrow facade on the street intersection remained without the figural decoration envisaged on previous versions of the design. It ends at the top in the glazed loggia of the conservatory. This motif goes back to the roof atelier so popular at the turn of the century, while formally it is the double of the south-facing glazed extension to Plečnik's own house in Trnovo. The concrete window bars are modelled on Perret's work and Plečnik placed a monumental outer mantle of columns in front of these, so providing the bold functionalist solution with a classical mask.

298

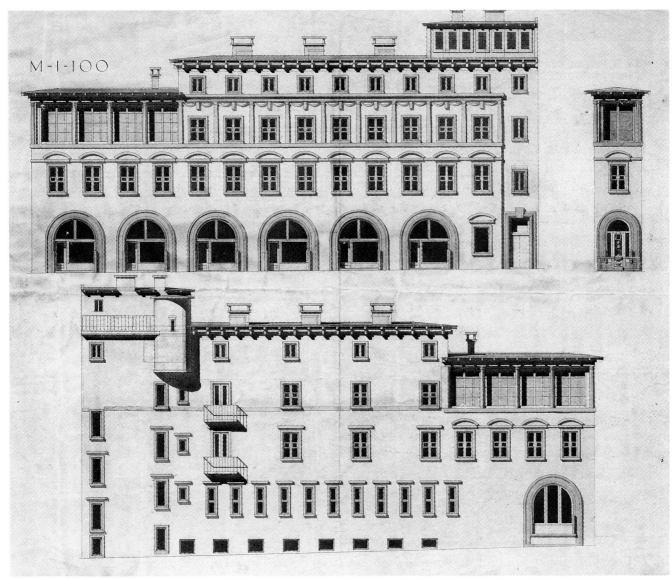

M·I·IOO

328. Facades of the 'Flat-Iron House', 1933

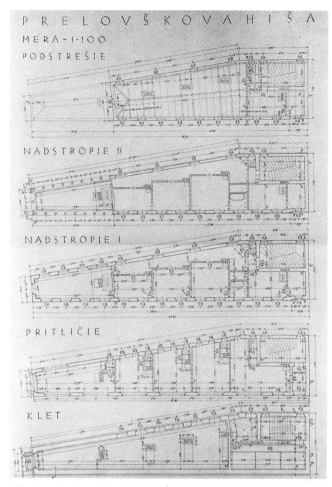

PRELOVŠKOVA HIŠA
MERA·1·100
PODSTREŠIE
NADSTROPIE II
NADSTROPIE I
PRITLIČIE
KLET

329. Ground plans of the 'Flat-Iron House', 1933

After much thought he decided to place a tall flagpole before the building (see fig. 198). Unlike the one for Prague Castle he made the pole of three parts, having these painted alternatingly with different 'flags' in three colours, to symbolize the 'trinity of the south-Slav people', which was then a highly topical issue. Three years after the house was finished the Prelovšeks sold it at cost price.

CEMETERY ARCHITECTURE

Plečnik attached greater importance to the religious aspect of the municipal cemeteries than his teacher Wagner, who saw the architect's task here primarily in regard to sanitation and function. After the death of his mother Plečnik, then still in Vienna, frequently pondered on the symbolic dividing line between the world of the living and the 'divine fields'. In Italy, the country cemeteries, with their white walls lit by the sun and their tall dark cypresses, had made a strong impression on him, and he frequently sketched cemetery portals, embellishing them with rich Secessionist symbols. In 1907, after his design for a grave for the Klimburg family had proved unsuccessful he wrote:

> God knows whether the City Council would permit what I am doing. In the cemeteries one sees nothing but sentimentality. But there is no room for that, either here or in church. It belongs in the corner – at home – in these rooms and places people need something positive – something great and sublime – perhaps they actually need something cheerful. These are only words. Fine words. But when the one or the other is finished, cheeks will blush red with shame. Man is a poor creature – full of longings – nowhere is he an embodiment – the devil of vanity draws – builds – the angel of humility humiliates.[662]

Plečnik built his first cemetery portal in the suburb of Vič in Ljubljana in 1935 with his assistant Valentinčič. He made it into a triumphal arch with proto-Doric concrete columns, and also made it a war memorial. Later it served as the starting-point for his propylaea in Žale.

Before he began to consider the problem of a central mortuary, he made energetic attempts to save the abandoned municipal cemetery attached to the church of St Christopher (sv. Krištof) in the suburb of Bežigrad. In 1927 he proposed to Matko Prelovšek that it should be converted it into a children's cemetery or a garden of remembrance for famous men,[663] and no doubt he had the cemetery in Vyšehrad in Prague in mind here. When his plan for the regulation of Ljubljana was approved he was commissioned to enlarge the old cemetery church of St Christopher for the new parish, which was in fact something he had proposed to the Bishop of Ljubljana ten years earlier.[664]

In 1932 he designed a cemetery to adjoin St Christopher's; it was to be dominated by a monumental Slovene pantheon (Hram slave) (fig. 331). As with the church of the Sacred Heart in Prague, he wanted a flattened bell-tower that would be visible from afar. The similarity of the details – a large round window with a clock – is due to the proximity of the two projects in time. The bell-tower in Ljubljana was to be nearly 20 metres higher than the one in Prague, as Plečnik wanted to give it a higher triangular projection both at the front and the rear. This unusual shape was probably the result of reworking the plan for the Žagar family vault in Rakek in 1930.[665] The integration of the main facade with the side of this memorial, using two different scales, could be based on an expressionist form of this kind without requiring concessions to modern art. The similarity

300

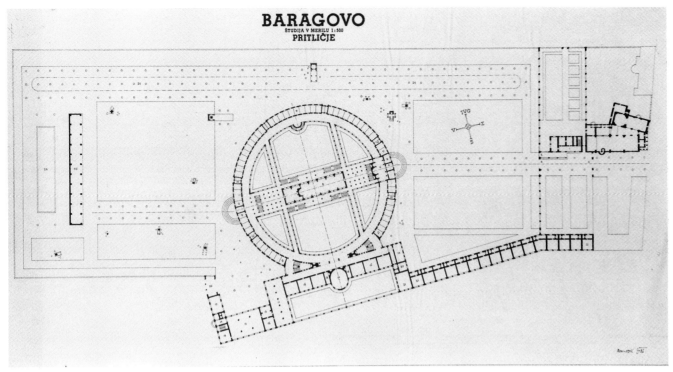

BARAGOVO
ŠTUDIJA V MERILU 1:500
PRITLIČJE

330. The Baraga seminary, 1932

of the Ljubljana church with Klint's church in Copenhagen may thus be quite unintentional, as Plečnik's plans are based on his elementary formal vocabulary.

But as no money was available for the Slovenian pantheon, Plečnik enlarged the existing cemetery church in 1933 and 1934, in such a way that later, had the whole complex been built, it could have been used as a parish hall. He supported the extension inside with arches, as Wagner had proposed in his study for the Interim churches, and was thus able to save money by making the walls thinner. Although it was only a provisional building, he did not position the whole length of the new extension against the existing church but made the irregular space between the two into a triangular nave. In this way he made the axis of the cemetery regular, and created a number of dynamic links between the old and the new space. When the church of St Christopher was demolished to make room for the new trade fair grounds in the 1950s, and Plečnik's extension was rebuilt in another location, his architecture lost its original point.

The decision by the Bishop of Ljubljana to build a seminary dedicated to the Slovenian missionary among the American Indians, Friderik Baraga, on the consecrated ground of the former main cemetery was not very fortunate. Moreover, the building proved too expensive to be realized

within the foreseeable future. In 1936 Plečnik created a design for a round seminary building with a chapel in a transverse section (fig. 330). The amphitheatre shape enabled him to link the main axes of the irregular site, and he also placed a lower wing with shops along Linhart Street (Linhartova cesta). However, this solution meant that he had to drop his project for the Slovene pantheon. The cemetery was divided into two sections and after the Second World War it quickly fell victim to Socialist town planning. In 1937, while the building preparations were being made, Plečnik changed the eastern part into a cemetery park (seen on the left of fig. 330) where he had some of the more important gravestones moved under the old arcades, which represented a modest substitute for a Slovenian pantheon. Some of the owners of the graves had already offered their gravestones for the foundations of the extension to the church, but Plečnik also piously incorporated some fragments into the new cemetery portal. The building work on the seminary was interrupted by the war, and only the essentials were finished. Plečnik had withdrawn at the start of the work, when the manager of the site, A. Suhadolc, changed the plans without consulting him.

A discussion of Plečnik's cemetery architecture would be incomplete without mentioning the many gravestones which he designed for Ljubljana, the Mura District and

301

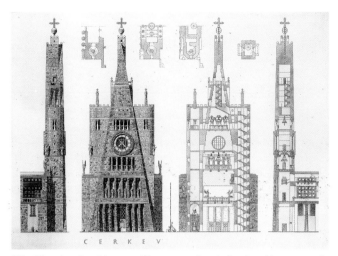

331. The church of honour (Slovene pantheon) for the old cemetery in Ljubljana, 1932

elsewhere in Slovenia. It was a subject he had hardly tackled in Vienna and Prague, but after his return to Ljubljana he began to work programmatically on the design of tombs and gravestones with his students, and he raised the art to an enviously high level. Tombstone architecture offered him the opportunity to take refuge from the materialism of the everyday world in pure architectural form. In its typology his repertoire ranged from simple stones bearing finely worked calligraphic inscriptions to wrought crosses, steles, vases, obelisks, mausoleums and temples, and he liked best to use the old forms in very free combinations and stylizations. His creations radiated faith in a new life through the contrast between the massive monument and the subtlety of its ornamentation. For the same reason Plečnik adorned the graves with the eternal flame and plants. In the outline or section he sometimes drew a cross, unswervingly testifying to his Christian faith, after the war in particular. A particular symbolic feature was the placing of the memorial stones on the edge of the grave or underpinning them with blocks in order not to have the weight of the stone on the body resting in the earth. He designed his own family grave as a miniature antique cemetery, with differently shaped steles and an archaic urn in the form of a house with the eternal light. In consideration for the harsh climate he chose the stones carefully, and made sure that they were precisely worked so that the ornament would literally evolve out of the block.

Plečnik also designed some communal graves for religious orders and in the first decades after the war these had an all-pervasive influence on memorial architecture in Slovenia. Finally, we should just briefly mention the unusual metal

urn which he designed around 1927 for Dr Emanuel Liska in Bohemia. It was on the model of Etruscan sepulchral chests and embellished with rich figural ornamentation.

ŽALE

As Ljubljana was growing rapidly it was becoming increasingly difficult to continue the practice of taking a funeral procession through the town to the distant cemetery. Hence, the municipal engineers had been considering a project for a central mortuary at the main cemetery since the mid-1920s, but the building department expressed doubts and in 1934 they refused to give permission for the work to start.

Two years later Plečnik, who was then working on the old cemetery at St Christopher's, put forward a different proposal for a new mortuary. The variant he drew in the summer of 1937 testifies to his efforts to give priority to the spiritual over purely functional needs. In the entrance, for example, he wanted a mighty columned portal, with rooms to left and right of this for the office staff, the clergy, flower shops and a room for a coffin to lie. On the axis of this peristyle he placed a round church, to be used exclusively for prayer, and only in the irregular rear part of the site did he place the building for the post-mortem examinations and the mortuary for infectious cases. A few months later he changed this idea, placing the post-mortem building in one of the two wings beside the entrance, allowing it to occupy almost all of this space. His experience in Vienna and Prague had taught him how demoralizing the display of the dead is in the mortuaries in big cities. For this reason he decided for a 'sacred grove', or a 'sacred garden', as he called it, in which some of the features of the traditional farewell to the dead could be preserved. He wanted to group smaller chapels around a central church, to be dedicated to the patron saints of the Ljubljana parishes. The rich architecture, the green and the dominant white would sublimate mind and thought.

So idealistic a plan would probably have had as little chance of being realized as his design for the university in Tivoli or the museum on Castle Hill, had not the energetic director of the Vzajemna Insurance Company, Stanko Sušnik, taken over as chairman of the administrative committee of the municipal mortuary. He thoroughly reorganized the enterprise and found ways to finance the project.[666] Building the new mortuary at the cemetery would save costs for the horse-drawn hearses, and some offices in the city would be vacated. For tactical reasons Plečnik did not offer everything he had in mind, and he made the extension dependent on the funds that were available. He maintained

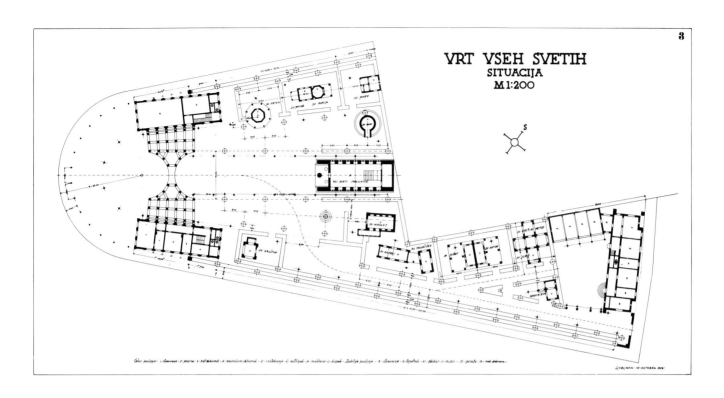

VRT VSEH SVETIH
SITUACIJA
M 1:200

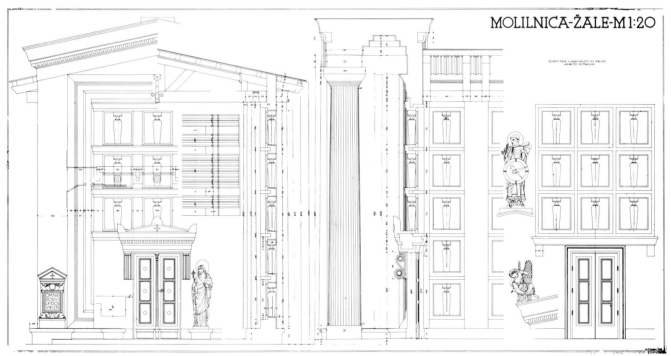

MOLILNICA-ŽALE-M 1:20

332–3. Site plan of Žale, 1938, and plan of the main chapel, 1939

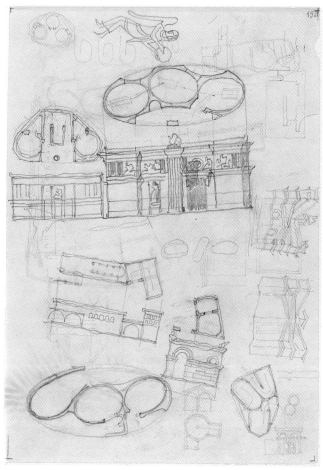

334. Sketches for a triple chapel for Žale, around 1938

a careful distance from the committee, and each time some-one cast doubts on his capabilities, he threatened, as he had done in Prague, to withdraw. To save his idea, which was being vehemently attacked on all sides, from the association of war veterans to the bishop's secretary Josip Dostal, he proposed attracting private sponsors. However, the committee refused to turn the small mortuaries into private chapels with family graves. A short time later, when the fate of the chapels again appeared to be in jeopardy, Plečnik wrote in resignation: 'I am not concerned about the realization; the designs are more important and more spiritual'.[667] He had insisted on the idealistic objectives since his very first talks with the mayor, and he wrote to him, saying: 'For God's sake, we don't want it to look like a remand centre, like the modern schools, where the light is measured in square metres and where they play around with hygienic jokes – this could, or it is supposed to be, a work that will last a hundred years.'[668] Hence he had endeavoured, as far as possible, not to encumber his city of the dead with prosaic

functionalist post-mortem facilities and similar ancillary buildings.

For Plečnik death also meant the right to equality before the Creator. It went against his conscience to differentiate his architecture, as he had been asked to do, according to seven classes. Disregarding the intended scale of charges he devoted the same care to all the chapels.

The portal is a mighty memento, reminding the visitor that this is the gateway to a different world, where the laws of human materialism no longer apply (see figs 211 and 214). The open view of the sky afforded between the columns and architraves is intended to soothe the distressed, and Plečnik took great care to ensure that the propylaea did not become a triumphal arch of death, although the idea of separating the two worlds of life and death actually seemed unChristian to him.[669] He wanted the columns in Podpeč marble, but this proved to costly. The Ljubljana cement firms colluded for the tender in order to put up prices so he also dropped the idea of artificial stone, deciding instead for the cheapest alternative, brick. On the other side of the city of the dead he wanted a monumental exit, but in the end he was only able to suggest this by making the neighbouring workshop building rather more ornate (figs 218 and 339). He grouped everything that in his view did not belong in a garden of memory, like the rooms for the carpenters, painters and decorators, the garages and vehicle wash facilities, on the north-eastern edge of the site, and this also saved the cost of an encircling wall.

Although the ensemble looks entirely homogeneous, the individual elements in fact only evolved while the building work was in progress. Plečnik was not always able to prevent misunderstandings. For example, when the builder, Emil Tomažič, started to work out the foundations for the chapels he believed they were all to be of the same size. After fruitless negotiations with the neighbours and the gardener Šimenc the chapels had to be very much reduced in size. Plečnik also had to squeeze them closer together (fig. 332), and he had recourse to hedges and double chapels to overcome some of the difficulties. When it became apparent that there would not be sufficient room for the ceremonies, the speakers and singers unless the green areas were made smaller, he set up a catafalque in front of the main chapel that could be used for all the solemn occasions (see fig. 212). Even before the Second World War broke out the director of the military hospital asked the Council to allow the chapels to be used for deceased soldiers, and this soon became an urgent need. In 1942, when new negotiations were being held on a part of the site that still needed to be acquired, Plečnik designed a military chapel in three sections; it was clad in stone and had a strongly profiled cornice, intended to resemble a triumphal arch. It stood beside the Gardeners' Pavilion.

Both these projects remained on the drawing board, as did the combined bier for the coffins and wreaths, which would have cut down the administrative costs and the number of pallbearers needed. It is also interesting in this context that Plečnik wanted the bearers to wear white uniforms, loosely cut in the archaic manner, with hats with broad brims and coloured ribbons.

His extremely personal interpretation of the funeral rites was never really understood. The architect's first disappointment came when the Garden of All Saints was renamed Žale, the Place of Mourning. It was a traditional name but very much more prosaic. A compromise was reached over the chapels, some of which bear the names of patron saints of the city's parishes and some the names of the most loved Slovenian saints. The last chapel was named Adam and Eve, in order to accommodate unbelievers or members of other religions, but this never proved a problem, as no religious differences ever arose over the funeral ceremonies. Plečnik wanted the funeral processions to leave Žale by the opposite gate on what was known as the Eternal Path, but in practice this was never accepted.

After nearly three years of building work Žale was officially opened in the summer of 1940. People rapidly came to accept it, but the polemics in the press went on. Few were interested in Plečnik's response to Antiquity. Dušan Grabrijan actually said he was bitterly disappointed, because he was unable to find in his teacher's latest work answers to the questions he was then concerned with, or any innovations in the use of material or construction.[670] His own functionalist orientation prevented him from recognizing the timeless quality of the architecture.

Although Plečnik had a wide range of historical models available to him, he avoided any association with cemetery building, apart from the tumulus, which he used to stress the Etruscan heritage (fig. 335). The chapels are individually stylized cult architecture, mainly antique in reminiscence (see fig. 216). With benches, memorial stones, a fountain and the rich building, Plečnik's city of the dead was intended to awaken hope and take away the fear of death. The fourteen chapels correspond to the Stations of the Cross on the way to human salvation.

The delight in forms, like the polychromy that was originally planned but could only be realized fragmentarily, is close to both Semper's description of Antiquity and the Slovenian tradition of art. A greater contrast to Gunnar Asplund's crematorium in Stockholm, which is of the same date, would be hard to imagine, although that is also influenced by traditional Italian cemeteries; it achieves almost

335. Žale, directly after the official opening, 1940

the same statements, but with extremely rational forms. Plečnik's metaphysical meditations on death, which he once said was the 'ultimate invention of philosophy', and his use of antique formal vocabulary ripened convincingly into absolute art. Thus, Žale is the architect's answer to Semper's premises, it is, so to speak, one of the possible realizations of the unwritten third part of *Stil*.

Although Plečnik looked to the past in some of his chapels, or even moved away from Western European civilization, the morphology of the individual architectural elements, like the walls, openings, floors, ceilings, roofs, ornamentation and lighting, remained his main concern. A good example is the main chapel, or church, with the baldachin (see figs 212 and 333). While the 1937 study for this was made under the influence of the mausoleum of Theoderich in Ravenna, the version actually built cannot be related to any known historical model. It consists of two pylons, between which stretches a rather lower section, while the whole has a low saddleback roof. This building is an important symbol, but it only acquires the desired monumentality through the setting between pylons. The chapel walls imitate columbaria, the Roman subterranean sepulchres with niches in the walls for cinerary urns, and in choosing this reference Plečnik wanted to show that the dead are close to God, or that the house of God grows out of our memories of the dead. To make the idea even clearer he was not afraid of the obvious association that would be aroused by urns in the shape of Egyptian ointment vessels, for in this sense Semper's theory negates the idea of transgression and grants Christian legitimation to any historical models when correctly used. As regards function, the open wall gave the room the necessary daylight (fig. 336), and this

336. Žale, 1939–40, the main chapel

337. The chapel of the Virgin Mary

338. The double chapel of St Joseph and St Anthony

339. The workshop

also enabled Plečnik skilfully to avoid the less monumental effect of modern glass.

There is a similar example in the light wall of the octagonal chapel of St Peter, which consists of three rows of metamorphosed ceramics. The chapel of St Nicholas is different, having concrete window frames in imitation of wood, and an interior with its inner row of columns which is an inverse variant of the composition of the conservatory in the Flat-Iron House (see fig. 217). The fenestration in Žale is thus solved with a variety of architectural means, adapted to the symbolic function required.

Let us go back, however, to the pylon on the entrance of the main chapel, which imitates a temple hall or vestibule (see fig. 212). The great Doric column, in itself a masterpiece of masonry, supports the broken entablature. Plečnik has avoided too evident a reference to a temple facade with a tympanon, and has made it plain that the existing rules can certainly be changed. The central position of the column is archaic in origin, and the tectonic syntax of the building is equally unclassical. In the traditional iconographic sense the column shifts the entrance symbolically into the funeral church. To prevent it from disappearing from sight behind the column Plečnik gave it a mighty mannerist gable.

Plečnik put a baldachin before the main chapel, with the catafalque and a lectern beneath. As he wanted to stress the typological independence of the baldachin he did not attach it to the chapel wall; moreover, the provisional nature of a canopy seemed to him irreconcilable with the monumental architecture of the chapel. By translating the textile ceiling above a wooden structure into a more permanent material, that is, concrete and copper, he indicated the original tectonic relation between the supporting elements and their loads, which he then in turn unified into an organic whole. The motif of hanging cloth, now repeated in artificial stone, illustrates Plečnik's characteristic synchronization of different stages of the formal metaphors with which he made the provenance of individual motifs clear.

The textures owe much to Semper. The different 'carpets' with their richly decorated borders in terrazzo before or in the chapels, and the decoration on the facades of the workshop building, are literal citations of textile art (see figs 217–18). Plečnik had been interested in similar questions while he was still working for Wagner, and his masterpiece is the facade of the university library building in Ljubljana. On the workshop building he combined klinker and pebblestone in geometric patterns, and the gradations of colour and the wave-shaped surface give the painterly impression of a woven carpet.

In contrast to this, the technique of mixing marble dust or glittering fragments of calcite into limestone plaster enables sharp edges to be formed, and it also makes the plaster more transparent. Semper actually maintains in *Stil* that the technique is older than the use of blocks of marble.[671] It was ideal

307

340. The 'Brezjanka' pavilion at Begunje, 1939, contemporary photograph

for the propylaea, which were to be transcendental rather than severe, and the main chapel.

Among the original architectural themes which Plečnik worked in Žale, faithfully following Semper, was the bladachin roof to the double chapel of St Joseph and St Anthony; it is based on the speculations on the Doric temple (fig. 338). According to Semper the Doric temple developed directly from the peripteros, and not from the temple in antis, as Vitruvius maintains, as the columns and the roof simply represent a great baldachin, protecting the cella without concealing it, and giving it symbolic significance.[672] The attraction of the direct contact with elementary architecture induced Plečnik to imitate antique building methods. He built the said chapel without previous static calculations, which represented a special challenge to him.[673]

The pavilions in the park of the former women's prison in Begunje of 1939 are a derivation of the same theme and not, as might perhaps appear at first glance, a variation of Laugier's purely functional primal hut. For the first pavilion Plečnik used tree trunks instead of columns, with a roof of concrete tiles above, which were made by the nuns to his instructions (fig. 340). The second pavilion, which was to be used for Corpus Christi processions and as a resting place for the Sisters of Mercy who worked in the prison, is a closed room under a pitched roof. The Doric columns with their mannerist rustication are striking; they are a rural metamorphosis of classical architecture.

The peak of this thematic search was reached in Plečnik's project for the social housing estate of 1943 and 1944 in the Ljubljana suburb of Krakovo (fig. 342). It came to be called the 'houses under a communal roof'.[674] With this project Plečnik wanted to rescue the almost idyllic village quality of this part of the town from the danger of dense building. He tried to persuade the Council to pay for a long roof and maintain it, under which the individual owner could build a small terraced house to his own design. These ideas can be compared with Le Corbusier's court building in Chandigarh in India of 1951 to 1955, and to a certain extent the 'floating' roof of the pilgrim church in Ronchamp can be compared with the workshop building in Žale. Although there is no formal similarity between the buildings, Plečnik's roof also 'floats' above the pillars, which lose some of their appearance of solidity by being painted.

Plečnik was certainly the only one of his contemporaries

308

to strive to give his works an older appearance. He could not have surmized that in the 1980s this would become the general practice of postmodern architects. In Žale he provided the double chapel of the Virgin Mary and St James, for instance, with concrete vases in the ancient manner (see fig. 215). He initially covered the tumulus with grass, again intending to recall ancient practices (fig. 335). And the placing of the chapels of St Andrew and St Francis, which was a result of the shape of the site, for the chapels are not coordinated with each other, was modelled on the organic growth of architecture of various periods.

In the encylopaedic treasury of architecture which Žale represents, where memories of the Acropolis certainly play a major part, Plečnik once more displayed the full range of his models. They include the chapel of St Maurus near Beuron of the 1860s, which served as a model for the side columns supporting the roof of the workshop building and the almost monochrome painting of the figures of saints. The animated cornice of the chapel of St Francis, and the rustication of the chapel of St Andrew are two of the few Secessionist influences. With the octagonal chapel of St Peter he imitated the silhouette of the covered fountain before Turkish mosques, and the 'Tower of the Winds' in Athens, which he greatly admired, while the neighbouring double chapel dedicated to the Virgin Mary and St James is a reference to Byzantine art. We encounter Gothic rose windows and doors reinforced with iron like in medieval times on several chapels.

In a description of the ensemble the columnar concrete candelabra and the many lights in the ceilings of the entrances should not be forgotten. On misty or snowy winter afternoons the artificial lighting is a major element in the mood the architecture creates. In such moments the Mediterranean clarity of form is transformed into a fairytale Nordic world, and we see that Plečnik was also heir to a different pole of the European cultural tradition, albeit one that he often denied.

341. Matko Prelovšek, Plečnik and the Mayor of Ljubljana, Juro Adlešič, inspecting the 'Brezjanka' pavilion, around 1940

Plečnik spent the war years anxiously. His abundant correspondence with Emilija Fon, a pharmacist in Kostanjevica in Lower Carniola reveals his uncertainty and the hardships he suffered. She was much younger than he and they had become acquainted in Prague where she was studying pharmacology;[675] but Plečnik could not commit himself to marriage – as several times before – for fear of losing his creative freedom.

With the end of the Second World War came a time that, to judge by its verbal proclamations, should have brought the realization of Plečnik's dreams; in reality things were different. During the last ten years of his life he experienced the most extreme phase of Communism and with it the intensification of the persecution of the Church. This became clear to him two years after the liberation, when, as a member of the Slovenian Academy of Science and Art, he and Fran S. Finžgar, one of the few Catholic intellectuals still tolerated by the authorities, protested at the removal of the Ursuline nuns from Ljubljana. When his nephew Karl Matkovič was imprisoned for several months Plečnik tried in vain to obtain the support of some of his former students who were then on the side of the new power-holders. There could be no further thought of monumental building projects, like the church for the suburb of Moste[676] that he had designed during the war. Some of his completed works were damaged. He was just able to rescue part of the interior of the Jesuit church of St Joseph in Ljubljana before it was taken over for secular use. He accumulated a number of sculptures and metal artefacts in the ancillary rooms in the nearby church in Trnovo. The church of Sts. Kyrillos and Methodios had to make way for the new trade fair grounds, and the architect's chapels disappeared from various other religious institutions. Acts of aggression against church officials were stepped up, particularly by the local authorities. The renovation of the church in Stranje, for instance, was impeded, the remnants of the graceful Baroque church in Šmartno in Tuhinj Valley (Tuhinjska dolina)[677] were blown up to prevent them being restored, and the timber already seasoned for the chapel at Velika planina was burned.

Architects began to be ashamed of accepting commissions from the Church, and Plečnik found himself taking on more work than ever. But it was not work that could have inspired architectural vision; rather he had to propose ways of making cheap adaptations with the very scarce funds that were available. Anything else soon proved to be utterly utopian. The prices for metals, marble and solid timber rose to hitherto unimaginable levels. In one case, for the church in Ribnica that had burnt down, Plečnik put a composition of

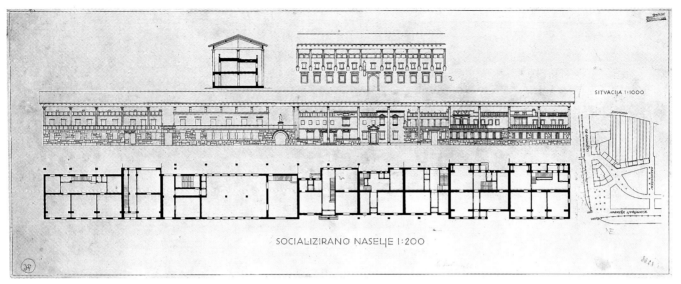

SITVACIJA 1:1000

SOCIALIZIRANO NASELJE 1:200

342. The 'houses under a common roof', 1944

classical elements in concrete on the two bell-towers to avoid the cost of an expensive lead roof (plan of 1956). He used a similar method for the lights for the church in Stranje, which he made in wood. Some of the metal workers who had been devoted to his art began to strive to earn more money, and no longer accepted work from him, much to his disappointment.

His preoccupation at this time was mainly with the applied arts, including book designs. This left its mark on his architecture in his emphasis on ornament. It is no coincidence that in advanced age Plečnik liked best to use the multi-coloured sgraffito, which Semper recommends.[678] In a certain sense he was coming back to his Secessionist beginnings in Vienna, and he liked to look for stimulus in his own early sketches. As he was unable to build monumental works he concentrated on designing vessels for Mass. In designing chalices he proceeded from Semper's description of archaic ceramics and he based his compositions on the contrasts between the monolithic effect of the product and the bowl that simply rests on the saucer, or the contrast between the visible tectonic core and its enclosure. According to Semper's *Stil* this is one of the fundamental themes of the potter's art. He was one of the few designers in the twentieth century to raise the quality of design of ecclesiastical vessels. The iconography of Plečnik's liturgical vessels, is often very subjective and was bound to honour the donor or the priest for whom the chalice was being made. Often, full of respect for the sacrifice involved, he would refrain from melting down the gold coins that had been carefully saved by relatives to make the chalice for a new priest's first

Mass but incorporated them in their original form in the chalice, etc.

The new political climate fundamentally changed views on art. That Soviet Classicism was not accepted in Slovenia was certainly due to the political conflict with the Soviet Union, but it was also due to the fact that the younger generation of architects wanted to build free of any historical tradition. Plečnik's constant preoccupation with the classics was an unacceptable to them as the orientation to Palladio was usual in the Soviet Union. Only Le Corbusier's theory seemed to lead away from the errors of 'bourgeois eclecticism'. The paradox was limited to architecture, and it had deeper roots, not least in the francophile inclination of the former kingdom of Yugoslavia. Some of Plečnik's graduates had attended the famous atelier in the Rue de Sèvres in Paris in the 1930s, and when later the flow of information was prohibited, Le Corbusier's ideas of that period were still having an impact in Ljubljana in the 1950s. An unusual syncretism was reached between the pre-war utopian fiction of the French architect and the post-war communist ideals: most of the architects knew Le Corbusier only from literature, as it was now hardly possible to travel abroad. The increasingly strong interference of politics with art which had to serve communist ideology was also reflected in Plečnik's unenviable position in the faculty. The more ambitious students generally attended the classes held by one of his graduates, Ravnikar, and he was left with female students, although he supposed architecture to be a typically masculine vocation. Attempts were made to exclude him from the faculty on the grounds that his teaching was not

343. Plečnik in his room at the Technical University, 1942

344. Plečnik with his pupil Vinko Glanz (left) inspecting the remains of the basilica (5th to 6th century A.D.) on Brioni, 1956

adapted to the new objectivity. Plečnik quietly took his revenge with ironic and biting remarks, incorporating these, as Wagner would have done, more or less conspicuously in his designs. 'Let us close the window, my son, and renounce the great wide world',[679] was his admission in the face of this new provincialism, which was in sharp contrast to the cosmopolitanism of pre-war Prague, or Vienna at the time of his studies.

In 1949 Plečnik experienced a slight rehabilitation when he was awarded the Prešeren Prize and a state medal. The two marks of recognition gave him the opportunity to erect war memorials throughout Slovenia.[680] In these works he combined the typology of tomb architecture with the formal ideas of his youth. The monument in the suburb of Trnovo, for example (1951/4), which consists of a base and huge sphere, can be compared with the model for the Gutenberg memorial of 1897. As Plečnik rarely had close contact with his clients, these works never went beyond the level of correct, enlarged clay maquettes. One exception is the monument for the Selce Valley (Selška dolina) victims of 1949/50 – a canopy placed sensitively in the landscape, with a broad flat saddleback roof on rusticated columns. Beneath the canopy he hung wooden posts to recall the martyrdom of the hostages, who were shot. He wanted to use a similar canopy to protect the excavations at the castle in Ptuj; in the 1940s these were still believed to be old-Slav cult places.

Although Plečnik wanted to meet President Tito and made two attempts to do so, they never did meet. His first major work for the president was the stone monopteros of 1956 on the Brioni Islands, where Tito had his summer residence. Here Plečnik was able to set the stone in a Mediterranean environment (fig. 345). As the sculptors were not capable of making anthropomorphic columns to antique models, he only provided the inner circle of oak supports with ornamental carvings. He had used similar beams before, carved to Nordic patterns, in 1915 in the Music Salon of the Zacherl Villa. In old age he remembered these in designing the christening chapels in Stranje and in the church of St Francis in Ljubljana, and certainly in designing the book for Finžgar's collection of fairytales, *Makalonca*, in 1944 (fig. 347). The pavilion for President Tito was the executed version of the classical antique theme which he had already proposed in 1949 for the unrealized mausoleum for the poet Prešeren in Vrba in Upper Carniola.

Plečnik did not seek to establish links with the new rulers, nor did he have many who spoke for him. The Minister of Culture, Ferdo Kozak, whose residence Plečnik had fitted out before the war, still supported him. To protect Plečnik from the unpleasantness in the faculty he proposed setting up a special chair of architecture for him at the Academy of Fine Arts.[681] Later he tried to obtain Plečnik's cooperation in the regulation of Ljubljana and for the Slovenian Parliament project (see figs 219–20). Finally, he played a major part in the award of the honours to Plečnik in the last years of his life. As the architect refused to allow any exhibition of his work to mark his eightieth birthday, the book *Napori* was published three years later, at Kozak's instigation. It introduces the work of Plečnik and his students. The author, France Stele, was forbidden by Plečnik to mention him either in *Architectura perennis* or in this volume, and so the text is very general; it illustrates the classical quality of Plečnik's works with historical excursions.

Nevertheless, the Minister of Culture was never really able to convince anyone of Plečnik's value. The communist rulers wanted to realize their radical urban visions, based on ideology, although they themselves felt most at home in the showy creations of inferior imitators of Plečnik's work. More out of courtesy towards the Nestor of Slovenian architecture than out of belief in his abilities they invited Plečnik to enter competitions for the opera house in New Belgrade (Novi Beograd) in 1947 and the Ministry of Defence in Belgrade in 1954. For the latter he worked out an inventive proposal for the dense urban context.[682] As he provided the project with columns and sculptures he could hardly have expected to be successful.

Plečnik's former students in Prague maintained contact with their teacher until the collapse of democracy in Czechoslovakia. Rothmayer in particular endeavoured to continue the regulation of Prague Castle as Plečnik would have wished. He visited his teacher a few times in Ljubljana, but after the war was not allowed to take any drawings or plans out of the country. When these direct contacts were also stopped, he honoured his teacher by reworking some of the elements Plečnik had used for Ljubljana University Library in the wedge-shaped antechamber to the Spanish Hall in Prague Castle. In 1947 he asked Plečnik for a sketch to complete the obelisk in the Third Courtyard. It was Plečnik's last contribution to Prague Castle.[683]

Plečnik's activities after the Second World War were no longer concentrated on Ljubljana. Among other things he was asked to work out planning guidelines for the towns of Kranj, Kamnik and Škofja Loka, but he made the greatest impact on Kranj, where he paved the square before the church, monumentalized the facade of the theatre and designed the steps by the nearby church of the Rosary. A particular problem here was the monument to the poet Prešeren, which was disproportionately large. Plečnik neutralized it with a green curtain. In 1953 he added a kind of antique proscenium to the theatre, with columns and

345. The pavilion on Brioni, 1956

346. The steps by the Rosary church in Kranj, 1954/5

313

347. Page of the book of fairytales, *Makalonca*, by Fran S. Finžgar, 1944

slender concrete arches, and garlands of artificial stone that recall Perret. A short time later he took up the theme again on the balcony in the court of the monastery of the Teutonic Knights (Križanke) in Ljubljana. In Kranj a simple fountain already stood above the hill leading to the church of the Rosary. Plečnik designed a new one to stand in the middle of his flight of steps (fig. 346), with the water tracing the line of movement of the flight as it flowed from one bowl to the next. Thematically he was following his Prague studies for the steps in the Paradise Garden, but in this case he combined the fountain with the obelisk. He defined the Rosary church with two horizontally and vertically shifted arcades, a motif that was very popular in English medieval church architecture. That is not to say that Plečnik knew of these sources, for he covered the existing Baroque arcades in the Ljubljana monastery of the Teutonic Knights with a new rhythm of beamed arches and had often corrected the exist-

ing irregular substance of a building in Prague in the same way. But the English influence is clear in the open framework of the wooden roof over the unified space of the church of the Virgin Mary in Grad in the extreme north-eastern part of Slovenia (1955).

After the end of the war Slovenia received back a considerable amount of territory in the west from Italy. This made the world of Karst which, being his father's homeland, had always been dear to his heart, and the Mediterranean accessible to Plečnik. When he visited the town of Koper by the Adriactic Sea he sketched a few patterns for the paving in front of the cathedral and tried to immerse himself in the authentic Venetian ambience. However, it was only a cautious step in his search for unity with the art he had always felt drawn towards; until then he had only been able to take up the dialogue with it in a middle European context.

Plečnik also received some commissions to enlarge churches in the regained territories, but he only executed the one for the church in Ponikve on the Šentvid plateau (Šentviška planota) (1951–7).[684] He enlarged the church, which had been burnt down during the war, gave it a different orientation and added a little tower like the one in Bogojina. With great piety he collected the remaining fragments of the nineteenth-century altar, that was not very valuable, and built them into the long wall. The flat roof, the ridge of which lies across the axis of the church, the open roof framework and the vestibule are traditional features of the architecture of the coastal region, and Plečnik has adapted his work to the *genius loci* here. Owing to his advanced age and because the church was difficult of access he left the supervision of the building work to his assistant Anton Bitenc, who carried out almost all his teacher's work after the war. This necessarily resulted in compromises that affected the quality of the work; moreover, Plečnik had hardly any chance to add to his ideas during the building work.

The situation was different with the church in Stranje that had been put to secular use during the war. The agile Franciscan monk Martin Perc had succeeded in persuading the architect to take over the renovation of the church and a few other tasks in the nearly town of Kamnik where the Franciscans had their monastery. Touched by the readiness of the villagers to restore the church with their own hands Plečnik helped them from 1946 until his death. The project in Stranje was not one of his major works, but formally and thematically it is rich in imaginative solutions, as he entered into the mental environment of the rural people and also took account of the modest means of the local craftsmen. The tradition of the Alpine region necessitated a richer ornamentation, but he consistently avoided compromising with folk art to achieve the desired effect. In some cases he translated classical or Renaissance stone elements into polished walnut, which took away the severity and gave them the more familiar appearance of furniture.

As the church in Stranje was Plečnik's last major realized religious work after the war it came to be very well known. The christening chapel (1947/8) under the bell-tower won particular praise, although it was in fact more a solution born of necessity. It gave rise to a number of similar commissions, and from then until his death Plečnik designed almost only fonts for churches in the Ljubljana diocese.

His native town, for which he had worked and designed untiringly for nearly twenty years, showed no further interest in him after the war. Only after he received public honours – on his eightieth birthday he was awarded an honorary doctorate by the Technical University in Vienna and another by the Technical University in Ljubljana – did the City Council entrust him with renovating the abandoned monastery of the Teutonic Knights, Križanke.[685]

Probably he would not have been given that commission either if the intention to add an extension to the School of Design, which had moved into the monastery building, on the foundations of the former city wall had not proved impossible. So in the last six years of his life Plečnik revitalized this neglected part of the old city of Ljubljana, giving it columns from the old Auersperg Palais, erecting portals from the houses demolished to make way for new town building and re-erecting old monuments. His colleagues often looked at the world of reminiscences that was being created within the monastery walls pityingly. In the 1950s the sgraffitto of the facades and the organic Secessionist line of the concrete lamp posts looked simply like bizarre flashes of thought from long forgotten times. The country was in the grip of industrial euphoria and there was general admiration for Scandinavian design. Anyone who could hastened north to see the works of Alvar Aalto.

In the monastery of the Teutonic Knights Plečnik relived his mature Prague phase once more in advanced age. He united almost all the themes that had once preoccupied him on the Prague Castle. He paved several courts, opened the wall on to the street with windows and enlivened the neglected, immobile masses of the building. He defined the spaces with minimal means and used lighting to take away

348. Monument to the War of Liberation in Trnovo, Ljubljana, 1953/4

some of their anonymity. One example is the small inner court which was intended for chamber music performances (see fig. 221). It has countless lamps set into the walls, and the architecture seems to melt with the lights and the music. Until then Ljubljana had not known such a Mediterranean room.

Plečnik retained his wealth of ideas and creativity right to the end. He died on 7 January 1957 in his house in Trnovo, and was given an official funeral in Žale. It seemed as if the Slovenian people wanted to apologize in advance for the speed with which he would be forgotten in the immediate future.

NOTES

1 F. Stele: 'Od obliča do velemojstra' ('From a plain to a great master'). *Koledar družbe sv. Mohorja za leto 1958*, Celje 1957 (reprinted in: *Plečnik*, 1968)
2 The reference is to the architect Friedrich von Schmidt (1825–91)
3 Plečnik's letter to A. Castelliz, dated 10.2.1929
4 Recorded by Strajnić
5 *The Zacherl Family Chronicle*, p. 235
6 M 171, undated
7 Plečnik's letter to Castelliz, dated 10.2.1929
8 Lenarčič
9 Recorded by Strajnić. It is not known exactly how the meeting with Wagner came about. Plečnik told Castelliz in a letter written in 1929 that after his failure with Luntz he went to Wagner personally; however, he told his students in Ljubljana that he gave Wagner's son his drawings and his future teacher agreed to see him the next day (Lenarčič).
10 Note on a drawing given to Boris Podrecca by Strajnić
11 Stele: *Plečnik v Italiji*, p. 230
12 Lenarčič
13 Recorded by Strajnić
14 Ibid
15 J. Hoffmann, letter to M. Mušič, dated 14.1.1952 (published in *Plečnik*, 1967)
16 Recorded by Strajnić
17 Plečnik's letter to Castelliz, dated 10.2.29. Emona was the Roman town on the site of the present Ljubljana.
18 W. Herrmann: 'Die Stellung Sempers zum Baustoff Eisen', in: Herrmann: *Semper*, p. 68
19 M 186, undated (May 1911)
20 Johnston: *Österreichische Kultur- und Geistesgeschichte*, p. 162
21 Wagner: *Moderne Architektur*, in Graf: *Wagner*, I, p. 276
22 See note 18
23 Semper: 'Vorläufige Bemerkungen über bemalte Architektur und Plastik bei den Alten', in Semper: *Kleine Schriften*, p. 217
24 See Semper: *Kleine Schriften*, pp. 233, 263
25 Wagner: *Moderne Architektur*, in Graf: *Wagner*, I, p. 276
26 According to Fabiani, he actually wrote the book down. Wagner invited him to stay in his villa in Hütteldorf for a time, and first went through the entire subject with him. See N. Šumi: 'Pismo Maksa Fabianija iz leta 1955' ('A letter by Maks Fabiani from 1955') in *Zbornik za umetnostno zgodovino*, New Series XXVII, Ljubljana 1991, pp. 121–2
27 See note 25, p. 266
28 'Architecture is the pure art of invention, for there are no ready prototypes in nature for its forms, they are free creations of human imagination and reason', Semper: *Kleine Schriften*, p. 292
29 Wagner: *Moderne Architektur*, in Graf: *Wagner*, I, p. 269
30 M 81, undated (May or June 1903)
31 Undated letter to Kotěra (June? 1906), in which Plečnik says: 'In the Wagner School I almost found it hard to bear – surface decoration . . .'
32 For more detail see H. Laudel: *Gottfried Semper. Architektur und Stil*, Dresden 1991, pp. 50–7
33 Kruft: *Geschichte der Architekturtheorie*, p. 358
34 W. Herrmann: 'Semper und Bötticher', in Herrmann: *Semper*, pp. 26ff.
35 G. Semper: 'Vorläufige Bemerkungen . . .' in Semper: *Kleine Schriften*, p. 225
36 Semper: *Stil*, I, Prolegomena, p. viii
37 Grabrijan: *Plečnik*, p. 91
38 Semper: *Stil*, II, p. 400
39 Quitsch: *Semper*, p. 72
40 Semper: *Stil*, I, p. 8
41 Ibid, pp. 436–7
42 Semper: 'Entwurf eines Systems der vergleichenden Stillehre', in: Semper: *Kleine Schriften*, p. 278
43 See W. Oechslin: *Stilhülse und Kern. Otto Wagner, Adolf Loos und der evolutionäre Weg zur modernen Architektur*, Zürich Berlin 1994, pp. 58–9
44 Semper: *Die vier Elemente der Baukunst*, pp. 52ff.
45 Semper: *Stil*, I, p. 445
46 Loos: *Sämtliche Schriften*, p. 106
47 Semper: *Stil*, I, p. 202
48 Moravánszky: *Die Erneuerung der Baukunst*, p. 74
49 Semper: 'Vorläufige Bemerkungen über bemalte Architektur und Plastik bei den Alten', in: Semper: *Kleine Schriften*, p. 226
50 Semper: *Kleine Schriften*, p. 239
51 Wagner: *Moderne Architektur*, in Graf: *Wagner*, I, p. 272
52 Semper: *Stil*, I, Prolegomena, p. xxviii
53 Wagner: 'Die Kunst im Gewerbe' (1899), in Graf: *Wagner*, I, p. 364
54 Semper: *Stil*, I, Prolegomena, p. xxii
55 Wagner: *Moderne Architektur*, in Graf: *Wagner*, I, p. 266
56 W.J.R. Curtis: *Le Corbusier, Ideas and Forms*, Phaidon Press 1986, p. 29
57 Semper: 'Entwicklung der Wand- und Mauerkonstruktion bei den antiken Völkern', in Semper: *Kleine Schriften*, pp. 383ff.
58 Wagner: *Moderne Architektur*, in Graf: *Wagner*, I, p. 276
59 Plečnik's letter to Castelliz, dated 10.2.29
60 E.E. Viollet-le Duc: *Dictionnaire raisonnée de l'architecture française du XIe au XVIe siècle*, 2 vols, Paris 1854–68
61 See Kruft: *Geschichte der Architekturtheorie*, pp. 375ff.
62 M 125, dated 31.7.1907
63 Kruft: *Geschichte der Architekturtheorie*, pp. 435ff.
64 Grabrijan: *Plečnik*, p. 92
65 Ibid, pp. 92–3
66 'Prešernov spomenik v Ljubljani' (Grabrijan: *Plečnik*, p. 114)
67 Lenarčič
68 Ibid
69 For A. Riegl see *Das holländische Gruppenporträt*, Vienna 1931, p. 181
70 M. Pozzetto: *Fabiani*, pp. 48–51
71 M. Pozzetto: 'Entwurf eines Systems der vergleichenden Stillehre', in Semper: *Kleine Schriften*, pp. 259ff.
72 Wagner: *Moderne Architektur*, in: Graf *Wagner*, I, pp. 273, 274
73 Lenarčič
74 M 139, undated (1909)
75 Lenarčič
76 Cf. Jacques Le Rider: 'Modernismus/Feminismus – Modernität/Virilität, Otto Weininger und die asketische Moderne', in *Ornament und Askese im Zeitgeist des Wien der Jahrhundertwende*, Vienna 1985, pp. 242–60
77 M 121, undated (1907)
78 M 31, undated (shortly after his return from his study tour to Italy and France)
79 The name was chosen analogous to '*Ver Sacrum*'
80 J. Kotěra: 'Jože Plečnik', in *Volné směry*, 1902, No. 5, p. 98
81 Kestranek's letter from New York, dated 5.2.1900 (AML)
82 M 70, undated (November 1902)
83 Plečnik's letter to Kotěra, undated (around 1908)
84 In June 1953 Fabiani sent M. Prelovšek an article on Plečnik, entitled: 'Jože Plečnik's Work as the Expression of a Personal and National Art', author's archive.
85 Fabiani: Obituary for Plečnik, letter to M. Mušič, 10.6.1957, published in *Plečnik*, 1967
86 Prelovšek: *Plečnik*, pp. 24–5, 192
87 Ibid, p. 17 (illus.), 182
88 Semper: *Stil*, I, Prolegomena, p. xxviii
89 Ibid, *Stil*, II, p. 374

90 Wagner: 'General regulierungsplan für Wien', in: Graf: *Wagner*, I, pp. 102–7

91 Prelovšek: *Plečnik*, pp. 16, 23

92 See R.J. Clark: 'Olbrich and Vienna', in *Kunst in Hessen und am Mittelrhein* 7, Darmstadt 1967, p. 36 and note 61

93 Prelovšek: *Plečnik*, p. 19 (illus., original in AML), 182

94 Original in AML

95 Ibid, 31, 182

96 Semper: *Stil*, II, p. 242

97 Kotěra: 'Jože Plečnik', in *Volné směry*, 1902, No. 5, p. 92

98 M 1a, undated

99 Ibid

100 V.S.: 'Gutenberg-Denkmal', in *Ver sacrum*, 1898, No. 2, pp. 2–3

101 Recorded by Strajnić; Prelovšek: *Plečnik*, pp. 13, 31, 33, 194; Forsthuber: *Moderne Raumkunst*, pp. 32–3

102 Draft of the letter from J. Jager to the deputies in the Carniolan parliament in 1899, SAZU manuscript collection

103 A. Loos: 'Interieurs. Ein Präludium', in Loos: *Sämtliche Schriften*, pp. 38–9

104 Ibid

105 Semper: *Stil*, I, pp. 66ff.

106 Ibid, II, p. 354 (illus.)

107 Prelovšek: *Plečnik*, pp. 33–5, 182

108 A. Loos: 'Aus der Wagner-Schule', *Neue Freie Presse*, 31.7.1898, in Loos: *Die Potemkin'sche Stadt*, pp. 50–1

109 See Graf: *Die vergessene Wagnerschule*, pp. 19–20

110 Prelovšek: *Plečnik*, p. 192

111 See note 108

112 Undated letter from his brother Andrej of 1897 (AML)

113 Documents from Plečnik's papers (AML)

114 Recorded by Strajnić

115 Letter to his mother, dated Rome 28.2.1891, in Stele: *Plečnik v Italiji*, p. 145

116 Ibid, p. 25 (illus.)

117 Letter to his mother, dated Turin 8.12.1898, ibid, p. 39

118 Diary note in Florence on 19.12.1898, ibid, p. 46

119 Diary note in Bologna on 16.1.1899, ibid, p. 105

120 Diary note in Florence on 3.1.1899, ibid, p. 73

121 Diary note in Bologna on 17.1.1899, ibid, p. 108

122 See Moravánszky: *Die Erneuerung der Baukunst*, p. 166

123 Letter to his brother, dated Rome 23.4.1899, in Stele: *Plečnik v Italiji*, p. 175

124 M 32, undated (1900)

125 Wagner's letter, dated Hütteldorf 4.2.1899 (AML)

126 Letter to his brother, dated Rome 8.2.1899, in Stele: *Plečnik v Italiji*, p. 134

127 Original in AML

128 'Aus der Wagner Schule', *Der Architekt*, Suppl. 5, 1899, p. 19; Stele: *Plečnik v Italiji*, pp. 269–70 (Plečnik dedicated the drawing to Strajnić, who gave it to the architekt M. Mušič)

129 See Pozzetto: *Die Schule Otto Wagners*, illus. 100, 102

130 Letter to his brother, dated Rome 10.3.1899, in Stele: *Plečnik v Italiji*, p. 151

131 A. Castelliz: *Reiseerinnerungen aus Italien 1898–1899*, Vienna 30.4.1899 (A. Castelliz papers, Albertina, Vienna)

132 Letter to his brother, dated Rome 9.5.1899, in Stele: *Plečnik v Italiji*, p. 186

133 Prelovšek: *Plečnik*, p. 183

134 Lenarčič

135 Prelovšek: *Plečnik*, p. 28 (illus.)

136 Graf: *Wagner*, I, p. 172, illus. 259

137 Letter to Kotěra, dated August 1901; Prelovšek: *Plečnik*, p. 183

138 Prelovšek: *Plečnik*, p. 183; Graf: *Wagner*, I, pp. 360 (illus. 538), 361 (illus. 539, 540)

139 Plečnik invested 100 gulden in the joint enterprise, and Wagner jun. sent the money back to him on 25.10.1900

140 M 33, dated Vienna 13.2.1900 (?)

141 Prelovšek: *Plečnik*, pp. 61–5, 183

142 Letter to Kotěra, dated August 1901

143 Wagner: *Moderne Architektur*, in Graf: *Wagner*, I, p. 273

144 Letter to Kotěra, dated 26.7.1901

145 *The Zacherl Family Chronicle*, p. 248

146 Prelovšek: *Plečnik*, pp. 66–8, 183

147 Letter to Kotěra, dated Palm Sunday 1903

148 A villa in Seewalchen on the Attersee, Atterseestrasse 67 built in 1902 and partially converted in 1984 (I am grateful to Alfred Weidinger jun. for the information and making it possible to see the house); see Prelovšek: *Plečnik*, pp. 67 (illus. 60, 61), 183

149 M 51, dated Vienna 12.5.1901

150 Semper: *Stil*, II, pp. 209ff.

151 See note 149

152 From Plečnik's offer of and commentary on the drawings dated 16.11.1900 (the photocopy of the document was kindly given to me by the architect Peter Zacherl)

153 Prelovšek: *Plečnik*, pp. 68–70, 183–4

154 Ibid, pp. 70–6, 184

155 Wagner's letter, dated 14.5.1902 (AML)

156 Prelovšek: *Plečnik*, p. 192

157 M 66, undated (summer or autumn 1901)

158 M 65, undated (May 1902)

159 M 34a, undated (February 1901)

160 Forsthuber: *Moderne Raumkunst*, pp. 29ff.

161 Prelovšek: *Plečnik*, p. 195

162 Ibid, p. 59 (illus. 48), 77, 190

163 Letter to Kotěra, undated (November 1902)

164 'This may be the best yet from the Secession – at least in appearance', he wrote to Kotěra (undated letter of 1900)

165 Letter to Kotěra, undated (with Kotěra's note January 1901)

166 Ibid

167 Letter from Janez Plečnik to his brother Andrej, dated 19.11.1901 (AML)

168 Grabrijan: *Plečnik*, p. 98

169 Prelovšek: *Plečnik*, p. 58

170 Letter to Kotěra, dated 20.1.1904

171 M 75, undated (26.12.1902)

172 Prelovšek: *Plečnik*, pp. 58, 79–80, 191

173 Letter to Kotěra, undated (early 1905)

174 Prelovšek: *Plečnik*, p. 195; Forsthuber: *Moderne Raumkunst*, pp. 107–8

175 L. Hevesi: *Acht Jahre Secession*, Vienna 1906, p. 494

176 Prelovšek: *Plečnik*, p. 195

177 Prelovšek: *Plečnik*, pp. 58, 134–5, 195; Forsthuber: *Moderne Raumkunst*, pp. 112–13

178 Prelovšek: *Plečnik*, p. 195

179 L. Hevesi: *Altkunst-Neukunst 1894–1908*, Vienna 1908, pp. 336, 338

180 H. Siebenmorgen: *Die Anfänge der 'Beuroner Kunstschule, Peter Lenz und Jakob Würger 1850–75'*, Sigmaringen 1983, p. 83

181 Ibid, p. 85

182 Prelovšek: *Plečnik*, p. 196; Forsthuber: *Moderne Raumkunst*, pp. 114–15

183 Letter to Kotěra, undated (October or November 1906)

184 Prelovšek: *Plečnik*, pp. 60, 196; Forsthuber: *Moderne Raumkunst*, pp. 138–9

185 Prelovšek: *Plečnik*, pp. 81–105, 185–6

186 Wagner: *Moderne Architektur*, in Graf: *Wagner*, I, p. 277

187 Semper: *Stil*, I, p. 87

188 Pozzetto: *Fabiani*,, p. 76

189 Semper: 'Entwurf eines Systems der vergleichenden Stillehre', in Semper: *Kleine Schriften*, p. 289

190 Pozzetto: *Fabiani*, p. 63

191 Sekler: *Hoffmann*, p. 82

192 Letter to Kotěra, undated (November 1900)

193 Plečnik's offer and commentary on the sketches (see Note 152)

194 *Der Architekt* VII, 1901, p. 48 and illus. 84

195 E. Bader: *Karl v. Vogelsang, Die geistige Grundlegung der christlichen Sozialreform*, Vienna 1900, pp. 201–16; based on the surviving chronicle, K. Sotriffer wrote a special monograph about the Zacherl family. The author analyses in detail the factory-owner's views and his political activity which increased parallel to the crisis which befell his enterprise during

World War I (K. Sotriffer: *Die Blüte der Chrysantheme. Die Zacherl-Stationen einer anderen Wiener Bürgerfamilie*, Vienna, Cologne, Weimar 1966).

196 Latin form of the Czech surname

197 Plečnik designed the covers for both books but he probably never read them, although he roughly learned about their contents from his talks with Zacherl.

198 Johnston: *Österreichische Kultur und Geistesgeschichte*, pp. 73ff.

199 Lenarčič

200 M 77, undated (March 1903)

201 'I wanted to build the Zacherl in brick – but with a difference – and they told me – and I still feel sick when I hear the word brick', he wrote to Kotěra, undated letter (October or November 1906)

202 *Bericht über den VIII. internationalen Architektenkongreß*, Vienna 1908, pp. 324ff.

203 M 110, undated (13.12.1904)

204 Semper: 'Bemerkungen zu des M. Vitruvius Pollio zehn Büchern der Baukunst', in Semper: *Kleine Schriften*, p. 196

205 Semper: *Stil*, II, pp. 373–4

206 Mušič: *Plečnik*, p. 87

207 Semper: *Wissenschaft, Industrie und Kunst*, p. 36

208 A. Loos: 'Die Baumaterialien', in Loos: *Sämtliche Schriften*, pp. 99ff.

209 A. Loos: 'The Chicago Tribune Column', in Loos: *Potemkin'sche Stadt*, p. 195

210 Semper: 'Entwicklung der Wand- und Mauerkonstruktionen bei den antiken Völkern', in Semper: *Kleine Schriften*, p. 392; Semper: *Der Stil*, I, p. 410

211 Semper: *Stil*, Prolegomena, p. xxviii–xxix

212 Semper: 'Entwurf eines Systems der vergleichenden Stillehre', in Semper: *Kleine Schriften*, p. 280

213 Prelovšek: *Plečnik*, p. 94; Forsthuber: *Modern Raumkunst*, p. 104

214 Semper: *Stil*, II, pp. 167–8

215 Ibid, p. 235

216 Undated letter from Peter Altenberg (Prelovšek: *Plečnik*, p. 100)

217 See Semper: *Stil*, I, Prolegomena, p. xliii

218 See note 216

219 M 69, undated (October/November 1902)

220 *Das Interieur* IV, 1903, Illus. 6

221 Prelovšek: *Plečnik*, pp. 75 (illus.), 76, 184

222 *Secesija na Slovenskem*, (*Art Nouveau in Slovenia*), exhibition catalogue, Ljubljana 1984

223 Prelovšek: *Plečnik*, pp. 77–9, 191; V.J. Behal: 'Two dining rooms from Graz', in *Furniture History*, Vol. xxvii, London 1991, pp. 161–5

224 Semper: *Stil*, I, p. 287; II, p. 341

225 The furniture is owned by the Zacherl family

226 Prelovšek: *Plečnik*, pp. 80, 191

227 V.J. Behal: *Möbel des Jugendstils, Sammlung des Österreichischen Museums für angewandte Kunst in Wien*, Munich 1988, pp. 204ff.

228 E. Leisching: 'Die Winterausstellung des k.k. Österreichischen Museums', in *Kunst und Kunsthandwerk* VII, 1904, p. 18 and unnumbered plate

229 Prelovšek: *Plečnik*, p. 191

230 M 119, dated 22.1.1906

231 Prelovšek: *Plečnik*, pp. 108–11, 187

232 Mušič: *Arhitektura in čas*, p. 287

233 Prelovšek: *Plečnik*, pp. 106, 107 (illus.), 187

234 Letter to Kotěra, dated September 1902

235 Prelovšek: *Plečnik*, pp. 117–18, 188

236 Strajnić: *Plečnik*, p. 19

237 *The Zacherl Family Chronicle*, p. 413

238 Prelovšek: *Plečnik*, pp. 118, 119 (illus.), 188

239 Strajnić: *Plečnik*, p. 25

240 Letter to Kotěra, undated (1907)

241 Letter to Kotěra, undated (18.1.1911)

242 Prelovšek: *Plečnik*. pp, 111–14, 188

243 M 138, undated (February? 1909)

244 Recorded by Strajnić

245 'Prešernov spomenik v Ljubljani'

246 Letter to A. Titl, dated 29.1.1930

247 See *Styl* I, 1909, pp. 115–16

248 Prelovšek: *Plečnik*, pp. 24, 182

249 Ibid, pp. 24 (illus.), 29

250 Letter from the architect Richard Vidale to Plečnik in Rome, dated 20.3.1899 (AML)

251 Original in AML

252 Wagner: 'Zur Studie: "Die Moderne im Kirchenbau" ', in Graf: *Wagner*, I, pp. 326ff.

253 M 21, dated Rome 23.4.1899, in Stele: *Plečnik v Italiji*, p. 173

254 Prelovšek: *Plečnik*, p. 39 (illus. 31)

255 Ibid, p. 182

256 Ibid, p. 123 (illus.)

257 M. Dreger: 'Die neue Bauschule, Ausstellung der Schüler Otto Wagners', in: *Ver Sacrum* II, No. 8, p. 22

258 Prelovšek: *Plečnik*, pp. 65, 66, 184

259 Ibid, pp. 131–2, 184

260 See H. Swoboda: *Konkurrenzen für eine einfache Pfarrkirche und ein Heiliges Grab*, Vienna, undated, p. 33

261 Prelovšek: *Plečnik*, pp. 136–7, 187

262 M 116, undated (1906?)

263 M 152, undated

264 Grabrijan: *Plečnik*, p. 104

265 See note 252, p. 328

266 Prelovšek: *Plečnik*, pp. 140–3, 188

267 B. Maksimović: 'Otto Wagner v spominih Ivana Vurnika', ('Otto Wagner in the memories of Ivan Vurnik') *Sinteza* 58–60, Ljubljana 1982, p. 192

268 Prelovšek: *Plečnik*, pp. 145–60, 188–9

269 Letter to A. Titl, dated 2.2.1932

270 Letter to A. Titl, dated 6.1.1933

271 Strajnić: *Plečnik*, p. 26; it is not clear from the text exactly which buildings are meant and how deeply Plečnik studied them.

272 Moravánszky: *Die Architektur der Donaumonarchie*, p. 133

273 F. Tomažič sketched the church briefly while Plečnik was giving his commentary, and he added: One of the designs for the church of the Holy Spirit (Tomažič's sketchbook, AML)

274 The originals are in AML; see Graf: *Wagner*, II, p. 544

275 M 162, undated (1910)

276 Ibid

277 According to reports by the architect Boris Kobe, 12.1.1980

278 F. Stele: 'Apologija moderne umetnosti', ('Apology for moderne art') *Čas* V, No. 9, pp. 401–15 and A. Plečnik's review, ibid, No. 10, p. 480

279 The originals are in AML

280 The original is in AML

281 Prelovšek: *Plečnik*, pp. 107 (illus. 102), 186

282 Strajnić: *Plečnik*, pp. 27, No. 19

283 Semper: *Die vier Elemente der Baukunst*, p. 103

284 See note 282

285 The original is in AML; Prelovšek: *Plečnik*, p. 154 (illus.)

286 On some of the capitals Plečnik has indicated ornamentation that appears in a perspective drawing of the crypt of 1910 (AML)

287 Pozzetto: 'Cemento armato, materiale nuovo nella scuola di Otto Wagner', in: *L'Industria Italiana del Cemento*, No. 6, 1981, p. 422

288 Letter to A. Titl, dated 16.11.1926

289 M 199, dated Vienna 26.12.1911

290 The balls reminded Plečnik of the holy graves in the churches in Ljubljana. In fact, this was a tradition that had started with the Baroque and spread along the Alpine region. The original intention to show the fifteen secrets of the rosary in the crypt would have been another reference to his homeland; the rosary played an important part in Plečnik's memories of his mother.

291 M 166, dated 1.10.1910

292 Letter to Kotěra, undated (January or February 1911)

293 Ibid

294 Letter to Kotěra, undated (1911)

295 M 264, undated (1913)

296 See Strajnić: *Plečnik*, No. 22

297 M 165, undated (1910)

298 Lenarčič
299 Letter from Janák, undated (AML)
300 Letter from Janák to Plečnik in Vienna, dated 5.12.1910 (AML)
301 Janák: 'Od moderní architektury – k architektuře', ('From modern architecture – to architecture'), *Styl* II, 1909–10, pp. 105–9
302 Tomažič's sketchbook (AML)
303 See note 301
304 P. Janák: 'Hranol a pyramida' ('A Prism and a Pyramid'), *Umělěcký měsíčník*, I, 1911–12, in Pechar Urlich, pp. 132ff.
305 Moravánszky: *Die Erneuerung der Baukunst*, pp. 148ff.; the most informative work to date on Czech Cubism is the exhibition catalogue *Kubismus in Prag 1909–1925* (*Cubism in Prague 1909–25*), Düsseldorf 1991
306 V. Hofman: 'Duch moderni tvorby v architektuře', ('The Spirit of Modern Creativity in Architecture') *Umělecký měsíčník* I, 1911–12, in Pechar/Urlich, p. 131
307 Prelovšek: *Plečnik*, pp. 162, 163 (illus.), 189, the sketches are in AML, in a private collection in Ljubljana and in the archive of the National Gallery (Národní galerie) in Prague
308 Plečnik: *Výběr prací školy pro dekorativní architekturu v Praze z roku 1911–1921*, Prague 1927, pp. 6, 7, 30, 31
309 Ibid., pp. 67–70
310 Ibid., p. 121; F. Burkhardt: *Vlastislav Hofman. Architektur des böhmischen Kubismus*, IDZ Berlin, undated, p. 8
311 *Umění* XXXV, 1987, No. 2, p. 104ff.
312 Feuerstein sent Plečnik several postcards from Moscow in 1913 (AML)
313 Letter from A. Král dated Brno 16.1.1947 (AML)
314 See O. Novotný: *Jan Kotěra a jeho doba*, Prague 1958, p. 44
315 M 194, undated
316 Mušič: *Arhitektura in čas*, pp. 293–7
317 Graf: *Wagner*, II, p. 804 (illus.)
318 Prelovšek: *Plečnik*, pp. 164–5
319 M 243, undated (Summer 1913)
320 H. Czech – W. Mistelbauer: *Das Looshaus*, Vienna 1976, p. 81
321 Prelovšek: *Plečnik*, p. 165
322 Ibid., pp. 165, 189
323 Ibid., p. 194
324 Z. Lukeš: 'L. Skřivánek', *Umění* XXXVI, 1988, No. 1, pp. 83–5
325 Z. Lukeš: 'Neznámá Plečnikova stavba v Praze', ('An Unknown Building of Plečnik in Prague') *Umění* XXXVII, 1989, No. 5, pp. 465–6
326 Prelovšek: *Plečnik*, pp. 65–6, 183
327 Ibid., p. 189
328 See note 325
329 National Gallery archive, Prague, S. Sucharda Fund, class. no. 3040. I am grateful to Dr Jindřich Vybíral for drawing my attention to this.
330 M 261, undated (1913)
331 Lenarčič; see also *Styl* IV, 1912, p. 192
332 M 212, dated 21.11.1912
333 See Prague Municipal Archive (Archiv hlavního města Prahy), VŠUP Praha, Fascicles 26–27 and two fascicles of the examination records
334 *Styl*, IV, 1912, p. 178
335 See note 333, Fascicle 55
336 Prelovšek: *Plečnik*, p. 194; see also: 'The chalice as a metaphor of antique ceramics', in *Plečnikovi kelihi (Plečnik's chalices)*, exhibition catalogue for Prague, Ljubljana 1996
337 Semper: *Stil* I, pp. 4–5
338 See M. Žunkovič: *Die Slawen ein Urvolk Europas*, Kremsier 1910
339 See. Plečnik's notebook of 1915 (owned by his heirs)
340 *Umetnost alpskih Ilirov in Venetov. Situle od Pada do Donave (The art of the Alpine Illyrians and Veneties. Situlae from the Po to the Danube)* exhibition catalogue, Ljubljana 1962, pp. 97–9
341 See note 333, fascicle of the conference records
342 *Styl* VI, 1920–1, pp. 52–6, and Supplements XXX–XLI; *Stavitel* I, 1919, No. 4, p. 79
343 *Stavitel* II, 1921–2, pp. 46–7; Plečnik: *Výběr prací školy pro dekorativní architekturu v Praze z roku 1911–1921*, p. 147
344 Plečnik, 1986, p. 148
345 Letter from V. Ložek, dated 12.2.1922 (AML)
346 Krečič: *Plečnik in jaz*, p. 160
347 M 281, dated 2.1.1920 and M 183 (end of first letter)
348 M 183 (2.1.1920)
349 Letter from A. Masaryk from Capri, dated 2.7.1921
350 Styl VI, 1920–1, unpag.; on Plečnik's appointment in Ljubljana see also P. Krečič: *Jože Plečnik*, Ljubljana 1992, pp. 96–7
351 *Stavitel* I, 1920, No. 8, p. 150; *Styl* VI, 1920–1, pp. 61–2; the data on Prague Castle is from V. Malá/D. Prelovšek: 'Faktografický přehled Plečnikova díla na Pražském hradě a v Lánech' Survey of Plečnik's work on Prague Castle and at Lány', in: *Josip Plečnik – Architekt Pražského hradu*, exhibition catalogue, Prague 1996, pp. 605–25
352 Plečnik later told his students in Ljubljana that the most significant fact about the presidential seat in Prague was that Masaryk was a great and profound philosopher. He did not believe that Jesus was the Son of God, but he did regard Him as the greatest man who had ever lived. Only unwillingly did the President sign death warrants, and each time he did so he made a black mark in his calendar. Plečnik added that Masaryk ate very sparingly, and he always stood up from the table hungry. (Lenarčić)
353 Letter from A. Masaryk from Lány, dated 14.8.1921
354 *Architektura ČSR* VII, 1948, No. 1, p. 13 (Masaryk's statement of 7.3.1920)
355 M 488, draft of a reply to an official of Prague Castle before World War II
356 Grabrijan: *Plečnik*, p. 72
357 Letter from the Prorektor of the Technical University in Zagreb, E. Schön, dated 6.12.1920 (AML). When the Technical University in Ljubljana was threatened with closure two years later, Schön renewed his offer, on 12.5.1922 (postscript to letter M 306)
358 'Úprava pražského hradu. Josef Plečnik hradním architektem,' ('Restoration of Prague Castle. Josef Plečnik appointed architect of the Castle') *Lidové Noviny* 1.12.1920 (reprinted in *Stavitel* II, 1920–1, p. XVII)
359 Letter from A. Masaryk, dated 13.5.1921
360 'In Italy art is alive – the feeling for form. We Slavs still need to find our forms – I believe you are one of the first. That has to be paid for with a bleeding heart'. (Letter from A. Masaryk, dated 13.8.1921)
361 This is well illustrated by the episode of the paving in the First Castle Courtyard. The account which Plečnik gave his students was purely for didactic purposes: 'I proposed paving the main court with granite; I shifted the axes slightly. When I asked which slabs would be most suitable the suppliers told me slabs 60 centimetres wide, of any length. I chose slabs 15 centimetres thick, asking for them to be smoothed on top and rough hewn beneath. A professor in the faculty, who was also the owner of the firm, undertook the work and sent an excellent polisher. So the first row was beautifully laid. Some wanted to underlay the slabs, and I suggested concrete; others wanted it all concreted. However, they only underlaid with sand, and the slabs sank unevenly, owing to their weight, although an untrained observer will hardly notice it. But just imagine, a matter of national prestige and they argue over a barrel of beer. When I saw what they had done I created a terrible stink!' (Grabrijan: *Plečnik*, p, 110) In fact Otto Rothmayer had to tell the stonemason how furious Plečnik was.
362 Letter from A. Masaryk from Lány, dated 7.3.1923
363 I am grateful to Dr Dalibor Veselý for drawing my attention to this
364 *Plečnik. Hradschin – Prag*, p. 101
365 M 306, dated 20.5.1922
366 Letter to a Ministry official F. Blažek, dated 28.1.1923, APH, class. no. 495/32, inv. no. 212
367 Letter from A. Masaryk from Lány, dated 7.3.1923
368 In this context Plečnik's account of his visit to the quarry is interesting, although it cannot be dated exactly: 'There was a terrible drumming noise, as the huge mass of granite slid over the steel tubes down the slope to the road. It was a thundering as if the Last Day of Judgement had come. For a time we stood as if transfixed. I could not move a step to escape the terrible danger that was hurtling down towards us. We shuddered, and some fled in naked fear for their lives. I remained rooted to the spot, staring at the raging fury of nature, from whose breast we had just torn so magnificent a monolith. Then there was smoke everywhere and we could hear a hissing noise. The steel tubes had heated until they were white hot, and they were bent and twisted out of all recognition. The mighty monolith lay before us like the body of a dead animal.' (Omahen: *Izpoved*, p. 113)

369 Sketch in Rothmayer's papers. (I am grateful to Dr Jana Horneková and Jan Rothmayer for allowing and arranging for me to see these.)

370 V. Weinzettel.: 'Mrákotínský monolit pro Pražský hrad' ('The Mrákotín monolit for Prague Castle'), *Kámen* IV, October 1923, pp. 137–9

371 Mušič: *Plečnik*, p. 189

372 *Styl* VI (XI), 1925–6, pp. 108–10

373 Copy of a letter from Plečnik to Dr Jan Svoboda, dated 14.5.1928 (Rothmayer's papers, Prague)

374 During the Second World War the Reich protector Reinhard Heydrich wanted to have the monolith removed, but President Hacha was able to prevent this. Only since the competition held in 1963 has the discussion on a new site ceased.

375 The inscription on the plan of 1926, now in the Prague Castle archive.

376 See Valena: 'Plečniks Gärten', p. 1491

377 See P. Janák: 'Josef Plečnik v Praze,' ('Josef Plečnik in Prague,') *Volné směry* XXVI, 1928–9, pp. 97–108

378 The historical data is from Valena: 'Plečniks Gärten', pp. 1482ff.; see also T. Valena; 'Nádvoří a zahrady – Plečnikovy úpravy v kontextu Pražkeho hradu' (Courtyards and gardens – Plečnik's interventions within the context of Prague Castle), in: *Josip Plečnik – Architekt Pražského hradu*, exhibition catalogue, Prague 1996, pp. 259–89.

379 As Plečnik did not approve of Kalvoda's sculpture, the Castle administration only purchased a version in half the original size. Before it was placed in its present position the administration considered whether it might be more appropriate in the smaller bellevue.

380 Omahen: *Izpoved*, pp. 28–30, illus. between pp. 40 and 41

381 Valena: 'Plečniks Gärten', note 21, p. 1489

382 Ibid, p. 1488

383 Removed in the early 1990s

384 Lenarčič

385 M 344, dated 11.9.1924

386 M 186, undated (May 1911)

387 See A. Jirásek; *Staré pověsti české (Old Bohemian Tales)*, Prague 1988, p. 46

388 Between 1963 and 1965 the sanded paths were asphalted and the roof terrace on the Winter Garden was enlarged

389 Valena: 'Plečniks Gärten', p. 1493

390 In 1962 the flagpoles, that had started to decay, were replaced by new ones, but these consist of several parts.

391 Letter from A. Masaryk, dated 21.4.1923

392 Archív Kanceláře prezidenta republiky, Prague, class. no. T 49/23, p. 380/1925

393 Grabrijan: *Plečnik*, p. 73

394 The copy of the part of the will referring to Plečnik is attached to a letter from A. Masaryk (AML)

395 Masaryk repeated his request to Plečnik to design a family tomb for Olšany-cemetery in Prague in his letter of 15.5.1932 (Masaryk Archive; I am grateful to Dr Rostislav Švácha for finding me these papers)

396 Letter from A. Masaryk, dated 15.12.1924

397 Ibid

398 Grabrijan: *Plečnik*, p. 55

399 Letter from A. Masaryk, dated 27.9.1921

400 Letter from A. Masaryk, dated 14.8.1921

401 Letter from A. Masaryk, dated 24.3.1924

402 Grabrijan: *Plečnik*, pp. 106–7

403 Ibid

404 E. Edgar: 'J. Plečnik doma', ('Plečnik at Home') *Kámen*, Prague 1941, No. 22, pp. 35–43

405 Prager Presse 7.3.1930; Omahen: *Izpoved*, p. 114 (Omahen erroneously states that he was referring to an object from the niche in the corridor).

406 Omahen: *Izpoved*, p. 166

407 M 332, dated 15.3.1924

408 The sentence is part of a longer Latin inscription translated into Czech

409 In the 1970s the library was moved from the second to the third floor and partially destroyed

410 Letter from A. Masarkyk to F. Stele, dated 7.10.1958

411 Grabrijan: *Plečnik*, p. 83

412 Semper: *Stil* II, p. 264

413 Ibid

414 See Note 212

415 Semper: *Stil* I, p. 287; *Stil* II, p. 341

416 Letter from A. Masaryk from Topolčianky, dated 15.10.1926

417 Letter from A. Masaryk, dated 16.–18.4.1924

418 Draft of Plečnik's letter to the President's office, dated 16.7.1924 (Rothmayer's Papers, Prague)

419 *Plečnik. Hradschin – Prag*, p. 56

420 'Die Burg im Jubiläumsjahr', *Prager Presse* 18.8.1928

421 See Z. Dvořáková: *Josef Zítek. Národní divadlo a jeho tvůrce*, (*Josef Zítek. The National theatre and its Founder*) Prague 1983, pp. 163–4

422 Replaced by a copy in 1965

423 Valena hypothetically notes that it calls in mind the log-house from the Libussa's prophecy (See note 378 'Nadvoří a zahrady . . . ', pp. 279–81)

424 The idea comes from Otto Wagner's facade cladding on the Post Office Savings Bank in Vienna

425 Semper: *Stil* I, p. 380

426 Semper: *Stil* I, p. 277

427 *Styl* IX (XIV), 1928/29, pp. 113–14; another indication that the beasts are related to folk art could be a photograph showing two oxen above the entrance to a farm near Zvolen in Slovakia, which Plečnik took on a school trip (in AML); see *Josip Plečnik – Architekt Pražského Hradu*, Prague 1996, p. 95

428 The postcard, dated 28.5.1927, is in the O. Rothmayer papers in Prague. See note 427

429 The reliefs are inv. nos. 552 and 554

430 Adolf Loos used a similar copper cladding on the ceiling of the dining room in the Villa Karma on Lake Geneva

431 Semper: *Stil* I, pp. 367–70

432 The Plečnik Hall was greatly changed in the 1960s (see Architektura ČSSR XXXV, 1976–7, pp. 292–303)

433 Valena: *Plečniks Gärten*, p. 1485

434 Only partly realized during the Second World War and in the 1950s

435 *Styl* II (VII), 1921–2, p. 33 and Supplement XXI

436 *Styl* III (VIII), 1922–3, pp. 32, 43

437 V. Šlapeta: '*Jože Plečnik and Prague*,' in: *Plečnik*, 1989, p. 92

438 Průchová: *Plečnik a Praha*, p. 451, Note 15

439 APH, Class. H 4032/46, Plečnik's Letter From 19.5.1936

440 P. Letarouilly: *Édifices de Rome moderne ou recueil des palais, maisons, églises, couvents, et autres monuments publics et particuliers les plus remarquables de la ville de Rome*, Paris 1840–57; see Semper: 'Bericht über die Abteilung für Architektur, Metall- und Möbeltechnik und praktisches Entwerfen', in: *Kleine Schriften*, p. 98; M 654, undated

441 Lenarčič; about Plečnik's school: M. Pozzetto: *Plečnikova šola v Ljubljani* (*Plečnik's school in Ljubljana*), exhibition catalogue for Prague, Ljubljana 1996

442 Ibid

443 See Omahen: *Izpoved*

444 E. Petruša-Štrukelj: *Ognjišče arhitektov akademikov*, exhibition catalogue, Ljubljana 1991

445 Semper: *Wissenschaft, Industrie und Kunst*, p. 63

446 Lenarčič

447 Ibid

448 Grabrijan: *Plečnik*, p. 84

449 Lenarčič

450 *Iz ljubljanske šole za arhitekturo* (*From the Ljubljana School of Architecture*), Ljubljana 1923

451 *Iz ljubljanske šole za arhitekturo* (*From the Ljubljana School of Architecture*), Ljubljana 1925

452 ZALj, I. državna realna gimnazija v Ljubljani, personnel file

453 M 385, dated St Jacob's Sunday, 1926

454 M 358, undated (April 1925)

455 Omahen: *Izpoved*, p. 143

456 Ibid, pp. 228ff.

457 Ibid, p. 263

458 M 356, undated (end 1924)

459 Mušič: *Plečnik*, p. 195

460 Letter to the architect N. Dobrović, dated 28.4.1927 (I am grateful to Ž. Škalamela for giving me a copy of this letter); see also Grabrijan: *Plečnik*, pp. 69–72

461 See M. Mušič: 'Plečnik and Beograd', ('Plečnik and Belgrade'), *Zbornik za likovne umetnosti*, Nr. 7, Matica srpska 1971, pp. 170ff.

462 His associate was the architect V. Lenarčič; D. Prelovšek: 'The Rojal Hunting Lodge Kamniška Bistrica', in: *Piranesi*, No. 2, Vol. 1, Ljubljana 1992, pp. 8–18

463 NŠALj, zgodovinski zapiski, Fascicle 30

464 M 333, undated (March, April 1925?)

465 *Iz ljubljanske šole za arhitekturo* (*From the Ljubljana School of Architecture*), Ljubljana 1925, pp. 58–67

466 See the parish chronicle (kept in the parish office)

467 Document in AML; V. Šlapeta: 'Joze Plečnik and Prague', in: *Plečnik*, 1989, pp. 92–4

468 *Iz ljubljanske šole za arhitekturo* (*From the Ljubljana School of Architecture*), Ljubljana 1923, unpag., original in the parish office of the church of the Sacred Heart in Prague

469 Draft of the article by A. Titl in AML

470 Lenarčič

471 See U. Schaf: *Die Kirche des heiligen Franciscus in Šiška*, Seminar work, Munich Technical University, summer semester 1989

472 *Styl* IV (IX), 1923–4, p. 14

473 M 394, dated 4.3.1927

474 *Architectura perennis*, p. 191

475 Grabrijan: 'Slabost in veličina arhitekta Plečnika', ('The Weaknesses and Greatness of the Architect Plečnik') in: Grabrijan: *Plečnik*, pp. 160–1

476 Letter to F. Škarda, dated 25.10.1918; on the church in Prague see also: F. Ondráš/R. Pavlíčková: *Chrám Nejsvětějšího Srdce Páně 1932–92* (*The Church of the Sacred Heart of Jesus 1932–92*), a brochure celebrating the 60th anniversary of the church, Prague 1992; I. Margolius: *Church of the Sacred Heart*, Phaidon Press 1995; D. Prelovšek: 'Kostel Nejsvětějšího Srdce Páně v Praze' (The Church of the Sacred Heart in Prague), in: *Josip Plečnik – Architekt Pražského hradu*, exhibition catalogue, Prague 1996, pp. 565–79.

477 Plečnik used Sitte's argument (C. Sitte: *Der Städtebau nach seinen künstlerischen Grundsätzen*, Vienna 1909, 4th edition, pp. 30 and 32)

478 M 291, dated 27.2.1921

479 J. Kuděla: 'Jože Plečnik v fondih Arhiva glavnega mesta Prage' (Plečnik in the materials of the Prague Municipal Archive) *Arhivi* XII, Ljubljana 1989, pp. 41–4

480 *Iz Ljubljanske šole za arhitekturo* (*From the Ljubljana School of Architecture*), Ljubljana 1923

481 *Lučine*, pp. 81–5, plan in the parish office of the church of the Sacred Heart in Prague

482 Letter to A. Titl, dated 16.12.1925

483 M 391, dated 8.1.1927

484 From Plečnik's description of the third project (Prague Municipal Archive), A. Titl papers, not class.

485 Semper: *Stil*, II, p. 375

486 Semper: *Stil*, I, pp. 40ff.

487 Semper mentions ermine as the symbol of supreme royal dignity (*Stil*, I, p. 108). O. Rothmayer confirmed to B. Podrecca that the texture of the facade was intended to simulate ermine. This is also mentioned in some contemporary publications.

488 Semper: *Stil*, I, p. 483

489 Lenarčič

490 See the illustration of the Pompeian candelabrum in Semper: *Stil*, II, p. 271

491 From Plečnik's letter to the priest I. Baša, dated 21.12.1926 (I am grateful to Professor Vilko Novak for drawing my attention to this). The book J. Smej: *Psalmi vaškega župnika* (*The Psalms of a Village Parish Priest*), Celje 1992, pp. 219–23 contains interesting recollections by the priest Baša of his work with Plečnik.

492 *Zbornik za umetnostno zgodovino* V, 1925, Nos. 1–2, p. 65

493 *Iz ljubljanske šole za arhitekturo* (*From the Ljubljana School of Architecture*) 1925, pp. 70–3

494 Omahen: *Izpoved*, p. 205

495 Grabrijan: *Plečnik*, p. 92

496 Semper: *Stil*, I, pp. 446–7

497 V. Novak: 'Izpovedi in pričevanja o Jožetu Plečniku' ('Statements about Yože Plečnik'), *Znamenje* VII, 1977, p. 60

498 V. Slugić: 'Fra Josip Markušić i prof. Jože Plečnik' (Father Josip Markušić and Professor Jože Plečnik) in: *Fra Josip Markušić*, Zagreb-Sarajevo 1982, p. 103

499 Some of the plans were published in: *Architectura perennis*, pp. 101, 103, 105–7

500 M 437, undated draft of a letter in German to an unknown recipient

501 'Cerkvica za Logarjevo dolino v Solčavi' (A little church for the Logars' Valley at Solčava) , *Dom in svet* XLIII, 1930, No. 5–6, p. 181

502 *Architectura perennis*, pp. 158–9

503 Plečnik's letter to the Franciscans in Bosnia, dat. 19.2.1930 (before the war in Bosnia in the Franciscan monastery in Jajce)

504 Ibid

505 The final work was directed by Plečnik's associate, the architect Janko Valentinčič, who also designed the two candelabra in the nave

506 M 59, dated 5.4.1901 (postmark)

507 Trnovo parish chronicle in Ljubljana; plans in AML; the history of the church is also recounted by F.S. Finžgar: *Leta mojega popotovanja* (*My travelling years*), Celje 1957, pp. 345–9

508 *Architectura perennis*, pp. 180, 181; *Lučine* (cont.)

509 The parish chronicle, written during the building work by K. Matkovič (archive of the parish of St Michael in Barje)

510 J. Kušar: *Plečnikova cerkev sv. Mihaela na Barju* (*Plečnik's church of St Michael at Barje*). Ed. and publ. by the Barje parish office, Ljubljana 1991, p. 7

511 A. Choisy: *Histoire de l'architecture*, Paris 1899, reprint: Inter-Livres 1991, Vol. I, p. 279

512 *Plečnik*, 1986, p. 81

513 See Semper: *Stil*, I, p. 284

514 *Architectura perennis*, p. 173

515 A. Hrausky: 'Plečnik in vojna' ('Plečnik and the War') *Arhitektov bilten* (*Architect's Bulletin*) XXV, November 1995, No. 126–7, pp. 47–8.

516 Plečnik: *Aedes Sancti Iosephi Patriarchae*, Ljubljana 1935

517 *Napori*, pp. II–IX

518 See Le Corbusier: *Vers une architecture*, new edition Paris 1977, p. 23; also *Napori*, pp. xxxvii (top), LII–LVII

519 *Architectura perennis*, pp. 124–9

520 See note 515 above.

521 *Architectura perennis*, pp. 94–9

522 Ibid, pp. 131–7, 220

523 *Napori*, pp. xl–xliv

524 Ibid, pp. lxviii–lxxvii

525 Ibid, pp. lxii–lxv

526 Letter to A. Castelliz in Vienna, dated 30.1.1929. See also Grabrijan: *Plečnik*, pp. 128–9.

527 M 428 (undated draft of Plečnik's answer to the letter from Tomažič from Celje, dated 26.8.1925)

528 Mušič: *Plečnik*, p. 204

529 M 382, dated 1.5.1926

530 Grabrijan: *Plečnik*, p. 111

531 Semper: *Kleine Schriften*, pp. 298–9

532 Semper: *Stil*, I, pp. 436–7

533 Ibid, p. 382

534 See D. Prelovšek: *Slovene Insurance Company Building*, Ljubljana 1985 (Engl. edition)

535 According to reports by the architect Janko Valentinčič in early 1985

536 Semper: *Stil*, I, p. 458

537 See Asenbaum/Haiko/Lachmayer/Zettl: *Otto Wagner. Möbel und Innenräume*, pp. 152–3

538 Vurnik: *Vseučiliška knjižnica ljubljanska*, p. 3

539 M 421, undated notebook, draft of a letter

540 Draft of the answer to the letter from the university secretary of 28.9.1935 (AML)

541 *Lučine*, pp. 64–5

542 The documents relating to the building of the library are in ZALj, Reg. IV, No. 1 and AS, Banovina, Technical Department VI-4, Fascicle 7311ff.

543 Plečnik: *Projekt univerzitetne biblioteke ljubljanske*; Graf: *Wagner*, II, p. 614

544 Graf: *Wagner*, II, pp. 738–40

545 Plečnik's postcard to the engineer Otahal, dated 5.1.1936 (AS, Banovina, Technical Department VI-4, Fascicle 7313)

546 Plečnik: *Projekt univerzitetne biblioteke ljubljanske*

547 Vurnik: *Vseučiliška knjižnica ljubljanska*

548 Draft of the letter to the regional president, dated 1.12.1935 (AML)

549 P. Krečič: *Plečnikova Ljubljana* (*Plečnik's Ljubljana*), Ljubljana 1991, p. 40

550 According to reports by the architect Janko Valentinčič in December 1982

551 According to reports by Plečnik's pupil, the architect Danilo Fürst

552 Semper: *Stil*, II, p. 358

553 According to reports by the architect Edvard Ravnikar

554 Semper: *Stil*, II, pp. 100–1

555 A. Vodopivec: 'Pogovor z Edvardom Ravnikarjem' ('Conversation with Edvard Ravnikar'), *Nova revija* IV, Ljubljana 1985, No. 35/36, p. 297

556 Semper: *Stil*, I, p. 368

557 Ibid, p. 385; A Choisy: *Histoire de l'architecture*, Paris 1899, I, p. 371 (See note 511)

558 Fabiani's letter to M. Prelovšek from Gorizia, dated 1.1.1954, published in: Maks Fabiani: *O kulturi mesta. Spisi 1895–1960* (*On the Culture of a Town, Essays 1895–1960*), Triest 1988, p. 178

559 Semper: *Stil*, I, p. 458

560 Letter to V. Glanz, dated 13.7.1938

561 Ibid, dated 24.3.1939

562 See Semper: *Stil*, I, pp. 276ff.

563 See K. Harather: *Haus-Kleider. Zum Phänomen der Bekleidung in der Architektur*, Vienna, Cologne, Weimar 1995, p. 46

564 Semper: *Stil*, I, pp. 376–7

565 The glass case for the Viennese silversmith I.C. Klinkosch of 1898, mentioned above in connection with Plečnik's church in Zagreb, is the most obvious example.

566 Semper: *Stil*, I, p. 381

567 See Asenbaum/Haiko/Lachmeyer/Zettl: *Otto Wagner. Möbel und Innenräume*, p. 79

568 The building was renamed the National and University Library and the Slovenian arm was placed above the entrance

569 Semper: *Stil*, I, p. 65

570 Lenarčič

571 S. Sušnik: 'Zavrženi lepoti in spomini na Plečnika' ('To the beauty rejected, and the recollections of Plečnik') (draft of an article kindly lent to me by the author)

572 M 338, dated 31.5.1924

573 Omahen: *Izpoved*, pp. 101–2

574 *Architectura perennis*, pp. 62–3

575 *Stavitel* II, 1920–1, p. 59; the building bears the date 1921 and parts have been converted

576 *Napori*, pp. clviii–clix

577 See note 555

578 Semper: *Stil*, II, p. 497 and p. 268

579 *Arhitektura* I, Ljubljana 1931, No. 1, pp. 7–9

580 M 598, letter to his nephew Karl Matkovič, dated 7.1.1928

581 Grabrijan: *Plečnik*, p. 165

582 M 382, dated 1.5.1926; A. Hrausky/J. Koželj/D. Prelovšek: *Plečnikova Ljubljana. Arhitekturni vodniki I* (*Plečnik's Ljubljana. Architectural guides I*), Ljubljana 1996

583 *Lučine*, p. 3

584 Plečnik: 'Studija regulacije severnega dela Ljubljane;' Plečnik: 'Studija regulacije Ljubljane in okolice'

585 Stabenow: *Plečnik*, p. 70

586 Grabrijan: *Plečnik*, p. 80

587 Plečnik: 'Studija regulacije severnega dela Ljubljane'

588 D. Prelovšek: 'Fabianijeva Ljubljana in njena aktualnost v poznejšem času' ('Fabiani's Ljubljana and its Topicality in Later Times') in M. Pozzetto: *Maks Fabiani. Nove meje v ahitekturi.* (*Maks Fabiani. New Borders in Architecture*), exhibition catalogue, Triest 1988, pp. 33–4

589 M Fabiani: *Regulacija deželnega stolnega mesta Ljubljane* (The Regulation of the Povincial Capital of Ljubljana), Vienna 1899

590 Letter from M. Prelovšek dated 19.4.1924 (AML)

591 Plečnik: 'Studija regulacije severnega dela Ljubljane'

592 Stabenow: *Plečnik*, pp. 64–6

593 Ibid, p. 88

594 V. Valenčič: 'Ljubljanski regulacijski načrti 1919–1945' ('Regulation plans for Ljubljana 1919–1945'), undated manuscript, p. 11; the best information on the history of the building of the northern part of Ljubljana is to be obtained from the minutes of the Council meetings ZALj, Cod. VIII)

595 Wagner: 'Erläuterungs-Bericht zum Entwurfe für den General-Regulierungs-Plan über das gesammte Gemeindegebiet von Wien' (Commentary on the General Regulation Plan for Vienna), in Graf: *Wagner*, I, p. 91

596 F. Stele: 'Marijin trg', ('The Virgin Mary Square') *Kronika slovenskih mest* IV, Ljubljana 1937, No. 3, pp. 147–55

597 B. Mihelič: *Urbanistični razvoj Ljubljane* (*The Urbanistic Development of Ljubljana*), Ljubljana 1983, pp. 18–21

598 M 601, letter to K. Matkovič, dated 22.1.1929

599 See Grabrijan: *Plečnik*, p. 167

600 According to reports by Gizela Šuklje, 5.1.1983

601 M 312, undated

602 See Graf: *Wagner*, I, p. 108

603 A. Loos: 'The Chicago Tribune Column', in Loos: *Die Potemkin'sche Stadt*, Vienna 1983, p. 155

604 J. Wester: 'Marijin spomenik na Sv. Jakoba trgu v Ljubljani' 'The Holy Virgin Memorial on St James's Square in Ljubljana', *Kronika slovenskih mest* V, 1938, No. 3, p. 167

605 Letter to M. Prelovšek, dated 21.1.1927. The letter is in the Lenarčič papers and was published in the periodical *Mladika* XXXV, Trieste 1991, No. 4, p. 72

606 Letter to M. Prelovšek, dated 14.4.1928

607 ZALj, Reg. IV. No. 52231/1932

608 Lenarčič

609 According to information from Lurška Curk who owned the company that reconstructed the monument

610 Wagner: *Moderne Architektur*, in Graf: *Wagner*, I, p. 280

611 *Napori*, p. CXXXVI; Grabrijan: 'O Plečnikovih propilejah', ('On Plečnik's Propylaea') in: Grabrijan: *Plečnik*, pp. 147–53

612 ZALj, Cod. VIII/37, Turistični odbor za Ljubljano (The Tourist Committee for Ljubljana), minutes of the meeting of 30.3.1939

613 Grabrijan: 'Slabost in veličina arhitekta Plečnika' (The Weakness and Greatness of the architect Plečnik's), in: Grabrijan: *Plečnik*, p. 174; F. Stele: 'Spomenik kralja Aleksandra I. Zedinitelja v Ljubljani', ('A memorial to King Alexander I in Ljubljana'), *Kronika slovenskih mest* VII, 1940, pp. 129–41

614 Letter to M. Prelovšek, dated 5.5.1940

615 *Napori*, p. xxvi

616 Ibid, pp. xxvi–xxix

617 *Slovenski narod* (daily paper), 10.3.1934

618 ZALj, Cod. VIII, Box 105, minutes of the meeting of the building department, 10.6.1930

619 See ZALj, Cod. VIII/4, minutes of the meeting, 21.11.1933

620 Plečnik: 'Frančiškansko mostovje'

621 Among the Plečnik drawings donated to SAZU by the architect Marjan Tepina

622 Stabenow: *Plečnik*, p. 132

623 Plečnik: 'Studija regulacije Ljubljane in okolice'

624 According to reports by the architect Franc Vardjan in March 1991

625 *Lučine*, p. 167

626 *Iz ljubljanske šole za arhitekturo* (*From the Ljubljana School of Architecture*), Ljubljana 1925, pp. 14–17, 127

627 ZALj, Cod. VIII/37, 1939, minutes of the meeting on 11.5.1939

628 Grabrijan: *Plečnik*, p. 21

629 See F. Stele: *V obrambo Rimskega zidu na Mirju v Ljubljani* (*In defence of the Roman wall at Mirje in Ljubljana*), Ljubljana 1928

630 See ZALj, Cod. VIII/27, 1934, minutes of the meeting of the building department technical committee, 1.5, 8.6 and 11.7.

631 Data on the regulation, see ZALj, Reg. IV, special Fascicle 3, No. 6; D. Prelovšek; 'Note on construction of the riverbank', *Lotus international*, No. 59, 1989, pp. 15–33

632 See Graf: *Wagner*, I, p. 106

633 Grabrijan: *Plečnik*, pp. 19–20; see also Mušič: *Plečnik*, p. 213; the sketch is published in: *Jože Plečnik. Lo spazio urbano a Lubiana*, exhibition catalogue, Oderzo 1996, p. 31, fig. 2

634 'Prešernov spomenik v Ljubljani' (Ljubljana)

635 *Iz ljubljanske šole za arhitekturo* (*From the Ljubljana School of Architecture*), Ljubljana 1925, pp. 18, 36

636 Ibid, p. 36

637 Plečnik: 'Frančiškansko mostovje'

638 Lenarčič

639 *Architectura perennis*, pp. 84, 85

640 Ibid, pp. 69, 71, 73

641 Ibid, p. 139

642 K. Dobida: 'K načrtu zatvornic na Ljubljanici' ('On the plan of the loch on the river Ljubljanica'), *Mladika*, Ljubljana 1935, No. 1. pp. 8, 12, 32

643 *Architectura perennis*, p. 75

644 Lenarčič

645 F. Stele: *Ljubljanski grad–slovenska Akropola* (*Ljubljana Castle – the Slovenian Acropolis*), Celje 1932

646 *Iz ljubljanske šole za arhitekturo* (*From the Ljubljana School of Architecture*), Ljubljana 1925, pp. 18, 126

647 Illus. in *Jože Plečnik, il ritorno del mito*, Venice 1983, p. 41

648 *Zbornik oddelka za arhitekturo na univerzi v Ljubljani 1946–1947* (*Deeds of the architectural department of Ljubljana University 1946–1947*), Ljubljana 1948, pp. 110–13

649 Ibid

650 See Note 646

651 *Napori*, pp. xxvi–xxix

652 Ibid, pp. xxii–xxv

653 The papers of the architect Ivo Spinčič, Ljubljana

654 *Lučine* (cont.)

655 See note 630, minutes of the meeting of the committee for the market and the regulation of the river banks

656 See Plečnik: *Seminar in Laibach*, pp. 50–71

657 Lenarčič

658 *Architectura perennis*, pp. 19, 21, 23, 25, 27, 29, 31, 33, 35, 37, 39, 41, 43, 45, 47, 49, 51, 53, 55, 57, 59, 61, 63, 65, 67

659 Ibid, p. 59

660 B. Podlogar/D. Prelovšek: *Jože Plečnik 'Peglezen'*, *Arhitekturni modeli* 2, Ljubljana 1986

661 D. Blaganje: 'Alcuni principi di composizione di facciate in J. Plečnik', in *Jože Plečnik, il ritorno del mito*, Venice 1983, p. 32

662 M 121, undated (March 1907)

663 See Plečnik, 1986, p. 116 (original in the author's archive)

664 NŠALj, zgodovinski zapiski, fascicle 30; on the new church see F. Stele: 'Hram Slave pri sv. Krištofu' (The Temple of Glory at St. Christopher's), *Dom in svet* XLVI, 1933, pp. 64–71, and in: *Naš Bežigrad v luči zgodovine, kulture, gospodarstva* (*Our Bežigrad District in the Light of History, Culture and Economy*), Ljubljana 1940, pp. 44–68

665 *Dom in svet* XLIII, 1930, illus. 72

666 On the building of Žale see ZALj, Cod VIII/35–36, 39 and Reg. IV, No. 1; D. Prelovšek/V. Kopač: *Žale by architect Jože Plečnik*, Ljubljana 1992 (Engl. edition)

667 Letter to S. Sušnik, dated 4.1.1939 (*Plečnik*, 1986, p. 119). I am grateful to Standko Sušnik for allowing me to see this correspondence.

668 Letter to Mayor J. Adlešič, dated 9.5.1937 (*Plečnik*, 1986, p. 118)

669 According to Vlasto Kopač, who worked as draughtsman on the plans

670 Grabrijan: 'Slabost in veličina arhitekta Plečnika' (The Weakness and Greatness of the architect Plečnik), in: Grabrijan: *Plečnik*, pp. 166–8

671 Semper: *Stil*, I, p. 467

672 Semper: *Stil*, II, p. 409

673 According to Vlasto Kopač

674 *Napori*, pp. XX–XXI

675 The letters are from the years 1930–55 and are kept in the AML after the death of Emilija Fon.

676 *Napori*, pp. lxxviii–lxxxi

677 Ibid, pp. xc–xciii

678 Semper: 'Die Sgrafflto-Dekoration', in Semper: *Kleine Schriften*, pp. 508–16

679 See *Napori*, p. 9

680 See *Spomeniki NOB Jožeta Plečnika in njegove šole* (*Monuments to the National Liberation War by Jaže Plečnik and his School*), exhibition catalgue, AML, Ljubljana 1975

681 Plečnik's reply to Kozak, dated 2.10.1945; Kozak's correspondence, manuscript collection is in Ljubljana National and University Library

682 *Napori*, pp. x–xix

683 The sketch recently disappeared from the Rothmayer legacy, and in 1995 it reappeared in the catalogue of one of the auction houses from London.

684 *Napori.*, p. lviii

685 ZALj, MLO, Glavni oddelek, No. 415/1954; sketches in the papers of the architect Anton Bitenc, Ljubljana

ABBREVIATIONS AND SOURCES

AML – Ljubljana Museum of Architecture

APH – Prague Castle Archive

Architectura perennis – F. Stele/A. Trstenjak/J. Plečnik: *Architectura perennis*, Ljubljana 1941 (reprinted 1993)

AS – Ljubljana, The State Archives of Slovenia

Asenbaum/Haiko/Lachmayer/Zettl: *Otto Wagner. Möbel und Innenräume* – P. Asenbaum/P. Haiko/H. Lachmayer /R. Zettl: *Otto Wagner. Möbel und Innenräume*, Residenz Verlag, Salzburg, Vienna 1984

Letter to A. Castelliz – Plečnik's letters to Alfred Castelliz are in the architect's papers in Vienna. In 1969 his daughter Ilse Castelliz kindly allowed me to see this correspondence. From 1996 Castelliz's Legacy has been kept in the Albertina, Vienna, but Plečnik's letters are missing.

Letter to V. Glanz – Plečnik's letters to his pupil Vinko Glanz are in the architect's papers and were kindly made available to me by Mrs Ana Glanz.

Letter to Kotěra – Plečnik's letters to Jan Kotěra are in the Architecture Archive of the National Technical Museum in Prague. They were kindly made available to me by the architect Vladimír Šlapeta.

Letter from A. Masaryk – Alice Masaryk's letters to Plečnik are in AML. Plečnik's letters to the President's daughter were destroyed during the war. Only a few unimportant fragments have survived.

Letter to M. Prelovšek – Plečnik's letters to Matko Prelovšek are in the author's archive.

Letter to F. Škarda – Plečnik's letters to the priest of Vinohrady, František

Škarda, are in the Municipal Archive in Prague. I am grateful to Dr Jiří Kuděla for making these available to me.

Letter to A. Titl – Plečnik's letters to Alexander Titl are in the Municipal Archive in Prague and were kindly made available to me by Dr Jiří Kuděla.

Forsthuber: *Moderne Raumkunst* – S. Forsthuber: *Moderne Raumkunst. Wiener Ausstellungsbauten von 1898 bis 1914*, Picus Verlag, Vienna 1991

Grabrijan: *Plečnik* – D. Grabrijan: *Plečnik in njegova šola*. (*Plečnik and His School*), Maribor 1968

Graf: *Wagner* – O.A. Graf: *Otto Wagner*, Vol. 1, *Das Werk des Architekten 1860–1902*, Vol. 2, *Das Werk des Architekten 1903–1918*, Böhlau Verlag, Vienna, Cologne, Graz 1985

Graf: *Wagnerschule* – O.A. Graf: *Die vergessene Wagnerschule*. Schriften des Museums des 20. Jahrhunderts 3, Vienna 1969

Herrmann: *Semper* – W. Herrmann: *Gottfried Semper. Theoretischer Nachlaß an der ETH Zürich, Katalog und Kommentare*, (*Theoretical writings deposited at the Technical University, Zürich, Catalogue and Commentary*) Birkhäuser Verlag, Basle, Boston, Stuttgart 1981

Johnston: *Österreichische Kultur- und Geistesgeschichte* – W.M. Johnston: *Österreichische Kultur- und Geistesgeschichte. Gesellschaft und Ideen im Donauraum 1848 bis 1938*, Böhlau Verlag, Vienna, Cologne, Graz 1974

Krečič: *Plečnik in jaz* – P. Krečič: *Plečnik in jaz*, Trst (Triest) 1985 (Plečnik and I, letters from J. Plečnik to A. Suhadolc, recollections of Plečnik by A. Suhadolc)

Kruft: *Geschichte der Architekturtheorie* – H.W. Kruft: *Geschichte der Architekturtheorie*, Beck Verlag, Munich 1986, 2nd edition. (English translation: *A History of Architectural Theory*, transl.)

Lenarčič: *Spomini na Plečnika* – Vinko Lenarčič: *Spomini na Plečnika* (*Recollections of Plečnik*, manuscript dating from the early sixties. I am grateful to Prof Marij Maver and the architect's son, Andrej Lenarčič, for this. An abbreviated version of the manuscript was published in serial form in the magazine *Mladika* in Trieste in 1991.)

Loos: *Potemkin'sche Stadt* – A. Loos: *Die Potemkin'sche Stadt. Verschollene Schriften 1897–1933*, Prachner Verlag, Vienna 1983

Loos: *Sämtliche Schriften* – A. Loos: *Sämtliche Schriften*, Herold Verlag, Vienna, Munich 1962

Lučine – *Iz ljubljanske šole z arhitekuro* (*Lučine*) (From the Ljubljana School of Architecture), 1928

Lučine (cont) – *Dela arhitektov na Tehniki Univerze v Ljubljani. Lučine, nadaljevanje 1929–1937*, Ljubljana 1937 (The work of the architects at the Technical University, Ljubljana, photo album, unpag.)

M – Provisional catalogue of Plečnik's letters to his brother Andrej and others, collected by his nephew, Karel Matkovič. Unless otherwise stated, Plečnik's letters to Andrej; the material is in AML.

Moravánszky: *Die Architektur der Donaumonarchie* – Á. Moravánszky: *Die Architektur der Donaumonarchie 1867–1918*, Corvina Verlag, Budapest, Berlin 1988

Moravánszky: *Die Erneuerung der Baukunst* – Á Moravánszky: *Die Erneuerung der Baukunst. Wege zur Moderne in Mitteleuropa 1900–1940*, Residenz Verlag, Salzburg, Vienna 1988

Mušič: *Arhitektura in čas* – M. Mušič: *Arhitektura in čas. Eseji in razprave*, (Architecture and Time. Essays and Articles), Maribor 1963

Mušič: *Plečnik* – M. Mušič: *Jože Plečnik*, Ljubljana 1980

Napori – *Napori. F. Stele: Esej o arhitekturi. J. Plečnik: Dela*, Ljubljana 1955 (*Stele: Essays on Architecture and Plečnik: Works*, joint title: *Endeavours*), reprinted 1993

NŠALj – Archibishop's Archive, Ljubljana

Omahen: *Izpoved* – J. Omahen: *Izpoved*. (*Statement*), Ljubljana 1976

Pechar/Urlich – J. Pechar/P. Urlich: *Programi české architektury* (Czech Architectural Programmes), Prague 1981

Plečnik, 1967 – B. Podreka: *Josef Plečnik 1872–1957*, Vienna, Prague, Ljubljana, exhibition catalogue, Vienna 1967 (new enlarged edition October 1967)

Plečnik, 1968 – L. Gostiša: *Arhitekt Jože Plečnik*, exhibition catalogue Ljubljana 1968

Plečnik, 1986 – *Arhitekt Jože Plečnik 1872–1957*, text by D. Prelovšek, exhibition catalogue, Ljubljana 1986

Plečnik, 1989 – *Jože Plečnik. Architect 1872–1957*, MIT Press, 1989

Plečnik, 'Frančiškansko mostovje' – J. Plečnik, 'Frančiškansko mostovie' (*'The Franciscan Bridge'*), Dom in svet XLII, Ljubljana 1929, pp. 150–151

Plečnik. Hradschin-Prag – *Josef Plečnik. Hradschin – Prag*, Seminar work 1979–1980 (tutor: N. Schuster), Chair of Design, Spatial Planning and Church Architecture, Technical University Munich 1980

Plečnik: *Projekt univerzitetne biblioteke ljubljanske* – J. Plečnik/F. Stele: *Projekt univerzitetne biblioteke ljubljanske*, (*The Ljubljana University Library Project*), Ljubljana 1933

Plečnik: Seminar in Laibach – *Josef Plečnik: Seminar in Laibach 1978–1979* (tutor: B. Podrecca), Chair of Design, Spatial Planning and Church Architecture, Technical University, Munich 1980 (published in 1983)

Plečnik: 'Studija regulacije Ljubljane in okolice' – J. Plečnik: 'Studija regulacije Ljubljane in okolice', ('Regulation study for Ljubljana and environs') Dom in svet XLII, Ljubljana 1929, No. 5, Supplement 4

Plečnik: 'Studija regulacije severnega dela Ljubljane' – J. Plečnik: 'Studija regulacije severnega dela Ljubljane', ('Regulation study for the northern part of Ljubljana') Dom in svet XLII, Ljubljana 1929, No. 3, p. 91

Plečnik: *Výběr prací školy pro dekorativní architekturu* – J. Plečnik: *Výběr prací školy pro dekorativní architekturu v Praze z roku 1911–1921*, (Selection of the work of the Prague School of Decorative Architecture, 1911–1921), Prague 1927

Pozzetto: *Die Schule Otto Wagners* – M. Pozzetto: *Die Schule Otto Wagners 1894–1912*, Schroll Verlag, Vienna, Munich 1980

Pozzetto: *Fabiani* – M. Pozzetto: *Max Fabiani. Ein Architekt der Monarchie*, Ed. Tusch, Vienna 1983

Prelovšek: *Plečnik* – D. Prelovšek: *Josef Plečnik. Wiener Arbeiten von 1896 bis 1914*, (*Works in Vienna from 1896 to 1914*), Ed. Tusch, Vienna 1979

'Prešernov spomenik v Ljubljani' – 'Prešernov spomenik v Ljubljani' (*The Prešeren memorial in Ljubljana*) (reprinted in Grabrijan; *Plečnik*, pp. 113–16) in: *Naši zapiski* III, October 1905, Nos. 10–11

Průchova: 'Plečnik a Praha' – Z. Průchova: 'Josef Plečnik a Praha', (*Plečnik and Prague*) in: *Umění* XX, 1972, pp. 442ff.

Quitsch: *Semper* – H. Quitsch: *Die ästhetischen Anschauungen Gottfried Sempers*, Akademie Verlag, Berlin 1962

SAZU – Slovenian Academy of Science and Art

Sekler: *Hoffmann* – E.F. Sekler: *Josef Hoffmann. Das architektonische Werk*, Residenz Verlag, Salzburg, Vienna 1982

Semper: *Die vier Elemente der Baukunst* – G. Semper: *Die vier Elemente der Baukunst*, Braunschweig 1851

Semper: *Kleine Schriften* – G. Semper: *Kleine Schriften*, Berlin, Stuttgart 1884

Semper: *Stil* – G. Semper: *Der Stil in den technischen und tektonischen Künsten oder Praktische Aesthetik*, Vol. 1, Textile Kunst, Frankfurt 1860, Vol. 2, Keramik, Tektonik, Stereotomie, Metallotechnik, Munich 1863

Semper: *Wissenschaft, Industrie und Kunst* – G. Semper: *Wissenschaft, Industrie und Kunst und andere Schriften*, Neue Bauhausbücher, Kupferberg Verlag, Mainz, Berlin 1966

Stabenow: *Plečnik* – J. Stabenow: *Jože Plečnik, Städtebau im Schatten der Moderne*, Vieweg & Sohn Verlag, Braunschweig, Wiesbaden 1996

Stele: *Plečnik v Italiji* – F. Stele: *Arh. Jože Plečnik v Italiji 1898–99*, (*Architect Jože Plečnik in Italy 1898–99*) Ljubljana 1967

Strajnić: *Plečnik* – K. Strajnić: *Josip Plečnik*, Zagreb 1920

Recorded by Strajnić – Material on Plečnik recorded by Kosta Strajnić in the manuscript collection of SAZU in Ljubljana

Valena: 'Plečniks Gärten' – T. Valena: 'Plečniks Gärten am Hradschin in Prag', *Bauwelt*, No. 39, Oct. 1986, pp. 1482ff.

Vurnik: *Vseučiliška knjižnica ljubljanska* – I. Vurnik: *Vseučiliška knjižnica ljubljanska*, (*Ljubljana University Library*), Ljubljana 1934

ZALj – Ljubljana Municipal Archive

The Zacherl Family Chronicle: The family chronicle was written about 1937 by the manufacturer's daughter Doris and her mother, and later about 20 copies were produced. It was kindly lent to me by the architect Peter Zacherl; all references are to the first volume.

INDEX OF NAMES

INDEX OF PLACES

329

ACKNOWLEDGEMENTS

The author and the publishers wish to express their grateful thanks to all the individuals and institutions who have helped to make this publication possible, in particular the Austrian Ministry of Science and Research in Vienna. They gratefully acknowledge all those who helped with the illustrations or gave information that facilitated the research work. Particular thanks are due to the architects Boris Podrecca, the Director of the Museum of Architecture in Ljubljana, Dr Peter Krecic, Dr Vera Mala from the Prague Castle Archive and Alenka Klemenc.

PHOTOGRAPHIC CREDITS

Architectura perennis 245, 267, 268
Der Architekt 40, 48, 49
Author's archive 47, 70, 71, 78, 158, 197, 209, 222, 251, 253, 256–61, 283–5, 308, 317, 328–9, 340–1
Archive of the 'Narodni dom' Athletic Association 304
Archiv Hlavniho města Prahy 225
Archiv Pražského hradu 1, 119, 120, 125, 126, 127, 128–35, 137–8, 144, 148–9, 152–5
Arhitekt Jože Plecnik (Exhibition Catalogue) 235, 241
Architectural Museum, Ljubljana 2–15, 17, 20–3, 31–2, 37, 39, 42–6, 50–5, 59–63, 65–8, 72, 74–7, 79, 80, 83, 85, 86, 115, 116, 118, 121–3, 139, 141, 145, 150, 157, 219, 220, 223, 227, 229, 240, 242–4, 247–50, 252, 255, 269, 279–80, 288–9, 294–6, 299, 300, 315, 321–2, 325–7, 330–1, 342
Arhiv Slovenije 156, 191
Anton Bitenc Estate 36, 58
Dom in svet 224
Einige Skizzen, Projekte und ausgeführte Bauwerke von O. Wagner 16
F.S. Finžgar: *Makalonca* 347
Damjan Gale 173, 184–6, 188, 192, 195, 198, 202, 210, 217, 218, 221, 236, 262, 301, 303, 305, 310–12, 318, 337–9, 346, 348
Lojze Gostiša 302, 316, 343–5
Historisches Museum der Stadt Wien 18
Janez Kališnik 107
Kancelář prezidenta republiky 93
Vlasto Kopač 332–4
Jože Kregar Estate 335
Kunst und Kunsthandwerk 64
Vinko Lenarčič Estate 313–14

Ljubljanski regionalni zavod za varstvo naravne in kulturne dediščine, Ljubljana 274–5
Lučine (cont) 297
T. G. Masaryk ve fotografii 142
Maca Matkovic Estate 88
Vilko Novak 237
Österreichische Nationalbibliothek 19
Parish Archive of the Sacred Heart, Prague 226, 228, 230–3
Nadškofijski arhiv Ljubljana 159–60
Plečnik: *Projekt univerzitetne biblioteke ljubljanske* 265–6; 'Studija regulacije Ljubljane in okolice' 286; 'Studija regulacije severnega dela Ljubljane' 287
Boris Podrecca 38
Borut Prelovšek 143
Damjan Prelovšek 108, 161, 168, 215, 238, 254, 272, 281–2, 336
Edo Primožič 263, 271, 273
Otto Rothmayer Estate 124, 140, 146, 151
Roberto Schezen 24–30, 32–5, 41, 56, 91–2, 95–101, 103–5, 112–14, 162–7, 169–72, 174–83, 187, 189, 190, 193–4, 196, 199–201, 203–8, 211–14, 216, 239, 246, 276–7, 290, 319
Ivo Spinčič Estate 298, 323, 324
Pavel Štecha 94, 102, 106, 109–11, 136
F. Stele: *Ljubljanski grad-slovenska akropola* 320
K. Strajnić: *J. Plečnik* 69, 73, 84, 87
Styl 81–2
Nenad Gattin and Nikola Vranić 147, 234, 278, 291–3, 309
Publicity Brochure for the Zacherl Firm 57
Zgodovinski arhiv Ljubljana 306
Marko Župančič 270, 307